Hans-Ulrich Krause, Dayanand Arora
**Key Performance Indicators for Sustainable Management**

Hans-Ulrich Krause,
Dayanand Arora

# Key Performance Indicators for Sustainable Management

A Compendium Based on the "Balanced Scorecard
Approach"

**DE GRUYTER**
OLDENBOURG

ISBN 978-3-11-059808-7
e-ISBN (PDF) 978-3-11-059809-4
e-ISBN (EPUB) 978-3-11-059934-3

**Library of Congress Control Number: 2019938958**

**Bibliografische Information der Deutschen Nationalbibliothek**
Die Deutsche Nationalbibliothek verzeichnet diese Publikation in der Deutschen
Nationalbibliografie; detaillierte bibliografische Daten sind im Internet über
http://dnb.dnb.de abrufbar.

© 2020 Walter de Gruyter GmbH, Berlin/Boston
Typesetting: Integra Software Services Pvt. Ltd.
Printing and binding: CPI books GmbH, Leck
Cover image: NicoElNino/iStock/Getty Images Plus

www.degruyter.com

**Dedicated to:**

My Parents
Ursula and Konrad Krause
*With special gratitude for their love and care*
– Hans-Ulrich Krause

My Parents
Subhadra and Ratan Lal Arora
*For their unforgettable role in my life*
– Dayanand Arora

# Preface

It is a matter of delight for us to present the first edition of our book "Key Performance Indicators for Sustainable Management". Our main purpose in writing this book is to organize and present major key performance indicators within the framework of the balanced scorecard approach. The book offers many thoughtful insights into the sustainable management of business operations in the modern world. We consider the book a valuable companion for business practitioners, students and teachers alike. We believe that even the reader with little or no knowledge of accounting and finance can benefit from this book.

The four perspectives (financial, customer, process, and learning/innovation) of the balanced scorecard can be viewed as interdependent and hierarchical. We believe that constant learning and innovation, at the firm level, leads to the refinement of internal processes, and helps in improving operational efficiency. This results in increased customer satisfaction and higher financial performance. We selected 180 ratios, and consider these to be a representative collection of key performance indicators, supporting all four perspectives of the balanced scorecard. With a compact and consistent profiling of all ratios, and supporting ideas for calculating and interpreting the key performance indicators, the book takes on the character of a reference manual.

The book also provides cutting-edge knowledge on several **key ecological indicators** linked to the four perspectives of the balanced scorecard approach. Among others, these include resource efficiency, carbon footprints, product related recyclability, emission volume of production related pollutants and awareness about energy sourcing. The ecological indicators seek to encourage an attitude of "long-term" strategic thinking in business decisions. In addition to this, we have introduced several key indicators for *"risk-related consciousness"* in evaluating business performance. We think that managers need to be continuously aware of indicators, such as value at risk, cash flow at risk, bankruptcy risk, expected process based risks, and the cost effectiveness of risk management initiatives.

In order to facilitate the implementation of the KPI project in a business, we propose the use of 28 SMART (Specific, Measurable, Achievable, Relevant and Timely) key performance indicators. The SMART indicators in this book are marked with the symbol (S) and offer at a glance a good overview of the major indicators for all kinds of business organization, and particularly for small and medium-sized enterprises.

We would like to place on record our gratitude to Dr Stefan Giesen, our publishing editor at De Gruyter for his encouraging ideas and support in the timely completion of this project. We are also thankful to David Peck for his hard work in the language editing of the text. Needless to say, any remaining mistakes in language

https://doi.org/10.1515/9783110598094-201

or content are still our responsibility, and we invite you to make suggestions to improve the next edition of the book.

Professor Dr. Hans-Ulrich Krause
hans-ulrich.krause@htw-berlin.de

Professor Dr. Dayanand Arora
arora@htw-berlin.de

# Contents

# Introduction

The subject area of business administration can well be considered an applied science. It comprises three typical activities: Describing (for example, a problem or an activity), Explaining (for example, its context and/or its parameters) and Managing (for example, developing, implementing and/or monitoring) a chosen solution. In order to accomplish these activities, a comprehensive range of tools and instruments have been developed over time. Key Performance Indicators (KPIs) are an important example of such instruments.

Though the usage of key performance indicators has a long tradition, its practical application has always been coupled with innovative ideas and the need for improvement. They represent the outcome of a continuous process of change, derived through various mutations in the economic, technical, social, political and ecological environment. Therefore, business firms of all sizes regularly call for effective tools to successfully plan, manoeuvre, and control their business operations.

Over the last few decades, systems with pyramid-like structured financial performance indicators have been dominant (for example, the DuPont System). Now, new approaches, such as the balance scorecard, are gaining ground. A performance evaluation system based on balance scorecard emphasizes the importance of using all types of information, both financial and non-financial, which is essential to remaining competitive. The accounting reports of a firm's performance are now often based on critical success factors in four different dimensions: the first dimension of financial information is usually supplemented with three non-financial dimensions (customers, business processes, and human resource/innovation). The management (including reporting) of non-financial issues and activities is increasingly becoming a proxy (through an analysis of cause-effect relationships) for evaluating the overall performance and abilities of a firm. Thus, balanced scorecard provides a basis for a more complete analysis than is possible with financial data alone. In this context, we proudly place on record the fact that our book is based on the balance scorecard approach, and is probably the first one of its kind.

An interesting trend in the business world is the decentralization of responsibility and authority. This has led to a sizable increase in the number of executives who not only have to understand key performance indicators, but also systematically influence them. Such professional requirements are expected, not only from the managers trained in business administration, but also from engineers, scientists, legal professionals, and others, who have, over time, risen to senior management positions in their firms. In addition, the increased internationalization of firms, with globally aligned sourcing, production and sales networks, makes the use of English in business communication indispensable. This is equally true for both internal and external reporting. We believe this book will be a useful reference guide, kept on the shelf of professionals, and used in their professional training.

https://doi.org/10.1515/9783110598094-001

In the academic world it is noticeable that students are increasingly expected to develop a sound understanding of modern management tools, including key performance indicators. This book provides both a basic as well as an advanced reference base for students of business administration, both at the undergraduate and graduate level. It is a compact introduction to the subject, even for students of interdisciplinary programs, such as industrial engineering or business law.

When using the key performance indicators, it is important that all concerned parties have a good understanding of their basic contents. Our book helps in achieving this goal in many ways. When searching for a suitable key indicator, its calculation and meaningful usage, the following questions should be answered carefully:

1. What kind of problem needs to be resolved? This would mean specifying the business aspect or the context, which needs to be analysed through an absolute or relative indicator.
2. What kind of data (physical, monetary and time value) is suitable and relevant for the purpose?
3. How can the needed data and information be obtained within the firm?
4. What is the typical value of the indicator, which should be targeted by the firm or which is achieved by other firms?
5. What possible actions are available, or can be applied, to improve the key indicator, which solve the problem or bring it closer to a solution?

This book explains key performance indicators, representing a new form of reference manual. We have developed business-related details for various groups or combinations of key indicators, with the following features:

– Structural navigation of the book around the four dimensions, or perspectives, of the balanced scorecard approach. The financial, customer, processes, human resource/innovation perspectives have been further classified into sub-groups to facilitate targeted referencing. The sub-groups, such as value-based management (VBM), project controlling, and supply-chain management, need to be highlighted, due to the increased need for key performance indicators in these areas.
– The core message of sustainable management is highlighted in this book. It is based on the idea of setting in motion a development process which satisfies the needs of the present generation without jeopardising the needs of future generations. With its emphasis on reporting and performance evaluation at the firm level, the application of the sustainability principle simultaneously tracks three top targets of economic benefits, social responsibility and ecological viability. Therefore, the selected ecological key performance indicators are not shown separately as the fifth perspective of the balanced scorecard approach but specifically integrated in each of the four perspectives.

- Compact indicator profiles with systematically consistent structures:

  `?` The analytical question answered by this indicator.

  `*` Definition or Formula for calculation, along with the dimension in which an indicator is expressed;

  `*` Calculation/Derivation of the indicator, with the source(s), where the information can be available or sought;

  `#` Interpretation and typical range of the indicator;

  `!` Useful suggestions for improving the indicator; and

  `&` List of related ratios and additional notes.

- The list of common synonyms for each key indicator provides more clarity about the terminology. In addition to that, a list of related indicators gives an opportunity for the reader to explore new aspects of the indicator under analysis.
- We have also offered specific instructions on which key indicators can be computed by external analysts without any problem, and those that can only be computed by internal analysts. Thus, external analysts can compute all key indicators, where input data is derived directly from the published annual reports, for example, profit indicators.

There are four Appendices at the end of the book: they provide additional suggestions for a systematic handling the subject of key performance indicators:

Appendix I offers a systematic explanation about how one can study and analyse the changes in the relative ratios.

Appendix II is devoted to explaining the basic linkages in the DuPont ratio system, and the three main drivers of return on equity.

Appendix III provides a tabular listing of all key performance indicators in an alphabetical order for easy referencing.

Appendix IV contains a tabular overview of 28 SMART (Specific, Measurable, Attainable, Relevant and Timely) KPIs with the related formulae for giving the reader a suggestive list of KPIs that we believe can give a quick profiling of the firm at a glance within the balanced scorecard framework.

We feel that our readers do not have to be experts in accounting and finance to understand the text. However, once they start understanding the information contained in the text, they will surely be on their way to becoming an expert on interpreting key performance indicators.

# 1 Basic Indicators

## 1.1 Technical Productivity

**Analytical Question** ?

How large is the technical (pure tangible) yield of an input factor, measured in terms of a particular output unit?

**Definition** *

$$\frac{\text{Output Quantity}}{\text{Input Quantity}}$$

or

$$\frac{\text{Output Quantity of Combined Factors of Production}}{\text{Input Quantity of Deployed Factors of Production}}$$

Examples of different factors of production are: raw material, labour-time, capital, supplies/utilities and area.

Various measures of quantity are: units produced, length, area in square meters, weight and time duration.

The measured value of efficiency may be expressed in units per hour (for example, produced quantity per hour), hours per customer (for example, time consumed per customer), square meter per unit (for example, required packing material quantity per machine) and Kg per hour (for example, produced chemical, measured in Kg per hour).

**Calculation/Derivation** »

The required data for this quotient is prepared from the internal cost accounting system, which is then processed and made available to decision makers in different cost types, cost-centres, and product costing.

**Interpretation and Typical Range** #

With the help of Technical Productivity, a *physical* measure of yield for all production factors is derived.

Since various combinations of production factors (each one measured differently) are used for a particular output, data for measuring Technical Productivity has to be collected and valued for each factor separately. Often the measured value shows individual and partial efficiency.

https://doi.org/10.1515/9783110598094-002

Therefore, it is not easy to recommend a typical range for this ratio. A useful interpretation of this ratio is possible over time, when intra-firm or inter-firm comparisons are made over several periods. When making international comparisons, the impact of other value drivers, such as changes in the bilateral exchange rate over time has to be carefully considered.

An important, though simplified, assumption made when calculating this quotient is that the input and output factors have a linear cause-and-effect relationship with each other. It should be emphasized that this assumption of linearity is not always true. Since the deployed factors of production are usually scarce, managers always try to achieve the highest possible yield, i.e. technical productivity.

## ! Useful Suggestions

The demand for targeted productivity has increased in firms and is often grounded in the need to improve future competitiveness. Through an improved (quantity-based) input-output relationship, the firm should make maximum use of scarce production factors. Improvements in productivity are focused at increasing the yield value of the deployed resource input. Thus, measuring productivity over time is an important step in process-optimization, which is often achieved through skilfulness in avoiding wasted time, energy or effort. Lean manufacturing provides an interesting example of process improvements, which supports the business benefits of rapid execution.

There is one more aspect that needs to be considered. If the input factors of production have substitutes, a part-improvement in productivity may not necessarily lead to total improvement in productivity. Moreover, an improvement in the productivity of a particular factor may well be due to increased consumption of another input factor.

A change in this ratio in the context of desired corporate goals can be achieved by a disproportionate increase or decrease in the achieved output (as numerator) and deployed input (as denominator). *For further details and systematic explanations of this argument, refer to the information in Appendix I.*

## & Related Ratios/Additional Notes

"Technical Yield" and "Output-Input Ratio" are often used as synonyms for Technical Productivity. In some cases, productivity is labelled as efficiency, such as material efficiency.

The inverse value of Technical Productivity (input quantity/output quantity) is known as "Production-Coefficient".

In order to make better judgments about the performance of a particular process, it is desirable to measure the outputs (the numerator) in monetary terms. This leads to the calculation of the so-called "economic productivity". If both output and input factors are measured in monetary units, the resultant value will be called "operating efficiency" In process reengineering, any change that increases economic productivity is considered as an economically efficient change.

## 1.2 Efficiency

### Analytical Question

How large is the relative yield of (or return from) an input factor in terms of a particular output unit? What is the quantifiable relative performance of a particular process, operation or a system?

### Definition

The term "efficiency" and various measures, which are related to or derived from it, are not uniformly defined. Some measures of Efficiency relate to "technical productivity", whereas other measures relate to "economic productivity". Mostly, Efficiency is named and described with reference to the input factor, such as material efficiency, labour efficiency (or employee efficiency), energy efficiency, etc.

$$\frac{\text{Output Value (Measured in Monetary Units)}}{\text{Input Value (Measured in Quantity or Monetary Units)}}$$

Some examples of efficiency are: production per employee, energy costs per machine hour, sales per square metre of sales area, and contribution margin per client.

Various measures of quantity are: units produced, length, area in square meters, weight and time-duration.

The measured efficiency value may be expressed in % (in the case of technical quantity-based efficiency) or in € per square meter, € per client, € per unit, € per hour (in the case of economic/value-based efficiency).

### Calculation/Derivation

The required data for this quotient is prepared from the internal cost accounting system, which is then processed and made available to decision makers in different cost types, cost-centres, and product costing.

### Interpretation and Typical Range

Put simply, Efficiency is a measure of performance. If it is measured in technical terms, it is similar to productivity and implies the yield of a particular production factor. Since various combinations of production factors (each one measured differently) are used for a particular output, data for measuring efficiency has to be collected and valued for each factor separately. Often the measured value shows partial efficiency.

Therefore, it is not easy to recommend a typical range for this ratio. A useful interpretation of this ratio is possible over time, when intra-firm or inter-firm comparisons are made over several periods. When making international comparisons, one has to consider carefully the impact of other value drivers, such as changes in the bilateral exchange rate over time.

An important, though simplified, assumption made when calculating this quotient is that the input and output factors have a linear cause-and-effect relationship with each other. It should be emphasized that this assumption of linearity is not always true. Since the deployed factors of production are usually scarce, managers always seek to achieve the highest possible economic yield, i.e., economic productivity.

### ! Useful Suggestions

Every measure of Efficiency is aimed at improving the value of the deployed resource input. Thus, measuring efficiency over time is an important step in process-optimization; this is often achieved through skilfulness in avoiding wasted time, energy or effort. Lean manufacturing is an interesting example of process improvement, which helps to achieve the business benefits of rapid execution.

If the input factors of production have substitutes, a part-improvement in efficiency may not necessarily lead to total improvement in efficiency. Moreover, an improvement in the efficiency of a particular factor may well be due to increased consumption of another input factor.

By comparison, producing something at a lower cost than competitors, or achieving a reduction in unit costs over time or reduction in time to complete a job, or reduction in inventory levels are other examples of efficiency improvements.

A change in this ratio in the context of desired corporate goals can be achieved by a disproportionate increase or decrease in the achieved output (as numerator) and deployed input (as denominator). *For further details and systematic explanations of this argument, refer to the information in Appendix I.*

### & Related Ratios/Additional Notes

The "Technical Efficiency" and "Economic Efficiency" are two variants of Efficiency. Various synonyms, such as "Output-input ratio", "Productivity" "Technical Productivity", "Technical Yield" or just "Yield", are commonly used for technical efficiency. Typically, the productivity is shown with reference to an input factor, such as material or energy.

The inverse value of technical productivity (input quantity/output quantity) is known as "Production-Coefficient".

Closely related to the concept of technical efficiency is another concept called Economic Efficiency, which is similar to economic productivity. If various input factors which are measured in heterogeneous dimensions, are made comparable by expressing them (in the denominator) in monetary terms, the resultant quotient is called Economic Efficiency.

## 1.3 Economic Efficiency

**Analytical Question**

?

How far is the computed value of the operational output-input ratio good enough, from the economic value perspective? Does the cost-benefit analysis of an operation lead to the creation of value?

**Definition**

*

The quotient for Economic Efficiency is an extension of technical and economic productivity, where both numerator and denominator are in monetary terms.

| Variant A: | Variant B: | Variant C: |
|---|---|---|
| $\dfrac{\text{Revenue}}{\text{Expenses}}$ | $\dfrac{\text{Benefits}}{\text{Costs}}$ | $\dfrac{\text{Budgeted Costs}}{\text{Actual Costs}}$ |

The Economic Efficiency is measured in multiples. The goal is to achieve a value above 1, for example, 1.2. If the values in the above variants are multiplied by 100, the result will be a percentage. Thus, a comparable goal is to achieve results above 100 %; for example, 120 %.

**Calculation/Derivation**

»

The required data for this quotient is prepared from the internal cost accounting or external accounting reports. In some cases, it is essential to have a direct costing (for segregating costs into variable and fixed) on the basis of budgeted and actual costs.

**Interpretation and Typical Range**

#

Economic Efficiency is a core criterion for making capital budgeting decisions. With the help of calculated economic efficiency, a *monetary* measure of yield is established for accepting or rejecting a project.

In all variants of Economic Efficiency, the rule of thumb is simple: the higher the quotient, the better the economic efficiency. However, sometimes values below 100 % are also possible, particularly in non-profit organizations (NPO), where the focus is not on profit-maximization. Instead, NPOs may choose projects based on the highest possible cost coverage.

**Useful Suggestions**

!

In order to influence this ratio positively, the numerator could be improved through a better price or volume strategy. The denominator (i.e., cost side) could be optimized through a more efficient use of the factors of production.

An important, though simplified assumption made for calculating this quotient is that the variable and fixed costs remain constant over time. However, if the output volume increases or reduces over time, the Economic Efficiency may change over- or under-proportionately because of the changing behaviour of the fixed costs (the so-called capacity effects).

Furthermore, as in similar ratios, the reduction of overheads or other cost-components should not lead to an over-proportionate reduction in performance; otherwise the expected improvement in economic efficiency may not be achieved. Simply speaking, the austerity measures should not create counter-productive effects.

A change in this ratio, in the context of desired corporate goals, can be achieved by a disproportionate increase or decrease in the achieved output or benefit (as numerator) and deployed input or costs (as denominator). *For further details and systematic explanations of this argument, refer to the information in Appendix I.*

**&** **Related Ratios/Additional Notes**

Economic Efficiency is also known as "Operational Efficiency" or "Cost-Benefit Analysis".

A closely related family of ratios that help in measuring Economic Efficiency is called "Profitability Ratios". Thus, various measures of profitability (with capital or sales as input variables) assist us in establishing economic efficiency.

Many banking institutions use the "Cost-Income Ratio". The ratio (actual-actual or budget-actual) helps in making diverse intra-firm and inter-firm comparisons, both in national and international contexts.

## 1.4 Profitability

**?** **Analytical Question**

How much is the relative Profitability, computed by comparing any indicator of periodic performance with the deployed resources? What is the ability of a business to generate profit (i.e. return) when compared with the capital employed or sales volume?

**\*** **Definition**

Four basic variants of Profitability are possible:

| Variant A: | Variant B: | Variant C: | Variant D: |
|------------|------------|------------|------------|
| $\dfrac{\text{Profit}}{\text{Capital}}$ | $\dfrac{\text{Profit}}{\text{Sales}}$ | $\dfrac{\text{Net Cash Flow}}{\text{Capital}}$ | $\dfrac{\text{Net Cash Flow}}{\text{Sales}}$ |

If the values in the above variants are multiplied by 100, the result will be as a percentage.

For computing the capital employed in the denominator, instead of the ending balance, the average volume of capital employed is often taken.

## Calculation/Derivation

The required data, depending upon the chosen profitability variant, can be obtained from the published external financial reports or from the internal cost accounting information system. The information may also be available in from the internal capital budgets or financial reports.

## Interpretation and Typical Range

Profitability is the most important measure of performance in any business decision. It is used to assess a business's ability to generate earnings in comparison to its expenses and is expressed as a relative measure.

For all capital or sales related profitability ratios, the valid statement is: the higher the Profitability, the better the earning-capacity and, consequently, the higher the self-financing capacity of the firm.

Unlike the "classical" Return On Sales (defined as operating profits/sales), in Cash Flow Margin (akin to EBITDA-turnover-yield), cash inflow is matched with sales, which cannot easily be influenced by balance sheet related policy decisions, and therefore, is considered more meaningful than any other measure based on earnings.

By comparison with the "classical" gross or net return on sales, the Cash Flow Margin Ratio carries the advantage of neutralizing many of the differences which arise because of divergent international legal directives and practices. Thus, international comparisons based on this ratio are useful.

In principle, for the calculation of Return On Equity, both profit *before* or *after* taxes can be taken. The calculations based on after tax profits (i.e., net income) are obviously more common. However, if non-incorporated firms (not liable to pay taxes) are compared with tax-liable corporate firms, it would be sensible to measure the profit before tax.

It is difficult to make recommendations about the target profitability. Obviously, the rule of thumb is that the Profitability should be higher than the financial costs. For orientation and benchmarking this ratio, one could take internal comparisons (such as the ratio in different organizational units or plan-actual values) or external comparisons where the branch-specific average period or the "best-practice" value may be used as a guide.

Assuming that the comparable firms have a similar structure of products, processes or potentials, any variance from the average values provides clear indication for serious reviews. These should help in analysing the positive and negative developments in the ratio, and steer them in the context of corporate goals.

## Useful Suggestions

In order to influence this ratio positively, the numerator could be improved through a better price/volume strategy on the sales side, and through a more efficient use of the factors of production on the cost side. Any business strategy that promotes high-yield (or discourages low yield) products and services would invariably lead to an improvement in profitability. In individual cases, one has to analyse the effects of those factors which cut across the time dimension; thus for example, products and services in varying life-cycle phases have different levels of profitability. Similarly, sometimes a product-mix-effect demands that products with lower-margins may be continued, in order to support and complement other high-margin products.

In the denominator, a reduction in the asset base could be achieved through selling of non-operating assets (at least at book value) or a reduction in inventory levels. Asset leasing is another common measure for reducing the denominator. Thus, even with constant (or declining) earnings, the profitability can be improved because of a lowered asset base.

A change in this ratio, in the context of desired corporate goals can be achieved by a disproportionate increase or decrease in the earnings (as numerator) and deployed assets or sales volume (as denominator). *For further details and systematic explanations of this argument, refer to the information in Appendix I.*

**& Related Ratios/Additional Notes**

Along with the classical measures of "Return On Equity", "Return On Assets" and "Return On Sales", in the recent past, there is a stronger tendency to calculate the cash flow based "Return On Equity" and "Return On Assets". *For details on these ratios, as well as for other ratios (such as ROI and CFROI) in the family of profitability ratios, refer to the appropriate terms in the Index.*

In the case of responsibility-centres (such as sales offices or profit-centres), which use profitability ratios for planning and controlling purposes but have no influence over financing and other decisions, the profitability ratios are generally calculated "Before Interest" and "Before Taxes".

## 1.5 Turnover Rate

**? Analytical Question**

How often is the average inventory of a particular asset turned over into sales during a period?

The ratio can be applied to a variety of assets or objects, for example, to inventories of different kinds.

**\* Definition**

$$\frac{\text{Average Sales, Need or Consumption}}{\text{Average Inventory}}$$

»

The ratio is expressed in terms of multiples and could have a decimal value as well.
    The numerator can be the average sales, need, consumption or outflow.

In the case of real assets, instead of using the quantity-based data for numerator and denominator, it is also common practice to take value-based data. However, for an inter-firm or time-series comparison of the value based result, it is important to check the consistency of the valuation base for the inventory amount. The valuation could be based on acquisition price or sales price, current price or average price, or appropriate production costs.

## Calculation/Derivation

The required data, depending upon the level of aggregation of the chosen products, can be obtained from the information system of (internal and external) accounting. For example, the data can be based on an ERP (Enterprise Resource Planning) system with a module-based structure. Among others, a familiar name of ERP software is SAP R/3 or S/4 HANA. The data could also be obtained from corporate capital budgeting documents.

## Interpretation and Typical Range

The Turnover Rate belongs to the category of "activity ratios". It shows the arithmetical intensity of an asset-use or consumption in the business processes.

    A general target range for this ratio cannot be determined. For orientation and benchmarking, one could take internal comparisons (such as the ratio in different organizational units or plan-actual values) or external comparisons where the branch-specific average period or the "best-practice" value may be used as a guide.

## Useful Suggestions

Assuming that firms in the same branch usually have similar production and asset structures, the ratio values, differing significantly from the averages, are clear candidates for serious reviews. These should help in analysing the positive and negative consequences and steering them in the context of corporate goals.

    In trading companies, Turnover Ratios constitute a central measure for steering the supply chain management. This is primarily because trading companies do not have any production of their own.

    The significance of the Turnover Rate is evident when we view stock number as "capital", particularly in the context of the ROI framework. The Profitability (Net Income/Capital) as a key ratio is extended into two ratios, where Return On Sales is based on EBIT/Sales and Asset Turnover is based on Sales/Average Assets. *For additional explanation about this multi-layered ratio systems, refer to the DuPont System in Appendix II as an example.*

    The multiplicative link between "Return on Sales" and "Asset Turnover" ratios in ROI shows that a firm can maintain its profitability despite a fall in the return on sales, if it is able to improve its asset turnover ratio. For this, the short, medium, and long-term impact of all the measures, which reduce the asset base without negatively influencing sales-generating capacity has to be carefully evaluated.

Similarly, a rise or fall in the profitability of the enterprise could be analysed with reference to return on sales and/or asset-turnover, and measures for improvement can be developed. This analytical perspective, and the derived conclusion, can be applied to all other ratios in the category of "turnover" as well.

A change in this ratio could be triggered by a disproportionate increase or decrease in sales as a measure of flow (as numerator) and inventory as a measure of stock (as denominator). *For further details and systematic explanations of this argument, refer to the information in Appendix I.*

**&** **Related Ratios/Additional Notes**

The word "Turnover Coefficient" is often used as a synonym for "Turnover Rate".

If the numerator and denominator are turned upside down, the resultant coefficient is called "turnover period" or "turnover time" or simply "coverage".

## 1.6 Elasticity

**?** **Analytical Question**

How strongly does the value of a dependent factor react to a change in the value of an independent factor, with both measured in percentages? For example, to what extent is the failure rate expected to change when the time allocated to the training of employees increases by 15 % in terms of error-prevention measures?

**\*** **Definition**

$$\frac{\text{Relative Change in dependent Factor}}{\text{Relative Change in independent Factor}}$$

Since both the numerator and the denominator are percentages, Elasticity is a dimensionless, usually non-integer value. Depending on the implicit relation between the two variables, it can be positive as well as negative (for example, -1.2).

**»** **Calculation/Derivation**

In practice, prerequisites are often lacking for (i) a system-based functional relation (backed up by calculations) or (ii) a regression analysis, which can produce statistically valid results. Therefore, either observation based on small patterns of reaction, or simple estimations based on previous experience, are carried out to derive common elasticity-assumptions.

**Interpretation and typical range**

Despite the insufficient availability of analytical data, determining robust and conclusive cause-effect-relationships or end-means-relationships is a matter of necessity and utmost importance in management control. When the relation between two values isn't directly based upon a mathematical operation (for example, gross price minus discount equals net price), all that remains in practice is the ability to make relatively well-founded assumptions and suppositions.

In the case of decisions involving multiple people, either through active participants, or through the inclusion of subordinates and superiors who need to be involved, the assumptions (such as those relating to elasticity) need to be objectively disclosed. This is important in encouraging rational corporate management as well as promoting mutual understanding for decision-making and action.

The economic and theoretical foundation of changing circumstances, and the intensity of their objective relationships are of essential importance for management, especially when various economic parameters are applied and, sometimes, their correlation in multi-layered KPI systems need to be understood. Thus, the validity of the tools in Balanced Scorecard is significantly reinforced by the quality of these objective dependency-relations (for example in the form of so-called strategy-maps with cost and value drivers).

Taking into account the variety of entrepreneurial malleable interdependent factors within a functional area, and between different levels of an organization, a generalized target value for the extent of each type of elasticity, obviously, cannot be determined.

For orientation and benchmarking elasticity, one could take internal comparisons (such as the ratio in different organizational units over time or budget-actual comparisons) and corresponding external comparisons, where the branch-specific average values or the "best-practice" values may be used as a guide.

**Useful suggestions**

In the name of simplicity, the fundamental form of the relationship between two variables is assumed to be implicit (so-called "mono-causality"). This is usually the basis for the implementation of various measures.

In most business decisions though, there are multiple parameters that are related in end-means-relationships, especially when one must take into account socio-cultural and environmental parameters because of sustainability concerns (so-called "multi-causality"). The complexity of this network of relationships is usually further increased by the fact that there is not just one but multiple targets, or a corporate goals-system with multiple levels of target priorities.

To be able to conduct the business activity in a company more effectively, the following areas of cause-effect-relationships between independent and dependent variables (in their respective corporate situations) have to be taken into account when determining elasticity:

- complementary, competing and neutral relationships
- linear (proportional) correlations but also those gradients having different levels of steepness over a period of time (so-called deviating correlations)
- progressive versus digressive trends
- stable or unstable, i.e. existentially threatened relationships in the time period being observed, potentially through disruptive internal or external influences
- immediate or lagged correlation between two variables (depending upon the length of delay).

The breadth of the fundamental spectrum of corporate areas of analysis during the derivation of cause-effect-relationships and the related calculation of elasticity should show how demanding the choice of appropriate indicators, and their integration into performance management systems are. This should adequately portray the reality of complex operational routines within a company.

**& Related Ratios/Additional Notes**
The concrete forms for special applications of elasticity concepts in management, especially in marketing and pricing policy are:
- Price Elasticity of Demand (Refer to KPI No. 3.3.6)
- Cross price elasticity of demand
- Income elasticity of demand

Other economic connections, in the form of cause-and-effect relationships, are also possible within the framework of this KPI.

## 1.7 Compound Annual Growth Rate (CAGR)

**? Analytical Question**
Relatively speaking, to what extent has a business parameter value changed on average within a multi-periodic comparison?

For example, by what percentage has the number of employees increased (called growth rate) or the revenue decreased (called decline rate) over a period?

**＊ Definition**

$$(1+v) = \left( \sqrt[n]{(1+v_1) \cdot (1+v_2) \cdot (1+v_3) \cdot \ldots \cdot (1+v_n)} \right)$$

Wherein:
- v – Compound average rate of change per period
- $v_i$ – rate of change in period I (i = 1, 2, 3. ..., n)
- n – maximum observed number of periods
- 1+v – average change factor per period

The rate of change is given as an absolute number. For example, a value of 0.15 corresponds (using the multiplying factor "100") to a growth rate of 15 %; a negative value of -0.028 corresponds (using the multiplying factor "100") to a decline rate of 2.8 %. The respective change factors in the calculation formula account for 1.15 and 0.972.

If in a practical case – and with continuous solely positive or continuous solely negative values – there are only the first and last observed values of a numerical series (with n periods) available, the simpler calculation formula can be applied:

$$(1 + v) = (\text{Final value}/\text{Initial value})^{(1/n)}$$

Rates of change are often (after multiplying by "100") interpreted as percentages (i.e. stated "in per cent", e.g. 1.8 % decline). In contrast, an increase or decrease in the rate of change is indicated "in percentage points" (the increase of the complaint rate has risen, e.g. from 4.2 % by 1.5 percentage points to 5.7 % or has halved by 2.1 percentage points to 2.1 %).

## Calculation/Derivation
The data for the purpose of this KPI has to be gathered from the equidistant time series. Furthermore, the data should be extracted in accordance with the issue under analysis (for example, external values with global, national or industry relevance or internal values with organizational structure relevance in a company) from the appropriate statistical sources, as well as from the accounting information systems.

## Interpretation and Typical Range
With the compound annual rate of change (v, henceforth CAGR), the average percentage change of a business relevant value per period within the course of time is determined. It may be an average increase (value of v > 0; e.g. increasing revenue), an average stagnation (value of v = 0; e.g. price stability), or an average decrease (value of v < 0, e.g. declining number of customers).

The choice of a periodic reference value depends highly on the research object – usually years, quarters or months are the corresponding reference periods for comparison. Basically, absolute stock values (e.g. inventory volume), absolute flow variables (e.g. operating incomes), as well as relative values (e.g. profit margins) can be considered as business issues worth analysing.

From a mathematical point of view, when determining the parameter CAGR, the so-called geometric mean of the changed values that belong to the individual periods is calculated. The issue of analysis needs to be ratio-scaled (indicating quantity, value or percentage, as for example number of pieces sold, fixed costs or capacity utilization) and all characteristic values need to present a solely positive or negative value (e.g. number of employees or partial loss). For a value-series with positive and negative values (for example gains and losses), it is not possible to determine a significant CAGR. Consequently, the geometric mean is arithmetically the $n^{th}$ root from the mathematical product of all observed change factors (i.e. all corresponding rates of change plus 1).

A generalized specification for the amount of the corresponding average rates of change is not determinable. With business-guided circumstances, the organizational goals, fixed by the company, serve as an important measuring stick. As an orientation for the magnitude of the rates of change, one could take internal comparisons (such as the ratio in different organizational units or budget-actual comparisons) and/or corresponding external comparisons, where the branch-specific average values or competitor's data or the "best-practice" values may be used as a guide.

**!** **Useful Suggestions**

As the CAGR represents a general mathematical measure for the percentage increase or decrease, it is useful for reporting, as well as universally applicable in all functional areas and on all organizational levels of management. Consequently, it is a central instrument for the numerical presentation of corporate growth.

As far as the subject of analysis is manoeuvrable over time, for example, contribution margins per product or fixed costs per factory site, appropriate management measures will have to be planned and implemented if the developments do not meet the target corporate goal. These days, managers increasingly choose relative targets (as against absolute targets), like "wanting to grow faster than the market" or "being more profitable than the biggest competitor".

In light of the widespread applications of the parameter CAGR, it is important to be aware of the substantial possibilities and limits of this interpretation. The shorter the observation period, the stronger the influence of individual (particularly positive or negative) fluctuations/volatilities on the average rate of growth or decline rate within the time period. By contrast, the longer the observation period, the greater is the likelihood of an alignment process and a levelling of extreme values happening. Seasonal fluctuations are not apparent from the average value. Likewise, one has to consider the so-called base effect; Identical increases in absolute values in relation to a smaller starting point, project a high growth rate, whereas in relation to an already high base, it projects a small growth rate.

Also, the difficulty of choosing a reference date or period (with a particularly low or high starting value) as a base for calculating the rate of change, needs to be considered for industry wide comparisons.

From the sole information of the CAGR, it is not possible to detect clear trends. The possible time series of change rates "10 %–8 %–6 %–4 %" or 4 %–6 %–8 %–10 %" lead to an identical average rate of change (v=0.0697, consequently 6.97 %), although completely contrary underlying developments are happening in each case.

Analogically, if this time series had negative percentage values as decline rates (for example for the yearly operational waste generation), an annotation could arise that distorts the real situation. The forward projection of future time periods is likewise, problematic. Only when making a comparison with earlier average rates of change can reliable findings be obtained.

**Related Ratios/Additional Notes**                                                    &

The term CAGR is a generic term for growth rate or decline rate. In many cases corresponding combinations of synonyms for both root words are used, for example, growth rate. Occasionally, in cases of shrinking markets, the term "negative growth rate" is used.

By comparison with the geometric mean, where compound average increases or decreases are calculated, the arithmetical mean calculates the average value of the observed absolute stock or flow values (for example average total assets or staff costs) or the average value of relatively expressed parameters (for example: equity ratio).

# 2 Financial Perspective

## 2.1 Profit Indicators

### 2.1.1 Earnings before Taxes (EBT)

**Analytical Question**  ?

How much are the earnings before taxes?

**Definition**  *

| | |
|---|---|
| | Net Income or Loss |
| + | Taxes on Income and Profits/(– Tax Refund) |
| = | EBT (Earnings before Taxes) |

The financial reporting under IAS/IFRS rules prohibits the explicit demarcation of extraordinary results. Instead, IAS/IFRS rules require a declaration of the "Results from Discontinued Operations".

The figure of EBT is stated in absolute currency units (for example, in €).

**Calculation/Derivation**  »

The data for this purpose can be obtained from the income statement contained in the annual reports (or quarterly reports).

**Interpretation and Typical Range**  #

The EBT is an indicator, belonging to the category of Pro forma ratios (the so-called "Earnings before..."-Family) which have emerged in the context of IFRS-Accounting.

To calculate the annual results, the revenues have to be added and expenses have to be subtracted. For specific analysis and information purposes, it may, however, be helpful to make special adjustments to the declared results. These adjustments, to a greater or lesser extent, lead to various intermediate or (as the case may be) to pro forma results, which deliver a subjective result. The "Earnings-before..." ratios provide estimates of earnings, as if the special adjusted expenses and/or revenues had not taken place in the firm. This helps in improving comparability over time and between firms. However, it can also lead to distortions and unclear comparisons, if unilateral changes in terminology made by the firm were not explicitly communicated.

The core of the EBT as an indicator represents the annual (or quarterly) net income, which according to the income statement is an *after-tax* number. However, the after-tax number is "neutralized" for the taxes paid. As a result, EBT is a pre-tax number.

https://doi.org/10.1515/9783110598094-003

For the absolute level of EBT, no generalization about a target number is possible. When comparisons are made over time (for the whole firm or parts thereof), a trend analysis (continuous increase or fall, highly fluctuating, etc.) of EBT over time has significant explanatory power. The explanatory value of EBT can be further increased by analysing it vis-à-vis sales or assets. This allows us to measure relative profitability which can be used for comparing firms of different sizes.

### ❗ Useful Suggestions

EBT should be used as a benchmark for comparing operating earning capacity in companies across different tax jurisdictions. An explicit calculation of results before income tax provides a good base, if the comparison is being drawn between firms having different forms of business organization or between firms in different tax regimes, and, last but not least, between firms operating internationally.

In order to influence this financial indicator, on the sales side, EBT could be improved by a better price or volume strategy. On the expense side, EBT could be improved by a more efficient use of the factors of production. As good examples of improving EBT, actions, such as focusing on profitable segments of products and services, careful price increases, and targeted control of variable and fixed costs be recommended.

### & Related Ratios/Additional Notes

Often, Profit before Taxes (PbT) is used as a synonym for EBT. However, some experts believe that the term "profit" includes both operating and non-operating profits.

Related ratios are: EBIT, EBITA, and EBITDA.

In general, the adjustments made in the calculation of "Pro-forma ratios" are non-recurring, mostly in abnormal and non-sustainable circumstances, which are shown in the income statement as business-related or non-business-related items. They are mostly viewed as "noise factors" which could influence a "fair view" of the wealth, financial and earnings position of the firm.

For deduction of taxes, one should consider only the taxes on income and profits. The other forms of taxes should not be deducted.

## 2.1.2 Earnings before Interest and Taxes (EBIT)

**Analytical Question**

How much are the earnings from operating business before interest and taxes?

**Definition**

> Net Income or Loss
> + Taxes on Income and Profits/(−Tax Refund)
> ─────────────────────────────────────────
> = EBT (Earnings/Income from Operating Business before Taxes)
> + Interest Expense
> ─────────────────────────────────────────
> = EBIT (Earnings/Operating Income before Interest and Taxes)

The financial reporting under IAS/IFRS rules prohibits the explicit demarcation of extraordinary results. Instead, IAS/IFRS rules require a declaration of the "Results from Discontinued Operations".

The figure of EBIT is stated in absolute currency units (for example, in €).

**Calculation/Derivation**

The data for this purpose can be obtained from the income statement contained in the annual or quarterly reports.

**Interpretation and Typical Range**

The EBIT is an indicator, belonging to the category of Pro forma ratios (the so-called "Earnings before…"-Family) which have emerged in the context of IFRS-Accounting.

The calculation of EBIT shows the operating earning capacity of a firm, independent of its capital structure and income tax burden. As an indicator, it is suitable for comparing profitability (when used along with sales or asset base), between firms, parts thereof, profit centres or segments.

The core of the EBIT as an indicator represents the annual (or quarterly) net income, which, according to the income statement, is an *after-tax* number. However, the after-tax number is "neutralized" for the tax payment and the interest expense. As a result, EBIT is a pre-tax number, which also removes the leverage effect (in the form of interest expense).

To calculate the annual results, the revenues have to be added and expenses have to be subtracted. For specific analysis and information purposes, it may be helpful to make special adjustments to the declared results. These adjustments, to a greater or lesser extent, lead to various intermediate or (as the case may be) to pro forma results, which deliver a subjective result. The "Earnings-before…" ratios provide estimates of earnings, as if the specially adjusted expenses and/or revenues had not occured in the firm. This can help in improving comparability over time and between firms. This can, however, also lead to distortions and unclear comparisons, if unilateral changes in terminology made by the firm were not explicitly communicated.

For the absolute level of EBIT, no generalization about a target number is possible. When comparisons are made over time (for the whole firm or parts thereof), a trend analysis (continuous increase or fall, highly fluctuating, etc.) of EBIT over time offers significant explanatory power. The explanatory value of EBIT can be increased by analysing it vis-à-vis sales or assets. This allows us to measure relative profitability, which can be used when comparing firms of different sizes.

### ! Useful Suggestions

EBIT should be used as a benchmark to compare the operating earning capacity between companies across different tax jurisdictions or compare companies with different capital structures. An explicit calculation of results before income tax provides a good base, if the comparison is being drawn between firms having different forms of business organization, or between firms in different tax regimes, or between firms operating internationally.

In order to influence this profit indicator, on the sales side, EBIT could be improved by a better price or volume strategy. On the expense side, EBIT could be improved by a more efficient use of the factors of production. As good examples of improving EBIT, actions such as focusing on profitable segments of products and services, careful price increases, targeted controlling of variable and fixed costs be recommended.

### & Related Ratios/Additional Notes

Sometimes, Profit before Interest and Taxes (PBIT) is used as a synonym for EBIT. However, some experts believe that the term "profit" includes both operating and non-operating profits.

Related ratios are: EBT, EBITA, and EBITDA. In the network of Pro forma ratios, along with these three, EBIT is the most widespread indicator of profitability.

In general, the adjustments made in the calculation of "Pro-forma ratios" are non-recurring, mostly in abnormal and non-sustainable circumstances, which are shown in the income statement as business-related or non-business-related items. They are mostly viewed as "noise factors" which could influence a "fair view" of the wealth, financial and earnings position of the firm.

In the deduction of taxes, one should consider only the taxes on income and profits. The other forms of taxes should not be deducted.

If both incomes and expenditures of a particular item (for example, interest expenses and interest income) are matched in the income statement for neutralizing the Pro forma ratios, it is called treatment parity. When only the revenue or expense side is considered, it is called treatment disparity. This approach is indeed the case in EBIT calculation, where only the interest expense is added back to the earnings.

If comparisons are made over time and between firms, it must be based on a clear and consistent foundation of definitions. Otherwise, the conclusions drawn may be of limited use.

Over time, there are many new variants, which have been added to the "Earnings before…" Ratios, and thus it is difficult to mention each variant. Some examples of the alphabets added to EBIT are as follows:

A   = Amortization
D   = Depreciation
DT = Deferred Taxes
I    = Interest
R   = Rents
SO = Stock Options
X   = Exploration Expenses

Thus, different kinds of interpretations are used in the internal reporting system for these indicators. Often, these indicators are not comprehensible to external parties, and have been exposed to increasing criticism.

### 2.1.3 Earnings before Interest, Taxes and Amortization (EBITA)

**Analytical Question**
How much are the earnings from operating business before interest, taxes and amortization (of intangible assets)?

**Definition**

| | |
|---|---|
| | Net Income or Loss |
| + | Taxes on Income and Profits/(−Tax Refund) |
| | EBT (Earnings/Income from Operating Business before Taxes) |
| + | Interest Expense |
| = | EBIT (Earnings/Operating Income before Interest and Taxes) |
| + | Amortization of Intangible Assets, including Goodwill |
| = | EBITA (Earnings before Interest, Taxes and Amortization) |

The financial reporting under IAS/IFRS rules prohibits explicit demarcation of extraordinary results. Instead, IAS/IFRS rules require a declaration of the "Results from Discontinued Operations".

The figure of EBITA is stated in absolute currency units (for example, in €)

**Calculation/Derivation**

The data for EBITA can be obtained from the income statement contained in the annual or quarterly reports.

**# Interpretation and Typical Range**

The EBITA is an indicator, belonging to the category of Pro forma ratios (the so-called "Earnings before..."-Family) which have emerged in the context of IFRS-Accounting.

The calculation of EBITA shows the operating earning capacity of a firm, independent of its capital structure and amortization of intangible assets (including goodwill). The last adjustment regarding amortization is integrated into reporting, primarily by those companies which find their EBIT reduced because of high amortization.

To calculate the annual results, the revenues have to be added and expenses have to be subtracted. For specific analysis and information purposes, it may, however, be helpful to make special adjustments to the declared results. These adjustments, to a greater or lesser extent, lead to various intermediate or (as the case may be) to pro forma results which deliver a subjective result. The "Earnings-before..." ratios provide estimates of earnings, as if the specially adjusted expenses and/or revenues had not occured in the firm. This can help in improving comparability over time and between firms. This can, however, also lead to distortions and unclear comparisons, if unilateral changes in terminology made by the firm were not communicated explicitly.

The core of the EBITA, as an indicator, represents the annual (or quarterly) net income, which, according to the income statement, is an *after-tax* number. The after-tax number is "neutralized" for the tax payment, the interest expense and the amortized amount. As a result, EBITA is a pre-tax number, which also removes the leverage (in the form of interest expense) and amortization policy effects.

The additional adjustment for amortization of intangible assets (including that of goodwill), should neutralize the differences in the earnings:
– Between firms which have grown internally and externally; in the case of companies with external growth, where acquisition price often contains a high amount of payment goodwill. Such acquired goodwill needs to be amortized over time, and during such periods of high amortization, the reported earnings (EBIT) may be conspicuously reduced.
– Between firms which have high license fees (for example, towards the acquisition of mobile-technology rights by telecom providers) and those which do not have such fees. In companies with high license fees, the reported earnings under EBITA are freed from amortization related encumbrances.

The significance of EBITA has grown since the introduction of the new rules for goodwill amortization, which, instead of a regular write off, allow an unscheduled amortization reference to an annual impairment test. But for the adjustment made in EBITA, the fluctuating write-off in the new rules makes EBIT more exposed to changes in amortization.

An explicit calculation of results before income tax provides a good base, if the comparison is being drawn between firms having different forms of business organization, or between firms in different tax regimes, and, or between firms operating internationally.

For the absolute level of EBITA, no generalization about a target number is possible. When comparisons are made over time (for the whole firm or parts thereof), a trend analysis (continuous increase or fall, highly fluctuating, etc.) of EBITA over time offers significant explanatory power. The explanatory value of EBITA can be increased by analysing it vis-à-vis sales or assets. This allows us to measure relative profitability which can be used in comparing firms of different sizes.

**Useful Suggestions**
EBITA should be used as a benchmark to compare companies across different tax jurisdictions or compare companies with different capital structures or companies with differing amortization policies and volumes.

In order to influence this financial indicator, on the sales side, EBITA could be improved by a better price or volume strategy. On the expense side, EBITA could be improved by a more efficient use of the factors of production.

**Related Ratios/Additional Notes**
Related ratios are: EBT, EBIT, and EBITDA.

In general, the adjustments made in the calculation of "Pro-forma ratios" are non-recurring, mostly as abnormal and non-sustainable circumstances, which are shown in the income statement as business-related or non-business-related items. They are mostly viewed as "noise factors", which could influence a "fair view" of the wealth, financial and earnings position of the firm.

In the deduction of taxes, one should consider only the taxes on income and profits. The other forms of taxes should not be deducted.

If both incomes and expenditures of a particular issue (for example, interest expenses and interest income) are matched in the income statement to neutralise the Pro forma ratios, it is termed as treatment parity. When only the revenue or expense side is considered, it is termed as treatment disparity. This approach is indeed the case in EBITA calculations, where only the interest expense is added back to the earnings.

If comparisons are made over time and between firms, it must be based on a clear and consistent base of definitions. Otherwise, the conclusions drawn can be of limited use.

### 2.1.4 Result from Continued Operations

**?** **Analytical Question**

Using the IFRS Accounting Standards, how much is the probable regular income to be achieved with the company's continued operations?

**✱** **Definition**

Operating Income + Financial Income

The "operating income" should primarily reflect all revenues and expenses that can be attributed to the operating line of business and are regularly attainable. The financial income includes all financial earnings and financial expenses that are of growing relevance, not least in view of the increasing interdependence of companies within the affiliated group of companies. According to IFRS accounting, both earning components may also include extraordinary income and expenses.

The "Result from Continued Operations" is expressed in absolute currency units (for example in €).

**»** **Calculation/Derivation**

With reference to disclosure requirements in accordance with IFRS accounting, this results in the so-called operating income:
- **using full-cost accounting:**

    Sales Revenue
    + Increase/( – decrease) in work in process and finished goods
    – Internally produced and capitalized assets
    – Cost of raw materials, consumables and supplies
    – Employee benefits and social security contributions
    – Employer's contribution to employees' retirement plans
    – Scheduled depreciation on property, plant and equipment
      and amortization of intangible assets (with finite useful lives)
    + Other incomes[1] /(–Other expenses[1])
    = Operating income (Based on IFRS)

- **using cost-of-sales accounting:**

    Sales Revenue
    – Cost of goods and services produced to generate sales (CoGS)
    – Sales and distribution expenses
    – General and administrative expenses
    – Research expenses
    + Other income[1] /(–Other expenses[1])
    = Operating income (Based on IFRS)

With reference to disclosure requirements under IFRS accounting standards, the so-called financial income is calculated as follows

   Interest (and similar) Incomes
−  Interest (and similar) Expenses
+  Dividend income
+  Income/( − expenses) from Investment Property
+  Income/( − expenses) from Associated Firms
+  Income/( − expenses) from License Fee and Royalty
+  Income/( − expenses) from Trust Business
=  Financial Income (Based on IFRS)

## Interpretation and Typical Range

In a growing number of companies, in addition to operational (mainstream business purpose) activities, financial activities are gaining in importance as success drivers (e.g. in the form of product-related services). Thus, making a clear distinction between "operating income" and "financial income" is becoming increasingly problematic. There is no generalizable guideline for the absolute amount of the "income from continuing operations" and its two sub-classifications – operating and financial incomes. When comparing actual results over time, or budget-actual ratios within the same period, the direction of change (continuously increasing or decreasing, strongly fluctuating, etc.) has an important interpretative power. This can be increased even further if these success factors are regularly viewed in relation to meaningful sales and capital values (such as Return on Sales or Return on Capital Employed).

## Useful Suggestions

In order to influence the operating income positively, the manager could work through a better price and/or volume strategy on the sales side. Similarly, on the input (cost) side, operating income could be optimized through a more efficient use of the factors of production. To cite a few examples, promoting profitable components of the product and service offering, selective use of the price variations, and targeted influencing of the variable and fixed costs development.

   The possibilities to influence the so-called financial income are diverse and depend on the specific circumstances of the company. As far as investments in other companies are concerned, strategic aspects of shareholding in other companies are of prime importance for example. A clearly negative financial result (for example, due to considerable interest expenses on borrowed capital) can also be desired,

---

1 As far as not related to any non-periodic results (such as amortization on Goodwill)

from an entrepreneurial point of view, if the return on equity is to be increased with the help of the leverage effect.

**& Related Ratios/Additional Notes**

Though most of the annual financial statements are largely based on the past, the management report does give some information about future developments. Thus, the external parties can only make limited and rough projections about future profitability, given their additional (industry-related) knowledge.

According to IFRS accounting standards, a further split of a firm's success can be made in the following form:
–   Operating and financial income (here combined into "Result from continuing operations")
–   Non-periodic income
–   Result from discontinued operations.

### 2.1.5 Result from Discontinued Operations

**? Analytical Question**

To what extent will the discontinued operations change the future performance of the enterprise?

**\* Definition**

The term "Result from Discontinued Operations" originated from IFRS accounting. It should be distinguished from other performance indicators, such as profit or loss from "Operating Business", "Non-operating Business" (for example, financial activities), and "Non-periodic Business".

This term "Result from Discontinued Operations" explicitly refers to the results of all those operations which the enterprise discontinued in the current year, or will be discontinuing in the future.

The "Result from Discontinued Operations" is stated in absolute currency units (for example, in €).

**» Calculation/Derivation**

With reference to the disclosure requirements of IFRS Accounting, the following calculation schema has been developed:

+   Revenues/(– Expenses) and Pre-tax Profit or Loss from Discontinued Operation(s)
+   Gain/(– Loss) resulting from the Valuation of Assets of Discontinued Operation(s)
+   Gain/(– Loss) resulting from the Sale of Discontinued Operation(s)
─────
=   Result from Discontinued Operations (Based on IFRS 5)

## Interpretation and Typical Range

A separate calculation for the results from discontinued operations increases the transparency of the annual financial statements, particularly towards the prognosis of future performance.

The magnitude of this individual figure depends to a great extent on the strategy (in particular the disinvestment strategy) of the enterprise under consideration, for example in the form of its regional or product divisional strategy.

## Useful Suggestions

The ability of the management to influence this figure depends significantly upon its strategic and operational policies.

## Related Ratios/Additional Notes

It is important to note that not all the results associated with the discontinued operations are included in this figure. In so far as gain or loss from the sale of non-current assets already sold or "classified as held for sale" not constituting part of a group, is not allowed to be shown as "Result from Discontinued Operations", such gains and losses should be captured as ordinary profit or loss.

### 2.1.6 Non-periodic Income

## Analytical Question

What is the volume of non-periodic income? How much income, in the period under consideration, is irregular and cannot be foreseen in advance?

## Definition

In the classification of performance indicators, the twin criteria of "linkage to business" and "regularity" are predominant. In the non-periodic income, attention is devoted to the irregularity of the circumstances. This indicator could well be further classified into operating and non-operating income.

This measure is collated with other performance indicators in IFRS accounting. It should be distinguished from other performance indicators, such as profit or loss from "Operating Business", "Non-operating Business" (for example, financial activities), and "Result from Discontinued Business".

The non-periodic income is stated in absolute currency units (for example, in €).

## Calculation/Derivation

According to the disclosure requirements under IFRS, non-periodic *operating* income is presented in the following formula:

> Other Incomes[2]
> – Impairment of Intangible Assets with an Indefinite Life, including Goodwill
> + Income from "Badwill" Settlement
> – Unscheduled Depreciation on Fixed Assets
> + Appreciation/(– Depreciation) in the value of Fixed Assets
> + Actuarial Mathematics related Gain/(– Loss) from Pension Obligations
> + Gain/(– Loss) from Exchange Translation
> + Inflation-related Gain/(– Loss) from Currency erosion
> + Gain/(– Loss) from Change in Estimates
> – Expenses[3]
>
> = Non-periodic *Operating* Income

According to the disclosure requirements under IFRS, non-periodic *non-operating* income is presented in the following schema:

> Other Incomes[4]
> + Valuation Gain/(– Loss) from Fair Value through Profit and Loss-Financial Instruments
> + Gain/(– Loss) from write-off of Available-for-sale and Held-to-maturity financial instruments
> + New-valuation Gain/(– Loss) of Investment property
> – Other Expenses[5]
>
> = Non-periodic *Non-operating* Income

**# Interpretation and Typical Range**

The annual financial statements become more transparent through separate identification of non-periodic incomes. This helps in improving the information value regarding the sustainability of income, which in turn, improves the forecasting of future earning capacity for the enterprise.

For the absolute level of operating income, no generalization about a target number is possible. When comparisons are made over time (for the whole firm or parts thereof), a trend analysis (continuous increase or fall, highly fluctuating, etc.) of non-periodic income over time, offers significant explanatory power.

---

2 To the extent they are not allocated to irregular non-operating income.
3 To the extent they are not allocated to irregular non-operating income.
4 To the extent they are not allocated to irregular operating income.
5 To the extent they are not allocated to irregular operating income.

**Useful Suggestions** !

The choices available to the management for influencing this performance indicator are no less significant. However, it is important to note that non-periodic income is a part of the periodic performance (IFRS rules), so that the main goal of increased transparency is adhered to.

**Related Ratios/Additional Notes** &

Both footnotes already hint at the problem that a clear differentiation of business transactions into "operating", "non-operating" and further into "regular" and "irregular" is not easy to determine. Ultimately, the information value of the calculated indicator suffers because of this weakness.

## 2.1.7 Net Operating Profit After Taxes (NOPAT)

**Analytical Question** ?

How much is the net operating profit after taxes (and before interest) of a firm?

**Definition** *

For many key figures, which have emerged recently in the literature, no exact terminology exists for individual components. Thus, the following definition represents a base-variant for defining NOPAT, which is used in literature and practice with several other adjustments:

> EBIT (Earnings/Operating Profits before Interest and Taxes)
> − Taxes on Income and Profits
> ───────────────────────────────────────────────
> = NOPAT (Net Operating Profit after Taxes and before Interest)

NOPAT is expressed in absolute currency units (for example, in €).

**Calculation/Derivation** »

The data for this ratio can be obtained from the annual financial statements.

In the literature and in practice, a series of additional adjustments are made to calculate NOPAT. Some examples are:

> + Amortization of Intangible Assets
> +/− Changes in Provisions (+ for increase and − for decrease)
> + Interest on Lease expenses
> +/− Changes in Capitalized R & D Costs (+ for increase and − for decrease)

For inter-firm comparisons, it is important to ensure the consistency of the definition for the adjusted periodic profits, as well as for the income and expenditure items.

**#** **Interpretation and Typical Range**

NOPAT shows the operating earning capacity of the firm, as if it is completely owner-financed (that is, as if it had no debt). This is because it does not include the tax savings which many firms get because they have existing debt. That is why, sometimes, NOPAT is described as Operating income before interest.

A general target for the optimum magnitude of NOPAT is not possible. The amount of NOPAT varies widely, depending upon branch-specific or size-specific characteristics. For comparison purposes, the branch-specific averages or best-practice values can be used as benchmarks. Similarly, observing the trend over time may provide useful information.

**!** **Useful Suggestions**

On the revenue side, NOPAT could be improved by a better price or volume strategy. On the expense side, it could be improved by more efficient cost management.

When recourse is made to the data available in the external accounting system, valuation based policies may influence NOPAT.

**&** **Related Ratios/Additional Notes**

NOPAT is used as the performance indicator for the calculation of Return On Invested Capital (ROIC), which in turn is used for value-added performance measurement, such as EVA (Economic Value Added).

NOPAT can also be calculated with the following formula, if operating profit can be taken as the base for taxation purposes:

NOPAT = Operating Profit x (1 − Tax Rate)

## 2.2 Profitability Indicators

### 2.2.1 EBIT-Turnover-Yield

**?** **Analytical Question**

What percentage of the turnover remains with the enterprise as profit (more precisely, as operating profit before interest and taxes)?

**\*** **Definition**

$$\frac{EBIT \cdot 100}{Sales}$$

Where EBIT is:

|   | |
|---|---|
|   | Net Income or Loss |
| + | Taxes on Income and Profits (– Tax Refund) |
| = | EBT (Earnings/Income from Operating Business before Taxes) |
| + | Interest Expense |
| = | EBIT (Earnings/Operating Income before Interest and Taxes) |

The financial reporting under IAS/IFRS rules prohibits explicit demarcation of extraordinary results. Instead, IAS/IFRS rules require a declaration of the "Results from Discontinued Operations".

The EBIT-Turnover-Yield is expressed as a percentage.

## Calculation/Derivation
The external parties can obtain the data for the purpose from the income statement contained in the annual or quarterly reports. The internal decision-makers can compute this ratio at shorter intervals within a year.

## Interpretation and Typical Range
The EBIT-Turnover-Yield is part of sales-based profitability ratios. It specifies the percentage of sales, which a firm is able to achieve as earnings (before interest and taxes) from its normal business. The ratio is, thus, a relative measure of the operating earnings capacity and the self-financing power of the enterprise. By comparison with the ratio "Return on Sales", EBIT-Turnover-Yield is a pre-tax measure, where the impact of interest payment is also eliminated. Thus, it could be considered as a "Gross Return on Sales".

Since the ratio is calculated before taxes, it represents the profit-generating capacity of the enterprise. Moreover, interest on borrowed funds is neutralized in the calculation, which makes the ratio independent of the capital structure (or financing effects). Therefore, the ratio is considered appropriate for comparing profitability between enterprises and business segments/divisions/profit centres. It is also used for judging the creditworthiness of enterprises.

EBIT-Turnover-Yield varies widely amongst different industrial branches and sectors. Therefore, it is difficult to recommend a target range. However, the higher the return, the better is the sales-related earning capacity of the enterprise. It is useful to compare a firm's EBIT-Turnover-Yield over time for trend analysis; an increasing, decreasing or stagnating trend over time provides more useful information about the operating performance of the enterprise.

## Useful Suggestions
A change in this ratio could be triggered by a disproportionate increase or decrease in the EBIT (as numerator) and sales (as denominator). *For further details and systematic explanations on this, refer to the information in Appendix I.*

On the (sales-related) revenue side, the EBIT could be improved by a better price or volume strategy. On the expense (payment) side, EBIT could be improved by more efficient cost management.

### & Related Ratios/Additional Notes
A closely related ratio is Return On Sales. If calculated with net income as numerator, the ratio is termed as Net Profit Margin.

Other related ratios are: EBITDA-Margin, Net Return On Sales and Cash Flow-to-Sales Ratio.

Sometimes, instead of sales, total output (comprising sales revenue, inventory changes and capitalization of internally-produced assets) is taken as the basis for calculation; this, however, does not change the interpretation of the ratio. When comparing this ratio with other enterprises, consistency of data should be ensured.

A calculation of return on sales, with earnings before tax, is recommended in all those cases where a comparison is drawn amongst different forms of organizations and, more so, for comparisons amongst enterprises in different taxation systems (such as enterprises from foreign countries).

To offset the effect of taxes, the taxes on income and profits should be considered. The other forms of taxes should not be offset.

If a firm has made a loss in a particular period (example: a negative EBIT), the calculated ratio is termed as "Burn Rate", implying the loss per currency unit of sales. For example, a negative EBIT of 8 cents per € of sales would mean a burn rate of 8 %.

### 2.2.2 Return On Sales (ROS)

### ? Analytical Question
What percentage of sales is available to the enterprise as profit (more specifically, as operating profit margin)?

Or how much profit is being produced per currency unit of sales?

### * Definition
In literature and practice, the term profit is numerously used, typical synonyms for profit are:
- net income,
- net income + Interest on debt,
- operating income, or
- earnings before interest and tax.

Whereas the first two indicators of profit are "after-tax" measures, the last two have a "before tax" character.

In general, return on sales is:

$$\frac{\text{Any Profit Indicator} \cdot 100}{\text{Sales}}$$

However, a specific (after-tax) definition is:

$$\frac{\text{Net Income} \cdot 100}{\text{Sales}}$$

Return On Sales is expressed as a percentage.

**Calculation/Derivation**                                                    »

The data for return on sales is available in the income statement of a particular financial report period

**Interpretation and Typical Range**                                          #

Return On Sales shows that part of sales which is available to a firm as profit. As an "after-tax" indicator, return on sales uses net income from the annual report as a measure of profit. This is, however, an aggregation at a very high level. In the framework for Return On Assets (ROA), the interest on debt needs to be considered as well. Thus, if the detailed definition of return on sales is not available, comparisons may not be easy.

As a "pre-tax" indicator, Return On Sales gives insight into how much profit (EBIT) is being generated from the normal operating business. Since the ratio is calculated before taxes, it represents the profit-generating capacity of the enterprise. Moreover, interest on borrowed funds is neutralized in the calculation, which makes the ratio independent of the capital structure (or financing effects). Therefore, the ratio is considered appropriate for comparing profitability between enterprises and business segments/divisions/profit centres.

Return On Sales is also used for judging the creditworthiness of enterprises. It varies widely amongst different industrial branches and sectors. Therefore, it is difficult to recommend a target range. However, the higher this return, the better the sales-related earning capacity of the enterprise. It is good to compare a firm's return on sales over time to look for trends; an increasing, decreasing or stagnating trend over time provides useful information about the operating performance of the enterprise.

For orientation purposes, one could make internal comparisons (such as the ratio in different organizational units or plan-actual values) or external comparisons, where the branch-specific average value or the "best-practice" value may be used as a guide.

**❗ Useful Suggestions**

A change in this ratio could be triggered by a disproportionate increase or decrease in the profit measure (as numerator) and sales (as denominator). *For further details and systematic explanations on this, refer to the information in Appendix I.*

On the (sales-related) revenue side, the EBIT could be improved by a better price or volume strategy. On the expense (payment) side, EBIT could be improved by a more efficient cost management.

**& Related Ratios/Additional Notes**

A closely related ratio is: EBIT-Turnover-Yield. If calculated with net income as numerator, the ratio is termed as Net Profit Margin.

Related ratios are: EBITDA-Margin, Net Return on Sales and Cash Flow-to-Sales Ratio.

Sometimes instead of sales, total output (comprising of sales revenue, inventory changes and capitalization of internally-produced assets) is taken as the basis for calculation; however, it does not change the interpretation of the ratio. When comparing this ratio with other enterprises, consistency of data should be ensured.

A calculation of Return On Sales with earnings before tax is recommended in all those cases where a comparison is drawn amongst different forms of organizations, and more so, for comparisons amongst enterprises across different taxation systems.

For offsetting taxes, only the taxes on income and profits should be considered. The other forms of taxes should not be offset.

If a firm has made a loss in a particular period, the calculated ratio is termed as "Burn Rate", implying the loss per currency unit of sales.

### 2.2.3 Return On Equity (ROE)

**❓ Analytical Question**

How good is the return on stockholders' equity?

How well has management used the stockholders' funds during the period?

**✳ Definition**

$$\frac{\text{Net Income} \cdot 100}{\text{Average Stockholders' Equity}}$$

Return On Equity is expressed as a percentage number.

**» Calculation/Derivation**

The data for net income is available in the income statement. The average stockholders' equity can be calculated with the beginning and ending balances from the balance sheets.

## Interpretation and Typical Range

Both present as well as potential investors are interested in the Return On Equity produced by the enterprise in the past, and more so, the expected Return On Equity in the future. Thus, enterprises have to integrate the minimum return expected by investors into their strategic planning.

The return on equity ratio is based on the balance sheet values of the stockholders' equity, and therefore, provides only a partial view of the enterprise's profitability. This is because it ignores the impact of stock price changes. For stockholders, Stock Yield is clearly a more comprehensive indicator.

In principle, for the calculation of Return On Equity, both profit *before* or *after* taxes can be taken. The calculation based on after tax profit (i.e. net income) is more common for external parties (for example, shareholders and analysts) and calculation based on before tax profit is more common for internal decision-makers. However, if non-incorporated enterprises are compared with tax-liable corporate enterprises, it would be sensible to take the profit before tax.

The Return On Equity, in the medium- or long-term range, should be well above the return on fixed-income securities. It is desirable to have a Return On Equity above the average market return on equity.

## Useful Suggestions

A change in this ratio could be triggered by a disproportionate increase or decrease in net income (as numerator) and in stockholders' equity (as denominator). *For further details and systematic explanations on this, refer to the information in Appendix I.*

On the revenue side, net income could be improved by a better price or volume strategy. On the expense side, net income could be improved by a more efficient cost management. An increase in Return On Equity could also be achieved through increased use of debt (leverage-effect).

## Related Ratios/Additional Notes

This ratio is also known as Return On Net Worth (RONW).

Related ratios are: Return On Sales, Return On Total Assets, Stock Yield, and Cash Flow-to-Equity Ratio. Another ratio called Leverage Factor shows the relation between Return On Stock and Return On Total Assets.

Effective analysis of a firm's return on equity also requires us to understand why its ROE differs over time and from those of its competitors. ROE profit driver analysis (also known as DuPont Analysis) breaks down ROE into three factors. These factors are called profit drivers and include Net Profit Margin, Asset Turnover and Financial Leverage. These three factors explain the effectiveness of the enterprise's operating, investing and financing activities respectively. *For additional explanation about the multi-layered ratio systems, refer to the DuPont System in Appendix II as an example.*

Instead of average stockholders' equity, the ratio may also be calculated with the beginning or end of the period stockholders' equity.

For non-corporate enterprises, an appropriate amount for owner's salary should be deducted from the net income to ensure the comparability with corporate enterprises.

### 2.2.4 Return On Assets (ROA)

**? Analytical Question**

How good is the return on total assets? How well has management used the invested assets to generate earnings?

**\* Definition**

$$\frac{(\text{Net Income} + \text{Interest Expense}) \cdot 100}{\text{Average Total Assets}}$$

Return On Assets is expressed as a percentage.

**» Calculation/Derivation**

The data for net income and interest expense is available in the income statement. The amount of interest expense should preferably be net of tax. The average total assets can be calculated with the beginning and ending balances from the balance sheet.

**# Interpretation and Typical Range**

Return On Assets show what earnings were (or will be) generated from total assets.

The ROA ratio is based on the balance sheet values for the assets, and therefore, provides only a partial view of the enterprise's profitability. This is because it ignores the impact of stock price changes. For stockholders, Stock Yield is clearly a more comprehensive indicator.

In principle, for the calculation of Return On Assets, both profit *before* or *after* taxes can be taken. The calculation based on after tax profit (i.e. net income) is more common for external parties (for example, shareholders and analysts) and calculation based on before tax profit is more common for internal decision-makers. However, if non-incorporated enterprises are compared with tax-liable corporate enterprises, it would be sensible to take the profit before tax.

It is not possible to give a desired target ratio for ROA. For orientation and comparison purposes, it is advisable to take the ROA ratio of competitors within the same branch, or listed (inter)national enterprises as a benchmark.

## Useful Suggestions

!

A change in this ratio could be triggered by a disproportionate increase or decrease in net income (as numerator) and average total assets (as denominator). *For further details and systematic explanations on this, refer to the information in Appendix I.*

In the numerator, net income could be improved by a better price or volume strategy. On the expense side, net income could be improved by a more efficient cost management. An increase in Return On Assets could also be achieved by encouraging high-return products or by reducing weaker products and services in the product portfolio. *For additional explanation about multi-layered ratio systems, refer to the DuPont System in Appendix II as an example.*

In the denominator, a reduction in the asset base could be achieved by disposing of non-operating assets (at least at book value) or a reduction in inventory levels.

## Related Ratios/Additional Notes

&

This ratio is also known as Return on Total Assets.

Related ratios are: Return On Investment (ROI), Return On Sales, Return On Equity, and Cash Flow-to-Total-Assets Ratio.

Instead of the average asset base, the ratio may also be calculated with the beginning or end of the period assets.

For non-corporate enterprises, an appropriate amount for owner's salary should be deducted from the net income to ensure the comparability with corporate enterprises.

## 2.2.5 Earnings Per Share (EPS)

### Analytical Question

?

What is the performance (earnings) of a company per share? How profitable is a company in relation to its outstanding shares?

### Definition

*

$$\frac{\text{Net Income}}{\text{Average Number of Outstanding Shares}}$$

Earnings Per Share is stated in absolute currency units (for example, in €).

Depending upon the accounting standards (IAS/IFRS, US-GAAP), a series of further variants of this ratio are calculated. For example, EPS may be based on types of shares or income (such as results from discontinued business). Thus, for inter-company comparisons, one should carefully check the underlying definition. If the firm has both common and preferred stock, the net income in the numerator should be adjusted for dividends paid for the preferred stock.

**»** **Calculation/Derivation**

The data for net income is available in the income statement. The information for dividends on preferred stock is usually available in the statement of stockholders' equity. The average number of outstanding shares can be computed by taking the beginning and end balances of common stock from the statement of stockholders' equity. However, it is more accurate to use the weighted average number of shares outstanding over the reporting period, because the number of shares outstanding may change over time. Thus, for example, if a company had 10 million shares for the first 3 months of the year and 15 million shares for the last 9 months of the year, the average outstanding will be 13.75 million shares (3/12 x 10)+(9/12 x 15). The freshly issued shares increases the number of shares outstanding, whereas repurchase of shares by the company decreases the number of average shares.

**#** **Interpretation and Typical Range**

"Earnings Per Share" serves as an effective indicator of profitability and is widely used in evaluating the performance of a company. It shows the portion of a company's profit allocated to each outstanding share of common stock.

The ratio provides a relative measure of profitability. Comparing the absolute earnings of one company with another does not really make sense, because it ignores the fact that two companies usually have a different number of outstanding shares. EPS is a good way of comparing the performance of the same company over time.

It is not possible to give a desired target ratio for EPS. For orientation purposes, it is advisable to take the earnings per share of competitors within the same branch.

**!** **Useful Suggestions**

"Earnings Per Share" is considered to be the single most important variable in determining a share's price. It is also an important component used to calculate the price-to-earnings valuation ratio. An improvement in the EPS of a company over time usually leads to positive reactions from investors, often leading to an increase in the share price.

A change in this ratio can be triggered by a disproportionate increase or decreases in net income (as numerator) and average number of outstanding shares (as denominator). *For further details and systematic explanations on this, refer to the information in Appendix I.*

While EPS is an effective measure, it can be misleading if there are significant differences in the market values of the shares being compared. Thus, if two companies have an EPS of €1.50, they might appear comparable. However, if shares in one company cost €10 and shares of the other cost €175, they are not comparable.

In order to improve the ratio, in addition to the financial possibilities of designing equity capital in the denominator, all measures which help a firm in earning decent distributable profits will have a positive impact on the EPS. For example, earnings could be improved through measures, which relate to the price and/or volume strategy on the sales side or through better organization of the input factors on the operational side.

**Related Ratios/Additional Notes**                                    &

As a synonym, "Profit per Share" can also be used.

A closely related variant of EPS is Diluted Earnings Per Share (Diluted-EPS). It expands on basic EPS by including the shares of convertibles, stock options (primarily employee based) and warrants outstanding in the average number of outstanding shares. With an unchanged numerator (net income) and expanded denominator, the diluted EPS is always lower than the basic EPS. Thus, it is considered to be a conservative measure and an indicator of a worst-case scenario. This is because it is unlikely that all convertibles, stock options and warrants would convert into common stock at once.

A related ratio is Cash Flow Per Share. This is a measure of financial performance that looks at the cash flow generated by a company on a per share basis.

Instead of average number of outstanding shares, the ratio may also be calculated with the number of outstanding shares at the end of the period.

### 2.2.6 Return On Investment (ROI)                                    Ⓢ

**Analytical Question**                                                ?

How good is the return on invested assets or employed capital? How well has the management used the invested assets to generate earnings? How efficient was an investment?

**Definition**                                                        ✱

The terminology used in the literature on the subject, as well as in the business world, is not uniform. The following two definitions exemplify the differences:

Variant A as a liberal version:

This definition of Return On Investment is identical with Return On Assets:

$$\frac{(\text{Net Income} + \text{Interest Expense}) \cdot 100}{\text{Average Total Assets 'or' Average Total Capital}}$$

or

Variant B as a conservative version:

This definition of Return On Investment uses operating income before interest and taxes in the numerator (with a neutrality towards the type of financing, the interest expense in not added back), and invested capital in the denominator:

$$\frac{\text{Earnings/Operating Income before Interest and Taxes (EBIT)} \cdot 100}{\text{Average Assets Employed}}$$

In either of the types, the numerator and denominator are logically linked to each other. Thus, Variant A relates the after-tax-income with total assets of the enterprise (where extraordinary incomes and incomes not relating to the current year are also included), and Variant B is based on pre-tax operating income and focuses on the operating business only.

Both of these definitions have their legitimacy and, in practice, they are used interchangeably. For inter-enterprise comparison, it is important to ensure the consistency of data used for different indicators.

ROI is expressed as a percentage.

## » Calculation/Derivation

The data for net income and earnings before interest and taxes and interest expense is available in the income statement. The average total investment can be calculated from the balance sheet. If assets employed differ from total assets, the appropriate information would have to be obtained from the internal accounting records. This information may not be available to external parties. The interest expense should preferably be net of tax.

As part of the internal reporting system, Return On Investment can also be calculated for periods shorter than a year. Thus, bi-annual, quarterly, and monthly ROI may be calculated for various segments/divisions of the enterprise.

## # Interpretation and Typical Range

Return On Investment shows the relative earnings generated (or which will be generated) from the invested capital (i.e. assets). The ROI is one of the most commonly used periodic ratios for finding out the return on invested capital.

In the key performance indicators pyramids, various composites of profitability ratios are commonly used. The Return On Investment is placed mostly at the top of such a pyramid with its various vertical and horizontal sub-divisions. The step-wise decomposition of the target ratio at various levels, allows for a systematic review of the drivers, which influence the return on investment. It is also referred to as the "DuPont Framework" (*refer to Appendix II for details*), because it is based on the pioneering work by this US American company.

For the sake of simplicity, ROI (Net Income/Invested Capital) is often presented with its multiplicative extensions. In the key performance indicator, the next level of ROI is also reorganized into "Return On Sales" (Net Income/Sales) multiplied by "Asset Turnover" (Sales/Total Assets),

In principle, in the calculation of profitability ratios, both profit *before* or *after* taxes can be taken. The calculation based on after tax profit (i.e. net income) is more common for external parties (for example, shareholders and analysts) and calculation based on before tax profit is more common for internal decision-makers. However, if non-corporate enterprises are compared with tax-liable corporate enterprises, it would be sensible to take the profit before tax. For non-corporate enterprises, an appropriate amount for owner's salary should be deducted from the net income to ensure the comparability with corporate enterprises.

It is not possible to give a desired target ratio for ROI. For orientation and comparison purposes, it is advisable to use the ROI of competitors within the same branch or of listed (inter)national enterprises as benchmark.

The ROI ratio is based primarily on the balance sheet values of the stockholders' equity, and therefore, provides only a partial view of the enterprise's profitability. This is because it ignores the impact of stock price changes. For stockholders, Stock Yield is clearly a more comprehensive indicator. Stock Yield shows the influence of stock-exchange-related factors, such as boom or slump in the market. However, it does not apply to the individual segments of the enterprise.

In the case that ROI, as in Variant B, is based on operating income, and the focus is on the profitability comparisons within the enterprise (and its divisions), the extraordinary and non-operating incomes/gains, as well as the aspects relating to the tax policy of the enterprise, are marked-off. Thus, the focus is placed on the actual operating performance of a particular unit, which a responsible manager can influence.

**Useful Suggestions**
A change in this ratio could be triggered by a disproportionate increase or decrease in net income (as numerator) and in invested capital (as denominator). *For further details and systematic explanations on this, refer to the information in Appendix I.*

In the numerator, net income could be improved by a better price or volume strategy. On the expense side, net income could be improved by more efficient cost management. An increase in Return On Investment could also be achieved by encouraging high-return products or by reducing weaker products and services in the product portfolio.

In the denominator, a reduction in the asset base can be achieved by disposing of non-operating assets (at least at book value) or a reduction in inventory levels.

The multiplicative link between "Return On Sales" and "Asset Turnover" ratios in ROI shows that a firm can maintain its profitability despite a fall in the Return On Sales, if it is able to improve its Asset Turnover Ratio. For this, a careful evaluation of the short, medium, and long-term impact of all the measures which reduce the asset base without negatively influencing the sales-generating capacity, should be carried out. Similarly, a rise or fall in the profitability of the enterprise could be analysed with reference to return on sales and/or asset-turnover, and measures for improvement can be developed. *For additional explanation about the multi-layered ratio systems, refer to the DuPont System in Appendix II as an example.*

**&** **Related Ratios/Additional Notes**

Related ratios are: Return On Assets (ROA), Return On Equity, Cash Flow-to-Total-Assets Ratio and Return On Sales.

Instead of average asset base, the ratio may also be calculated with end of the period assets.

### 2.2.7 Return On Invested Capital (ROIC)

**?** **Analytical Question**

How good is the return on invested capital? How good is the return on required capital? How well is management able to allocate capital within its operations?

**\*** **Definition**

$$\frac{\text{NOPAT} \cdot 100}{\text{Average Invested Capital}}$$

Where:

| | EBIT (Earnings/Operating Profits before Interest and Taxes) |
|---|---|
| + | Taxes on Income and Profits/(− Tax Refund) |
| = | NOPAT (Net Operating Profit after Taxes and before Interest) |

and
Average values of the following:

| | Required Working Capital |
|---|---|
| − | Non-Interest Bearing Current Liabilities |
| | Net Working Capital |
| + | Fixed Assets |
| = | Average Invested Capital |

Return On Invested Capital is expressed as a percentage.

**»** **Calculation/Derivation**

The data for this ratio can be calculated from the annual financial statements. In the category of non-interest bearing current liabilities, advance payments received from customers (for goods and services to be delivered) are also included. The amount of average invested capital can be calculated from the beginning and closing balances available on the balance sheet.

**Interpretation and Typical Range**                                    `#`
Return On Invested Capital shows how effectively the capital was invested.

The Return On Sales and Return On Assets are considered as base measures of business performance. However, for special kinds of analysis, these ratios provide a very general view. Therefore, a series of new variants have been developed. At the centre of ROIC, the immediate link is provided between earnings from normal operations and the invested capital.

It is not possible to give a desired target ratio for Return On Invested Capital. For orientation and benchmarking this ratio, one could take internal comparisons (such as the ratio in different organizational units or plan-actual values) or external comparisons, where the branch-specific average value or the "best-practice" value may be used as a guide.

**Useful Suggestions**                                                  `!`
A change in this ratio could be triggered by a disproportionate increase or decrease in NOPAT (as numerator) and in capital invested (as denominator). *For further details and systematic explanations on this, refer to the information in Appendix I.*

Earnings could be improved through direct measures, which relate to the price and/or volume strategy on the sales side or through better organization of the input factors on the operational side. The ratio can also be improved though a "lean" deployment of invested capital. An increase in ROIC could also be achieved by encouraging high-return products or by reducing weaker products and services in the product portfolio.

Comparing a firm's ROIC with its cost of capital (WACC) reveals whether invested capital was used effectively.

**Related Ratios/Additional Notes**                                     `&`
The following ratios are often used as synonyms: Return On Capital Employed (ROCE), Return On Capital (ROC), Return On Net Assets (RONA), and Return On Net Operating Assets (ROOA or RONOA).

As a related ratio, Return On Assets (ROA) is considered to be the closest. It relates all components of earnings (including interest expense on borrowings) to all (both own and borrowed) components of capital.

Instead of the average asset base, the ratio may also be calculated with the end of the period invested capital.

### 2.2.8 Return On Capital Employed (ROCE)

**?** **Analytical Question**

How well is the return on capital employed? How profitable is the capital employed?

**＊** **Definition**

$$\frac{\text{EBIT} \cdot 100}{\text{Average Capital Employed}}$$

Where:

| | Net Income or Loss |
|---|---|
| + | Taxes on Income and Profits/(– Tax Refund) |
| = | EBT (Earnings/Operating Profit before Taxes) |
| + | Interest Expense |
| = | EBIT (Earnings/Operating Profits before Interest and Taxes) |

Financial reporting under IAS/IFRS rules prohibits explicit demarcation of extraordinary results. Instead, IAS/IFRS rules require a declaration of the "Results from Discontinued Operations".

And average values of the following:

| | Stockholders' Equity |
|---|---|
| + | Pension Reserves |
| + | External Borrowings |
| = | Average Capital Employed |

Return On Capital Employed is expressed as a percentage.

**»** **Calculation/Derivation**

The data for EBIT is available in the income statement. The average capital employed can be calculated with the beginning and end balances from the balance sheet. Sometimes, only long-term external borrowings are used in the calculation of capital employed.

**#** **Interpretation and Typical Range**

The main profitability ratios, such as Return On Sales or Return On Assets, are not always suitable for specific purposes. Therefore, a series of new ratios have recently emerged. In ROCE, the main focus is on establishing a relationship between the results of operating business vis-à-vis the capital employed.

For the calculation of EBIT, net income, which is an after tax value, is adjusted for taxes and interest expense. In effect, EBIT is a pre-tax figure, which eliminates the impact of the financing decision. The use of ROCE is recommended in all those cases, where a comparison is being drawn between enterprises having different forms of business organization or between enterprises in different tax regimes, such as international enterprises.

ROCE represents the operating earning capacity of the business independent of its capital structure and, therefore, is particularly suitable for comparing the profitability across enterprises (as an aggregated unit or divisions/profit centres).

The use of ROCE is recommended in all those cases, where a comparison is being drawn between enterprises having different forms of business organization or between enterprises in different tax regimes, such as international enterprises.

It is not possible to give a desired target ratio for ROCE. For orientation purposes, one could make internal comparisons (such as the ratio in different organizational units or plan-actual values) or external comparisons, where the branch-specific average value or the "best-practice" value may be used as a guide.

**Useful Suggestions**
A change in this ratio could be triggered by a disproportionate increase or decrease in EBIT (as numerator) and capital employed (as denominator). *For further details and systematic explanations on this, refer to the information in Appendix I.*

In the numerator, net income can be improved by a better price or volume strategy. On the expense side, net income can be improved by a more efficient cost management. An increase in ROCE can also be achieved by encouraging high-return products or by reducing weaker products and services in the product portfolio.

In the denominator, a reduction in capital employed could be achieved by disposing off non-operating assets or reducing the inventory levels. Sometimes, it is desirable to categorically separate the employed assets from the assets which are *indeed* not being employed in operations.

**Related Ratios/Additional Notes**
As synonym for this ratio, we could consider Return On Net Assets (RONA) or Return On Net Operating Assets (RONOA/ROOA)

Related ratios are: Return On Investment (ROI), Return On Assets (ROA). As a related ratio, ROA ranks above ROI, because as the name implies, it compares all the financial resources (owners' capital and borrowed funds) with all earnings generated through these resources (including the interest expense on borrowed funds).

Instead of the average asset base, the ratio may also be calculated with beginning or end of the period assets.

### 2.2.9 Return On Net Assets (RONA)

**? Analytical Question**

How good is the return on assets needed in normal operations? How well has management used the operational assets to generate earnings?

**\* Definition**

$$\frac{\text{EBIT} \cdot 100}{\text{Average Net Assets}}$$

Where:

|   | Net Income or Loss |
|---|---|
| + | Taxes on Income and Profits/(− Tax Refund) |
| = | EBT (Earnings/Operating Profits before Taxes) |
| + | Interest Expense |
| = | EBIT (Earnings/Operating Profits before Interest and Taxes) |

The financial reporting under IAS/IFRS rules prohibits explicit demarcation of extraordinary results. Instead, IAS/IFRS rules require a declaration of the "Results from Discontinued Operations".

The denominator is calculated with the average values for the following:

|   | Required Working Capital |
|---|---|
| − | Non-Interest Bearing Current Liabilities |
| = | Net Working Capital |
| + | Fixed Assets |
| = | Average Net Assets |

Return On Net Assets is expressed as a percentage.

**» Calculation/Derivation**

The data for net income and interest expense is available in the income statement. The amount of average net assets can be calculated from the data available on the balance sheet. In the category of non-interest bearing current liabilities, it is important to include the advance payments from customers primarily for the goods and services to be delivered.

**# Interpretation and Typical Range**

Return On Net Assets shows what earnings were generated from the operational assets.

The basic ratios of Return On Sales and Return On Assets measure performance. However, for special kinds of analysis, these ratios provide a very general view.

Therefore, a series of new variants have been developed. At the centre of RONA, the immediate link is provided between earnings from normal operations and the net assets needed for the purpose.

The main point in calculating RONA is the direct linkage of profitability to the earnings from ordinary business when compared with the assets needed for the purpose.

Since the ratio is calculated before taxes, it represents the profit-generating capacity of the enterprise. Moreover, interest on borrowed funds is neutralized in the calculation, which makes the ratio independent of the capital structure (or financing effects). Therefore, the ratio is considered appropriate for comparing profitability between enterprises and business segments/divisions/profit centres.

The use of RONA is recommended in all those cases where a comparison is being drawn between enterprises having different forms of business organization or between enterprises in different tax regimes, such as international enterprises.

It is not possible to give a desired target ratio for RONA. For orientation and comparison purposes, it is advisable to take the Return On Net Assets ratio for competitors within the same branch, or listed (inter)national enterprises as a benchmark.

**Useful Suggestions**
A change in this ratio could be triggered by a disproportionate increase or decrease in EBIT (as numerator) and in net assets (as denominator). *For further details and systematic explanations on this, refer to the information in Appendix I.*

In the numerator, EBIT could be improved by a better price or volume strategy. On the expense side, EBIT could be improved by a more efficient cost management. An increase in RONA could also be achieved by encouraging high-return products or by reducing weaker products and services in the product portfolio.

In the denominator, a reduction in the asset base could be achieved by disposing off non-operating assets (at least at book value) or a reduction in the inventory levels. More efficient use of net assets can also lead to improvements in the return on net assets.

**Related Ratios/Additional Notes**
Often the following ratios are used as synonyms: Return On Capital Employed (ROCE), Return On Capital (ROC), and Return On Net Operating Assets (ROOA or RONOA).

As a related ratio, Return On Assets (ROA) or Return On Capital is considered to be the closest. It relates all components of earnings (including interest expense on borrowings) to all (both own and borrowed) components of capital.

Instead of the average asset base, the ratio may also be calculated with end of the period net assets.

### 2.2.10 Risk Adjusted Return On Capital (RAROC)

**?** **Analytical Question**

In the banking and financial services business, how good is the risk adjusted financial performance of the enterprise? How good is the relative quality of earnings from individual business lines and/or business units in relation to a minimum return (so-called "hurdle rate")?

**\*** **Definition**

$$\frac{\text{Economic Profit} \cdot 100}{\text{Economic Capital}}$$

Where:

Economic Profit  = Return generated by a business line in excess of cost of equity capital

*And*

Economic Capital = Capital attributed to each business line on the basis of market risk, credit risk and operational risk

Because there is an adjustment made both in numerator and denominator, it would be more appropriate to call this ratio as Risk Adjusted Return On Risk Adjusted Capital (RARORAC). However, it is more common to use RAROC.

Risk Adjusted Return On Capital is expressed as a percentage.

**»** **Calculation/Derivation**

The needed data for this ratio should be available to a financial institution internally, in an accounting system which is based on a Risk Adjusted Performance Metrics (the RAPM).

**#** **Interpretation and Typical Range**

The ratio RAROC is used by banks for risk and value oriented management and is derived from RAPM-concept, which is a pillar of capital market theory. The primary goal is to create a linkage between risk management and value management, where the bank tries to achieve the return-expectations of stockholders under the restrictions imposed by risk-factors.

It is not possible to give a desired target ratio for RAROC. The benchmarking is largely dependent on the return expectations of investors. Possible orientation for minimum return expectations could come from average return in a particular business segment or "best-practice" values.

**Useful Suggestions** !

A change in this ratio could be triggered by a disproportionate increase or decrease in risk adjusted economic profit (as numerator) and in economic capital invested (as denominator). *For further details and systematic explanations on this, refer to the information in Appendix I.*

The concrete measures for impacting this ratio constitute the core of a bank's management practices. The bank will have to decide how to measure a particular type or level of risk associated with a business activity is. It will also show the types of business activities in which economic capital should be invested, so that overall performance can be optimized.

**Related Ratios/Additional Notes** &

There is a close relationship between RAROC and RORAC, which is the Return On Risk Adjusted Capital.

### 2.2.11 Cost-Income Ratio (CIR)

**Analytical Question** ?

What is the volume of operating costs (of a firm or a bank) in relation to gross revenues?

Or, how many cents should be spent on average for every € of revenue earned?

**Definition** *

$$\frac{\text{Operating Costs}}{\text{Gross Revenues}}$$

With reference to a bank, the definition is:

$$\frac{\text{Non-interest Expenses}}{\text{Interest Revenue} + \text{Non-interest Revenue}}$$

The CIR is expressed as a percentage.

**Calculation/Derivation** »

Assuming that all costs are equal to expenses, the required data can be taken from the income statement; the operating costs would be the sum of salaries, wages, and other general expenses. Gross revenues would be the sum of all normal operating revenues (which is the total of interest, fee, trade, and other income, including extraordinary income).

**#** **Interpretation and Typical Range**

CIR is considered one of the main ratios when carrying out internal and external comparative analysis in efficiency at financial institutions. In making national or international inter-firm comparisons, it is important to ensure that the institutions being compared have a similar business structure.

The lower the CIR, the more economically operated (and consequently, more efficient) is the business segment or the entire bank. Since in a single period, operating expenses may be relatively fixed, it is not uncommon that fluctuations in good and bad years are compared.

**!** **Useful Suggestions**

A change in CIR could be triggered by a disproportionate increase or decrease in operating costs (as numerator) and gross revenues (as denominator). *For further details and systematic explanations on this, refer to the information in Appendix I.*

Along with efforts at directly influencing the operating income through a better price or volume strategy, appropriate strategies towards more efficient use of the factors of production can be attempted.

It is relevant to note that any attempt at reducing overheads and other operating costs should, as with other ratios, impact less than proportionally on the revenue side, i.e. the reduction in overheads should not cause an equal or proportional reduction in revenues and incomes. Otherwise, the goal of improving operative efficiency is not achieved.

**&** **Related Ratios/Additional Notes**

Through CIR, a firm or a bank can provide a (general) quantitative expression of its efficiency.

## 2.3 Liquidity Indicators

### 2.3.1 Cash Ratio

**?** **Analytical Question**

How good is the so-called cash liquidity?

**\*** **Definition**

$$\frac{(\text{Cash} + \text{Cash Equivalents}) \cdot 100}{\text{Current Liabilities}}$$

This ratio specifies a percentage rate. The ratio can also be expressed as a multiple of current liabilities, in which case it should not be multiplied by 100.

## Calculation/Derivation

The term "Cash and Cash Equivalents" includes cash at hand, cash at bank and checks. The amount of current liabilities is derived from the liabilities side of the balance sheet.

## Interpretation and Typical Range

The Cash Ratio is part of the cash-balance-oriented liquidity analysis and is considered as an indicator of the short-term liquidity. With reference to the closing date, it shows a comparison between liquid cash and short-term payment obligations. If the Cash Ratio is analysed by external parties based on the annual financial statements, the interpretation of ratio may be less meaningful because the cash position after the financial accounts closing date may have changed significantly.

The higher the percentage rate, the more stable the liquidity. Since Cash Ratio is sensitive to small events and the timing of transactions, it is more helpful if interpreted along with Quick Ratio and Current Ratio. In general, the Cash Ratio should give a value exceeding 100 %. It could as well be below 100 %, in which case, it should be assumed that the enterprise has easy access to bank loan facilities.

## Useful Suggestions

Despite the indispensable need to maintain financial solvency, one has to be mindful of the cost-effectiveness of maintaining high cash positions which do not earn any or very low interest. Through detailed financial and liquidity planning, a firm should estimate its daily receipts and payments to ensure solvency. All surplus cash should be invested preferably in high-yield short-term investments. Thus, the interpretive power of the Cash Ratio is limited.

## Related Ratios/Additional Notes

Other names for this ratio are: cash liquidity and absolute liquidity ratio.

In literature, and also in practice, there are different levels of liquidity. Most common are Level I (Cash Ratio), Level II (Quick Ratio) and Level III (Current Ratio). Whereas at level II, short-term investments and accounts receivable are included in the numerator, at level III, all current assets are compared with all current liabilities.

### 2.3.2 Quick Ratio

**? Analytical Question**

How far do the cash and near cash assets of the enterprise exceed its short-term liabilities?

**\* Definition**

$$\frac{(\text{Current Assets} - \text{Inventory}) \cdot 100}{\text{Current Liabilities}}$$

This ratio specifies a percentage rate. The ratio can also be expressed as a multiple of current liabilities, in which case it should not be multiplied by 100.

**» Calculation/Derivation**

The term "near cash assets" includes cash at hand, cash at bank, checks, short-term investments and accounts receivable (net of the allowance for doubtful debts) or, simply stated, all current assets *minus* inventory should give the same value. The amount of current liabilities is derived from the liabilities side of the balance sheet.

**# Interpretation and Typical Range**

The Quick Ratio is part of the account-balance-oriented liquidity analysis and is considered as an indicator of the short-term liquidity. With reference to the closing date, it shows a comparison between near cash assets and short-term payment obligations. If Quick Ratio is analysed by external parties based on the annual financial statements, the interpretation of ratio may be less meaningful because the cash position after the financial accounts closing date may have changed significantly.

The higher the percentage rate, the more stable the liquidity. Since Quick Ratio is sensitive to small events and the timing of transactions, it can be better interpreted collectively, along with Cash Ratio and Current Ratio. In general, the ratio should give a value equal to 100 % or so-called 1:1 in the Acid Test Ratio.

**! Useful Suggestions**

Despite the indispensable need to maintain financial solvency, the cost-effectiveness of maintaining high cash positions, which do not earn any or very low interest should be considered. Through detailed financial and liquidity planning, a firm should estimate its daily receipts and payments to ensure its solvency. All surplus cash should be invested, preferably in high-yield short-term investments.

**Related Ratios/Additional Notes**    &

Other names for this ratio are: Net Quick Ratio or Acid Test Ratio. The term comes from the way gold miners would test whether their findings were real gold nuggets. Unlike other metals, gold does not corrode in acid; if the nugget didn't dissolve when submerged in acid, it was said to have passed the acid test. Likewise, if a company's financial statements pass the figurative acid test, you can use this as an indication that there isn't any accounting gimmickry going on and that its bank account actually does contain gold!

In literature, as also in practice, there are different levels of liquidity. Most common are Level I (Cash Ratio), Level II (Quick Ratio) and Level III (Current Ratio). Whereas in the stringent Cash Ratio, only cash and cash equivalents are included in the numerator, in Current Ratio all current assets (including inventory) are compared with all current liabilities.

### 2.3.3 Current Ratio    Ⓢ

**Analytical Question**    ?

How far are short-term liabilities covered by short-term assets?

**Definition**    ✱

$$\frac{\text{Current Assets} \cdot 100}{\text{Current Liabilities}}$$

This ratio specifies a percentage rate. The ratio can also be expressed as a multiple of current liabilities, in which case it should not be multiplied by 100.

**Calculation/Derivation**    »

The term "current assets" includes cash at hand, cash at bank, checks, short-term investments, accounts receivable (net of allowance for doubtful debts) and inventory of raw material, work in process and finished products. Assets which have been paid partly by customers, or cannot be sold within a year, should not be included in the list of current assets. The amount of current liabilities is derived from the liabilities side of the balance sheet.

**Interpretation and Typical Range**    #

The Current Ratio is part of the account-balance-oriented liquidity analysis, and is considered as an indicator of short-term liquidity. With reference to the closing date, it shows a maturity matching between short-term assets and short-term payment obligations. If the ratio is analysed by external parties, based on annual financial statements, the interpretation may be less meaningful because the relevant position after the financial accounts closing date may have changed significantly.

The higher the percentage rate, the more stable the liquidity position of the enterprise. In general, the ideal ratio should give a value equal to 200 % or the so-called 2:1 (A 2:1 current ratio is, sometimes, referred to as "Banker's rule".) As a reverse argument, a 2:1 ratio implies that 50 % of the current assets should be financed by long-term liabilities.

**! Useful Suggestions**

Despite the indispensable need to maintain financial solvency, the cost-effectiveness of maintaining high cash positions which do not earn any or very low interest should be considered. Through detailed financial and liquidity planning, a firm should estimate its daily receipts and payments to ensure its solvency. All surplus cash should be invested preferably in high-yield short-term investments.

**& Related Ratios/Additional Notes**

Another name for this ratio is: Banker's rule.

In the literature, as also in practice, there are different levels of liquidity. Most common are Level I (Cash Ratio), Level II (Quick Ratio) and Level III (Current Ratio). Whereas in the stringent Cash Ratio, only cash and cash equivalents are included in the numerator, in Quick Ratio, all current assets (excluding inventory) are compared with all current liabilities.

### 2.3.4 Working Capital

**? Analytical Question**

How much of the interest-earning funds are committed to short-term assets?

**✳ Definition**

|  |
|---|
| Short-term Assets |
| − Advance Payment Received from Customers |
| − Short-term Liabilities |
| = Working Capital (or Net Working Capital) |

The resulting figure for Working Capital is stated in absolute currency units (for example, in €).

**» Calculation/Derivation**

The information for calculating Working Capital is derived from the balance sheet.

**# Interpretation and Typical Range**

The Working Capital, also known as net current assets, is part of the account-balance-oriented liquidity analysis and is considered as an indicator of short-term liquidity. It shows the difference between the interest-earning short-term funds (this is why the advance received from customers is not included here) and short-term external funds. Thus, working capital shows that part of the short-term assets, which are financed by long-term funds.

When a firm targets 'achieving a positive working capital', the goal is to cover the short-term liabilities through short-term assets. Often, a working capital target is recommended, in which the short-term liabilities should not exceed 75 % of short-term assets.

In some cases, however, a negative working capital can also be positively interpreted. This could be, in those cases, where suppliers are willing to finance the sales through accounts payable, depending on the negotiation power of the firm.

**Useful Suggestions**
In order to optimize the deployment of capital in the enterprise, it is desirable to achieve a sustained reduction in the capital locked up in operations. The working capital is increasingly considered as a starting point for improving operational performance. It not only helps to improve the performance, but also provides additional funds for eventual expansion plans.

When planning Working Capital, the client-needs and competitive aspects of inventory levels for finished products, as well as optimization of inventory levels for raw-materials, supplies and work-in-process should be carefully analysed. Similarly, the accounts receivable should also be analysed, and, if not yet in place, it is good to install an active receivable management system.

**Related Ratios/Additional Notes**
Instead of subtracting the short-term assets from short-term liabilities, the working capital logic is also shown through a division of short-term assets, by short-term liabilities. Such a figure is termed as "Working Capital Ratio".

## 2.3.5 Cash-burn Rate

**Analytical Question**
What is the volume of cash which a company needs per period?
During what period is a company likely to exhaust its available liquidity?

**Definition**

$$\frac{\text{Liquid Resources (+ Near-liquid Assets)}}{\text{Net Cash Outflow}}$$

The ratio is mentioned in units of time (for example, in years or months).

**>> Calculation/Derivation**

External parties can derive the data for this ratio from the reported numbers in annual financial statements.

**# Interpretation and Typical Range**

The Cash-burn Rate is grouped in the category of liquidity ratios. It is based on estimates about when a firm would exhaust its liquidity.

This ratio originated in the context of young growth-oriented start-ups which applied it for predicting insolvency. It also indicated the time horizon, when a company uses up its venture capital, before generating positive cash flows from operating activities. However, the interpretative value of this ratio is based on very restrictive assumptions (for example, that past developments can be extrapolated or fresh liquidity cannot be obtained). In a dynamic environment, we notice that the prognostic value of balance sheet figures is limited. Some decisive qualitative changes, such as expected additional/large contracts, cannot be incorporated into the accounting statements.

The shorter the period of Cash-burn Rate, the more exposed the firm is (or a project, which needs more financial resources) to risks of bankruptcy.

**! Useful Suggestions**

A firm has many options to explain its future investment plans to interested parties, which go beyond the extrapolated estimates of the past data. A company can clarify the planned developments to outsiders with the help of voluntary disclosures.

**& Related Ratios/Additional Notes**

The denominator is also called negative cash flow (entry without minus sign). Because of various reasons, which limit the prognostic value of Cash-burn Rate for young growth-oriented firms, it is used only as a starting point for deeper analysis. Thus, with the help of a liquidity indicator, like Cash-burn Rate, the financial strains can be evaluated. For concrete information, the working capital is estimated with reference to the periodic expected operating expenses in the immediate future.

## 2.4 Tests of Solvency

### 2.4.1 Debt-to-Equity Ratio

**? Analytical Question**

How stable is the firm's financing? What proportion of debt and equity is the firm using to finance its assets? What is the relationship between the amount of capital provided by creditors and owners?

**Definition**                                                                                    ✳

> Total Liabilities
> ───────────────────
> Total Owners' Equity

Sometimes, only interest bearing, long-term debt is used instead of total liabilities.

This ratio can be expressed in multiples (for example, debt is 2.7 times of equity) or in percentages (in which case, the result should be multiplied by 100).

**Calculation/Derivation**                                                                        »
The values for this ratio could be drawn, with some adjustments (for examples, advance payments and accruals) from the balance sheet.

**Interpretation and Typical Range**                                                              #
This ratio belongs to the category of "Capital Structure Analysis" which is also named "Financing Analysis". The ratio occupies itself with the types and durability of the available capital. Through this ratio, the financial risk and creditworthiness of the firm can be estimated.

The Debt-to-Equity Ratio is an important example of the leverage effect. It shows the significance of equity in the credit-standing check by banks and rating agencies. A high ratio suggests that a company relies heavily on funds provided by creditors. The higher the ratio, the riskier the firm's financial position; the firm may not be able to meet its contractual financial obligations during a business downturn.

It is not possible to fix a general, operationally logical norm for this ratio. As with the Equity Ratio, sometimes a smaller ratio, or one equal to 3 times (300 %) or 2 times (200 %) may be employed. The appropriate target depends on the branch-specific characteristics and the legal form of the firm.

**Useful Suggestions**                                                                            ❗
A change in this ratio could be triggered by a disproportionate increase or decrease in total liabilities (as numerator) and owners' equity (as denominator). *For details on this, refer to the explanation in Appendix I.*

On the equity capital side, the ratio can be influenced, for example, through a capital distribution and allocation program as well as through dividend payout and retention policies. On the debt side, the need for borrowed funds can be reduced by disposing of the non-operational assets (minimum at book value) or by reducing working capital requirements. Assuming a constant owners' equity, a reduction in the volume of borrowed money would lead to a reduction in the debt-to-equity ratio.

There are four reasons, which call for a lower Debt-to-Equity Ratio:
- Owners' equity attracts more capital. A high amount of owners' equity, with its basic characteristic of safe capital, makes it noticeably easier to obtain credit;

- With increasing share of owners' equity, the commitment of the firm increases, so that the risk of insolvency by excessive indebtedness is reduced;
- By comparison with borrowed funds, financing through equity capital does not create any obligation to make payments for interest and principal; and
- Lower influence of the creditors, such as banks.

In the context of leverage effects (also reflected in the indicator "Financial Leverage Index"), a higher Debt-to-Equity Ratio may be desirable within certain limits. As long as the return on total capital is higher than the interest rate on borrowed funds, the leverage effect will be visible in the improved return on equity.

**&  Related Ratios/Additional Notes**

Since the total capital is the sum of owners' equity and external liabilities, the equity ratio (equity/total capital), the debt ratio (total liabilities/total capital) and Debt-to-Equity Ratio are three different forms of the same financial structure analysis. The conclusion drawn, remains the same in each of the ratios.

In certain situations, the basic variant of Debt-to-Equity Ratio can be slightly modified, for example, for certain balance sheet positions like advance payments and accruals. Such adjustments help in removing various balance sheet related changes, and allow for a better comparison between firms and over time.

By comparison with the Debt-to-Equity Ratio, the Debt-to-Cash Ratio provides a better perspective because it shows the relationship between net borrowed funds and net cash flows.

### 2.4.2 Debt-to-Cash Ratio

**?  Analytical Question**

What is the length of time in which the present effective debt (or the net financial debt) can be repaid through periodic cash flows?

**✳  Definition**

$$\frac{\text{Effective Debt}}{\text{Cash Flow}}$$

or

$$\frac{\text{Net Financial Debt}}{\text{Cash Flow}}$$

Where:

> Short- and Medium-term Debt
> + Liabilities with a maturity >5 years
> − Monetary Value of Current Assets (− Receivable with a maturity >1 Year)
> ───────────────────────────────
> = Effective Debt (Level I)
> + Provisions for Pension and similar Liabilities
> ───────────────────────────────
> = Effective Debt (Level II)

and

> Bonds issued
> + Liabilities towards Banks
> + Acceptance Commitments
> + Interest-bearing debt in other Borrowings
> − Cash and Near Cash Assets
> − Short-term Securities in Current Assets
> ───────────────────────────────
> = Net Financial Debt

The ratio is expressed in units of time, usually in years (it can also be in fractions of a year, such as 2.4 years).

### Calculation/Derivation

The values for the numerator can be taken from the asset and liabilities mentioned in the balance sheet. The cash flow can be calculated by adjusting the figure of annual net income for all non-cash expenses and revenues.

### Interpretation and Typical Range

The Debt-to-Cash Ratio combines a stock value (Effective Debt) with a flow value (Cash Flow) for calculating the payment capacity of a firm. It represents a common measure of financial risk. Thus, the cash flow becomes an indicator of the borrowing capacity and points out the period (under specific conditions) in which the liabilities can be cleared with the help of self-generated financial resources. Examples of specific conditions may include that the cash flow will not be used for investments, dividend and interest payments or that the level of debt will not be increased through other business activities.

### Useful Suggestions

A change in this ratio could be triggered by a disproportionate increase or decrease in effective debt or financial debt (as numerator) and cash flows (as denominator). *For details on this, refer to the explanation in Appendix I.*

Apart from various possibilities for directly influencing the cash flow, it can be improved by a better price or volume strategy. On the debt side, the need for borrowed funds can be reduced by disposing of non-operational assets (minimum at book value) and/or by reducing working capital requirements.

**& Related Ratios/Additional Notes**
As synonyms, sometimes "Repayment Period" is also used.

In the Anglo-Saxon world, the volume of effective debt is often used to connote the sum of all kinds of outstanding debts.

### 2.4.3 Interest Coverage Ratio

**? Analytical Question**
How much resources are generated by the company from its operating business to meet its current interest obligations?

**\* Definition**

$$\frac{\text{EBIT} \cdot 100}{\text{Interest Expense}}$$

Where:

|   | Net Income or Loss |
|---|---|
| + | Taxes on Income and Profits/(– Tax Refund) |
| = | EBT (Earnings/Income from Operating Business before Taxes) |
| + | Interest Expense |
| = | EBIT (Earnings/Operating Income before Interest and Taxes) |

The financial reporting under IAS/IFRS rules prohibits explicit demarcation of extraordinary results. Instead, IAS/IFRS rules require a declaration of the "Results from Discontinued Operations".

This result obtained through this ratio is expressed as a percentage.

**» Calculation/Derivation**
The data for both numerator and denominator can be taken from of the income statement.

**# Interpretation and Typical Range**
The Interest Coverage Ratio shows the amount of resources generated for each € of interest expensed. A high ratio indicates an extra margin of protection in the event of deteriorating profits. Analysts are particularly interested in a company's ability

to meet its required interest payments because failure to do so could result in bankruptcy.

This ratio illustrates a measure of risk which, however, is not sufficient if considered alone. A general target cannot be given for this ratio because the interest burden of a firm is considerably influenced by its financing strategy. Through careful utilization of the leverage effect, the Interest Coverage Ratio can in fact be reduced, despite increasing the interest expense burden in absolute numbers. As long as the operating results increase faster, the ROA would exceed the interest cost on borrowed funds.

**Useful Suggestions**

A change in this ratio can be triggered by a disproportionate increase or decrease in EBIT (as numerator) and Interest Expense (as denominator). *For further details and a systematic explanation on this, refer to the information in Appendix I.*

The ratio can be influenced by focusing on the business results of the firm. Thus, on the sales side, measures towards a better price or volume strategy and, on the expense side, measures towards a more efficient use of the factors of production can be helpful. It can also be influenced through reduction of the interest burden; possibly by negotiating better terms of credit, greater use of discounts offered by suppliers, and reduction in capital blocked in some assets (such as working capital).

Analysts should consider the company's long-term strategy when using this ratio; a rapidly growing company may have a high interest burden because of its investment in future operations, but no significant increase in income at the beginning.

**Related Ratios/Additional Notes**

The ratio is also known as "Times Interest Earned (TIE)" or "Interest Charges (or Fixed Interest) Coverage".

The formula for Interest Coverage Ratio can be written also as:

$$\frac{\text{Interest} + \text{Principal Payments on Debt per Period} \cdot 100}{\text{Cash Flow per Period}}$$

In this case, the analytical question will be: how much is the burden on operating income for the payment of interest expenses? As a consequence, the interpretation would be: the ratio shows the share of operating income which is needed for covering the interest expense on borrowed funds. The lower the ratio, the lower the risk or burden of an increase in interest rates on the results of the firm.

Some analysts prefer to compare interest expense with the amount of cash a company can generate. By relating the interest expense with cash flow, a direct relationship is established with the payment capacity of the firm.

## Ⓢ 2.4.4 Debt Service Coverage Ratio (DSCR)

### ❓ Analytical Question

What is the cash flow amount, available in a period, in relation to the annual interest and principal repayment on debt?

### ✴ Definition

$$\frac{\text{Cash Flow per Period} \cdot 100}{\text{Interest} + \text{Principal Payments on Debt per Period}}$$

The KPI "Debt Service Coverage Ratio" (henceforth DSCR) is expressed as a "%" or as a multiple, if the formula in not multiplied by 100.

### » Calculation/Derivation

The data for the numerator and denominator can be taken from the budgeted cash flow statements of the company. For cash flow purposes, the "operating cash flow" is used, with slight adjustments, if necessary. Occasionally, EBITDA is used as a proxy for this purpose, which, from a business point of view, is not without problems.[6] Borrowing costs include all interest expenses from interest-bearing liabilities, but not interest for pension provisions or other bank charges. Sometimes, lease rent on financial leases is also included in the borrowing costs.

### # Interpretation and Typical Range

The DSCR illustrates the extent to which the company has the ability to make further payments in addition to payments for interest on borrowed funds and repayment of principal. This ratio is particularly important for lenders because, the higher the percentage of DSCR, the lower the risk for the lender.

DSCR is therefore of considerable importance when raising additional debt, especially if the company in question is already financed with relatively small equity. In principle, companies with strong equity capital are in a better position to pay the necessary debt ratio, which is arithmetically reflected in a better percentage value for the DSCR. If additional funds are borrowed and/or if interest rates rise while the debt level remains constant, the value of this KPI deteriorates.

The DSCR of a company should always be at least 100 % in order to ensure that interest and principal repayments on borrowed capital are always made on an accrual basis. A further and general guideline on the ideal range as to by how much the 100 % limit should be exceeded cannot be given because the respective risk

---

6 Details on the terminological peculiarities and possible demarcations can be found in the respective independent profiles for these KPIs in the compendium.

assessment strongly depends on the individual company's situation, expected developments, industry conditions and the general economic climate.

**Useful Suggestions**

Changes in this relative ratio can be achieved by disproportionate increases or decreases in the related cash flow type (in the numerator) and the payments for interest and repayment of borrowed funds (in the denominator). *For further details and systematic explanations on this, refer to the information in Appendix I.*

The cash flow values can be improved through direct measures which relate to the price and/or volume strategy on the sales side, or through better organization of the input factors on the operational side. The debt servicing per period depends, on the one hand, on a reduction or increase in the interest burden (e.g. through efficient management of the terms of debt) and, on the other hand, on the amount of contractually agreed repayments (and any changes in repayment amounts or, in individual cases through their targeted deferral).

In business terms, the DSCR is part of the KPI family of "Financial Covenants". At its core, also including the Debt-to-Equity Ratio (KPI No. 2.4.1), Debt-to-Cash Ratio (KPI No. 2.4.2), Interest Coverage Ratio (KPI No. 2.4.3) and the liquidity indicators (KPI category 2.3). Financial covenants are typically ancillary contractual arrangements in credit transactions in the sense of a set of tools for early crisis prevention. For the creditor, the primary objective is to ensure that the interest and principal repayments, agreed with the debtor, are secured by complying with the agreed KPI targets.

For companies as debtors, it is important to achieve the contractually agreed ratios through suitable strategic and operational measures, and to inform the lender regularly about this through actual results or the budgeted-actual comparisons. This is important so as to not endanger lending in the future, and to avoid payment difficulties. From the company's point of view, this obligation to report key figures is also driven by efforts to reduce debt costs.

**Related Ratios/Additional Notes**

Another common synonym for the ratio "DSCR" is: Principal Service Coverage Ratio.

In analogy to the Interest Coverage Ratio, the DSCR is also determined as the inverse of the version described above, according to the following definition:

$$\frac{\text{Interest} + \text{Principal Payments on Debt per Period} \cdot 100}{\text{Cash Flow per Period}}$$

In this case, the question is: How high is the relative burden of interest and principal repayment on cash flow per period? The following statement should now apply to the interpretation of its meaningful value: the lower the percentage, the lower the risk, in the event of rising interest rates or falling cash flows, that the firms would slip into liquidity problems.

### 2.4.5 Bankruptcy Prediction Score

**?** **Analytical Question**

What is the likelihood that a company may go bankrupt in the near future?

**\*** **Definition**

$$Z\text{–Score} = 3.3 \cdot \frac{EBIT}{Total\ Assets} + 1.0 \cdot \frac{Sales}{Total\ Assets} +$$

$$0.6 \cdot \frac{Market\ Value\ of\ Equity}{Total\ Book\ Debt} + 1.4 \cdot \frac{Retained\ Earnings}{Total\ Assets} + 1.2 \cdot \frac{Working\ Capital}{Total\ Assets}$$

The Z-Score model, developed by Edward Altman, represents a popular and commonly used statistical model to predict the likely bankruptcy of a firm. Each of the formula's ratios[7,8,9] describes a different credit-relevant aspect of the company's operation.[10] Six basic accounting values and one market-based value are combined into five ratios. As a result, liquidity, cumulative profitability, asset productivity, market based financial leverage and capital turnover are addressed respectively. All of the ratios are weighted by coefficients and form a linear combination.

The values are expressed in a score format, with an extension into decimals.

**Variant for privately-held companies**

In 1983, Altman developed a revised Z-score model for privately held firms. As a result, the new model ratios are:

$$Z\text{–Score} = 0.717 \cdot \frac{Working\ Capital}{Total\ Assets} + 0.847 \cdot \frac{Retained\ Earnings}{Total\ Assets} + 3.107 \cdot \frac{EBIT}{Total\ Assets}$$

$$+ 0.420 \cdot \frac{Book\ Value}{Total\ Liabilites} + 0.998 \cdot \frac{Sales}{Total\ Assets}$$

**Variant for privately-held and non-manufacturing firms**

In order to minimize a potential industry effect created through the asset turnover value of the formula, Altman revised his model excluding the Sales/Total assets ratio. As a result, the Revised Four variable Z-score Model was composed:

---

**7** Details for Return on Assets can be found in KPI No. 2.2.4
**8** Details for Asset Turnover Ratio can be found in KPI-No. 2.8.4
**9** Definition of Working Capital can be found in KPI-No. 2.3.4
**10** (Brealey, 2020)

$$Z\text{–Score} = 6.56 \cdot \frac{\text{Working Capital}}{\text{Total Assets}} + 3.26 \cdot \frac{\text{Retained Earnings}}{\text{Total Assets}} + 6.72 \cdot \frac{\text{EBIT}}{\text{Total Assets}}$$
$$+ 1.05 \cdot \frac{\text{Book Value of Equity}}{\text{Book Value of Total Liabilities}}$$

## Calculation/Derivation

Given the following KPIs of a *publicly-listed* company XY,

$$\frac{\text{EBIT}}{\text{Total Assets}} = 0.12$$

$$\frac{\text{Sales}}{\text{Total Assets}} = 1.4$$

$$\frac{\text{Market Value of Equity}}{\text{Total Book Debt}} = 0.9$$

$$\frac{\text{Retained Earnings}}{\text{Total Assets}} = 0.4$$

$$\frac{\text{Working Capital}}{\text{Total Assets}} = 0.12$$

the company's Z-score is as follows =

$$(3.3 \cdot 0.12) + (1.0 \cdot 1.4) + (0.6 \cdot 0.9) + (1.4 \cdot 0.4) + (1.2 \cdot 0.12) = 3.04$$

As a result, the score is above the cut-off level for predicting bankruptcy, and therefore, the company can be considered favourably in its creditworthiness. *(Refer to the details about the typical range below to interpret the Z-Score.)*

The financial ratios are based on the balance sheet and income statement data of a firm.

Therefore, the information can be derived through its posted annual report or stock market platforms.

Considering the example of a *privately-held* company AB with the following ratios:

$$\frac{\text{Working Capital}}{\text{Total Assets}} = 0.09; \qquad \frac{\text{Retained Earnings}}{\text{Total Assets}} = 0.12$$

$$\frac{\text{EBIT}}{\text{Total Assets}} = 0.12; \qquad \frac{\text{Book Value}}{\text{Total Liabilities}} = 0.8$$

the company's Z-score is as follows =

$$(0.717 \cdot 0.09) + (0.847 \cdot 0.12) + (3.107 \cdot 0.12) + (0.420 \cdot 0.8) + (0.998 \cdot 0.09) = 0.965$$

Since the Z-score, in this case, is below 1.23 it can be seen that this company AB is likely to go bankrupt.

Considering the example of a *privately-held non-manufacturing company* LM, which has the following ratios:

$$\frac{\text{Working Capital}}{\text{Total Assets}} = 0.08; \quad \frac{\text{Retained Earnings}}{\text{Total Assets}} = 0.04$$

$$\frac{\text{EBIT}}{\text{Total Assets}} = 0.05; \quad \frac{\text{Book Value of Equity}}{\text{Book Value of Total Liabilities}} = 0.07$$

the company's Z-score is as follows =

$$(6.56 \cdot 0.08) + (3.26 \cdot 0.04) + (6.72 \cdot 0.05) + (1.05 \cdot 0.07) = 1.065$$

As a result, the company LM is deemed to be bankrupt, since its score is below 1.10.

## # Interpretation and Typical Range

The Z-score model by Altman presents a commonly used multiple, discriminate analysis to predict the bankruptcy of a firm.

Most bankrupt firms have a Z-score below 2.7 before they become bankrupt, whereas most non-bankrupt firms have a Z-score above this level. As a result, a firm having a score above 2.7 is considered as having a favourable creditworthiness. A firm having a Z score lower than 1.81 indicates that it is bankrupt. Firms with scores between 1.23 and 2.30 are considered to be in a grey area or zone of ignorance.

Analysing the values for privately held firms with scores of < 1.23 indicate bankrupt firms, and scores of > 2.90 indicate non-bankrupt firms. Firms having a score between 1.23 and 2.90 are determined to be in the zone of ignorance or grey area.

Finally, the scores for the Revised Four Model predict that a company having a score lower than < 1.10 is bankrupt whereas a company with a score higher than > 2.60 is deemed to be non-bankrupt. Scores between 1.10 and 2.60 are considered in a grey area.[11]

## ! Useful Suggestions

The formula can predict financial efficiency or bankruptcy up to 2-3 years in advance. One year prior to bankruptcy, the model predicts financial failure correctly for 95% of firms. Accuracy decreases to 72% two years out and to 52% three years prior to insolvency.[12]

Given that the predictive value of the model has an accuracy of 95% in predicting chance of financial failure within a year's range, Investors can use the Altman's score to determine whether they should buy or sell a particular stock. Investors many consider purchasing a stock if its Altman's Z-Score is closer to 3 and selling it if the value is closer to 1.8.

---

**11** (S. Vasantha, 2013)
**12** (Eugene F. Brigham, 2010)

**Related Ratios/Additional Notes**                                    &

Altman suggested a multiple discriminant analysis (MDA) as the appropriate statistical technique, but there are further uni-variate and multivariate scores that can be used to determine the bankruptcy of companies. As an example, the "Distance to Default score" by Morningstar represents a model that claims that a company has defaulted when the market value of the assets drops below the book value of the liabilities. In contrast to the Z-score, the model does not specifically address the cash accounting values or the financial covenants that are typically examined.[13]

There are a number of ways to carry out credit analysis. A number of techniques have been developed to calculate the credit score. Mostly, the creditworthiness of a firm is assessed through its capacity to meet its obligations. The liquidity indicators (KPI category 2.3), Tests of solvency (KPI category 2.4), cash flow measures (KPI category 2.5) and cash flow ratios (KPI category 2.6) mentioned in this book give a broad range of indicators which can be utilized for assessing the creditworthiness of a firm. Most of these indicators can be computed with the help of the published financial statements of a company.

## 2.5 Cash Flow Measures

### 2.5.1 Cash Flow

**Analytical Question**                                                ?

How much is the cash flow surplus or deficit generated by the enterprise during the period under consideration? Did the company generate enough cash flow internally, to meet its obligations and finance necessary investment?

**Definition**                                                         *

There is no other financial measure in which the definitions are as numerous as in Cash Flow. Since the intention in writing this book is to achieve some degree of clarity about various terms, we will limit ourselves to providing the basic variations and offer explanations for the following elements of the cash flow family: Cash Flow, Gross and Net Cash Flow, Free Cash Flow and Operating Cash Flow. There are no legal or binding rules on the subject; therefore, several terms and definitions have developed over time. An attempt is made here to offer clear demarcations of terms, before explaining their financial significance.

The variety of ways in which Cash Flow is calculated (in theory and in practice) makes it imperative to check which method of cash flow computation was applied. This is particularly important when cash flow is differentiated into various categories I, II and III without clarifying. In principle, there are two methods for

---

**13** (Miller, 2009)

calculating cash flows: a direct method and an indirect method, both of these obviously lead to the same results.

Direct Method:

> Revenues generating Cash Inflows
> − Expenses causing Cash Outflows
> ―――――――――――――――――――
> = Cash Flow

Indirect Method:

> Net Income or Loss
> + Non-cash Expenses
> − Non-cash-Revenues
> ―――――――――――――――――――
> = Cash Flow

In order to provide clarity in the following content, two examples for various definitions are presented, which have become widespread in the academic and business worlds:

> The so-called "Practitioner's Formula":

> Net Income or Loss
> + Depreciation (− Appreciation) of Fixed Assets
> + Increase (− Decrease) in Long-term Provisions
> ―――――――――――――――――――
> = Cash Flow

The key figure of Cash Flow is stated in absolute currency units (for example, in €).

## » Calculation/Derivation

Following the indirect method, the calculation of cash flow can be made with sufficient precision, even by an external party, when based on the published annual report; in particular, when using the income statement and balance sheet. For the direct method of calculating cash flow, detailed information from the accounting data of the enterprise is needed.

## # Interpretation and Typical Range

Cash Flow, as a key parameter, indicates the financial resources, which were generated by a firm from its sales activities during a particular period (mostly 12 months). Thus, these resources can be used during the year for investment (in fixed and current assets), repayment of loans, distribution of profits, repayment of owners' equity and increasing its cash balances. The cash flow surplus should be considered as a "flow-measure", and does not represent concrete liquidity on a particular balance sheet date.

From an external perspective, Cash Flow is considered as an important indicator of the financial power and profitability of a firm. The volume of net income shown in the income statement can be grossly affected by balance sheet related measures (such as depreciation). Through various adjustments in net income, which are made to calculate cash flow, all balance sheet related possibilities are neutralized. The significance of cash flow is derived primarily from this fact.

A general target for cash flow cannot be determined. There is a fundamental rule for the cash flow volume: the larger the better; however, the amount of depreciation involved needs to be considered. Thus, a positive cash flow, which arose out of an annual loss and a huge depreciation, cannot necessarily be considered as a positive indicator of the financial strength and business performance.

## Useful Suggestions

Cash Flow, as a sales-related measure, shows very clearly the self-financing capacity of the enterprise through its main business. In order to influence this financial indicator, on the inflow (i.e. sales) side, cash flow can be improved by a better price or volume strategy. On the outflow (i.e. expense) side, cash flow can be improved by more efficient use of the factors of production.

In strengthening business planning, steering, and controlling internal processes, cash flow can be an important component in independently managed active business units, such as divisions, profit centres, regions, customers and/or product groups, marketing channels, etc. Within the structures of such segment-based information, cash flow can also be used for particular purposes, such as fixing the liquidity-oriented lowest prices.

## Related Ratios/Additional Notes

The absolute value of Cash Flow is not very suitable for comparisons with other enterprises. The information value of cash flow is more if it is related to other key parameters, for example, with sales, stockholders' equity and total capital. The relative ratio, thus, helps in understanding what percentage of sales, equity or total capital was available as cash inflow in a particular period.

Additional information as to how much cash was used, for what purpose, and where it came from, is available in the cash flow statement.

*For further details about the strengths and weaknesses of various cash flow variants, refer to the terms, Gross and Net Cash Flow, Free Cash Flow and Operating Cash Flow.*

## 2.5.2 Gross or Net Cash Flow

**? Analytical Question**

What is the internal financing capacity of the enterprise?

**\* Definition**

Since there are many different ways in which the term cash flow is put into practice, it is proposed that one should carefully check the details to find out which definition of cash flow is being used.

In many practical situations, the difference between "Gross" and "Net" Cash Flow refers to whether it is pre-tax or after-tax cash flow. The following example clarifies the point:

|   | Annual Net Income or Loss |
|---|---|
| + | Depreciation of Fixed Assets (– Appreciation of Fixed Assets) |
| + | Increase in Long-term Provisions (– Decrease in Long-term Provision) |
| = | Net Cash Flow |
| + | Taxes on Income and Profit |
| = | Gross Cash Flow (or Cash Flow before Taxes) |

*In the direct method for estimating cash flows,* another difference between gross and net cash flow is that gross cash flows are associated with all cash inflows whereas net cash flow is the residual figure after all outflows have been subtracted from all inflows.

All variants of Cash Flow are stated in absolute currency units (for example, in €).

**» Calculation/Derivation**

According to the indirect method, the calculation of cash flow can be made with sufficient precision even by an external party, based on the published annual report (in particular through the income statement and balance sheet). For the direct method of calculating cash flow, detailed information from the accounting data of the enterprise is needed.

**# Interpretation and Typical Range**

Any performance measure which is calculated before tax is recommended in all those cases, where a comparison is drawn amongst different forms of organizations and, more so, for comparisons amongst enterprises in different taxation systems (such as enterprises from foreign countries).

From an external perspective, cash flow is considered an important indicator of the financial power and profitability of a firm. The volume of net income shown in the income statement could be grossly affected by the balance sheet related measures (such as depreciation). Through various adjustments in the net income, which are made to calculate cash flow, all balance sheet related possibilities are neutralized. The significance of cash flow is derived primarily from this fact.

A general target for Gross or Net Cash Flow cannot be determined. There is a fundamental rule for the cash flow volume: "the larger the better"; however, one has to consider, particularly, the amount of depreciation and changes in reserves involved. Thus, a positive cash flow, which arose out of an annual loss and a huge depreciation, cannot necessarily be considered as a positive indicator of the financial strength and business performance.

## Useful Suggestions

Cash Flow, as a sales-related measure, shows very clearly the self-financing capacity of the enterprise through its main business. In order to influence this financial indicator, on the inflow (i.e., sales) side, cash flow could be improved by a better price or volume strategy. On the outflow (i.e., expense) side, cash flow can be improved by a more efficient use of the factors of production.

To strengthen business planning, steering and controlling of internal processes, Gross Cash Flow can be an important component to manage independently active business units (such as divisions, profit centre, regions, customers and/or product groups, marketing channels, etc.). The chosen details and classification of cash flow levels, which are mostly multi-dimensional and multi-layered, depend on the circumstances and needs of each enterprise. Within the structures of such segment-based information, cash flow can also be used for particular purposes, such as fixing the liquidity-oriented lowest prices.

## Related Ratios/Additional Notes

The absolute value of cash flow is not very suitable for comparisons with other enterprises. The information value of cash flow is more, if it related to other key parameters, for example, with sales, stockholders' equity and total capital. The relative ratio thus helps in understanding what percentage of sales, equity or total capital was available as cash inflow in a particular period.

Additional information about how much cash was used, for what purpose, and where it came from, is available in the cash flow statement.

*For further details about the strengths and weaknesses of various cash flow variants, refer to the terms, Cash Flow, Free Cash Flow and Operating Cash Flow.*

### 2.5.3 Free Cash Flow (FCF)

**? Analytical Question**

How much free cash does a firm generate during a particular period (for example, in a year)?

**✱ Definition**

FCF denotes the amount of "free" funds which are available to a firm, after the planned (re)investments in fixed and current assets have been considered. FCF is calculated as follows:

|   |   |
|---|---|
| | Cash Flow from Operating Activities |
| − | Cash Flow from Investing Activities |
| = | Free Cash Flow (FCF) |

The FCF is stated in absolute currency units (for example, in €).

**» Calculation/Derivation**

According to the indirect method, the calculation of Free Cash Flow can be made with sufficient precision even by an external party based on income statement and balance sheet contained in the annual report. For the direct method of calculating free cash flow, detailed information from the accounting data of the enterprise is needed. In a shareholding companies' data, FCF can be found on the statement of cash flows.

**# Interpretation and Typical Range**

The basic interest in analysing FCF lies in its utility as a planning and controlling instrument. It conveys whether a firm is able to generate surplus cash, after laying out the money needed for rationalization, substitution and expansion related investment. The FCF offers the resources needed for undertaking new business opportunities. FCF has gained a central position in business valuations and in value-based management.

In a period of normal business, FCF should be positive in the long-run (over many periods under consideration). Only then, a firm is assumed to be generating financial value. In the case of so-called start-ups, FCF could be negative for a long period initially; it could signal that the new company is making large investments. If these investments earn a high return, the strategy has the potential to pay dividends in the long-run. If a company is not able to count on a positive FCF in the foreseeable future, it could be threatened with bankruptcy.

**! Useful Suggestions**

FCF shows very clearly the self-financing capacity of the enterprise through its main business. It is a measure, which maps the internal financing of the enterprise, based on the operational business.

In order to influence this financial indicator, on the inflow (i.e., sales) side, FCF could be improved by a better price or volume strategy. On the outflow (i.e. expense) side, FCF could be improved by a more efficient use of the factors of production. Thus, on the one hand, FCF can be improved by pushing more profitable (or by reducing the less profitable) products and services. On the other hand, a conscious and restrictive investment strategy could help improve FCF in the short-run, though it may be disadvantageous in the medium to long term.

**Related Ratios/Additional Notes**

When using the cash flow based measures for management-controls, FCF is preferable because it is free (legitimately and legally) of various balance sheet influences.

The terms which relate to the category of cash flow measures have grown considerably in the past. Thus, which term is considered more suitable for analysing a business process must be examined carefully.

### 2.5.4  Operating Cash Flow (OCF)

**Analytical Question**

How much cash does a firm generate from running its business?

**Definition**

Since there are many different ways in which the term cash flow is put into practice, it is proposed that the details to find out which definition of cash flow is being used should be carefully checked. In addition, the definition of different business purposes should be clearly laid out, because a conservative definition of "ordinary business" could make the extraordinary component larger, and conversely, a liberal definition could reduce the extraordinary component. Based on the distinction of ordinary and extraordinary business, OCF can be calculated as follows:

|  | |
|---|---|
| | Cash Flow |
| + | Extraordinary (neutral or non-periodic) Expenses |
| − | Extraordinary (neutral or non-periodic) Revenues |
| = | Operating Cash Flow (= ordinary or effective Cash Flow) |

Another common method for calculating OCF is to pool the cash received from the customers and reduce it by the cash paid for purchase of goods and services, salaries and wages, income taxes and interest on liabilities. It is relevant to note that the direct and indirect methods for calculating cash flow are primarily applied with reference to OCF.

The OCF is stated in absolute currency units (for example, in €).

**» Calculation/Derivation**

The calculation of cash flow, according to the indirect method, can be made with sufficient precision, even by an external party, based on the published annual report, in particular through income statement and balance sheet. For the direct method of calculating cash flow, detailed information from the accounting data of the enterprise is needed. In shareholding companies, OCF can be found on the statement of cash flows.

**# Interpretation and Typical Range**

The OCF describes the surplus of regular receipts over the operational payments of a firm. OCF provides a financial "flow-measure" which reflects on the liquidity of a period. OCF is a measure of the liquidity-generating capacity of a firm, and thus represents the internal financial latitude available through self-earned funds.

**! Useful Suggestions**

OCF shows very clearly the self-financing capacity of the enterprise through its main business. It is a dynamic liquidity measure, based on the operational business, and maps the internal financing of the enterprise.

In general, the larger the OCF, the better the liquidity position. A large OCF provides resources for repaying debts, making investments and distributing dividends. However, this statement should be analysed with reference to the branch-specifics; thus, capital-intensive firms usually have a high OCF because of high depreciation. Though often used for assessing liquidity, OCF is also appropriate as a measure for analysing the profitability of a firm and for predicting crises.

OCF can also be used as a check on the quality of a company's earnings. If a firm reports high earnings but negative OCF, it may be using aggressive sales or accounting techniques.

When OCF is viewed in relation to current liabilities, it is called the OCF Ratio. It is a measure of how well current liabilities are covered by the cash flow generated from a company's operations.

**& Related Ratios/Additional Notes**

Synonyms for OCF are: Cash Flow provided by Operations, (Net) Cash Flow from Operating Activities, Ordinary Cash flow.

In the framework of various national and international standards, most companies prepare a statement of cash flows where all the cash-related activities are mapped. In this statement, a 3-staged description of cash flows is provided:
- Cash Flows from Operating Activities;
- Cash Flows from Investing Activities; and
- Cash Flows from Financing Activities.

Cash flows from investing activities are cash inflows and outflows related to the purchase and disposal of long-lived productive assets and investments in the securities of other companies. Cash flows from financing activities include ex-change of cash with creditors and owners.

A further classification is made under extraordinary (non-periodic) and neutral (non-business) cash flows. The extraordinary cash flows provide a separate classifi-cation of extraordinary activities contained in the above-mentioned three catego-ries. The goal of this classification is to increase the transparency in the inflow and outflow of liquid resources.

When using the cash flow based measures for management-controls, OCF is preferable because it is free of various balance sheet influences (both legitimately and legally).

The terms relating to the category of cash flow measures have grown consider-ably in the past. Thus, it must be examined carefully which term is more suitable for analysing which business process.

Further details about the strengths and weaknesses of different cash flow var-iants can be taken from terms such as "Cash Flow", "Gross or Net Cash Flow" and "Free Cash Flow".

### 2.5.5 Cash Flow at Risk (CFaR)

**Analytical Question**
How large is the variance of actual cash flow (or liquid funds) from a budgeted value, with a given probability, in a particular period under review? For Example, this could relate to a project, an organizational segment (subsidiary, business divi-sion, etc.) or a company as a whole.

**Definition**
Cash Flow at Risk (henceforth CFaR) is defined as an analytical method for measur-ing, with a high degree of probability, the risk of cash flow shocks for a non-financial firm.[14]

The CFaR is generally the lowest cash flow that is to be achieved, with a certain predetermined probability, during the period under review (marked with a dot in the figure). In general, a probability distribution should be determined for a business-related, risky financial indicator (here the cash flow) and (using a selected confidence level, for example, 95 %) the resulting value is to be recorded as CFaR.

---

[14] Given that there is a multi-layered method for computing CFaR, a detailed description of the method for computing this KPI is not made for the sake of brevity. Instead, a diagram should pro-vide a visual clarification involved in the computation of CFaR. For further reading on the subject, refer to Romeike/Hager (2013), p. 193 ff., particularly p. 482 ff.; Vanini (2012), p. 181 ff., particularly p. 192 ff.; Diederichs (2012), p. 117 ff.

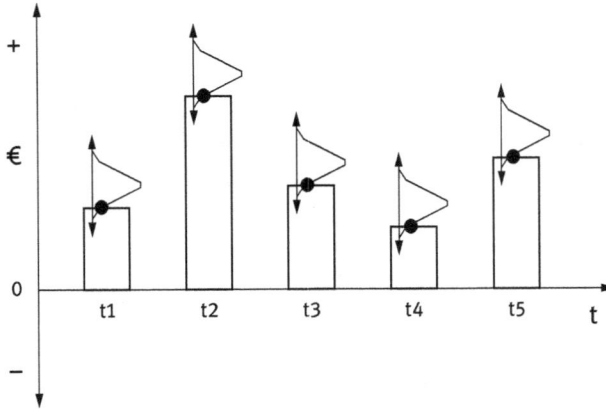

**Diagram 1**

The following explanation applies to the diagram:
The X-axis shows the individual time periods $t_1$, $t_2$, etc. On the Y-axis, the monetary units are displayed (here in €). The numbers below the zero line show the negative period values and, the numbers above zero line, show positive cash flows.

## » Calculation/Derivation
The data for this KPI are cash receipt and payment figures, and risk assessments associated with these receipts and payments. The data can be found in the corporate investment and operational financial planning and, if necessary, in a project's financial plan.

## # Interpretation and Typical Range
The key value CFaR, as a monetary risk measure, is derived and applied in a modified form from the Value-at-Risk (VaR) approach, but is not primarily geared to the needs of financial institutions, but rather to non-financial and merchandize companies.

However, the CFaR only stipulates one (critical) probability distribution point – by specifying the confidence level – as a statistical key value. By contrast in the case of investment project comparisons, it is not apparent how high the greatest possible loss could be (if applicable, in the sense of a potential threat to the company's existence). A maximum small level in the CFaR in an unfavourable case clearly has to be assessed differently from a potentially enormously large amount for the CFaR which initially appears to be tolerable, so CFaR is not suitable as the sole criterion for assessing risk.

Focusing this indicator on falling below a certain value of business performance being observed, also gives it the character of an asymmetric downside risk measure that does not reflect the possible (positive) excess of certain upper limits (so-called upside potential).

It is not possible to determine a specific general target for the order of magnitude of the corresponding CFaR. In particular, the specific financial circumstances and expectations of the organizational unit under consideration must be taken into account.

**Useful Suggestions**                                                     !
Within the framework of an efficient entrepreneurial risk management, risk analyses, risk-assessments and risk-control measures must be taken at various aggregation levels, and for both real and financial indicators (e.g. sales volumes, raw material prices or exchange rates).

In addition to selecting a suitable performance indicator, such as cash flow (or period-related earnings with the corresponding indicator designated as earnings-at-risk), the future pattern of the characteristic values of the key figure must be predicted in a meaningful way.

**Related Ratios/Additional Notes**                                        &
In addition to the key figure for dynamic capital budgeting called "Net Present Value", there is another, but much simpler risk measure of significance within the scope of capital budgeting, which determines the end of the period that is (probably) required to achieve a net present value of zero (the so-called Payback Period).

### 2.5.6 Earnings before Interest, Taxes, Depreciation and Amortization (EBITDA)

**Analytical Question**                                                     ?
How much are the Earnings from operating business *before* considering the following four items: *Interest, Taxes, Depreciation (of tangible assets) and Amortization (of intangible assets)*?

**Definition**                                                             *

|   | |
|---|---|
|   | Net Income or Loss |
| + | Taxes on Income and Profits/(–Tax Refund) |
|   | EBT (Earnings/Income from Operating Business before Taxes) |
| + | Interest Expense |
| = | EBIT (Earnings/Operating Income before Interest and Taxes) |
| + | Amortization of Intangible Assets, including Goodwill |
| = | EBITA (Earnings before Interest, Taxes and Amortization) |
| + | Depreciation of Tangible Assets |
| = | EBITDA |

The financial reporting under IAS/IFRS rules prohibits explicit demarcation of extraordinary results. Instead, IAS/IFRS rules require a declaration of the "Results from Discontinued Operations".

The figure of EBITDA is stated in absolute currency units (for example, in €).

## » Calculation/Derivation

The data for EBITDA can be obtained from information contained in the annual or quarterly reports.

## # Interpretation and Typical Range

The calculation of EBITDA shows the self-financing capacity of a firm, independent of its capital structure and depreciation/amortization policies. The ratio of EBITDA to sales (the so-called EBITDA margin) is often considered to be one of the most relevant measures for the intrinsic business profitability, allowing meaningful inter-firm comparisons. It is equally good for comparisons between firms having different forms of business organization, or between firms in different tax regimes, and lastly, between firms operating internationally.

By comparison with the regular formulas for calculating the cash flow (Net Income + Depreciations – Appreciations + changes in provisions), there are some people in academia and industry, who believe that EBITDA could be seen as a proxy measure for cash flows, since it considers only those revenues and expenses that have an impact on cash. *(For basic differences between EBITDA and cash flow, please refer to additional notes at the end of this description.)*

The EBITDA is an indicator, belonging to the category of Pro forma ratios (the so-called "Earnings before..."-Family) which have emerged in the context of IFRS-Accounting.

To calculate the annual results, the revenues have to be added and expenses have to be subtracted. For specific analysis and information purposes, it may, however, be helpful to make special adjustments to the declared results. These adjustments, to a greater or lesser extent, lead to various intermediate or (as the case may be) to pro forma results which deliver a subjective result. The "Earnings before..." ratios provide estimates of earnings, as if the special adjusted expenses and/or revenues had not occurred in the firm. This can help in improving comparability over time, and between firms. This can, however, also lead to distortions and unclear comparisons if unilateral changes in terminology made by the firm were not explicitly communicated.

The core of the EBITDA, as an indicator, represents the annual (or quarterly) net income, which, according to the income statement, is an *after-tax* number. The after-tax number is "neutralized" for tax payment, the interest expense. Through the additional adjustments of depreciation and amortization, the balance sheet policy related issues are also neutralized.

The ratio comparing EBITDA to the value of the enterprise (net market value of equity) serves as a measure of the vulnerability of the firm to a takeover. This ratio

(Value/EBITDA) provides an estimate of the number of years needed for an acquirer to recover the capital invested in an acquisition. The lower the ratio, the smaller the number of years until payback, and the more attractive is a business, all other things being equal, to a potential buyer.

For the absolute level of EBITDA, no generalization about a target number is possible. When comparisons are made over time (for the whole firm or parts thereof), a trend analysis (continuous increase or fall, highly fluctuating, etc.) of EBITDA over time offers significant explanatory power. The explanatory value of EBITDA can be increased by analysing it vis-à-vis sales or assets. This allows us to measure relative profitability, which can be used for comparing firms of different sizes.

## Useful Suggestions
The greater the number of adjustments we make to the net income, the stronger the focus on the spectrum of measures which belong to the product or services related processes in the enterprise. In order to influence this financial indicator, on the sales side, EBITDA could be improved by a better price or volume strategy. On the expense side, EBITDA could be improved by a more efficient use of the factors of production.

## Related Ratios/Additional Notes
Related ratios are: EBT, EBIT, and EBITA. In the network of pro-forma ratios, along with EBT and EBIT, EBITDA is one of three widespread indicators of profitability.

In general, the adjustments made in the calculation of pro-forma ratios are non-recurring, mostly as abnormal and non-sustainable circumstances, which are shown in the income statement as business or non-business related items. They are mostly viewed as "noise factors" which could influence a "fair view" of the wealth, financial and earnings position of the firm.

For the deduction of taxes, only the taxes on income and profits should be considered. The other forms of taxes should not be subtracted.

If both incomes and expenditures for a particular issue (for example, interest expenses and interest income) are matched in the income statement for neutralizing the pro-forma ratios, it is termed as treatment parity. When only the revenue or expense side is considered, it is termed as treatment disparity. This approach is indeed the case in EBITDA calculation, where only interest expense is added back to the earnings.

If comparisons are made over time and between firms, it must be based on a clear and consistent base of definitions. Otherwise, the conclusions drawn can be of limited use.

The main differences between EBITDA and Cash Flow are related in particular to the following points:
- Appreciation is not considered;
- Changes in provisions are not included;
- Amortization of Goodwill is not taken into account;

- Income taxes are included; and
- Interest expense (and in case treatment parity, also interest income) are considered.

The last two items are not *non-cash* expenses or income, though they provide typical business-related examples in the computation of cash flows.

## 2.6 Cash Flow Ratios

### 2.6.1 Cash Flow Margin

**?** **Analytical Question**
How much is the free operating cash flow from sales?

**\*** **Definition**

$$\frac{\text{Operating Cash Flow} \cdot 100}{\text{Net Sales}}$$

Where: Net Sales = Gross Sales – (Sales Returns + Allowances for Damaged or Lost Goods + Discounts Allowed)

The "Cash Flow Margin" is expressed as a percentage.

**»** **Calculation/Derivation**
The data for operating cash flow can be obtained from the cash flow statement or calculated from the income statement. The figure for net sales needs to be calculated from the income statement and notes contained in the annual or quarterly reports.

**#** **Interpretation and Typical Range**
The "Cash Flow Margin" is part of sales-based profitability ratios. It specifies the percentage of sales which a firm is able to achieve as cash inflow from its normal business. The ratio is thus a relative measure of the operative earnings capacity and self-financing power of the enterprise.

The "Cash Flow Margin" varies widely amongst different industrial branches and sectors. Therefore, it is difficult to recommend a target range. However, the higher the return, the better the sales-related liquidity of the enterprise.

It is good to compare a firm's cash flow margin over time to make a trend analysis. An increasing, decreasing or stagnating trend over time provides more useful information about the operating performance of the enterprise.

## Useful Suggestions

Unlike the "classical" Return On Sales (defined as operating profits/sales), in Cash Flow Margin (akin to EBITDA-turnover-yield), cash inflow is matched with sales, which cannot be easily influenced by balance sheet related policy decisions, and therefore, is considered as more meaningful than any other measure based on earnings.

A change in this ratio can be triggered by a disproportionate increase or decrease in the operating cash flow (as numerator) and net sales (as denominator). *For further details and systematic explanations on this, refer to the information in Appendix I.*

Cash Flow Margin, as a sales-related measure, shows very clearly the self-financing capacity of the enterprise through its main business. In order to influence this financial indicator, on the cash inflow (i.e., sales) side, Cash Flow Margin could be improved by a better price or volume strategy. On the cash outflow (i.e., expense) side, Cash Flow Margin could be improved by a more efficient use of the factors of production.

## Related Ratios/Additional Notes

Another name for this ratio is: Cash Flow Rate.

Sometimes, Cash Flow Profit Margin is mentioned as a related ratio. However, because of the word "profit", it could be misleading.

Another variant of this ratio is "total cash flow/total sales", which is easier to calculate from the available data.

The information value of this ratio can be further improved by using free cash flow as a numerator which reflects the remaining cash flow after the needed investment in fixed and current assets.

By comparison with the "classical" gross or net return on sales, the cash flow margin ratio carries the advantage of neutralizing many of the differences which arise because of divergent international legal directives and practices. Thus, international comparisons based on this ratio are useful.

Cash Flow Margin is also used for judging the creditworthiness of enterprises. In particular, this ratio is relevant for creditors and investors because it pinpoints the capacity of the enterprise (or parts thereof) to undertake investments, repay borrowed money, repurchase stock and/or pay dividends.

### 2.6.2 Cash Flow Return On Investment (CFROI)

## Analytical Question

How much is the cash-based return on capital employed?

## Definition

$$\frac{\text{Cash Flow} \cdot 100}{\text{Market Value of Capital Employed}}$$

This formula shows the static approach for calculating the CFROI. *For other approaches, refer to the additional notes.*

The CFROI is expressed as a percentage.

**» Calculation/Derivation**

The data for cash flow can be obtained from the net income (or loss) and adjusted for the non-cash revenues and expenses. Market value of capital employed can be calculated by multiplying the number of shares issued by the market price per share.

**# Interpretation and Typical Range**

In the framework for value-based management, cash flow based indicators are increasingly used.

The valuation related advantage of cash flow lies in its ability to neutralize the policy issues impacting on the balance sheet and to provide a transparent insight into the financial earning capacity of the firm. The ratio compares the cash generating capacity with reference to the market value of capital employed. Thus, CFROI refers to the valuation premise that the stock market sets prices based on the cash generating capacity of the firm and, not necessarily, on corporate performance or earnings.

**! Useful Suggestions**

A change in this ratio could be triggered by a disproportionate increase or decrease in the cash flow (as numerator) and market value of capital employed (as denominator). *For further details and systematic explanations on this, refer to the information in Appendix I.*

Cash flow, as a sales-related measure, shows the self-financing capacity of the enterprise through its main business very clearly. In order to influence this financial indicator, on the cash inflow (i.e., sales) side, it could be improved by a better price or volume strategy. On the cash outflow (i.e., expense) side, it could be improved by a more efficient use of the factors of production. Thus, an increase in cash flow could be achieved by encouraging high-return products or by reducing weaker products and services in the product portfolio.

**& Related Ratios/Additional Notes**

Another variant for calculating the CFROI is as follows:

$$\frac{(\text{Cash Flow} + \text{Interest on Borrowed Funds}) \cdot 100}{\text{Total Capital}}$$

The information about interest on borrowed funds and total capital can be obtained from the income statement and the balance sheet respectively.

Several other approaches have been developed in the past (for example, the discounted cash flow approach of CFROI by the Boston Consulting Group) for measuring ratio. Therefore, for inter-firm comparison, it is important to ensure the consistency of data and definitions used for computing this ratio.

Like the classification of Return On Equity (ROE) and Return On Assets (ROA), because of its economic significance, the calculation of Cash Flow Return On Equity (CFROE) is considered equally. While calculating CFROE, interest payment on borrowed funds is ignored in the numerator and year-end equity is used in the denominator. Similar to the classical ROE, the impact of financial decisions is masked and the realized cash flow is compared directly vis-à-vis equity capital.

### 2.6.3 Cash Flow Return On Equity (CFROE)

**Analytical Question**

How much is the cash-based return on stockholders' equity? How much cash can the firm afford to return to its stockholders?

**Definition**

$$\frac{\text{Free Cash Flow} \cdot 100}{\text{Year-end Stockholders' Equity}}$$

The CFROE is expressed as a percentage.

**Calculation/Derivation**

The data for free cash flow can be obtained from the cash flow statement or calculated from the income statement (in which case, the net income has to be adjusted for non-cash items). The figure of stockholders' equity can be taken from the balance sheet contained in the annual or quarterly reports.

**Interpretation and Typical Range**

Cash flow based analysis is beneficial for valuation purposes, because it neutralizes the balance sheet related policy measures. Moreover, it provides a transparent view of the financial profitability of a firm. In CFROE, free cash flow is viewed in relation to the *book value* of stockholders' equity.

In value-based systems for corporate management, cash flow oriented ratios and numbers are increasingly used.

In general, the per cent value of CFROE lies well above the classical return on equity calculated for the same period, because depreciation as a large non-cash item is added to the numerator in computing the cash flow.

**❗ Useful Suggestions**

A change in this ratio could be triggered by a disproportionate increase or decrease in the free cash flow (as numerator) and stockholders' equity (as denominator). *For further details and systematic explanations on this, refer to the information in Appendix I.*

Cash flow, as a sales-related measure, shows very clearly the self-financing capacity of the enterprise through its main business. In order to influence this financial indicator, on the cash inflow (i.e., sales) side, the ratio could be improved by a better price or volume strategy. On the cash outflow (i.e., expense) side, the ratio could be improved by a more efficient use of the factors of production and alternatives towards increasing the cash flow, such as negotiating longer payment conditions with suppliers.

The ratio can be influenced on the owners' capital side, by withdrawing or injecting capital as well as by distributing dividends or retaining profits.

**& Related Ratios/Additional Notes**

Related ratios are: Cash Flow Return On Investment (CFROI) and Return On Equity (ROE).

Similar to the classically defined ROE (net income/Stockholders' equity) the calculation of CFROE also has its financial significance. In this ratio, only cash flow is considered in the numerator and stockholders' equity is applied to the denominator. The financial structure of the enterprise (and the interest burden on borrowed money) is not considered here. From the business perspective, this makes more sense, particularly for individual business divisions or segments, which do not have any influence on the capital structure decisions of the firm. Thus, the comparison is carried out with the assumption, as if the business were financed with only the owners' equity.

### 2.6.4 EBITDA-Turnover-Yield

**❓ Analytical Question**

What is the contribution of sales in the cash flow generated out of the operating business? What percentage of the operating turnover remains with the enterprise as cash inflow?

**✳ Definition**

$$\frac{EBITDA \cdot 100}{Sales}$$

Where EBITDA is:

| | |
|---|---|
| | Net Income or Loss |
| + | Taxes on Income and Profits/(–Tax Refund) |
| = | EBT (Earnings/Income from Operating Business before Taxes) |
| + | Interest Expense |
| = | EBIT (Earnings/Operating Income before Interest and Taxes) |
| + | Amortization of Intangible Assets, including Goodwill |
| = | EBITA (Earnings before Interest, Taxes and Amortization) |
| + | Depreciation of Tangible Assets |
| = | EBITDA (Earnings before Interest, Taxes, Depreciation and Amortization) |

The financial reporting under IAS/IFRS rules prohibits explicit demarcation of extraordinary results. Instead, IAS/IFRS rules require a declaration of the "Results from Discontinued Operations".

The EBITDA-Turnover-Yield is expressed as a percentage.

## Calculation/Derivation
The data for numerator (as a proxy for cash flow) and denominator can be obtained from the income statement contained in the annual or quarterly reports.

## Interpretation and Typical Range
The EBITDA-Turnover-Yield is part of the sales-based profitability ratios. It specifies the percentage of sales which a firm is able to achieve as cash inflow from its normal business. The ratio is thus a relative measure of the operative earnings capacity and self-financing power of the enterprise. By comparison with Cash Flow Margin, EBITDA-Turnover-Yield is a pre-tax measure in which, other than interest payment and taxes, changes in long-term provisions (such as for pensions) and appreciations are not included.

EBITDA-Turnover-Yield varies widely amongst different industrial branches and sectors. Therefore, it is difficult to recommend a target range. However, the higher the return, the better the sales-related liquidity of the enterprise. It is good to compare a firm's EBITDA-Turnover-Yield over time to make a trend analysis; an increasing, decreasing or stagnating trend over time provides more useful information about the operating performance of the enterprise. It is also used for judging the creditworthiness of a firm.

## Useful Suggestions
Unlike the "classical" Return On Sales (defined as operating profits/sales), in EBITDA-Turnover-Yield (akin to cash flow margin), cash inflow is matched with sales which

cannot easily be influenced by balance sheet related policy decisions, and therefore, is considered as more meaningful than any other measure based on earnings.

A change in this ratio could be triggered by a disproportionate increase or decrease in the EBITDA (as numerator) and sales (as denominator). *For further details and systematic explanations on this, refer to the information in Appendix I.*

EBITDA is often considered to be one of the most relevant measures of the intrinsic business profitability, allowing meaningful inter-enterprise comparisons. It also shows the self-financing capacity of the enterprise through its main business. In order to influence this financial indicator, on the cash inflow (i.e., sales) side, EBITDA could be improved by a better price or volume strategy. On the cash outflow (i.e., expense) side, EBITDA could be improved by a more efficient use of the factors of production.

**&** **Related Ratios/Additional Notes**

As a synonym, Operative (EBITDA) Margin is often used.

Related ratios are: EBIT-Turnover-Yield and Cash Flow Margin.

By comparison with the "classical" gross or net return on sales, EBITDA-turnover-yield carries the advantage of neutralizing many of the differences, which arise because of divergent international legal directives and practices. Thus, international comparisons based on this ratio are useful.

## 2.7 Financial Structure Indicators

### 2.7.1 Equity-To-Fixed-Assets Ratio (Level I)

**?** **Analytical Question**

How stable is the enterprise's financing?

To what extent are the long-term assets, used in the firm, covered by equity capital?

**\*** **Definition**

$$\frac{\text{Stockholders' Equity} \cdot 100}{\text{Long-term Assets}}$$

This ratio is expressed as a percentage rate.

**»** **Calculation/Derivation**

The values for stockholders' equity and long-term assets are drawn from the balance sheet. The items included in stockholders' equity include authorized capital of the enterprise, the reserves, retained earnings and net income for the year. The items included in long-term assets are land, building, machinery, equipment, furniture and fixtures.

## Interpretation and Typical Range

Equity-To-Fixed-Assets Ratio (Level I) belongs to the category of static-long-term ratios for balance sheet based liquidity analysis. It is grounded in the principle of investment financing with identical maturities. It is a comparison between equity capital (in the numerator) and long-term assets (in the denominator). The assets, tied up in the company on a long-term basis (here the focus is on non-current assets), should be self-financed and from sources which are available over equally long time horizons. As a recommended target, one should strive to achieve a ratio which is greater than 100 %.

## Useful Suggestions

If this ratio provides a cover for long-term assets under 100 %, it implies that parts of the long-term assets have been financed by external debt, and follow-up financing may become necessary during the life of the long-term assets. Such follow-up financing could be available only at a higher interest rate so that, eventually, the enterprise might face a liquidity squeeze, or see lower returns. In the case that the enterprise is not able to raise funds long-term, in extreme circumstances, sale of short-term assets (mostly with financial losses) may become necessary.

To avoid the risk of jeopardizing normal business operations, it is, therefore, important to match the duration of the resource assets locked in for the duration of the committed funds.

A change in this ratio can be achieved by disproportionate changes in equity capital (in numerator) and long-term assets (in denominator). *For further details and systematic explanations on this, refer to the information in Appendix I.*

On the equity capital side, the ratio can be influenced, for example, through capital distribution and allocation programs as well as through dividend pay-out and retention policies. On the asset side, the starting point could be a change in the investment and disinvestment policy. The long-term assets can also be acquired on a rental or lease basis (by using the so-called off-balance sheet policy).

## Related Ratios/Additional Notes

The context used in describing the Equity-To-Fixed-Assets Ratio is also described as the "golden rule of financing", which requires that long-term investments should not be financed with short-term funds.

Another synonym for this ratio is: Fixed Asset Coverage Ratio. The segregation into I – II – III levels is also shown under the categories A – B – C.

An extended version of this ratio, which, over and above equity capital, adds long-term borrowing in the numerator, is referred to as Equity-To-Fixed-Asset Ratio (Level II).

If parts of current assets (minimum inventory level) are included in the denominator, the ratio is referred to as the Equity-To-Fixed-Asset Ratio (Level III).

### 2.7.2 Equity-To-Fixed-Assets Ratio (Level II)

**[?] Analytical Question**

How stable is the enterprise's financing?

To what extent are the long-term assets used in the business covered by equity capital and long-term external borrowing?

**[*] Definition**

$$\frac{(\text{Stockholders' Equity} + \text{Long-term Debt}) \cdot 100}{\text{Long-term Assets}}$$

This ratio specifies a percentage rate.

**[»] Calculation/Derivation**

The values for stockholders' equity, long-term debt and long-term assets are drawn from the balance sheet. The items included in stockholders' equity include authorized capital of the enterprise, reserves, retained earnings and net yearly income. Long-term debt means all the liabilities with a maturity of over one year. The items included in long-term assets are land, building, machinery, equipment, furniture and fixtures.

**[#] Interpretation and Typical Range**

Equity-To-Fixed-Assets Ratio (Level II) belongs to the category of static-long-term ratios for balance sheet based liquidity analysis. It is grounded in the principle of investment financing with identical maturities. It is a comparison between equity capital and long-term external debt (in the numerator) and long-term assets (in the denominator). The assets, tied up in the company on a medium and long-term basis (here the focus is primarily on non-current assets), should be financed from sources (equity or debt) which are available over comparable time horizons.

As a recommended target, one should strive to achieve a ratio which is larger than 100 %.

**[!] Useful Suggestions**

If this ratio provides a cover for long-term assets under 100 %, it implies that parts of the long-term assets have been financed by short-term external borrowings and, a follow-up financing could become necessary during the life of the long-term assets. Such follow-up financing could be available, among others, only at a higher interest rate, so that eventually the enterprise might face a liquidity squeeze, or have lower returns. In the case that the enterprise is not able to raise funds long-term, in extreme circumstances, the sale of short-term assets (mostly with financial losses) may become necessary.

To avoid the risk of jeopardizing the normal business operations, it is, therefore, important to match the duration of the resources locked in assets with the duration of the funds committed.

A change in this ratio can be achieved by disproportionate changes in the total equity capital and long-term external borrowings (in numerator) and in long-term assets (in denominator). *For further details and systematic explanations on this, refer to the information in Appendix I.*

On the equity capital side, the ratio can be influenced, for example, through stock repurchase and fresh equity issues, through dividend pay-out and retention policies, as well as through reshuffling of short-term debt into long-term debt. On the asset side, the starting point could be a change in the investment and disinvestment policy. The long-term assets can also be acquired on a rental or lease basis (by using the so-called off-balance sheet policy).

### Related Ratios/Additional Notes &
The context used in describing the Equity-To-Fixed-Assets Ratio (Level II) is also described as the "golden rule of financing", which requires that long-term investments should not be financed with short-term funds.

Another synonym for this ratio is: Fixed Asset Coverage Ratio. The segregation into I – II – III levels is also shown under the categories A – B – C.

A conservative or tighter version of this ratio, which takes only equity capital in the numerator, is referred to as Equity-To-Fixed-Asset Ratio (Level I).

If parts of current assets (for example, minimum inventory level) are included in the denominator, the ratio is referred to as Equity-To-Fixed-Asset Ratio (Level III).

### 2.7.3 Equity-To-Fixed-Assets Ratio (Level III)

### Analytical Question ?
How stable is the enterprise's financing?

To what extent are the long-term assets and working capital used in the business, covered by equity capital and long-term external borrowing?

### Definition *

$$\frac{(\text{Stockholders' Equity} + \text{Long-term Debt}) \cdot 100}{(\text{Long-term Assets} + \text{Long-term Component of Working Capital})}$$

This ratio specifies a percentage rate.

## » Calculation/Derivation

The values for this ratio, other than the long-term component of working capital, are drawn from the balance sheet. The long-term component of working capital, such as minimum inventory level, is fixed individually by companies, and is available only to internal decision makers. The external analysts have to depend on the information in the annual financial statements.

The items included in stockholders' equity include authorized capital of the enterprise, the reserves, retained earnings and net yearly income. Long-term debt means all the liabilities with a maturity of over one year. The items included in long-term assets are land, building, machinery, equipment, furniture and fixtures.

## # Interpretation and Typical Range

Equity-To-Fixed-Assets Ratio (Level III) belongs to the category of static-long-term ratios for balance sheet based liquidity analysis. It is grounded in the principle of investment financing with identical maturities. It is a comparison between equity capital and long-term debt (in the numerator) and long-term assets (in the denominator). The assets, tied up in the company on a medium and long-term basis (here the focus is primarily on non-current assets), should be financed from sources (equity or debt) which are available over comparable time horizons.

As a recommended target, one should strive to achieve a ratio which is larger than 100 %.

## ! Useful Suggestions

If this ratio provides a cover for long-term assets under 100 %, it implies that parts of the long-term assets have been financed by short-term external borrowings and, a follow-up financing could become necessary during the life of the long-term assets. Such follow-up financing could be available, among others, only at a higher interest rate, so that eventually the enterprise might face a liquidity squeeze or have lower returns. In the case that the enterprise is not able to raise funds long-term, in extreme circumstances, sale of short-term assets (mostly with financial losses) may become necessary.

To avoid the risk of jeopardizing normal business operations, it is, therefore, important to match the duration of the resources locked in assets with the duration of the funds committed.

A change in this ratio can be achieved by disproportionate changes in the total of equity capital and external debt (in numerator) and in the total of long-term assets and the long-term component of working capital (in denominator). *For further details and systematic explanations on this, refer to the information in Appendix I.*

On the equity capital side, the ratio can be influenced, for example, through capital distribution and allocation programs, through dividend pay-out and retention policies, as well through reshuffling of short-term debt into long-term debt. On the asset side, the starting point could be a change in the investment and disinvestment policy. The long-term assets can also be acquired on a rental or lease basis (by using the so-called off-balance sheet policy).

### Related Ratios/Additional Notes &

The context used in describing the Equity-To-Fixed-Assets Ratio (Level III) is also described as the "golden rule of financing", which requires that long-term investments should not be financed with short-term funds.

Another synonym for this ratio is: Fixed Asset Coverage Ratio. The segregation into I – II – III levels is also shown under the categories A – B – C.

A conservative or tighter version of this ratio, which takes only equity capital in the numerator, is referred to as Equity-To-Fixed-Asset Ratio (Level I).

By comparison with level I, a somewhat liberal version of this ratio also includes, in addition to the equity capital, long-term debt in the denominator. This ratio is referred to as Equity-To-Fixed-Asset Ratio (Level II) or the "golden" balance sheet rule, which requires that fixed assets be backed up by long-term capital and short-term assets, by short-term funds.

### 2.7.4 Equity Ratio Ⓢ

### Analytical Question ?

How is the relative financial strength of the firm in terms of equity capital? What is the loss-absorption capacity of the firm?

### Definition *

$$\frac{\text{Total Owners' Equity} \cdot 100}{\text{Total Capital}}$$

or

$$\frac{\text{Total Owners' Equity} \cdot 100}{\text{Total Assets}}$$

This ratio is expressed as a percentage.

### Calculation/Derivation »

The values for this ratio could be drawn from the balance sheet.

### Interpretation and Typical Range #

This ratio belongs to the category of "Capital Structure Analysis", which is also named "Financing Analysis". The ratio occupies itself with the types and durability of available capital. Through this ratio, the financial risk and creditworthiness of the firm can be estimated.

The Equity Ratio shows the share of equity capital in total capital at the end of a period or closing date. It shows the significance of equity in the credit-standing check by banks and rating agencies. A high ratio suggests that a company relies more on funds provided by owners. The higher the ratio, the more secure the firm's financial position; in which case a firm is considered to be financially stable and independent from creditors. Thus, it is considered as a measure of the firm's ability to withstand financial risks.

It is not possible to fix a general, operationally logical norm for this ratio. An Equity Ratio of greater than or equal to 25 % (or 33.3 %) is usually expected. The appropriate target ratio depends on the branch-specific characteristics and the legal form of the firm.

## ! Useful Suggestions
A change in this ratio could be triggered by a disproportionate increase or decrease in owners' equity (as numerator) and total assets (as denominator). *For further details and a systematic explanation on this, refer to the information in Appendix I.*

On the equity capital side, the ratio can be influenced, for example, through capital distribution and allocation programs as well as through dividend pay-out and retention policies. On the debt side, the need for borrowed funds can be reduced by disposing of the non-operational assets (minimum at book value) or by reducing working capital requirements. Assuming a constant owners' equity, a reduction in the volume of borrowed money would lead to a reduction in the Equity Ratio.

There are four reasons which call for a higher equity ratio:
– Owners' equity attracts more capital. A high amount of owners' equity, with its basic characteristic of safe capital, makes it noticeably easier to obtain credit;
– With an increasing share of owners' equity, the commitment of the firm increases, so that the risk of insolvency by excessive indebtedness is reduced;
– By comparison with borrowed funds, financing through equity capital does not create any obligation to make payments for interest and principal; and
– Lower influence of the creditors, such as banks.

In the context of leverage effects (also reflected in the indicator "Financial Leverage Index"), a lower equity ratio may be desirable within certain limits. As long as the return on total capital is higher than the interest rate on borrowed funds, the leverage effect will be visible in improved return on equity.

## & Related Ratios/Additional Notes
Shareholder Equity Ratio is a common synonym for this ratio. Together with debt ratio (total debts/total assets or capital), it completes the total capital; both should add up to a 100 %.

Since the total capital is the sum of owners' equity and external liabilities, the equity ratio, the debt ratio (total liabilities/total capital) and debt-to-equity ratio (debt/equity) are three different forms of the same financial structure analysis. The conclusion drawn remains the same in each of the ratios.

In certain situations, the basic variant of equity ratio can be slightly modified (for example, through proportional assignment of long-term reserves). Such adjustments help in removing various balance sheet related changes and allow for better comparison between firms, and over time.

The equity ratio also hypothetically shows the percentage of assets on which shareholders have a residual claim. For example, with an equity ratio of 40% and total assets of €600 Million, the shareholders would receive, in the event of liquidation at book values, €240 Million (40% · 600). The higher the ratio, the more shareholders may receive in the event of liquidation.

The value of equity capital, shown on the balance sheet, does not show the actual value of the firm owners' commitment. One of the main reasons for this difference lies in undisclosed reserves. Thus, the market value of owners' equity could be much higher than what is reported on the balance sheet, and the firm may have a much higher equity ratio.

### 2.7.5 Financial Leverage Index

**Analytical Question**                                                      ?

How effective is the capital structure of the firm?

**Definition**                                                               ✳

$$\frac{\text{Return On Equity}}{\text{Return On Assets}}$$

The result obtained through this ratio is expressed in numerical value (say, an index of 1.5) or as a coefficient.

**Calculation/Derivation**                                                   »

The raw-data for the computation of Financial Leverage Index is derived from the income statement (for each numerator of the profitability ratio) and from the balance sheet (for each denominator of the profitability ratio).

**Interpretation and Typical Range**                                         #

The so-called "Leverage Analysis" is considered to be a major building-block in analysing financial statements.

If the index has a value of more or less than 1 (implying a divergence between return on equity and return on assets), it indicates a "Leverage-Chance" or

"Leverage-Risk", respectively. It is desirable to examine whether an increase or decrease of debt-equity ratio (debt/equity) could improve the return on equity.

It is not possible to fix a general, operationally logical norm for this ratio. Apart from normal business opportunities and risks (analysed in operating leverage and not a point of discussion here), the question of designing an appropriate financial structure is the main concern in the financial leverage index.

### ! Useful Suggestions

A change in this ratio could be triggered by a disproportionate increase or decrease in return on equity (as numerator) and return on assets (as denominator). *For further details and a systematic explanation on this, refer to the information in Appendix I.*

The index can be influenced by focusing on the business performance of the firm. Thus, on the sales side, measures towards a better price or volume strategy and, on the expense side, measures towards a more efficient use of the factors of production could be helpful. The leverage index can also be influenced through reduction in the asset base (reducing capital employed) as well as through changes in the debt-equity ratio.

The following classical equation for the leverage effect, provides more clarity on the basic factors involved and the areas which management can focus:

$$ROE = ROA + (ROA - COD) \cdot (D/E)$$

Where:
ROE = Return On Equity
ROA = Return On Assets
COD = Cost of Debt (which is the after tax interest rate on borrowed fund)
D = Debt
E = Equity

As long as the ROA is higher than the interest rate on borrowed funds, the leverage effect will be visible in the improved return on equity. Most companies have such positive leverage effect. However, in crisis situations, the positive effect may change, when ROA is lower than the COD (after-tax). This would have the impact of reducing the profit available for stockholders.

Given the environmental factors and the firm-specific factors, the management should evaluate various opportunities and risk scenarios and, based on this, should develop a suitable financing strategy.

### & Related Ratios/Additional Notes

A related measure is the Financial Leverage Percentage (ROE – ROA) which basically has the same interpretation: it measures the advantage or disadvantage that occurs when a company's ROE differs from its ROA.

In the context of the leverage index, there are three ratios which are interrelated: the equity ratio (equity/total capital), the debt ratio (total liabilities/total capital) and the debt-to-equity ratio (debt/equity) which are three different forms of the same financial structure analysis. The conclusion drawn remains the same for each of the ratios.

### 2.7.6 Cost and Revenue Structure related Ratios

**Analytical Question**

What relative importance does a specific cost (or revenue) category have in the total costs (or revenues) of a relevant business object, in a particular period?
- Classified into different cost categories (e.g. material, human resource, energy, and other contracted services. When appropriate, these could be further subdivided according to their individual or fixed overhead character)
- Classified into different revenue categories (e.g. related to product, regional and/or customer segments. When appropriate, these could be further subdivided according to transaction-dependent and transaction-independent internal revenue categories).

Appropriate business objects could be fixed within the whole firm according to the required level of detail. For example, individual business areas, profit centres, strategic business units (SBUs), and divisions or plants are common business objects.

**Definition**

$$\frac{\text{Specific Cost or Revenue Category in a Period} \cdot 100}{\text{Total Costs or Revenues per Reference Object in a Period}}$$

All variants of the "cost structure parameters" as well as the "revenue structure parameters" are indicated as a "%" dimension. The choice of periodic reference value, strongly depends on the object of analysis. Accordingly, months/quarters/years are the most common reference periods.

**Calculation/Derivation**

The necessary data can be extracted from the computer based accounting department information systems. How frequently the data will be collected depends on the decision-makers' need for information and is, in many cases, made in regular cycles, and if necessary, depending on the situation, at short notice and outside the regular schedule.

**# Interpretation and Typical Range**

In many companies, the material costs and human-resource costs represent the biggest cost pools. Many times, energy costs also significantly affect the total costs. Thus, in order to maintain and increase the competitiveness, it is crucial to analyse the amount and movement of respective cost positions over time, and when for example, external disturbances occur, manage these actively.

As the "cost and revenue related ratios" are always indicated in percentages, the mathematical constellation has to be considered carefully when carrying out economic interpretation of changes. This is because when an increase of the vertical intensity of manufacturing, or a price decline, leads to fall in total material costs, with all other conditions being equal, the proportion of other cost categories rise in the total (and vice versa when the opposite constellation applies). This should not be taken to mean that the other cost categories have increased.

It has been a revealing fact for years that, not only in the classical business models like B2B or B2C, but also in other business models, pre and (even more so) post-sale services are gaining an increasing portion in the revenue structure of the overall business.

This stronger revenue-side differentiation is particularly significant for business models in the digital economy. Here, structural distinctions must be made between direct revenue generation from transaction-based connection, royalty fees (like the pay-per-view or pay-per-click) and transaction-independent installation and basic fees (like the pay-per-period).

Similarly, for generating indirect revenues, transaction-based provisions (for example, pay-per-lead or pay-per-sale) can be compared with transaction-independent revenues (for example, as pay-per-period) from data mining and, if applicable, banner advertising.

It is difficult to make any operational generalization about the desired levels for a particular "cost and revenue structure". A general target range for this ratio cannot be determined. For orientation and benchmarking this ratio, internal (such as the ratio in different organizational units or plan-actual values) or external comparisons should be made, where the branch-specific average period or the "best-practice" value may be used as a guide.

**! Useful Suggestions**

Based on the premise that firms in a particular industry have similar cost and revenue structures, the key performance values which significantly differ from the industry average values, provide useful hints when focusing on the positive or negative developments, and steering these towards corporate goals.

In general, the spectrum of actions directly influencing relevant cost as well as relevant revenue categories can be developed from price and/or volume controlling measures.

When, for example, the use of specific high tech-components (with correspondingly expensive purchase prices) represents significant potential to gain, maintain or expand competitive advantages, a comparatively high proportion of material expenses can be deliberately desirable.

Similarly, the possibilities for generating further revenues with modern forms of price bundling and a hybrid range of services in classical business fields, has to undergo another economic review. The combination, and expected weightage of forms of revenue, generated by different business models within the digital economy, is targeted at using the appropriate willingness of direct customers as well as of third parties (among others, advertising companies) in the sense of a multi revenue stream optimization in each of the "net economy's" field of application.

In principle, a change in this ratio, in the context of desired targets, can be achieved by a disproportionate increase or decrease in the achieved output (as numerator) and deployed input (as denominator). *For further details and systematic explanations, refer to information in Appendix I.*

**Related Ratios/Additional Notes**

From the direct and appropriate combination of cost and revenue items, based on the marginal and full costing and supplemented with reasonable database supported applications using methods like multidimensional fix-cost calculations or process costing, appropriate period-related and unit-related success indicators (per-unit profits, contribution margins, etc.) can be derived.

The various possibilities to capture, process and prepare large volumes of data in real-time, according to specific (assignment and calculation) rules, offer companies an excellent basis to communicate information about cost and revenue structures internally and, if applicable, also externally, which is useful for decision making. This can also be used to translate the information into successful business strategies with reasonably derived measures.

### 2.7.7 Provisions Rate

**Analytical Question**

What part of the total capital is financed through provisions? What is the proportion of provisions in the total capital of the company?

**Definition**

$$\frac{\text{Sum of Provisions and Contingent Liabilities} \cdot 100}{\text{Total Capital}}$$

The "provisions rate" is expressed as a percentage.

Both the numerator and the denominator are to be taken at balance sheet date.

**» Calculation/Derivation**

The required data for this key indicator can be derived from externally published financial reports of the company, along with the footnotes provided for an understanding of different types of provision and contingent liabilities. The data can be further classified for finer evaluation internally, e.g. for understanding the maturity period of each type of provision and contingent liability.

Under IFRS rules, recognition and measurement of provisions and contingent liabilities is covered by IAS 37 and IAS 19. Thus, under IAS 37, provisions are defined as liabilities of uncertain timing and amount[15] and contingent liabilities are defined as possible obligations, depending upon whether some uncertain future event occurs. Under IAS 19, a company has to recognize and provision for payments for post-retirement benefits (such as pensions or lump-sum payments). To calculate the sum of all provisions in this KPI, the provisions under IAS 37 and IAS 19 should be added together.

The term total capital in the denominator for this KPI, refers to the sum of long-term debt and total shareholders' equity. Conversely, it can be calculated by excluding short-term liabilities from the liabilities side of the balance sheet.

One has to distinguish between short-term and long-term provisions to understand this indicator. Whereas short-term provisions have a maturity of less than one year (such as provisions for bad-debts, sales allowances, inventory obsolescence, provision for income tax, etc.), long-term provisions relate to maturities of more than one year (such as provision for retirement benefits, law suits and warranties). The indicator "provisions rate" is calculated with long-term provisions and contingent liabilities and excludes short-term provisions.

**# Interpretation and Typical Range**

The "provisions rate" is an indicator of the extent to which the company is financed by provisions set aside for accrued liabilities, contingent liabilities and accrued retirement benefits. When provisions are made for specific purposes, the amount is shown in the income statement as an accrued expense and the equivalent amount is shown on the balance sheet, on the liabilities side as a purpose-specific (expected or contingent) liability. Basically, these provisions (though meant for the specific-purpose liabilities) are available to the company as funds for financing. To this end, "provisions rate" describes a segment of the capital structure, because it shows the provisions' portion of the total capital.

As with many other key indicators, the interpretation and comparison of concrete values for this ratio may not be easy, particularly in certain kinds of

---

15 Any present obligation, as a result of past events, where settlement is expected to result in an outflow or resources (i.e. a payment).

companies where noticeably extensive content relating to external legal standards has to be implemented. Nevertheless, to begin with, the collection and reporting of this indicator makes it clear that the firm is pursuing a preventive strategy for securing risk management and corporate compliance, in a world full of uncertainties and regulatory regimes.

However, for orientation and benchmarking, internal (such as the ratio in different organizational units or budget-actual comparisons) and corresponding external comparisons can be taken, where the branch-specific practices or the risk-management frameworks adopted by competitors may be used as a guide.

## Useful Suggestions

If we exclude the provisions for retirement benefits (which are computed, based on national legal systems or contractual agreements between employer and employees), the sum total of all provisions can also be interpreted as a benchmark for the risk-management framework for the firm. Many companies follow the policy of provisioning pre-emptively on the probable risk of losing a lawsuit and, consequently, for payment of penalties. Similarly, many companies also provision for onerous loss-making contracts, for probable warranty claims, possible restructuring or eventual environmental clean ups.

It also has a strong linkage with the corporate governance framework, established by the firm for compliance with national regulations and directives. Other factors that influence the value of this ratio are the size of the firm, complexity of the firm's business, type of business model (e.g. local, national or international), and risk-tolerance capacity of the firm.

## Related Ratios/Additional Notes

One should categorically distinguish between "provisions rate" and "reserves rate". Reserves are an appropriation of net income, and signify that part of net income which is not distributed as dividend to shareholder but retained as part of the equity. The KPI "reserve ratio" should be understood as an indicator of the solvency of the company, because of its linkage to the shareholders' equity. In IFRS, reserves include fair value reserves, hedging reserves, revaluation reserves, foreign currency translation reserves and other statutory reserves.

The interpretative power of "provisions rate" is limited, because of the low informative value of high long-term provisions.

According to IFRS, measurement of provisions which have a maturity of more than one year, are made at discounted present values, using pre-tax discount rates that reflect the current market assessment of the time and monetary value and the risk specific to the liability (IAS 37.45 and 37.47)

## 2.8 Efficiency Ratios

### 2.8.1 Average Collection Period

**? Analytical Question**

How long does it take, on an average, for a customer to pay his/her accounts? How effective are the credit-granting, payment conditions and collection activities of the firm towards its customers?

**✳ Definition**

$$\frac{\text{Average Accounts Receivable} \cdot 360}{\text{Net Sales Revenue}}$$

Where:

Average Accounts Receivable = (Beginning Accounts Receivable + Ending Accounts Receivable)/2

Net Sales               = Gross Sales – (Sales Returns + Allowances for Damaged or Lost Goods + Discounts Allowed)

The ratio is computed in number of days.

**» Calculation/Derivation**

For internal analysis, the average accounts receivable can be computed from the accounting department data, at desired intervals, such as quarterly or monthly. The external analysts, however, can compute the average accounts receivable only from the balance sheet in the last published annual report and net sales out of the income statement contained therein.

**# Interpretation and Typical Range**

This ratio provides information about the average payment time taken by the customers. Conversely, the ratio shows the effectiveness of credit sales, payment conditions and collection activities. The shorter the collection period, the faster the availability of financial resources (out of the invoiced sales) for other business activities would be. When a customer exceeds the average collection period substantially, the chance of recovering the outstanding receivable from him falls proportionately.

A general target for this ratio is not possible. However, if other conditions remain constant, shorter collection periods are preferable to longer ones. To benchmark this ratio, one could take the branch-specific average collection period or the "best-practice" value.

## Useful Suggestions

A change in the average collection period could be triggered by a disproportionate increase or decrease in the accounts receivable in the numerator and net sales in the denominator. *For details on this, refer to the explanation in Appendix I.*

If a customer is not able to pay within the period allowed for payment, it could be because of:
–   A complaint. The invoice will be paid only after the problem has been resolved;
–   the customer has changed his readiness to make speedy payments; or
–   a relatively poor market position of the firm (such as dependence on a few customers) is misused by some clients.

In addition to the measures taken to reduce the above problems (improving quality, careful selection of customers by analysing their credit standing, or increasing the client-mix), some financial measures can be implemented as well:
–   Expediting the process of sending reminders;
–   increasing the use of "direct-debiting" the customer for invoice amounts and/or increasing the use of electronic-banking for collection;
–   use factoring (in domestic markets and, in particular, in some foreign markets); or
–   offering better payment incentives by increasing the discount rate for earlier payments.

The proposed suggestions for reducing the collection period should be checked carefully, not just for their liquidity improvement effect, but also for their impact on profitability. Thus, an increase of the discount rate for earlier payment will not only reduce the collection period, but would also reduce the firm's income. It is good to search for an optimum solution in this case.

## Related Ratios/Additional Notes

This ratio is also called Days Sales Outstanding (DSO).

The ratio is sometimes calculated in two steps:
–   Receivable Turnover Ratio (Net Sales/Average Accounts Receivable) is calculated first followed by
–   Average Collection Period (360/Receivable Turnover Ratio).

The net result, however, is the same.

In many countries, instead of 360, 365 days are taken for the purpose of calculating this ratio.

Average Collection Period is one of the ratios, where both financial and business-performance measures support each other and lead to collective success.

### 2.8.2 Average Payment Period

**[?] Analytical Question**

How long does it take for the firm to pay its suppliers on average? How efficient is the management in availing suppliers' credit and in meeting obligations to suppliers?

**[*] Definition**

$$\frac{\text{Average Accounts Payable} \cdot 360}{\text{Cost of Goods Sold}}$$

Where:
Average Accounts Payable = (Beginning Accounts Payable + Ending Accounts Payable)/2
Cost of Goods Sold = Beginning Inventory + Purchases − Ending Inventory

Because of the multiplier "360", the ratio is to be expressed in number of days. Similarly, the ratio will be expressed in months if the multiplier is "12".

**[»] Calculation/Derivation**

For internal analysis, the average accounts payable can be computed from the accounting department data, at desired intervals, such as quarterly or monthly. The external analysts, however, can compute the average accounts payable only from the balance sheet in the last published annual report. The cost of goods sold can be obtained from the income statement.

**[#] Interpretation and Typical Range**

This ratio provides information about how far the firm takes advantage of the average payment conditions granted by suppliers. Conversely, the ratio measures how quickly management is paying trade accounts. The longer the average payment period, the longer the duration over which the financial resources (out of the unpaid invoices) are available for other business activities.

Given a particular average payment period, it is good to check the cost of such "implicit" credit by suppliers; maybe the supplier offered a discount for early payments, but this was not availed of by the firm.

A general target for this ratio is not possible. For benchmarking this ratio, one could take the branch-specific average collection period or the "best-practice" value.

**Useful Suggestions**

A change in average payment period could be triggered by a disproportionate increase or decrease in the accounts payable in the numerator or cost of goods sold in the denominator. *For details on this, refer to the explanation in Appendix I.*

If the average payment period availed of by the firm, increases over time, it could be because of:

- A complaint. The invoice will be paid only after the problem has been resolved;
- the financial support through bank credit is not available to the firm; or
- the relatively strong market position of the firm (such as dependence of the supplier on the firm) is utilized.

In real life, taking advantage of the credit provided by the suppliers is considered to be an advantage. The following aspects should, however, be considered in the process:

- the simplicity of the trade-credit (there are no special credit formalities to be complied with);
- the firm's dependence on bank credit does not increase; or
- the ease of obtaining credit, as soon as a liability arises, the credit facility becomes available.

The proposed suggestions should be carefully checked, not just for their liquidity improvement effect, but also for their impact on profitability. Thus, a decision by the firm to delay the payment could provide more time. However, this could be at the cost of sacrificing the discount offered by the supplier. One should search for an optimum solution in this case.

**Related Ratios/Additional Notes**

This ratio is also called Days Payable Outstanding (DPO).

This ratio is sometimes calculated in two steps:

- Payable Turnover Ratio (Cost of Goods Sold/Average Trade Accounts Payable) is calculated first, followed by
- Average Payment Period (360/Payable Turnover Ratio).

The net result, however, is the same.

In many countries, instead of 360, 365 days are taken for the purpose of calculating this ratio.

Average Payment Period is similar to the Average Collection Period and one of the ratios where both financial and business-performance measures support each other, and lead to collective success. Both of these indicators are important elements in managing the "Cash-to-Cash Cycle".

Ⓢ **2.8.3 Cash-to-Cash Cycle**

▣ **Analytical Question**

What is the length of time during which liquidity is tied up in the operating cycle? How much time does the firm take in order to convert resource inputs into actual cash flows?

✱ **Definition**

Days Inventory Outstanding + Days Sales Outstanding – Days Payable Outstanding

Where:
Days Inventory Outstanding (DIO):

$$\frac{\text{Inventory} \cdot 360}{\text{Net Sales}}$$

Days Sales Outstanding (DSO):

$$\frac{\text{Average Trade Accounts Receivable} \cdot 360}{\text{Net Sales}}$$

Days Payable Outstanding (DPO):

$$\frac{\text{Average Trade Accounts Payable} \cdot 360}{\text{Cost of Goods Sold}}$$

The ratio is computed in number of days.

» **Calculation/Derivation**

For internal analysis, the needed data can be obtained from the accounting department. The external analysts, however, will have to depend on information contained in the last published annual report.

\# **Interpretation and Typical Range**

In the "stock-based" liquidity analysis, the ratios calculated at the end of a period, usually have the disadvantage of being merely a snapshot. Cash-to-Cash Cycle is part of the "flow-based" liquidity analysis. It allows the projection of future developments, with the help of payment streams (and the related turnover periods) from the past.

A general target for this ratio cannot be given without considering the overall position of the firm, and its branch-specific features. However, the shorter the cash-to-cash cycle, the shorter the period during which the capital is blocked and, obviously, the more successful the working capital management.

**Useful Suggestions** !

A change in this ratio could be triggered by a disproportionate increase or decrease in the reported balances of different items (inventory, accounts receivable and accounts payable) in the numerator and reported flow items (net sales and cost of goods sold) in the denominator. *For details on this, refer to the explanation in Appendix I.*

The formula for the calculation of Cash-to-Cash Cycle has three components, and the additive and subtractive linkage between these components clearly shows the direction in which the desired measures should be implemented: A drop in DIO and DSO, and an increase in DPO would help in improving the ratio.

**Related Ratios/Additional Notes** &

– This ratio is also known as "Cash Conversion Cycle". Sometimes, Operating Cycle is also used as a synonym.
– Out of the three components of Cash-to-Cash Cycle, DSO and DPO are known also as Average Collection Period and Average Payable Period respectively.

### 2.8.4 Asset Turnover Ratio

**Analytical Question** ?

How effective is the management in utilizing assets to generate revenues? How many € worth of sales is generated for each € of assets? How often is the invested capital turned over through sales revenue in a period?

**Definition** *

$$\frac{\text{Net Sales}}{\text{Average Capital}}$$

or

$$\frac{\text{Net Sales}}{\text{Average Net Assets}}$$

Where:
Average Net Assets = (Beginning + Ending Assets net of depreciation)/2

This ratio is expressed in terms of multiples.

Depending upon the business level being analysed, the denominator could be invested capital, operating assets or fixed assets.

### » Calculation/Derivation

The data for sales and asset base could be obtained from annual financial statements. When other denominators, such as operating assets are being used, additional information may be required from the accounting department. This information however, may not be accessible to external analysts.

### # Interpretation and Typical Range

The Asset Turnover Ratio is grouped in the category of turnover, or activity ratios, and explains the average period during which assets are locked in the business process. The economic significance of asset turnover is visible in the ROI ratio. Thus, profitability ratio ROI (Net Income/Assets) is split into return on sales (Net Income/Sales) and asset turnover (Sales/Assets). *For additional explanation about the multilayered ratio systems, refer to the DuPont System in Appendix II for an example.*

The absolute value of the Asset Turnover Ratio is branch-specific. In principle, the higher this ratio, the higher the ROI with a given return on sales. However, it is interesting to note that firms with a low-margin price strategy usually have high asset turnover while those with relatively high-margin price strategy have low asset turnover.

### ! Useful Suggestions

A change in the Asset Turnover Ratio could be triggered by a disproportionate increase or decrease in the net sales (as numerator) and average assets (as denominator). *For further details and systematic explanations on this, refer to the information in Appendix I.*

The splitting of ROI into two multiplicative components of return on sales and asset turnover ratio suggests that, despite falling return on sales, the profitability of a firm can be maintained if the asset turnover can be increased. For this purpose, various short- and long-term steps towards reducing the assets locked in operations, without negatively impacting upon the sales generating process will have to be considered.

Similarly, a fall or rise in the profitability of the firm could be analysed with reference to a change in return on sales, or in the asset turnover ratio, and corrective measures could be applied.

A lower or declining asset turnover ratio may indicate that a firm is expanding by acquiring additional assets, which will impact on future sales. Conversely, a rise in the ratio could be a signal that a firm is cutting back on capital expenditure because of an expected economic downturn. Thus, related information must be analysed before drawing conclusions from changes in this ratio.

### & Related Ratios/Additional Notes

The choice of the denominator in asset turnover is dependent on what kind of numerator is used. Thus, when operating results or EBIT is used, operating assets as the corresponding denominator should be taken. In this case, asset turnover is calculated with a narrowly defined numerator (only operating income) and a narrowly defined denominator (only operating assets and not total assets).

For inter-firm comparison, it is important to ensure the consistency of data and definitions used for computing the asset turnover ratio.

### 2.8.5 Asset Coverage Period

**Analytical Question**
How long will the available asset be sufficient to cover a given consumption or need pattern? How long will a particular asset be available?

The ratio can be applied to a variety of assets or objects (inventory, cash at hand, etc.) and could be individually calculated for raw-material, supplies, work-in-process, finished products and cash/cash equivalents.

**Definition**

$$\frac{\text{Average Daily Inventory} \cdot 360 \text{ Days}}{\text{Average Daily Need or Consumption}}$$

The ratio is expressed in terms of time, depending upon the chosen multiplier. For 360 as a multiplier, the result would be "in days", for 52, it would be "in weeks" and for 12, it would be "in months".

The denominator can be the average need or consumption or outflow.

In the case of real assets, instead of using the quantity based data for numerator and denominator, in practice it is also common to take value based data. For an inter-firm or time-series comparison of value based result, it is important to check the consistency of the valuation base for the inventory amount. The valuation could be based on acquisition price or sales price, current price or average price, or appropriate production costs.

**Calculation/Derivation**
The required data, depending upon the level of aggregation of the chosen products, can be obtained from the information system of (internal and external) accounting. For example, the data can be based on an ERP (Enterprise Resource Planning) system, with a module-based structure. The data could also be obtained from corporate capital budgeting documents.

**Interpretation and Typical Range**
The coverage ratios deliver information about the supply position of the asset under consideration. The higher the ratio value, the more stable and longer is the supply secured for the market. However, the longer the turnover period, the higher

the capital commitment, and also various direct and indirect costs of managing the warehouse are therefore higher.

A general target range for this ratio cannot be determined. For orientation and benchmarking this ratio, internal (such as the ratio in different organizational units or plan-actual values) or external comparisons should be made, where the branch-specific average period or the "best-practice" value may be used as a guide.

## ! Useful Suggestions

Assuming that firms in the same branch usually have similar production and asset structures, the ratio values, differing significantly from the average, are clear candidates for serious reviews. These should help in analysing positive and negative consequences, and steer them in the context of corporate goals.

Along with cost-oriented analysis, it is important not to ignore the market-oriented perspective. A sizable reduction in the turnover period could jeopardize the expected delivery plan of the customer. In such cases, however, it is good to consider the firm-specific pros and cons of all business aspects. For example, it is good to check whether the longer delivery times are accepted by customers and, in certain cases, longer delivery times are viewed as a positive signal, such as in the luxury goods market.

## & Related Ratios/Additional Notes

The word "turnover period" is often used as a synonym for "coverage period".

If the numerator and denominator are turned upside down, the resultant coefficient is called "turnover-coefficient" or simply "turnover".

### 2.8.6 Accumulated Depreciation to Fixed Assets Ratio

## ? Analytical Question

What is the degree of asset depreciation relating to plant property and equipment as an aggregate? What part of total fixed assets has already been depreciated?

## * Definition

$$\frac{\text{Total Accumulated Depreciation on Fixed Assets}}{\text{Total Value of the Fixed Assets (based on historical costing)}}$$

Total accumulated depreciation includes the amount of depreciation related to all the fixed assets (other than land) shown on the balance sheet.

The total value of the fixed assets relates to the acquisition cost of the plant, property and equipment (based on the historical cost) as on the balance sheet date.

The ratio "accumulated depreciation to fixed assets" is expressed in decimal values. Thus, the resultant number would always be between zero and one.

## Calculation/Derivation

»

The data for total accumulated depreciation and value of the fixed assets can be obtained from the fixed asset accounting database of the financial accounting department. The asset accounting method may be based on national or international financial reporting standards (IFRS). If the company has adopted IFRS, IAS 16 applies to the accounting treatment for property, plant and equipment (henceforth PPE). Under IAS 16.73, a company has to disclose for each class of PPE, information about the basis for measuring the carrying value, depreciation method(s) used, useful life or depreciation rates, and details about additions and disposals, etc.

It is important to note that land is not included in the value of PPE because it is not treated as a depreciable asset.

The computation of this ratio demands that we use the aggregated value of accumulated depreciation for all assets, which exist on the balance sheet on a particular date. It also takes all the PPE as an aggregated group, without distinction of age or valuation method. However, as a variation, the accumulated depreciation ratio for a particular type of asset, such as computer hardware, can be computed to make a judgment about their condition or age.

## Interpretation and Typical Range

#

Investors and managers use the "Accumulated Depreciation to Fixed Assets Ratio" as a measure of the productiveness of the fixed assets. Often, banks ask for this information from their borrowers, to assess the useful life and productive capacity of the fixed assets owned by the borrower. A very low ratio in this case could mean that many fixed assets have recently been acquired, and they still have plenty of useful life left. Conversely, a high ratio suggests the opposite. This means that most assets have a high average age, and this may have a negative impact on their productivity. It is also a signal to the management to plan for upcoming asset replacement. If the company does not have enough capital to replace the worn-out fixed assets, this ratio is most likely to continue to climb. Thus, for example, a ratio of 30 % does not raise any alarms, but a ratio of 70 % may be an important call for securing loans ready for making fresh investments in fixed assets.

The ratio has a strong branch specific character. Like many other financial indicators, this ratio is also highly connected with the company's line of business, and industry standards. In general, it is a significant parameter for managers in manufacturing companies. An economically meaningful interpretation on the desirable targets for this ratio can, therefore, only be achieved by an in-house and/or inter-plant multi-period comparison over time (eventually, involving further partial efficiencies). It may be equally helpful to compare the replacement policies of other competitors in the industry, before raising any alarms, based on this ratio.

**❗ Useful Suggestions**

It is important to note that the "accumulated depreciation to fixed assets ratio" is highly dependent on the company's depreciation policy. If the depreciation method corresponds to the useful economic life of fixed assets, this ratio can be a good indicator of the age of the assets.

Under IAS 16, fixed assets can be re-valued, so that their carrying values reflect fair values. If the new depreciation is computed on the basis of the re-valued assets, the ratio between the newly accumulated depreciation (after revaluation of fixed assets) and re-valued asset values, provides a better interpretation of the remaining useful economic life of the fixed assets.

**& Related Ratios/Additional Notes**

The indicator "accumulated depreciation to fixed assets ratio" is also known as "degree of asset depreciation" or "total depreciation ratio".

The ratio may be less comparable between two firms in the same business if one has obtained its fixed assets under leasing, and the other has all its fixed assets under its ownership. In such cases, the amount shown in the denominator will differ between the two companies, leading to distortions in interpretations of the value.

The differences in the computation of acquisition costs under IFRS and other standards may also cause this ratio to assume different values.

## 2.9 Value Based Management (VBM)

### 2.9.1 Cash Value Added (CVA)

**❓ Analytical Question**

How much is the cash-based value enhancement (value added) of the firm, or parts thereof, in a particular period?

**✳ Definition**

(CFROI – Capital Cost Rate) · Gross Investment

Where:
CFROI (in %) = (Cash Flow/Market Value of Capital Employed) · 100

Another formula for computing CVA is:

Operating Cash Flow (OCF) – Operating Cash Flow Demand (OCFD)

Where:

OCFD = Operating Cash needed to cover the Capital Costs (in currency units)

This indicator of value added is measured in currency units (for example, in €).

## Calculation/Derivation                                                    »

For the internal decision-makers, the needed data for this indicator could be taken from the accounting department. The external parties have to rely on reported numbers in the annual financial statements to derive the required data, where several adjustments may be needed.

The cost of capital rate is usually drawn from the Weighted Average Cost of Capital (WACC) approach.

## Interpretation and Typical Range                                          #

CVA emerged from the conceptual background relating to Value-Based-Management (VBM), where the market value of the equity is viewed as the main indicator of performance measurement. As a periodic excess return, which is viewed explicitly as added value, CVA shows value enhancement if the calculated indicator is positive, and value destruction if the indicator is negative. The simple logic is that, given a particular opportunity cost, the use of capital for another purpose should have led to a higher return.

A general target for the optimum range of CVA is not possible. For comparison purposes, branch specific or best practice estimates are usually applied. However, the higher the value added over a period of time, the better is the positioning of value-based-management philosophy in the firm.

## Useful Suggestions                                                        !

In addition to the methodical details, which can help (as with any other complex calculation system) influence the value of CVA up to a limit, the important drivers to improve this ratio are: rate of return on individual business segments or divisions and the growth rate.

## Related Ratios/Additional Notes                                          &

The Boston Consulting Group uses CFROI as a relative indicator of value added or "extra yield".

Like any other complex methodical system, CVA has some strengths (such as its integrative approach towards value-enhancement and its clarity), and some weaknesses (such as the large number of ways in which CVA is calculated, with all its incomprehensible variants). Therefore, for comparison between and amongst firms, it is always important to ensure the consistency of the definitions and methods used. A time-series, where comparisons are made over several years, could help improve the explanatory power of the measure.

### 2.9.2 Economic Profit (EP)

**?** **Analytical Question**

How much is the value creation by the firm in one period?

**\*** **Definition**

(ROIC – WACC) · Invested Capital

or

NOPLAT – (WACC · Invested Capital)

Where:
ROIC = Return on Invested Capital
WACC = Weighted Average Cost of Capital
NOPLAT = Net Operating Profits Less Adjusted Taxes

This indicator for value added is measured in currency units (for example, in €).

**»** **Calculation/Derivation**

For the internal decision-makers, the needed data for this indicator could be taken from the accounting department. The external parties have to rely on reported numbers in annual financial statements for deriving the required data, where several adjustments may be needed.

**#** **Interpretation and Typical Range**

The EP should be grouped under the category of value-based management indicators. This so-called "operating excess profit" shows the valued added for the period in question. Though in the form of absolute currency units, this indicator is a leading indicator for value added, and can be further divided into other value-drivers, such as ROIC, WACC and Invested Capital.

A general target for the optimum range of EP is not possible. For comparison purposes, branch specific or best practice estimates are usually applied.

However, the higher the value added over a period of time, the better the positioning of value-based-management philosophy in the firm.

**!** **Useful Suggestions**

In the context of value-based-management, different composites (key performance indicator pyramids) are used for planning and controlling. The EP is mostly placed at the top of such a pyramid, with its various vertical and horizontal sub-divisions, such as ROIC, WACC and Invested Capital. *For additional explanations about the multi-layered ratio systems, refer to the DuPont System in Appendix II* as an example. The step-wise decomposition of the target ratio at various levels allows for a systematic review of the value drivers in order to influence the economic profitability of the firm. Through a conscious linking of financial and non-financial indicators (for example, with the help of the Balanced Scorecard tool), concrete operational measures for the implementation of strategic goals at various decision-levels can be aimed at.

The periodic performance measure EP can be calculated both for the whole firm as well as for its divisions and segments. Over and above its use in the valuation of existing economic units (such as profit centre), EP can also be used in the context of planned mergers, acquisitions and joint-ventures.

## Related Ratios/Additional Notes &

The concept of EP can be traced back to Copeland/Kollar/Murrin as consultants at McKinsey & Company.

Like any other complex methodical systems, EP has some strengths (such as its integrative approach towards value-enhancement and its clarity), and some weaknesses (such as the large number of ways in which EP is calculated, with all its incomprehensible variants).

Therefore, for comparisons between and amongst firms, it is always important to ensure the consistency of definitions and methods used. A time-series, where comparison is made over several years, could help improve the explanatory power of the measure.

## 2.9.3 Economic Value Added (EVA)

### Analytical Question ?

How much is the periodic contribution (typically one year) of value added for the firm which exceeds the expected minimum return on capital? How much is the true economic profit of the firm?

### Definition *

NOPAT – (WACC · Capital Employed)

or

Operating Profit – Capital Charge

Where:

| | | |
|---|---|---|
| NOPAT | = | Net Operating Profit After Taxes |
| WACC | = | Weighted Average Cost of Capital |
| Capital Employed | = | Assets needed in Operating Business (Including the book value of undisclosed reserves and goodwill) |

EVA, as also the MVA (Market Value Added), is the registered trademark of value-based measures of Stern and Stewart.

This indicator for value added is measured in currency units (for example, in €).

## » Calculation/Derivation
The extraction and preparation of needed data for this indicators comes from the accounting department, which requires several adjustments (the total number of all adjustments could be as much as 160) to the numbers derived from the reported statements.

## # Interpretation and Typical Range
EVA belongs to the category of "residual-income" indicators and measures the true economic profitability of the firm. Thus, given that a firm has a total EBIT of €15 million, and a tax rate of 30%, its NOPAT would be €10.5 Million. Further, given a total capital employed of €80 Million and a WACC of 9%, its capital charge would be €7.2 Million. Thus the EVA of this firm would be €3.3 Million (€10.5 − €7.2 Million).

With the above example, and with the help of several adjustments to the performance indicators in external reporting, various ratios are calculated (with EVA as the top indicator in the pyramid) which contribute to the goal of maximizing shareholders value. Basically, EVA calculates the operating "excess-profit" which is a measure of extra return on capital employed over and above the comparable minimum return.

A general target for the optimum range of EVA is not possible. As benchmarks, internal or external (within the branch competitors) best-practice values could be used. However, various firm-specific adjustments make a comparison between firms difficult.

## ! Useful Suggestions
One could focus on three different measures towards improving EVA:
- Improving the operating profits of the firm (assuming that capital employed remains constant);
- Realizing investment only in those projects which offer a yield above the capital costs; and/or
- Exiting from those investment projects where the expected yield is below capital costs.

## & Related Ratios/Additional Notes
The EVA was originally developed by the founder and partner of the consulting firm "Stern Stewart & Co". Depending upon the conceptual design, a variety of adjustments and corrections have to be made to calculate EVA, some of which have

been explicitly proposed by the firm. However, in practice, these adjustments are not made consistently. Therefore, the significance of each adjustment must be made with reference to the specific and situational demands of each firm.

Closely related to the concept of EVA, is the indicator Market Value Added (MVA) which represents the present value of all expected EVAs of the firm.

### 2.9.4  Weighted Average Cost of Capital (WACC)

**Analytical Question**

What should be the minimum expected return from the capital employed? What minimum return should be expected from projects?

**Definition**

$$WACC = \left( K_e \cdot \frac{E}{E+D} \right) + \left( K_d \cdot \frac{D}{E+D} \right)$$

Where:

E   =   Equity Capital
D   =   Debt (particularly the interest carrying debt)
$K_e$   =   Cost of Equity
$K_d$   =   Cost of Debt

When the WACC calculation includes the tax aspect, the formula is:

$$K_e \cdot \frac{E}{E+D} + K_d \cdot (1-t) \cdot \frac{D}{E+D}$$

Where:
t = Corporate Income Tax Rate

The ratio is expressed in percentage terms.

**Calculation/Derivation**

The calculation of WACC is based on the weighted average cost of equity, and the cost of debt.

The cost of equity ($K_e$) can be computed with the help of the Capital Asset Pricing Model (CAPM).

The formula for the computation of $K_e$ is as follows:

$$K_e = R_f + ß \cdot (R_m - R_f)$$

Where:

$R_f$   =   Interest rate on risk-free securities (such as Government Bonds)

ß     =   Beta factor representing specific risk.

           If ß >1, it shows that the value of the stock fluctuates more than the whole market.

           If ß <1, it shows that the value of the stock has lower volatility than the whole market

$R_m$   =   Market return (the average return on a particular stock market, based on capital gains and dividend paid)

## **#** Interpretation and Typical Range

The ratio represents the minimum expected return on capital employed. It is also used as a discount factor for the computation of net present value (NPV) in all discounted cash flow methods for capital budgeting and valuation.

Generally, the average WACC depends upon the risk-free interest rate, branch specific factors (with ß as the proxy for branch specific risks), and capital structure of the firm. It lies typically in the range of 7% to 12%. In some cases, because of high risk premiums (for example, associated with high growth firms), the 12% limit may be exceeded.

## **!** Useful Suggestions

It is imperative that the business activities initiated by the management, should earn a return which is larger than WACC. In practice, one could ensure through appropriate incentive systems that all value-generating projects are implemented, unless there are financial limitations in doing so. It is particularly important to ensure that value-generating projects are not rejected. Through this practice, one can ensure that the absolute volume of operating surplus grows further, though the relative value added (compared to WACC) may grow slowly.

## **&** Related Ratios/Additional Notes

WACC has become an important comparative measure in recent years. It is particularly used in the context of concepts relating to value-based management, such as Economic Profit (EP) and Economic Value Added (EVA).

## 2.9.5 Value at Risk (VaR)

**Analytical Question**

What is the largest expected loss, on a particular investment position, over a given period of time, for a specified confidence level?

**Definition**

Value at Risk (henceforth VaR) is a statistical measure that quantifies the level of financial risk within a firm, a portfolio, or a specific asset position over a specified period of time. The following example illustrates how VaR works:

Let us assume that a company's stock is trading on the stock exchange for 5 years, and an investor is keeping a daily record of returns on this stock for the last 1400 days. He finds out that the stock had an average return of 1% over 270 days of the total time. On the lower end of the daily average returns, he finds out that over 70 days (representing 5 per cent of all daily records), the return varied between losses of 4% to 8%. Thus, we could say that, based on historical data with a 95% confidence level, the expected maximum daily loss (VaR) will not exceed 4% of the invested amount. Conversely, VaR implies that the investor is confident at the 95% level, that his gain will exceed −4%.

If we want to move to a confidence level of 99%, daily return records suggest that, on about 14 days, there was an average loss of 8%. Thus, with a 99% confidence level, we can say that the daily expected loss will not exceed 8%. Conversely, the investor is confident at the 99% level, that his gain would be more than −8%.

Usually VaR is computed, based on standard deviation of daily returns over the period of observation. If the standard deviation for daily returns, on the same stock above is 2%, the formula for calculating the VaR (assuming a normal distribution for daily returns) for an expected daily return of 0.1% is as follows:

$$\text{VaR (at 95\% confidence level)} = \text{Expected Daily Returns} - (1.98 \cdot \text{Standard Deviation})$$

Filling in the values of 2% standard deviation and an expected return of 0.1%, the VaR shall be

$$\text{VaR (at 95\% confidence level)} = 0.1\% - (1.98 \cdot 2\%) = -3.86\%$$

Thus, if the investor has a $20 million investment in the above stock, his maximum daily loss in dollars would be:

$20,000,000 \cdot (-3.86\%) = \$772,000$ representing the VaR at 95% confidence level and standard deviation of daily returns at 2%.

It is important to note that the computation of VaR, for a 99% level, demands that the standard deviation is multiplied with 2.33 instead of 1.65.

**»** **Calculation/Derivation**

The data for this KPI is based on historical stock returns computed from stock values published by the stock exchanges and is widely available online. However, the frequency of data for the KPI depends upon the time horizon for which the VaR needs to be computed. For example, if a bank's trading-portfolio is invested in highly liquid currencies, a one-day horizon is acceptable. For an investment manager balancing and valuing his portfolio on a monthly basis, a 30-day horizon is desired. Accordingly, the VaR is computed on a monthly time horizon.

The choice of confidence level is dependent on the purpose of computing VaR. If the purpose is to find out how much capital an institution must have, to cover the possible maximum loss of value which most banks have to provide, computing VaR for higher confidence levels is important. However, if the VaR is being computed just to compare the risk across markets, the confidence level is not so significant.

**#** **Interpretation and Typical Range**

VaR is intended to warn the investors about the potential maximum value loss that could occur over a particular time period, such as a day, week, month or year. If the investor is uncomfortable with the potential value loss that could occur in a day or a week, they can revise their investment portfolio to make it less risky, though one has to keep in mind the transaction costs of reshuffling the portfolio.

While VaR can be used by any entity to measure its risk exposure, it is mostly used by commercial banks and investment banks to capture the potential loss in value of their traded portfolio, from adverse market movements over a specified period. This potential value loss is then compared with their available capital and cash reserves, to ensure that the loss can be covered without putting the firm at risk.

VaR focuses on falling below a certain value of the business performance indicator to be observed which gives it the character of an asymmetric downside risk measure that does not reflect the possible (positive) excess of certain upper limits (so-called upside potential).

In many cases, investors calculate the VaR of a portfolio and compare it with a benchmark index to check whether the portfolio outperforms or underperforms the benchmark. If a portfolio tracks a benchmark fairly well, the active return will be small, and so there will be a smaller risk.

**!** **Useful Suggestions**

Within the framework of an efficient and entrepreneurial risk management, risk analyses, risk-assessments, and risk-control measures must be taken at various aggregation levels and for both real and financial indicators (e.g. sales volumes, raw material prices or exchange rates).

In addition to selecting a suitable performance indicator such as cash flow (or period-related earnings with the corresponding indicator designated as earnings-at-risk), the future pattern of the characteristic values of the key figure, e.g. using probability distributions (using parametric or simulation methods) or benchmark scenarios and the use of sensitivity analyses on the basis of business risk models must be predicted in a meaningful way. Reference is made to a related KPI "Cash Flow at Risk" which explains the value exposure of any underlying asset or a portfolio.

### Related Ratios/Additional Notes &

There are many approaches to computing VaR. In the formula above, firstly, VaR computation was based on historical returns and secondly, on the basis of standard deviation of daily returns. In the third approach, VaR can also be computed by applying the stock beta instead of standard deviation of daily returns.

VaR is also calculated on the basis of Monte Carlo simulation.[16] Monte Carlo simulation involves developing a model for future stock price returns and running multiple trials through that model. Thus, if we run 100 hypothetical trials of monthly returns, and found out that the worst 5% of outcomes were less than −15%, the conclusion would be that, with a 95% confidence level, we do not expect to lose more than 15% in any given month.

In addition to the key figure of dynamic capital budgeting, called "net present value", there is another, much simpler risk measure of significance within the scope of capital budgeting, which determines the completion of the period that is (probably) required in order to achieve a net present value of zero (the so-called payback period).

## 2.10  Capital Market Tests

### 2.10.1 Market-to-Book Ratio

**Analytical Question** ?

How is the growth in the value of a particular investment, reflected by the change between market and book value of the stocks?

**Definition** *

$$\frac{\text{Market Value per Share}}{\text{Book Value per Share}}$$

Where: Book Value per Share =

$$\frac{(\text{Stockholders' Capital} + \text{Retained Earnings}) - \text{Preferred Stock}}{\text{Number of Outstanding Shares}}$$

---

**16** Monte Carlo simulation refers to any method that randomly generates trials, but by itself does not tell anything about the underlying methodology.

This ratio is expressed in terms of a percentage.

### » Calculation/Derivation
The information about stock prices (latest spot price or average price for a defined period) could be obtained from stock exchange sources where the stock is traded. The book value of a share is equal to equity per share, and can be calculated from the balance sheet as on a particular reporting date.

### # Interpretation and Typical Range
The market-to-book ratio delivers the relationship between the market value of a share and its book value on the balance sheet. In the broadest sense, it gives information about the hidden potential (even about undisclosed reserves) which the market assumes, and which is reflected in the estimates of likely supply and demand for this stock.

Since the book value of a share is the equity capital per share, it gives information about how much the book value is above the nominal value of the share and as a consequence, the proportion of disclosed reserves in total equity.

The higher the value of this ratio, the more the price which an investor must pay for a share in the equity of the firm. For existing stockholders, increase in this ratio means (unrealized) improvement in the value of the share.

### ! Useful Suggestions
Assuming that firms in a particular industry have similar revenue and cost structures, ratios above or below the average for the industry give clear indications for chasing the positive or negative developments more carefully and for influencing these if possible.

Since the market price of the stock is guided by the supply and demand conditions on the stock exchange, it cannot be influenced directly by firms. However, a firm can indirectly influence the positive development of the stock prices through a transparent and open information policy. All measures which help a firm in earning decent distributable profits, will have a positive impact on the market price of the stock. For example, earnings could be improved through measures which relate to the price and/or volume strategy on the sales side or through better organization of the input factors on the operational side.

If the market-to-book ratio is lower than average for the branch, it means that the stock is undervalued. It could also mean that something is fundamentally wrong in the company. The ratio also reveals whether one is paying too much for what would be left if the company were to go bankrupt immediately.

A change in market-to-book ratio could be triggered by a disproportionate increase or decrease in the market price per share (as numerator) and book value per share (as denominator). *For further details and systematic explanations on this, refer to the information in Appendix I.*

**Related Ratios/Additional Notes**&

Price-to-Book Ratio (or P/B ratio, as it is commonly called) is another synonym for this ratio.

## 2.10.2 Stock Yield

**Analytical Question**?

How rewarding is the investment in a particular stock?

**Definition**＊

$$TRS_1 = \left( D_1 + \frac{P_1 - P_0}{P_0} \right) \cdot 100$$

Where:
$TRS_1$ = Total Return on Stock after period 1
$D_1$ = Dividend received during period 1
$P_1$ = Price at the end of period 1 (or sale price)
$P_0$ = Price at the beginning of the period 1 (or purchase price)

For the sake of simplicity, the tax aspect has been kept out. The appropriate after-tax value depends upon the tax regulations in the relevant country, and the individual circumstances of the taxpayer.

This ratio is expressed as a percentage.

**Calculation/Derivation**»

The data for this ratio can be derived from the published information on the stock exchange, where the stock is traded.

**Interpretation and Typical Range**#

The Stock Yield shows the total return on investment. It is a major information tool for companies vis-à-vis their shareholders, potential institutional investors, private investors and financial analysts. As a relative measure, it demonstrates the appreciation of value which an investor achieves by holding the shares of a company for a particular period (for example, one year). However, this ratio does not explicitly take into account the risk undertaken by the investor.

A benchmarking of this ratio depends upon the individual aspiration level of the investor. Possible orientation for a benchmark could come from, for example, the average stock yield in a particular industrial sector, the risk-free rate of return (like on fixed-interest securities), or an individual's risk-benefit attitude. In general, the adequacy of the calculated yield depends upon whether the investor is compensated for the risk assumed, or not.

**! Useful Suggestions**

Typical reasons for a falling stock yield could be:

– The dividend is lowered or omitted by the company.
– The stock price is dropping or has dropped below the strike price.

In addition to conducting its business effectively so as to generate distributable profits, it is important to provide a more transparent picture of the financial and operational position of the company through an open investor relations policy. As a consequence, the enterprise could stimulate investors' interest, which would reflect itself in the rising price of the stock.

**& Related Ratios/Additional Notes**

Two other common names for this ratio are: Stock Return and Total Return on Common Stock. The related ratios are: Dividend Yield, Price-Earnings Ratio and Price-to-Cash Flow Ratio.

The Stock Yield is used mostly with reference to past data. It is a calculated number and has a notional value. A real capital gain or loss arises only sell his shares. When calculating the ratio during the year, the factor X/360 could be used to develop a comparable number out of the annual ratio.

It is relevant to note that the end-of-the-period ratio does not give any information about the positive or negative trends or interim changes during the year.

The ratio, often labelled as "performance", serves as a benchmark for comparing the performance of investment managers. However, the ratio does not explicitly take into account the risk undertaken.

### 2.10.3 Dividend Yield

**? Analytical Question**

What is the cash return on investments on the stocks of a company?

**\* Definition**

$$\frac{\text{Dividends per Share} \cdot 100}{\text{Market Price per Share}}$$

This ratio is expressed as a percentage.

## Calculation/Derivation

The amount of dividends per share can be taken from annual reports (prepared according to IFRS/IAS). For potential stock investors, the relevant market price is the current stock price. For existing stockholders, the original stock price at the time of purchase should be taken.

## Interpretation and Typical Range

The Dividend Yield ratio is calculated when analysing the return on stock investment. It shows the relationship between distributable dividends or paid dividends and the stock price.

For investors, the information about dividend yield provides an important clue comparing various investment opportunities, and constitutes a major component for analysing annual financial statements. However, the dividend yield ratio ignores the impact of stock price fluctuations (i.e., capital gain or loss) and therefore, indicates only the cash flow related performance for the investment.

The estimation or evaluation of this ratio, similar to Stock Yield, depends upon the individual aspiration level of the investor. For example, a possible orientation for a benchmark could come from the average stock yield in a particular industrial sector, the risk-free rate of return (like on fixed-interest securities), or an individual's risk-benefit attitude.

## Useful Suggestions

A change in dividend yield ratio could be triggered by a disproportionate increase or decrease in the dividends (in numerator) or stock prices (in denominator). *For further details and systematic explanations on this, refer to the information in Appendix I.*

Since the market price of the stock is guided by the supply and demand conditions on the stock exchange, it cannot be directly influenced by the enterprises. However, a firm can indirectly influence the positive development of the stock prices through a transparent and open information policy. All measures, which help a firm in earning decent distributable profits will have a positive impact on the market price of the stock.

For example, earnings could be improved through measures which relate to the price and/or volume strategy on the sales side, or through better organization of the input factors on the operational side. Any decision to reduce the retained earnings component of net income can also help in increasing the distributable profits in the form of dividends.

## Related Ratios/Additional Notes

The related ratios are: Stock Yield, Dividend Rate Ratio (where the denominator is the nominal price and not the market price), Price-Earnings Ratio, and Price-to-Cash Flow Ratio.

### 2.10.4 Price-Earnings Ratio (P/E Ratio)

**? Analytical Question**

Is a share worth the money? Or, by how many times, the earning per share is rolled over in the stock price?

**\* Definition**

$$\frac{\text{Stock Price per Share}}{\text{Earnings per Share (EPS)}}$$

This ratio is expressed as a multiple. For example, if a company's earnings per share over the last 12 months were €1.95, and its stock is currently trading at €43 a share, the price-earnings ratio for the stock would be 22.05 (i.e., €43/€1.95).

**» Calculation/Derivation**

The information about stock prices is available from stock exchange sources. The data about earnings per share can be computed from annual reports by dividing the net income by the average number of total shares in a period.

Because of various alternatives, available for preparing the annual financial statements, it is important to make various adjustments in the earnings per share of companies, in order to ensure the comparability of numbers.

**# Interpretation and Typical Range**

The Price-Earnings Ratio is a measure of relative value. The higher the ratio between stock price and earnings per share, the more expensive the stock. Accordingly, the lower the yield on the stock, the longer the period in which the stock price (assuming constant earnings per share over time) would take to amortize. Conversely, the lower the ratio between stock price and earnings per share, the cheaper the stock. Accordingly, the higher the yield on the stock, the shorter the period in which the stock price (again under the assumption of constant earnings per share over time) would take to amortize.

Mostly, a high price-earnings ratio suggests that investors are expecting higher earnings growth in the future when compared to companies with a lower price-earnings ratio. It is more useful to compare the price-earnings ratios of one company to other companies in the same industry, to the market in general, or against the company's own historical price-earnings ratio. For example, it would not be useful to compare the price-earnings ratio of a technology company (high P/E) with a utility company (low P/E), as each industry has very different growth prospects.

In general, there is no such thing as a target price-earnings ratio. For orientation and assessment purposes, it is advisable to take the price-earnings ratio of competitors within the same branch, or listed (inter)national enterprises as a benchmark.

**Useful Suggestions**

!

A change in the price-earnings ratio could be triggered by a disproportionate increase or decrease in the stock prices (as numerator) and earnings per share (as denominator). *For further details and systematic explanations on this, refer to the information in Appendix I.*

Since the market price of the stock is guided by the supply and demand conditions on the stock exchange, it cannot be directly influenced by the enterprises. However, a firm can indirectly influence the positive development of the stock prices through a transparent and open information policy. All measures, which help a firm in earning decent distributable profits will have a positive impact on the market price of the stock. For example, earnings could be improved through measures which relate to the price and/or volume strategy on the sales side, or through better organization of the input factors on the operational side.

The reasons for an increase of the price-earnings ratio could be:

– Change in numerator: Increase in the stock price through positive news, directly from the enterprise and/or improved assessment of the enterprise's performance by financial analysts. The announcement of a dividend increase is usually reflected in the stock price.
– Change in Denominator: The enterprise is planning a stock repurchase and, through this action, reduces the base value.

For a fall in the price-earnings ratio, one could anticipate contrary reasons.

**Related Ratios/Additional Notes**

&

The Price-Earnings Ratio is often mentioned as P/E Ratio or PER.

A related ratio is the Price-to-Cash Flow Ratio. This ratio is very similar to the price-earnings ratio, except that the cash flow is less influenced by balance sheet and valuation-related choices than by earnings. Cash flow is often treated as an indicator of the earnings and self-financing capacity of a firm.

### 2.10.5 Price-To-Cash Flow Ratio

**Analytical Question**

?

Is a share worth the money, based primarily on the criteria of the self-financing capacity of a firm? Or, by how many times, the cash flow per share is rolled over in the stock price?

**Definition**

*

$$\frac{\text{Stock Price per Share}}{\text{Cash Flow per Share}}$$

This ratio is expressed as a multiple.

## » Calculation/Derivation

The information about stock prices is available from stock exchange sources. The internal data about cash flow per share should be available from the accounting department of the enterprise. For external parties, it can be computed from annual reports, by dividing the Net Cash Flow by the average number of total shares in a period.

Since there are so many variants of cash flow terminology, it is necessary to have a common definition for comparison purposes. It is a matter of choosing a definition for cash flow, which reflects as closely as possible the sustained earnings of the enterprise. The best cash flow indicator for the earnings of the enterprise, is the net cash provided by operating activities.

## # Interpretation and Typical Range

The Price-To-Cash Flow Ratio provides, in a special way, a relative measure of the value of a stock vis-à-vis its cash flow. The higher the ratio, between stock price and cash flow per share, the more expensive the stock. Accordingly, the lower the yield on the stock, the longer the period in which the stock price takes for recovery (assuming constant cash flow per share over time). Conversely, the lower the ratio between stock price and cash flow per share, the cheaper the stock. In either case, however, we notice that cash flow is utilized for financing various business activities. Therefore, the numerical value of this ratio is primarily notional.

From the expectations perspective, the Price-To-Cash Flow Ratio is a measure of the market's expectation of a firm's future financial health. Since this measure deals with cash flow, the effects of depreciation and other non-cash factors are removed. Since accounting laws on depreciation vary across jurisdictions, this ratio can allow investors to compare foreign companies from the same industry with greater ease.

In general, there is no such thing as a target Price-To-Cash Flow Ratio. For orientation and comparison purposes, it is advisable to take the Price-to-Cash Flow Ratio of competitors within the same branch, or listed (inter)national enterprises as a benchmark.

## ! Useful Suggestions

A change in Price-To-Cash Flow Ratio could be triggered by a disproportionate increase or decrease in stock prices (as numerator) and cash flow (as denominator). *For further details and systematic explanations on this, refer to the information in Appendix I.*

The reasons for an increase in the Price-To-Cash Flow Ratio could be:
- *Change in numerator*: Increase in the stock price through positive news directly from the enterprise and/or improved assessment of the enterprise's performance by financial analysts.
- *Change in denominator*: The enterprise is in a highly competitive business area, with increasing price competition, and, thus, could maintain its sustainable cash flow only at a lower level. In such a case, the base for the stock price would be lowered though a particular stock which becomes less attractive (or more expensive) for the potential investor and may not be in the interest of a growth-oriented enterprise.

Since the market price of the stock is guided by supply and demand conditions on the stock exchange, it cannot be influenced directly by the enterprises. However, a firm can indirectly influence the positive development of the stock prices through a transparent and open information policy. All measures which help a firm generating higher sustainable cash flows will have a positive impact on the market price of the stock.

### Related Ratios/Additional Notes &
A related ratio is Price-to-Free Cash Flow Ratio. It compares a firm's market price to its level of annual free cash flow which reduces operating cash flow by capital expenditure.

This ratio is very similar to the Price-Earnings Ratio, except that cash flow is less influenced by balance sheet and valuation-related choices than by earnings. Cash flow is often treated as an indicator of the earnings and self-financing capacities of a firm.

## 2.10.6 Cash Flow per Share

### Analytical Question ?
How much (free) cash per share does a firm generate during a particular period (for example, in a year)? What is the cash or self-financing capacity per share?

### Definition *

$$\frac{\text{(Free) Cash Flow}}{\text{Number of Shares Outstanding}}$$

The ratio is stated in absolute currency units per share (for example, € per share).

### Calculation/Derivation »
The Cash Flow per Share is determined by dividing the total (free) cash flow by the total number of shares outstanding. The data needed to calculate the cash flow per

share for the past is derived from the corporate reports, based on annual financial statements. For calculating the expected value of this ratio, the financial analysts have to depend on annual financial statements.

**#** **Interpretation and Typical Range**

Cash flow is the sum of net cash flow from operating activities, net cash flow from investing activities and net cash flow from financing activities. Free cash flow is the residual net cash from operating activities, after planned expenditure for replacement investment has been considered.

From the absolute size of cash flow and its growth over time, one can draw conclusions about the self-financing capacity of the firm. If cash flow is calculated per share, it can help in making inter-company comparisons; particularly amongst (inter)national firms in the same branch.

**!** **Useful Suggestions**

A change in Cash Flow per Share could be triggered by a disproportionate increase or decrease in the (free) cash flow in the numerator, and number of outstanding shares in the denominator. *For further details and systematic explanations on this, refer to the information in Appendix I.*

Cash flow, as a sales-related measure, shows very clearly the self-financing capacity of the enterprise through its main business. In order to influence this financial indicator, on the inflow (i.e., sales) side, cash flow can be improved by a better price or volume strategy. On the outflow (i.e., expense) side, cash flow can be improved by more efficient use of the factors of production.

If a company has issued fresh capital during the period under consideration, leading to an increase in the number of outstanding shares, the average number of shares should be taken as the denominator.

**&** **Related Ratios/Additional Notes**

The Cash Flow per Share serves as the basis for the calculation of a similar ratio called "Price-To-Cash Flow Ratio". This ratio is used for analysing the developments in the financial power of a company, and also for making inter-enterprise comparisons. By comparison with the Price-Earnings Ratio, cash flow per share and price to cash flow ratios are less influenced by balance sheet related policies.

When (free) cash flow per share is divided by the market price per share, it is called (free) cash flow yield. The lower the ratio, the less attractive is the firm and vice-versa. The logic is that investors would like to pay as little as possible for as much earnings as possible.

In some countries, the opposite of cash flow yield is very popular. It is termed as "Price-To-Cash Flow Ratio".

## 2.11 Capital Budgeting Tests

### 2.11.1 Payback Period

**Analytical Question** `?`

What is the length of time for recovering the cost of investment in a project?

**Definition** `*`

$$\frac{\text{Acquisition Cost}}{\text{Average Cash Inflow per Period}}$$

This ratio is expressed in units of time (i.e., in years/months/weeks). The unit of time could as well be in fractions. For example, if a project costs €100,000 and is expected to return €40,000 annually, the payback period would be 2.5 years.

**Calculation/Derivation** `»`

The data for this ratio should be recorded in the form of cash inflows and outflows and could be derived from the firm's investment and financial plans. The data could also be derived from a project accounting system, which is established for project management purposes. In practice and for the sake of simplicity, the payback period is calculated with the help of projected sales and costs, or with projected cash inflows and outflows.

**Interpretation and Typical Range** `#`

In addition to the measures for the economic profitability of the planned investment in absolute and relative terms (for example, profit contribution or return on investment), the Payback Period covers a special risk-factor (i.e. time), which should be used as supplementary information to other performance measures.

The time needed for recovery of the cost of investment is, arithmetically, the point of time, when the sum of all cash inflows exceeds all cash outflows.

The calculation of the Payback Period is based on the fact that, the farther we plan into the future, the more difficult the planning process and, as a consequence, the higher the risk associated with the recovery of the invested amount. Payback Period, which is primarily a time based ratio, offers only a rough assessment of a project's quality.

Unlike other methods used in capital budgeting, the Payback Period does not explicitly consider the time value of money; only the average cash inflow per period is considered in this ratio. Ignoring the time value of money can lead to serious distortions in results, and could lead to wrong decisions by the management.

A generally applicable payback period target cannot be determined. As orientation, the payback period should not exceed the product life-cycle or the technical (or economic) life of a machine.

## ! Useful Suggestions
Since the Payback Period method does not consider the changes in periodic cash inflows and the time of their occurrence, it should only be used for evaluating short-term investment projects, such as investment for plant updating etc.

## & Related Ratios/Additional Notes
The ratio is also known as Pay-off Time, Pay-out Period.

The main problem with the payback period method is that it ignores the time value of money. Furthermore, it ignores all the benefits that occur after the payback period. Another method, which removes these two problems, is the Discounted Cash Flow Method. It estimates the period, using an appropriate discount rate, and changes in the periodic cash inflows which are needed to recover the capital invested in a project.

### 2.11.2 Time Adjusted or Discounted Payback Period

## ? Analytical Question
What is the length of time for recovering the cost of investment in a project, along with an appropriate yield towards the required rate of return? When does the net present value arrive at zero for the first time?

## * Definition

$$A_0 = \sum_{t=1}^{w} (e_t - a_t) \cdot (1+i)^{-t} = 0$$

Where:
$A_0$ = Net Present Value
$t$ = Time Period
$w$ = Total number of periods under consideration
$e_t$ = Receipts in period t
$a_t$ = Payments in period t
$i$ = Interest Rate

This ratio is expressed in units of time (i.e., in years/months/weeks). The unit of time could as well be in fractions.

## Calculation/Derivation

The data for this ratio should be recorded in the form of cash inflows and outflows and could be derived from the firm's investment and financial plan.

## Interpretation and Typical Range

In addition to measures for the economic profitability of the planned investment, in absolute and relative terms (for example, profit contribution or return on investment), the Time Adjusted Payback Period covers a special risk-factor (i.e. time), which should be used as supplementary to other performance measures.

The time needed for recovery of the cost of investment is, arithmetically, the point of time when the net present value of the investment reaches zero for the first time.

The calculation of the Time Adjusted Payback Period is based on the fact that, the farther we plan into the future, the more difficult the planning process and, as a consequence, the higher the risk associated with the recovery of the invested amount. Payback period, which is primarily a time based ratio, offers only a rough assessment of a project's quality.

Unlike other methods for capital budgeting, the payback period does not explicitly consider the time value of money; only the average cash inflow per period is considered in this ratio. Ignoring the time value of money can lead to serious distortions in results, and can lead to wrong decisions by the management.

A generally applicable payback period target cannot be determined. As orientation, the payback period should not exceed the product's life-cycle or the technical (or economic) life of a machine.

## Useful Suggestions

In the framework for capital budgeting or investment-controlling, the plausibility of the data provided by the project-initiator or leader should be carefully checked. In addition to providing methodical support towards planning and preparation of investment application, one should also collect regular data about the progress of the approved projects. Such information is useful for timely identification of serious variances and for corrective actions. Once the project is complete, the final costing of the project should be calculated in order to derive useful lessons for future projects.

Through systematic and targeted sensitivity analysis, the critical contribution of input factors towards project profitability and towards improving the target payback period should be analysed.

## Related Ratios/Additional Notes

The ratio *is not* synonymous with Pay-off Time or Pay-out Period.

In practice, the *static* payback period is a related measure which is still very often used "as a rule of thumb" for investment decisions. The static payback period delivers the length of time needed for recovering the cost of investment in a project, without considering the time value of money.

The main problem with the payback period method is that it ignores all the benefits (positive or negative) that occur after the payback period. The inclusion of the residual or salvage value of a project can make a huge difference in the selection of profitable projects; it could even change the ranking of economically preferred projects.

### 2.11.3 Net Present Value

**? Analytical Question**

To what extent can an investment project be considered as financially profitable or beneficial? Or what is the monetary "value-added", generated by the investment project when viewed from today's perspective?

**\* Definition**

$$A_0 = \sum_{t=1}^{w} (e_t - a_t) \cdot (1+i)^{-t}$$

Where:

$A_0$ = Net Present Value
$t$ = Time Period
$w$ = Total number of periods under consideration
$e_t$ = Receipts in period t
$a_t$ = Payments in period t
$i$ = Interest Rate

The KPI is measured in monetary units (e.g., in €).

**» Calculation/Derivation**

The data for this KPI relates to the cash inflows and outflows. It can be derived from corporate investment and financial plans as well as from a separate project capital-budgeting plan, if available.

**# Interpretation and Typical Range**

The KPI "Net Present Value" (NPV) represents the central financial parameter in capital budgeting and investment controlling. In the context of dynamic capital budgeting decision, this KPI is the most important decision criterion for the so-called "Discounted Cash Flow (DCF)" and is also known as the DCF method.

The NPV is calculated as the difference between the present value of the future cash inflows to be expected over the entire duration of an investment project, and (the present value of) the investment-related cash outflows at the time the project starts. The economic value of an investment project is, therefore, assessed by discounting the future cash flows over time.

A NPV of zero implies that, based on the underlying assumptions regarding the amount and timing of cash flows on the one hand, and the investor's required rate of return on the other hand, the investor recovers the invested capital along with the interest at the required rate of return. Accordingly, a positive NPV means that a project is worth more than it costs. So, if a firm is making investment in such a project, it is making its shareholders better off. If the required rate of return chosen for discounting the cash flows corresponds to the profitability of a comparable investment (with a similar risk profile), the amount of positive NPV of the investment project in question would have to be interpreted as the absolute monetary benefit of this alternative.

The quality of the economic significance of the NPV is essentially determined by the extent to which the methodological requirements (e.g., with regard to comparable maturities and accountability of cash flows, etc.) are met in practice, and inaccuracies in forecasting the cash flows (risks and opportunities) avoided.

It is not possible to determine a concrete general target for a positive NPV. In principle however, the following applies for alternative evaluation with otherwise comparable boundary conditions: the higher the NPV, the better the project. However, the NPV is ultimately strongly influenced by the scope of the respective project and risk-reward profile of the expected cash flows. Above all, the NPV depends on the type of investment project: In the case of cost-cutting and streamlining projects, it is to be assumed at an early stage that cash inflows will remain more or less constant. Meanwhile, in the case of innovative investments, the desired noticeable cash flows can only be expected after the introduction phase, with correspondingly high growth rates.

**Useful Suggestions**

In addition to a proper collection/computation of the capital-budgeting data, the main emphasis should be on the transparency of the input data, and a decent interpretation of the results. This includes checking the plausibility of the cash flows mentioned in the investment application, particularly the amount, the time of their probable occurrence, and the choice of the required rate of return for discounting the cash flows.

It is a good practice to conduct capital budgeting with so-called "scenario analysis". Thus, one should consider the possible deviations from "safe" and single-value expectations ("normal values" of a so-called base case) into their positive forms and opportunities ("optimistic values" of a so-called best case) and their negative forms as risks ("pessimistic values" of a so-called worst case) on the basis of arguments. Likewise, possible variants of different required rates of returns, and their consequences for the NPV results, must also be examined. Similarly, evaluations with the inclusion of so-called "critical values" for certain critical parameters (such as cost-optimization, exchange rate changes, etc.) applied individually and/ or in combination, as well as the use of sensitivity analysis, are typical measures to achieve meaningful results. In addition, dynamic amortization KPIs, such as (discounted) Payback Period can also be used.

### & Related Ratios/Additional Notes

Common synonyms are: Present Value; DCF (Discounted Cash Flow).

In addition to the central key figure "NPV", the "Discounted Payback Period", which determines the end of the period that is (probably) required to reach a NPV of zero and the "NPV Index", which is a special Profitability Index that relates the NPV to invested capital, are other KPIs of significance in measuring the riskiness of projects.

### 2.11.4 Profitability Index

### ? Analytical Question

What is the profitability of an intended investment? What is the ratio of net present value to required investment?

### * Definition

$$\frac{\text{Net Present Value}}{\text{Required Initial Investment}}$$

This KPI is measured in multiples or in fractional values. Alternatively, if you multiply the formula by 100, the result can be expressed as a percentage as well.

### » Calculation/Derivation

The data can be derived from corporate investment and financial plans as well as from a separate project capital-budgeting plan, if available.

### # Interpretation and Typical Range

In the context of capital budgeting and investment controlling, the key figure "profitability index" is a special type of profitability indicator in the form of a relative measure. It supplements the well-known absolute performance indicator, net present value (henceforth NPV).

For the "profitability index", the NPV of the project under consideration is determined using the discounted cash flow method, and then the calculated NPV is related to the required capital expenditure in the form of the initial investment.

This shows the NPV of the discounted cash flows in relation to the required investment outlay on the start date.

The project profitability for various investment alternatives, expressed in indexed multiples, provides a ranking of projects, even when the company uses no hard capital rationing, i.e. the company has no limits on capital available for investment per period.

The formal and substantive conditions related to the derivation of NPV (see the detailed information – including the spectrum of useful guidelines – in KPI No. 2.11.3) are equally applicable to the profitability index.

It is not possible to determine a concrete general target for profitability index. In principle however, the following applies for evaluating alternatives with otherwise comparable boundary conditions: the higher the profitability index, the better the project.

**Useful Suggestions**

The idea of putting NPV as an absolute value in relation to the investment volume for the key figure "profitability index" shows, for example, that at a comparable level of the NPV, the respective lower capital requirement becomes a decisive factor for the assessment of the economic ranking of several projects. In business life, however, it may be necessary that a required replacement investment with a comparatively lower profitability index has a higher priority than normal projects. After such an investment is made, rest of the available capital can be invested on the basis of the corresponding ranking of the profitable "desired" projects.

Changes in this relative ratio can be achieved by disproportionate increase or decrease in the related NPV (in the numerator) and invested funds (in the denominator). *For further details and systematic explanations on this, refer to the information in Appendix I.*

The price and quantity related influences on the cash inflows/outflows and their temporal allocation are to be checked as plan values for their plausibility in the same way as the expected amount of the initial investment. With suitable sensitivity analyses, conceivable "range of expectations" can be disclosed. On the other hand, the assumption of a limited investment budget must also be examined with a view to achieve a certain degree of flexibility. This can help to implement additional financially attractive projects or rather launch these in stages or start with a delay in a manageable framework.

**Related Ratios/Additional Notes**

In addition to the central key figure "NPV" as risk measures, especially the "Discounted Payback Period" and the "Cash Flow at Risk" are of business significance in the method network of dynamic investment calculation.

## 2.12 Finance-related Ecological Indicators

### Ⓢ 2.12.1 Resource Efficiency

**❓ Analytical Question**

How large is the yield, on an ecologically significant resource-input in a company, measured in quantity units, in terms of a given economic output, measured in monetary units?

**✳ Definition**

The inclusion of the term "efficiency" as part of any KPI's name is not uniform in literature and practice: the comparison of two quantity units is basically a (technical) productivity, but it is often synonymously called efficiency. The specific expression of the first part of the name of an individual efficiency KPI is usually based on the input resource (e.g. energy or material efficiency).

$$\frac{\text{Monetary Value of the Output (measured in Revenue or Yield)}}{\text{Amount of the Ecological Input (measured in Quantity Units)}}$$

The input quantity is usually measured in units, length, area and volume units, weight/mass, other physical size and time-space units.

Depending on the examined relation, the respective dimensions result in the ratio of a value unit (numerator) and a quantity unit (denominator), in terms of economic efficiency, e.g. "€/m3 water" or "€/kwh".

**» Calculation/Derivation**

The prerequisite for obtaining the required data for these resource-oriented KPI types is the existence of an appropriate and detailed, computer-based corporate Environmental Information System (EIS). The prime tasks of an EIS, in the context, includes the collection, processing and preparation of ecologically relevant data, especially for:

- the quantity- and value-based collection (e.g. resource consumption and emissions quantity),
- the documentation for external reporting obligations (required by laws, directives, etc.),
- the creation of meaningful KPIs in order to present complex interrelationships in a condensed manner, and to enable,
- the comparison of facts and developments over time within the company, as well as externally.

**Interpretation and Typical Range**

Since business processes are characteristically distinguished by the combination of several production factors which are measured in different dimensions and usually create more than one product and/or service type, only uni-dimensional, so-called partial resource efficiencies, can be determined and interpreted.

Quotient formations or ratios implicitly assume a causal relationship that is often assumed to be proportional, but does not always have to be. For example, if a part of energy input consists of a (fixed) base-load and another part is variable and production-quantity-dependent, the determination of energy efficiency could possibly lead to a distorting proportional treatment of the fixed resource input.

An economically meaningful interpretation on the desirable targets can, therefore, only be achieved by an in-house and/or inter-plant multi-period comparison over time (eventually, involving further partial efficiencies). In the case of internationally oriented comparisons, any interim changes in foreign exchange rates should also be taken into account, if value measures are involved.

**Useful Suggestions**

Every measure of efficiency is based on the principle of productivity and/or profitability. In terms of sustainability and the careful use of scarce resources, the systematic measurement of efficiency over time forms an important element in the continuous process optimization, e.g. to gradually reduce fresh water consumption for cooling purposes.

However, as the factors of production are often substitutable, the intended increase in a fractional efficiency does not necessarily imply an improvement in the overall efficiency, particularly, if the increase in efficiency of one factor results in increased use of another factor of production.

A change in this ratio could be triggered by a disproportionate increase or decrease in the chosen output measure (in numerator) and resource-category as input measure (in denominator). *For further details and systematic explanations on this, refer to the information in Appendix I.*

**Related Ratios/Additional Notes**

The above-mentioned definition of resource efficiency is focused on the sense of an "economic" efficiency. Often these terms are combined with an input prefix, such as "material efficiency" or "energy efficiency" etc.

The reciprocal of "resource efficiency", the same state of affairs represented by the exchanged numerator and denominator, is called "resource coefficient".

## 2.12.2 Sustainable Value

### ? Analytical Question

How much is the sustainable value[17] of a firm expressed in terms of monetary units? How much is the resource-efficiency of a firm in relation to a representative comparable object? How big is the sustainable value (comparable with a benchmark), which is created (or destroyed) by a firm through its deployment of a particular bundle of economic, ecological and social resources?

### ✳ Definition

$$\frac{\text{Sum Total of Resource Value Added}}{\text{Number of Incorporated Resources (Indicators)}}$$

The ratio "Sustainable Value" is expressed in monetary units (for example, in €).

### » Calculation/Derivation

In order to obtain the required internal data for this ratio, a perquisite is the existence of an appropriate and detailed (computer based) operative-environment information system. For external analysts, access to the cumulative data of the whole firm is needed to compute this ratio. This kind of cumulative data could be based on an informative sustainability report.

To determine a particular benchmark, the data could be obtained from macroeconomic statistics. If the data is required for a specific comparable group, it could be taken from appropriate data banks (such as branch-specific statistics).

The mathematical derivation of sustainability value, in terms of the above definition, can be explained with the following steps (a parallel example should help in easily understanding this):

### Step 1:
### Selecting the earnings-indicator and measuring its size during the period under consideration:

At the firm's level, the earnings-indicator could be the "net value added". For easy access of data, "EBIT plus labour costs" could be taken. To find a comparable object (benchmark) as an earnings-indicator, for example, "macroeconomic net value added" in the form of Gross Domestic Product (GDP) after depreciation of fixed assets could be used.

---

17 For a detailed description of this ratio refer, among others, to Figge and Hahn et al. (2007) – http://www.new-projekt.de/downloads/newstudielangversion.pdf, downloaded on 9.9.2009

**Step 2:**
**Selecting the types of resources (Indicators) and measuring their quantity during the period under consideration, both for the firm and the benchmark:**
In the basic model, (proposed by Figge and Hahn[18]) the chosen 10 economic, ecological and social indicators are: capital employed, carbon dioxide emissions, nitrogen oxide emissions, sulphur oxide emissions, emissions of light volatile organic compounds (so-called VOC-emissions), water consumption, waste generation, dust emissions, number of jobs and number of reportable accidents.

**Step 3:**
**Computing the individual resource efficiencies separately for the firm (F) and for the Benchmark (B): This is based on the following formula:**

$$\frac{\text{Value of the Earnings-Indicator}}{\text{Resource Quantity}}$$

As an example, the resource efficiency of a firm (F) with an earnings-indicator of 800 € and resource quantity of 20 tons, is equal to (800 €/20 tons) 40 € per ton. Similarly, resource efficiency for a benchmark (B), with an earnings-indicator of 30,000 € and resource quantity of 1,000 tons, is equal to (30,000/1,000) 30 € per ton.

**Step 4:**
**Computing, for each resource, the achieved resource specific earnings, separately for the firm and the benchmark, on the basis of firm's resource quantity:**
Resource Efficiency (F) · Resource Quantity (F) = Resource Specific Earnings (F)
(for the firm, it is 800 € = 40 € per ton · 20 tons)
Resource Efficiency (B) · Resource Quantity (F) = Resource Specific Earnings (B)
(for the benchmark, it is 600 € = 30 € per ton · 20 tons)

**Step 5:**
**Computing the resource value added, respectively for each of the incorporated indicators for the firm:**
This means an arithmetical comparison of the firm's achieved Specific Resource Earnings should be carried out for each resource with the Specific Resource Earnings of the benchmark (the opportunity cost):

| Resource Value Added | = | Resource Specific Earnings (F) | − | Resource Specific Earnings (B) |
|---|---|---|---|---|

---

18 Figge/Hahn (2007)

**Step 6:**
**Computing the ratio "Sustainable Value" as the arithmetical average for all the resource value added for the firm:**
(as shown in the above definition).

### # Interpretation and Typical Range

The ratio "Sustainable Value" allows assessment of the sustainable performance of a particular firm in terms of a single monetary value. It makes use of the "time-tested" principle of opportunity cost: The "price" of a particular unit of economic, ecological or social resource is determined by the lost output value of an alternative use of the same resource.

The "Sustainable Value" is achieved by a firm if it is able to use the resources more efficiently than the benchmark. This is arithmetically reflected in the resultant value of step 6. Thus, the ratio contributes to a higher transparency and comparability for sustainability performance. This helps in reviewing the operational origins and causes of differences in sustainability performance.

The sustainability value concept allows an integrated monetary "triple-bottom-line-value" for firms. The social and ecological aspects can be measured in the same way, which has been common for the use of economic capital for many years now. Instead of a single target of high return on capital (ROI), the firms and its stakeholders can now aim at a high sustainable efficiency, measure it comprehensively and influence it through various remedial measures.

In general, it is not possible to mention any desirable target for sustainable value and no concrete number can be given which would be operationally justifiable. As an orientation, one should set the general goal of improving the resource efficiency. The firm could make comparisons between budgeted and realized levels of resource efficiency. The branch-specific averages or "best-practice examples" could also be used as desired targets.

It is important to note that, because of the continuously changing methods of data recording and collection, as well as because of intermittent purchase/sales for some parts of the firm, the number presented by a firm, in its consolidated reports, are not always comparable.

### ! Useful Suggestions

The ratio "Sustainable Value" delivers a monetary value, which uses the quality of resource-efficiency in a firm as a measuring-scale for sustainable management.

Assuming that most firms are increasingly guided by the basic performance idea of conserving natural resources both on the input and output side, there are a large number of measures, which can be applied for consumption efficiency in resources.

It is always beneficial to plan, steer and control the flow of resources, such as raw-materials, energy and water. Analysing and, if needed, changing the flow of these resources can be a useful exercise. Included in the list of measures are:
- identifying technical or organisational weaknesses;
- initiating improvements for reducing the energy and material flows (if possible by implementing a circular flow or recycling system);
- developing ideas for improving the emissions, volumes and environmental impact of the production processes; and
- encouraging environmentally-conscious behaviour of employees and rewarding employees for such behaviour in the framework of a compensation system.

Since most of the emissions have an (increasing) price, a reduction in the volume-driven emission should, in general, lead to (assuming constant environment protection costs) a cost reduction.

### Related Ratios/Additional Notes

The sustainable value approach, proposed by Figge and Hahn is an open concept. Beyond the main idea of using the opportunity cost principle for ecological and social resources (in addition to economic resources), the sustainable value approach leaves open the following elements in the decision framework:
- selection of earnings indicators;
- type and number of resources (economic, ecological and social) considered;
- weighting of the resource value added which contributes to sustainable value; and
- selection of the benchmarks (for example, national economy, branch, and other performance target values).

The 10 indicator model described above is, therefore, only one of the variants, though the most popular one, on sustainable value preposition.

Although it is the first such concept which draws upon the value-based opportunity costs for sustainability management, some conceptual and methodical problems cannot be ignored: Usually, capital and/or resource intensive firms/branches perform poorer in macroeconomic comparison. Sometimes within the same branch, firms have considerably differing values and this demands further analysis. Because of a serious shortage of available data, the computation of "sustainable value" is still confined to individual firms and does not allow for its measuring individual products and the whole supply chain in a branch.

In order to compare the "sustainable values" of firms with varying sizes, the earnings to opportunity cost relationship can be used. This would help create a relative number.

Thus, in the example mentioned above, the relative "sustainable value" could be shown as 1.3 (800 € as earnings-value (F)/600 € as opportunity costs), implying that this firm has generated 30 % more value than its benchmark equivalent would have generated with the same resources. This shows that the firm is, on average, 30 % better than the national economy. In this way, the firms can be compared with each other in a sustainable value ranking, independent of their size.

### 2.12.3 Disposal Costs Ratio

**?** **Analytical Question**

What is the share of disposal costs in the total production costs?

**\*** **Definition**

$$\frac{\text{Disposal Costs per Period}}{\text{Production Costs per Period}}$$

The ratio is expressed as a percentage.

**»** **Calculation/Derivation**

A prerequisite for obtaining the required data for this ratio is the existence of an internal and detailed (computerized) cost accounting system. This system should allow for separate and systematic collection of environment related cost-types and, when required, should also provide a special cost centre for the purpose. Thus, a firm may have a cost centre for product-return, for recycling, where a firm might record its own costs towards product-return or costs arising out of external services (such as regular product-dismantling).

Because of the lack of extensive standardisation of data, a comparison of these costs over time may be more useful than comparison across firms.

**#** **Interpretation and Typical Range**

To review the effects of various business activities, it is important for the firm to ensure the comprehensiveness and consistency of disposal costs related information. This would help the firm to operate more resource-efficiently on the input side, and emission efficiently on the output side.

The disposal costs ratio should contribute towards improving the transparency and relative significance of disposal costs, which arise during the production process (for example, costs towards waste disposal, waste-water disposal and exit-air disposal) or during/at the end of product-consumption process (for example, the responsibility of the producing firm to take back the spare or worn-out parts and old products).

As orientation and for comparison purposes, internal benchmarks between various units within the firm (such as locations/plants) can be used. The performance over time can be analysed with the help of budget-actual comparisons. External benchmarks could be taken from the branch-specific averages, or best-practice values.

The percentage value of this ratio is dependent on several factors. The typical range of disposal costs is not only guided by commercial decisions made by the firms towards resource consumption (such as austerity measures), but is also influenced by regulatory frameworks, which leads to the emergence of disposal costs through various directives.

## Useful Suggestions

On the supposition that firms in the same branch usually have similar production structures, the ratio values, differing significantly from the averages, are clear candidates for serious reviews. This should help in analysing the positive and negative developments, or consequences, and in manoeuvring them in the context of corporate goals.

Through careful, systematic and foresighted management, a firm can use a life cycle assessment approach, where alternative materials and supplies are analysed for their environmental impact from raw-material extraction to consumption and final recycling or disposal. Through environmental targets, a firm can develop specifications towards material consumption efficiency, recycling capability, energy saving, emission standards and noise-reduction.

Thus, an optimal recycling concept begins with the design and conceptual phase of new products. In many situations, the producer has to develop and operate a network for the taking back of spare and worn-out parts, consumed materials (such as used oil), as well as old products and disposal of these materials.

A firm can reduce disposal costs by managing the wastewater and waste materials carefully. Sometimes, these costs can be reduced by treating the wastewater for reuse in production. All efforts at reducing the quantity of waste materials and waste water on the one hand, and at avoiding the use of dangerous materials (which are expensive to dispose of) on the other hand, can provide positive measures in this direction.

In the framework of sustainability management, a firm can develop various strategic and operative initiatives which can contribute towards managing disposal costs.

## Related Ratios/Additional Notes

Related ratios, which have similar goals, are Recycling Quota, Rejection Ratio, Disposal Costs per Unit of Output, and Non-Conformity Costs Ratio.

The so-called "Demolition Costs", which involve dismantling of machines and demolition of buildings, are usually not included in disposal costs. This is because of the infrequent nature of such costs, related to dismantling and demolition.

# 3 Customer Perspective

## 3.1 Customer Relationship Management (CRM)

### 3.1.1 Customer Acquisition Rate

**Analytical Question**

By what percentage did the number of customers increase in a period? How big is the proportionate addition of new customers in relation to the sum total of all the existing customers?

**Definition**

$$\frac{\text{Number of New Customers Added in a Period} \cdot 100}{\text{Total Customers at the Start of a Period}}$$

The period-oriented (such as annual or quarterly) customer acquisition rate is calculated in percentage terms.

**Calculation/Derivation**

The required data for this quotient is derived from the information system (which is upstream of external accounting) of marketing, sales, or distribution departments (statistics, customer and order database). In this context, the criteria for treating a customer as "new customers" should be carefully considered. For example, what should be the time gap between the last and the latest order from this customer to call him/her "new"?

**Interpretation and Typical Range**

The Customer Acquisition Rate belongs to the category of customer relationship management (CRM). More precisely, it is related to the third "R" of relationship marketing (the first R is the recruitment/acquisition; the second R is retention and the third R is recovery/win-back). It shows the results of marketing efforts of the firm towards acquiring new customers with reference to the existing client-base, in the period under consideration. Thus, it has its relevance primarily as an early-warning indicator about the increase in future sales and the related (possible) surge in income.

To obtain a full view of the situation, it is good to include the mirror image of the "customer churn rate". This helps in calculating the net growth or decline in the customer base. Moreover, general market developments and the performance of main competitors should also be included in the analysis, in order to find out whether the firm has above or below-average performance.

https://doi.org/10.1515/9783110598094-004

A general target for this ratio is not possible. For benchmarking this ratio and for orientation purposes, the branch-specific average values or the "best-practice" value can be taken.

## ! Useful Suggestions

The centre stage for acquiring customers is occupied by all those measures which help in meeting the first time needs of the customers or which help in offering preferential treatment to entice customers from competitors. Under the assumption that comparable firms in a particular branch have similar costs and income structure, any significant change in this ratio, above or below its average, offers clear signals for careful analysis of positive or negative developments. This also helps to counter-influence developments in ways commensurate with the firm's objectives.

## & Related Ratios/Additional Notes

Two synonyms of the customer acquisition rate are, New Customer Ratio or New Customer Intensity.

In the formula for customer acquisition rate, the numbers of customers (quantity based variant) could also be substituted or combined with the sales weights (value based variant). In the value based variant, it is possible to see the volume of sales associated with new clients. Similarly, the ratio can be adjusted with the reduction in the contribution margin or Customer Lifetime Value (CLV).

Sometimes, the ratio is also calculated with the "average" customer base. In this case, the reference point of analysis includes 50% of customers acquired and 50% of customers lost, and this may "water-down" the results.

### 3.1.2 Customer Churn Rate

## ? Analytical Question

How much is the attrition of customers as a percentage? How big is the proportionate departure of customers, in relation to the sum total of all the existing customers?

## * Definition

$$\frac{\text{Number of Discontinued Customers in a Period} \cdot 100}{\text{Total Customers at the Start of a Period}}$$

The period-oriented (such as annual or quarterly) Customer Churn Rate is calculated in percentage terms.

## Calculation/Derivation
The required data for this quotient is derived from the information system (which is upstream of external accounting) of the marketing, sales, or distribution departments (statistics, customer and order database).

## Interpretation and Typical Range
The Customer Churn Rate belongs to the category of customer relationship management (CRM). More precisely, it is related to the third "R" of relationship marketing (the first R is the recruitment/acquisition; the second R is retention and the third R is recovery/win-back). It shows what percentage of the customer base did not buy from the firm in the period under consideration. Thus, it has its relevance primarily as an early-warning indicator concerning the decline in future sales, and the related downturn in income.

To obtain a full view of the situation, it is good to include the mirror image of "customer acquisition rate". This helps to calculate the net growth or decline in the customer base. Moreover, the general market developments and the performance of main competitors should also be included in the analysis in order to find out whether the firm has above or below average performance.

A general target for this ratio is not possible. For benchmarking this ratio and for orientation purposes, the branch-specific average values or the "best-practice" value can be taken.

## Useful Suggestions
In order to obtain useful information, it is good to initiate an additional analysis about what led to the departure of customers, over and above the percentage analysis in certain situations. In this connection, loss of sales or revenues could also be highlighted. It is important to check whether the "lost" clients belong to A, B, or C category of customers.

The starting point for analysing the churn rate relates to determining the reasons for the "departure" of customers, who may have:
- Some concrete dissatisfaction about the quotation of the firm;
- Opted for some preferred promotion campaign from competitors; or
- Personal reasons for changed demand behaviour.

The centre stage for recovering profitable customers is occupied by all those measures, which help in fetching back all lost customers and also those who may be "lost" in the foreseeable future. Included in these measures are: a survey of the reasons for customer departure; how to eliminate these reasons; the concrete efforts at regaining customers; and close supervision. It is relevant to note that departures of customers, that made (or would have made) little or no contribution to the firm's income, provide new opportunities for focusing on financially attractive business relations.

**&** **Related Ratios/Additional Notes**

Customer Turnover Rate is a common synonym for customer churn rate. Sometimes, Attrition Rate is also used as a synonym.

In this context, it is relevant to note that customer turnover rate is handled in various ways. Thus, showing it as a quotient between "customers acquired" and "customers lost" may lead to misleading interpretations, if the absolute numbers for numerator and denominator are unknown. For example, if customers acquired were equal to customers lost, the quotient would be 1. However, if the absolute number of total customers is small, this may be a good sign. Conversely, with a large absolute number, careful analysis of the reasons for the shift of customer base needs to be carried out for its opportunities and risk impact.

In the formula for churn rate ratio, the number of customers (quantity based variant) could also be substituted or combined with the sales weights (value based variant). In the value based variant, it is possible to see the loss of sales associated with the lost clients. Similarly, the ratio can be adjusted with the reduction in the contribution margin or Customer Lifetime Value (CLV).

Sometimes, the ratio is also calculated with the "average" customer base. In this case, the reference point of analysis includes 50 % of customers acquired and 50 % of customers lost, and this may "water-down" the results.

### 3.1.3 Customer Retention Period

**?** **Analytical Question**

What is the average time span of a business relationship, or a customer-supplier relationship, in a particular customer-segment?

**\*** **Definition**

The Customer Retention Period is that span of time, during which a steady (often secured through a contractual agreement) exchange of goods and/or services takes place between a firm and its customer.

The indicator is expressed in units of time, mostly in years.

**»** **Calculation/Derivation**

The required chronological dates (opening dates when customers start buying from the firm and closing dates when contractual obligations are completed) are derived from the information system (which is upstream of external accounting) of marketing, sales, or distribution departments (statistics, customer and order database).

**#** **Interpretation and Typical Range**

The Customer Retention Period belongs to the category of customer relationship management (CRM). More precisely, it is related to the second "R" of relationship marketing (the first R is the recruitment/acquisition; the second R is retention and the third R is recovery/win-back). It shows the average time endurance of a customer relationship, which may be classified further in different segment-based criteria. In addition to its help in estimating the achievable sales (and profit) forecasts for the period, the indicator can also provide further insights for CRM. The retention period can be classified for A, B, and C categories of clients, which could assist in designing a different marketing-mix for each type of customer need.

In determining a desirable retention period, internal benchmarks can be used for comparison between different business units, or between plan and actual values. If available, external benchmarks, such as branch-average or best-practice values, could also be used.

**Useful Suggestions**

To obtain a complete view of the situation, it is good to include the developments in "customer acquisition rate" as well as in "customer churn rate". This helps to assess the turnover-intensity in the customer base. Moreover, general market developments and the performance of main competitors should also be included in the analysis, in order to find out whether the firm has above or below average performance.

A general hypothesis linked to efforts at increasing the customer retention period is as follows: a longer customer retention period reduces the customer acquisition costs and, along with falling communication costs over time, leads to improved profitability for a particular relationship. The firm should check the efforts made at customer retention to find out whether these factors are important.

To achieve a profitable customer relationship, all the measures contributing to increased customer loyalty may be applied:
- Consolidating and strengthening the business relationships through loyalty management (efficiency measurement through customer-satisfaction analysis), and
- Stabilization of vulnerable relations and avoidance of cancellations from (protesting as well as non-protesting) customers, through an effective complaint-management system.

The centre stage for recovering the profitable customers is occupied by all those measures which help in fetching back all lost customers and also those who may be "lost" in the foreseeable future. Included in these measures are: a survey of the reasons for customer departure, how to eliminate these reasons, the concrete efforts at gaining back customers through revitalization.

**Related Ratios/Additional Notes**

In the mass-media branch, particularly in business divisions such as book clubs, instead of customer retention period, "Mortality Period" is used as a synonym. This refers to individual customers and the period of their membership.

### 3.1.4 Customer Significance Level

**?** **Analytical Question**

Whether the departure of a particular customer could push the firm into losses?

**\*** **Definition**

$$\frac{\text{Sales attributed to the Customer (in \%)}}{100\,\% - \text{Breakeven Capacity (in \%)}}$$

The ratio is measured in the resultant value as a decimal (such as 0.8).

The term "breakeven capacity" is often expressed as "capacity level".

**»** **Calculation/Derivation**

To obtain the needed data to calculate this ratio, the direct or marginal costing system is required, which systematically classifies costs into variable and fixed components. The ratio also assumes the availability of sales data, classified according to clients' name.

**#** **Interpretation and Typical Range**

The Customer Significance Level is an indicator of risk associated with a customer's departure. It demonstrates the dependence of a firm on its large customers, in the sense of "major customers". It illustrates whether a firm would go below its breakeven point without a particular customer.

If the ratio results in a quotient of larger than 1, the customer should be a "significant" one, and departure would lead the firm (at least in the short-run) into losses.

Since the risk analysis (which is also calculated in anticipation of the likelihood) based on this ratio is linked to the foundations of breakeven analysis, the methodical limitations of this instrument should be considered when interpreting this ratio.

**!** **Useful Suggestions**

The instrument used for calculating the customer significance level is the breakeven analysis. Although the instrument is (in its basic variant) based on various limiting assumptions (for example, one product model or static costs), its clarity explains its intensive use in the short-run.

The short-term time horizon of direct (or marginal) costing, and the basic version of breakeven analysis, allows only a limited spectrum of measures. Thus, there are only 3 parameters in the definition of breakeven point (price per unit and variable costs per unit, which help in calculating the contribution margin per unit, and the fixed periodic costs) that can be manoeuvred. Through a combined effort on pricing policy on the one hand, and cost management (by reducing variable costs per unit and sometime total fixed costs) on the other, a firm can achieve a reduction of its breakeven point.

In particular, this ratio should help to identify the dependence on individual customers and show the negative consequences of such dependence. It should also aid in finding measures to avoid negative consequences with the help of a strengthened customer base through new acquisition of clients.

### Related Ratios/Additional Notes
The Customer Significance Level belongs to the category of breakeven analysis. The other ratios in this category are Breakeven Point (expressed in quantity), Margin of Safety (measured in currency or quantity units), Margin of Safety Factor (measured in %) and Cash Point. If these ratios/indicators are linked together with individual products, product groups or specific market segments, they offer significant insights into the short-term success or risk involved in the object under review.

In terms of its orientation, this ratio also analyses the situational aspects of issues (in this case, linked with a customer) of safety margin and safety margin factor.

## 3.1.5 Cross-Selling Ratio

### Analytical Question
What is the volume of additional (not so far purchased) products and services (from other business divisions) which the firm is able to sell to its existing customers?

### Definition
Reference to an individual customer or a customer-group:

$$\frac{\text{Sales Volume of Other (or New) Products and Services} \cdot 100}{\text{Sales Volume of Existing Products and Services}}$$

The cross-selling ratio is expressed in percentage terms.

### Calculation/Derivation
The required data for this quotient is derived from the information system (which is upstream of external accounting) of marketing, sales, or distribution departments (sales statistics, customer and order database). The actual sales could be obtained from the financial bookkeeping. For planning cross-selling potential, customers should be grouped in specific segments depending upon their demands and behaviour indicators.

**#** **Interpretation and Typical Range**
The Cross-Selling Ratio belongs to the category of customer relationship management (CRM). More precisely, it is related to the second "R" of relationship marketing (the first R is the recruitment/acquisition; the second R is retention and the third R is recovery/win-back). It shows the relative increase in the intensity of customer relationship, which is reflected in the ordering of new products and services by the customer.

This ratio is particularly relevant to firms with many product divisions (both in manufacturing industry as well as in banks and insurance firms), where an attempt is made to extend the customer relationship to other products. Depending upon the volume of existing product divisions, the percentage value of cross-selling may be small in the beginning; however, with the passage of time, it should help in increasing customer loyalty and customer retention.

**!** **Useful Suggestions**
The presence of a good internal cost accounting and external financial accounting system is the prerequisite for a successful cross-selling strategy; it allows for a multi-stage computation of the customer-profitability. A customer-profitability can be achieved or increased through cross selling of new products or services. Often, a firm tries to attract a customer based on a standard or initial product, to buy additional products or services. The loyalty of the customer is carried over from existing products to other (or new) products.

**&** **Related Ratios/Additional Notes**
Some companies use the word "attaching" to convey the cross-selling strategy. When more expensive upgrades or add-ons are offered in a cross-selling strategy, it is called "up-selling".

Cross-Selling Ratio is a measure of customer loyalty and is related to improving customer satisfaction. Thus, one should combine this ratio with other early or late indicators (for example, "Customer Satisfaction Index" or Sales Volume per Customer, etc.).

The values in the numerator and denominator should both be expressed either in terms of quantity or in value (for example in €).

### 3.1.6 Customer Lifetime Value (CLV)

**?** **Analytical Question**
How much is each present or potential customer worth to the firm, when viewed in terms of his capitalized value? How much should the marketing department be willing to spend to acquire or retain a customer?

**Definition**                                                                                          ✱

With the help of the discounted capital budgeting method, the net present value (NPV) of a customer over the total period of a relationship is measured. Thus, CLV represents the calculated NPV.

$$A_0 = \sum_{t=1}^{w} (e_t - a_t) \cdot (1+i)^{-t}$$

Where:

$A_0$ = Net Present Value
t  = Time Period
w = Total number of periods under consideration
$e_t$ = Receipts in period t
$a_t$ = Payments in period t
i  = Interest Rate

The CLV is measured in terms of monetary units (such as €).

**Calculation/Derivation**                                                                              »

In this ratio, the business relationship with a customer is viewed as an investment project and its value is estimated. The required forecasts for timing and magnitude of all probable cash inflows and outflows which relate to a particular customer or customer groups, are based on estimates of appropriate indicators. In the case of private customers, factors such as age, profession, wealth, and life style are used for the purpose. In the case of business customers, branch- or firm-specific factors such as market growth, competitive positioning, financial stability and technical competence are considered as possible clues for measuring CLV.

**Interpretation and Typical Range**                                                                    #

The CLV is the result of a dynamic method where the future value of a customer relationship is estimated. It calculates the net present value of a particular customer. Like in any other discounted capital budgeting method, it is important to recognize the existence of various uncertainties, which relate to:
– the assumption about the future,
– the developments in the customer life cycle, and
– the resulting cash flows.

In CLV, financial implications of a customer relationship are measured in the form of the "wealth" generated, which in turn is related to achievable future sales/profits and when the firm would reach its breakeven point through customer retention.

**❗ Useful Suggestions**

The CLV belongs to the category of customer relationship management (CRM). More precisely, it is related to all the "Rs" of relationship marketing (the first R is the recruitment/acquisition; the second R is retention and the third R is recovery/winback). Therefore, the spectrum of possible measures for improving the CLV is broad. In the following, some examples are given:

– Exhausting all potentials in respect of: a direct-sales volume expansion through up-selling/cross-selling and an indirect-sales volume expansion through a positive personal sales promotion;
– Exhausting all potential in respect of customer willingness to pay higher prices, which may be reflected in customer satisfaction and loyalty. Indirectly also, the higher price potential could be achieved by personal sales promotion;
– Exhausting all potential in respect of achieving below average costs for promotion and customer support, as well as the reduced cost of acquiring new customers. This could also be achieved by personal sales promotion.

**& Related Ratios/Additional Notes**

There are other typical questions which could be asked with reference to CLV:

– Is a present or potential customer relationship valuable from the capital budgeting perspective?
– How can the customer relationship be made more profitable through cross-selling or upselling?
– Is the "departure" of a particular customer a "loss"? Does the present value of the customer relationship have a positive or negative impact?

**Ⓢ 3.1.7 Customer Satisfaction Index**

**❓ Analytical Question**

What is the level of customer satisfaction with regard to products and services delivered by the firm?

Is the firm considered as a preferred provider of the products and services?

**✴ Definition**

The Customer Satisfaction Index (CSI) represents a ratio which maps the complex aspects of customer satisfaction in a simple manner. It can be measured in many ways, and one of the methods for measuring CSI is explained as follows:

$$\frac{\sum (\text{Average Satisfaction Score for each Parameter} \cdot \text{Relative Weight})}{\text{Total of all Relative Weights}}$$

The resultant value of CSI can be expressed as a percentage.

## Calculation/Derivation

The customer satisfaction scores are derived mostly from specific customer surveys, which are usually performed periodically by the marketing/sales department or by external institutes hired for the purpose. The weights are based on the importance attached by customers (typically, on a scale of 0 to 10) to a set of key parameters (such as quality, price level, packaging, and delivery commitments).

The following example illustrates the calculation. The customers' satisfaction score (on a scale of 0 to 10, where 10 represents the highest level of perceived satisfaction) on each parameter (column B) multiplied by the relative weights (in column C) is summed up and later divided by the total of the relative weights. The resultant number is the CSI.

| Parameter P | Absolute Weights A | Average Satisfaction Score B | Relative Weights C = A/Average Weight | Weighted Score D = B · C |
|---|---|---|---|---|
| P1 | 7 | 8 | 1.17 | 9.36 |
| P2 | 5 | 4 | 0.83 | 3.32 |
| P3 | 9 | 8 | 1.50 | 12.00 |
| P4 | 3 | 3 | 0.50 | 1.50 |
| P5 | 6 | 4 | 1.00 | 4.00 |
| | Average = 6.00 | Average = 5.40 | Sum = 5.00 | CSI = 6.04 |

Where:
  A = Absolute Weights assigned by all respondents for each parameter
  B = Average Satisfaction Score assigned by all respondents for each parameter
  C = Relative Weights based on = Absolute Weight (as in column A)/Average Weights (Both absolute and average weights obtained from column A. For parameter 2, the relative weight, for example, is 5/6 = 0.83)
  D = Satisfaction Score · Relative Weight (= B · C)
  CSI = Average of Weighted Scores – in this example:(9.36 + 3.32 + 12.00 + 1.50 + 4.0)/5 = 6.04

Since the scale used was 0 – 10, CSI of 6.04 is equal to 60.4 %. This implies that the firm is 60.4 % successful in satisfying its customers.

## Interpretation and Typical Range

The customer satisfaction index is a quantification of how far the company is able to fulfil the expressed and implied expectations of customers. Though the calculation is based on subjective survey results, it offers a clear indication of whether the firm has met or exceeded customer expectations.

Every firm can track its performance against stated requirements of quality and timeliness in so far as appropriate documentary evidence is available. Some internal indication of whether the firm is meeting the requirements can also be obtained from data on scrap rates, parts-per-million (PPM), complaints quota (indicators of negative satisfaction), sales improvements, repeat orders, positive customer audit reports (indicators of positive satisfaction), etc. However, when it comes to measuring intangible expectations, the firm has to rely on measures like CSI.

A general target range for the desired level of satisfaction cannot be recommended. However, the higher the CSI, the better the customers' perception about performance. For orientation and benchmarking this ratio, a firm could use internal time series comparisons and if it possible, external comparisons with branch-specific average or best-practice values may be used as a benchmark.

## ! Useful Suggestions
Mostly, there is an obvious and strong link between customer satisfaction and customer retention. Customers' perception of service and quality of a product will determine the success of the product or service in the market.

With better understanding of customers' perceptions, companies can tune their actions better to meet customer needs. They can identify their own strengths and weaknesses, where they stand in comparison to their competitors, chart out future progress and improvement. Customer satisfaction measurement helps to promote an increased focus on customer outcomes and stimulate customer-oriented improvements in the work practices and processes used within the company.

The CSI can also be used for quantifying the overall satisfaction level of one customer. Plotting this CS of the customer against a time scale shows how well the firm is accomplishing the task of customer satisfaction over a period of time. In order to reduce the subjectivity and bias due to individual perception of one respondent within the customer's organization, several respondents (buyer, user, inspector, etc.) could be contacted. Surveying a number of respondents for each customer gives a complete perspective of customer satisfaction. However, it may be necessary to devise a different questionnaire for each of them.

## & Related Ratios/Additional Notes
A ratio, which is often used as an indicator of customer (dis)satisfaction, is termed as "Customer Complaint Ratio". It shows the number of returned or claimed products vis-à-vis the total number of products sold. A higher complaint ratio refers to unfulfilled expectation and/or falling satisfaction.

### 3.1.8 Customer Complaint Ratio

**Analytical Question**

What is the relative size of customer complaints involving the products and services delivered by the firm?

**Definition**

In literature, there are two kinds of meanings attached to this measure: one is product-related, when the bought product is claimed/returned to the seller and the other is customer-related, when he/she protests about something not done properly. In the following, both product-related and customer-related ratios are shown:

Product-related:

$$\frac{\text{Number of Returned Products/Services} \cdot 100}{\text{Total Number of Sold Products/Services}}$$

or

Customer-related:

$$\frac{\text{Number of Complaints} \cdot 100}{\text{Total Number of Clients}}$$

In either variant of this ratio, the resultant number is expressed as a percentage.

**Calculation/Derivation**

The values for the denominator can be obtained from the general sales statistics of the firm. The details about the numerator could be collected through a special recording system, possibly through a systematic claim/complaint management. The information should give concrete insight into the reasons for claims and/or complaints.

**Interpretation and Typical Range**

The Customer Complaint Ratio specifies that part of the sold products/services which the customer returned because of defects. In the customer-related variant, it specifies those customers who have complained about something. It is a central aspect of the business complaint management, which dedicates itself to a targeted overcoming or reduction in the expressed dissatisfaction.

The Customer Complaint Ratio is often used as a qualitative indicator and is applied in the context of measuring the customer satisfaction. However, it is important to note that only the directly notified cases are considered in this ratio. This means that the true level of defects or complaints could be much higher; the lodged complaints are only part of the "annoyance-iceberg". Furthermore, the quantification of the claims/complaints does not give any details about which types of complaint-reasons are responsible for this.

Theoretically, the complaint ratio should show a small value. However, when the customers know about systematic and targeted complaint management, it often leads to a greater readiness on the part of unsatisfied customers to complain.

A general target range for this ratio cannot be determined. For orientation and benchmarking, a firm could use internal time series comparisons and, if possible, external comparisons with branch-specific averages may be used as a guide.

**❗ Useful Suggestions**

An important prerequisite for the effective interpretation of the ratio is the conviction that claims or complaints are a very important source of information for the firm. Through a detailed analysis of the information collected, the firm is able to improve the quality of the offered products and services and avoid a silent departure of dissatisfied customers.

In various researches, it has been found that a major proportion of dissatisfied customers do not complain. Thus, as part of systematic complaint management, a firm could implement a series of measures which may help in "evidence-controlling":

- Reduce the number of unvoiced complaints, which could be measured with the following formula:

$$\frac{\text{Number of Non-complaining Dissatisfied Customers}}{\text{Total Number of all Dissatisfied Customers}}$$

- Reduce the number of unofficial complaints (voiced informally to an employee), which could be measured by the following formula:

$$\frac{\text{Number of Not-registered Complaints}}{\text{Total Number of Complaints}}$$

In either case, the purpose is to reduce the knowledge deficit in terms of incorrect estimation of the nature of customer satisfaction. The knowledge deficit may lead to investigation into those areas of improvement, which are not considered urgent from the customer perspective. Figuratively speaking, both measures are intended to reduce the size of the "annoyance-iceberg" under water.

With the help of increased discovery rate, and the following formula

$$\frac{\text{Number of Registered Complaints}}{\text{Total Number of Dissatisfied Customers}}$$

a system for a detailed and extensive information base can be established to understand the reasons for customer annoyance.

If the Customer Complaint Ratio is compiled for each product or product group, the information obtained could be seen as an indicator of the product quality from the customers' perspective. The products which have a high return rate or where the cause of the complaint cannot be specified, could as be withdrawn from the product-portfolio or a change of supplier forced.

**Related Ratios/Additional Notes**  &

To complement the two variants (both of which are quantity-based) of the ratio above, the Customer Complaint Ratio could also be shown as a value-based measure. In this case, the numerator is the sales value of the returned goods/services and the total sales of the period are the denominator.

The so-called complaint-cost intensity (or the complaint-cost ratio) is a related ratio, which shows the costs (such as payment of a claim) arising out of a customer complaint vis-à-vis the total sales to this customer.

Like other ratios, the Customer Complaint Ratio can be modified to suit the business needs of a firm. It is quite acceptable to differentiate among various types of complaints and have the ratio for each complaint-group separately.

For external comparison, the consistency of the definition used for this purpose should be ensured.

### 3.1.9 Flop Rate

**Analytical Question**  ?

How high is the flop rate for newly introduced products or services?

**Definition**  *

$$\frac{\text{Number of Unsuccessful Product and/or Service Innovations} \cdot 100}{\text{Total Number of all Product and/or Service Innovations}}$$

The Flop Rate is expressed as a percentage.

**Calculation/Derivation**  »

Although Flop Rate represents an obvious and easily comprehensible fact, the collection of data for this purpose is not without problems. Firstly, there has to be a uniform definition of which "new launch" or innovation can be called as a marketable product or service. Secondly, it is necessary to have objective and comprehensible criteria for measuring what may be called a flop. In addition to that, there should be agreement on a time-horizon, which a product or service must outlive to be called a flop.

The information for this ratio has to be collected internally through special surveys.

## # Interpretation and Typical Range

In the framework for strategic product planning, development of a balanced portfolio of products and services is very important. The Flop Rate is a measure of the successful acceptance of a new launch in the market, though it is negatively measured in terms of what is not accepted by the market. It is desirable to keep the flop rate to the minimum possible, though a flop rate of zero will be an illusion. It is not rare that the percentage of flops is influenced by the innovation and product-succession strategy of the firm.

The need for definitional clarity is important here, so that managing such things can be done more meaningfully. The choice of economic criteria for determining "success" needs to be made carefully.

An inter-firm comparison of the flop rate, depending upon the availability of data, should be done with caution, because of the differences in the terminologies used. However, empirical studies have shown that for certain categories of products, particularly in foods, the flop rate could be as high as 60 % to 95 %.

## ! Useful Suggestions

Since innovations are mostly coupled with heavy personnel, material and financial resources, a firm always strives to reduce the flop rate in the market. In the framework for innovation management, many companies have multi-staged valuation and selection methods (coupled with technical feasibility studies and market research studies) for analysing the expected return and the success probability.

## & Related Ratios/Additional Notes

A synonym for Flop Rate is "Failure Rate".

## 3.2 Marketing Communication Indicators

### 3.2.1 Media Coverage Level

**Analytical Question**    `?`

How many contacts can be made with a particular group of people through a communication medium or a media-combination within a particular period?

**Definition**    `*`

In the majority of the cases, various quantitative variants of the term are used. Depending upon the number of times a medium was used or the number of different media used, the following variants could be mentioned:

- Gross Coverage: total individual coverage for each communication medium
  (In the case that several mediums are used, the data is not adjusted for multiple contacts per person)
- Net Coverage: external coverage-overlapping is eliminated
  (Here the data is adjusted for multiple contacts per person)
- Cumulative Coverage: internal coverage-overlapping is eliminated
  (Here the data is adjusted for multiple contacts per person)
- Combined Coverage: external and internal coverage-overlapping is eliminated
  (Here the data is adjusted for all kinds of multiple contacts).

These variants of media coverage are expressed in absolute numbers, such as "number of contacts" or "number of persons".

**Calculation/Derivation**    `»`

The required data for this measure is obtained from extensive market research surveys. There surveys regularly update the data about the use of individual medium by readers, listeners and viewers.

**Interpretation and Typical Range**    `#`

The Media Coverage Level shows how many people or contacts were reached through a particular medium (or a combination of media) at least once. In the framework for communication policy (as an element of marketing-mix), it represents the leading decision criterion for the selection of an appropriate medium.

When the media coverage is linked to the costs of using different media, the so-called "cost per thousand", which helps in comparing the economic efficiency of different communication media can be used.

**❗ Useful Suggestions**

Since the use of communication media does not always fully correspond with the target group of the advertisement, it is desirable to use a weighted coverage, where share of desired target group in the total user base could be taken as weight.

Although the Media Coverage Level is an undisputed basis for decisions about advertisement-budget deployment (in inter-media or intra-media selection), the measure does not give any clues about contact-quality (duration and intensity of observation in an advertisement) and the real contact-impact. Furthermore, when decisions are made about allocating the advertisement budget to different communication vehicles, the time component and the assumed impact should also be analysed. For example, with respect to the choice of timing, time-intervals between two advertisements or the number of repetitions are important.

**& Related Ratios/Additional Notes**

As alternative variants of quantitative measures for media coverage, the area aspect of media coverage, where the geographical reach of the communication medium is analysed, should also be talked about. There could be a qualitative media coverage, which checks the effective reach of a campaign in the target group of people.

### 3.2.2 Click Through Rate (CTR)

**❓ Analytical Question**

In what proportion did an online advertising banner induce an Internet user to take a concrete step and click on the banner?

**✳ Definition**

$$\frac{\text{Number of AdClicks} \cdot 100}{\text{Number of AdImpressions}}$$

The Click Through Rate is expressed as a percentage.

**» Calculation/Derivation**

The term AdClicks (Advertisement Clicks) implies the number of mouse-clicks on an advertising banner and AdImpressions (Advertisement Impressions) implies the number of times the banner was delivered. The AdClicks and AdImpressions are collected through special scripts on the internet-server. This kind of data-collection is referred to as "campaign-tracking".

## Interpretation and Typical Range

CTR is considered to be the main performance indicator of online marketing. As a measure of efficiency for online advertising, it shows the success of the online campaign. By comparison with classical marketing campaigns, online advertisement allows a direct measurement of campaign success, as indicated by the visitors' decision to pick up the contact through a click.

A relatively high success rate implies that the banner design and its content were good at inducing the visitor to click on it. Whether the intended target group was indeed reached, can be checked or estimated only through a deeper analysis of the data.

Banner advertisement CTRs have fallen over time, often measuring significantly less than 1%. Thus, according to prevailing opinion, a CTR of 0.3% to 0.8% is considered usual. However, in some individual cases, CTRs have also been higher.

## Useful Suggestions

In the framework of comprehensive online marketing, controlling can encompass a broad spectrum of possible business actions (for example, in the area of CRM).

As such, the CTR does not offer any specific interpretation about the success of the campaign or accessing the target group. Thus, a CTR of less than 0.1% for a particular campaign could be more effective than a CTR of more than 2% in another campaign, if exactly the same target group accessed the advertisement and placed the orders. Whether the same visitor, who clicked on the banner, also placed the order can easily be checked through the "conversion rate". However, if the visitor to the banner used another distribution channel to buy the product, a clear identification can be made only through direct survey of the buyers.

## Related Ratios/Additional Notes

Click Rate and AdClick Rate are two other synonyms for CTR.

In the family of online ratios for evaluating the performance of online marketing, Conversion Rate, Cost per Click and Cost per Order are other common ratios.

### 3.2.3 Conversion Rate

## Analytical Question

In what proportion were the online banner contacts transformed into online-orders?

## Definition

$$\frac{\text{Number of Online-Orders} \cdot 100}{\text{Number of AdClicks}}$$

Where:

The term AdClicks (Advertisement Clicks) implies the number of mouse-clicks on an advertising banner by an internet user.

The Conversion Rate is expressed as a percentage.

## » Calculation/Derivation

The actual AdClicks are collected through special scripts on the internet-server. This kind of data-collection is referred to as "campaign-tracking".

## # Interpretation and Typical Range

Conversion Rate is one of the performance indicators of online marketing. It shows the transformation rate between customer-contact (through CTR) and the decision to buy. The resultant Conversion Rate may show (though not necessarily) the periodic causal connection between customer contact and order placing.

In practice, the Conversion Rate lies mostly between 1% and 2%.

## ! Useful Suggestions

Like other comparable measures, which provide information for grasping the effectiveness of marketing communications, similar rules apply for conversion rate as well. Thus, in order to draw better conclusions from the volume for the conversion rate, one should analyse all the relevant relationships with the customers. If, in an extreme situation, the internet is the only source of communication with the customer, the conversion rate will provide a clear message about the effectiveness of communication. However, in majority of the practical situations, there are many communication channels for approaching potential customers, so that this measure for the conversion rate cannot give clear conclusions without supporting data. Similarly, there could be various channels for placing orders. For example, the order may be placed by letter, fax, telephone, email, online or in the traditional personal form, where the customer visits one of the outlets.

The Conversion Rate can be enhanced through strong target group oriented banners.

A change in this ratio (in the context of target business goals) could be achieved by a disproportionate increase or decrease in the number of online orders (as numerator) and in number of AdClicks (as denominator). *For further details and systematic explanations on this, refer to the information in Appendix I.*

## & Related Ratios/Additional Notes

In the family of online ratios for evaluating the performance of online marketing, Click Through Rate (CTR), Cost per Click, Cost per Order and Contact Price per Thousand are often used ratios.

### 3.2.4 Usage Intensity of Internet-based Media

**Analytical Question**

The term "Internet-based Media" covers all types of internet-based organizations that contribute to any kind of digital execution of information, communication and/or transaction processes between firms, customers and governments.

How high is the number of customers in an entertainment concern, within one month, who uses the eService portal for mobile music? or

In terms of value, how high is the procurement share in an industrial firm for production goods of type B and C[1], that are purchased within one quarter, through an electronic sourcing platform? or

How many minutes per day does a user stay, on average, on an information website of a trading company or social media?

**Definition**

Method of Absolute Indicator:

Number or Value of monitored Objects of one specific Type of Internet-based Media within one Period

The values for the method of absolute parameter, is indicated in units of quantity, time or money.

Method of Relative Indicator:

$$\frac{\text{Number or Value of monitored Objects of one specific Type of Internet-based Media within one Period}}{\text{Target Indicator per Period from a carefully selected Population Basis}}$$

The values of the method of relative indicator are shown as a number or (when multiplied by a factor of 100) as a percentage.

**Calculation/Derivation**

A significant part of the information relating to the generation of appropriate specifications for the usage intensity can be extracted from data analyses of webserver-log-files and cookie-applications. Here, for example, the specialized software tools like WebAnalytics or GoogleAnalytics can be employed. The information regarding income and cost elements for usage intensity can be obtained from the data created for internal and external accounting.

---

1 If the firm follows ABC classification system, the B and C category of goods would imply all goods other than the most valuable/important goods in category A.

**#** **Interpretation and Typical Range**

Because of the complementary interaction amongst various developments in the digitalization of data, the miniaturization of technical components, sharply increased computer computational performance and the global linkage of transmission paths, the electronic-network economy has become significantly important, not only for existing industrial and service companies but also for innovative start-ups. The technologies relating to Big-Data-Analytics (BDA) have improved the decision-making process by helping to analyse usage related information at several levels.

For the development and implementation of fast-growing web-based business models (so called Electronic Business/E-Business or Management by Internet/ Digital Management), as well as for planning, management and control of corresponding business processes (e.g. in terms of an E-Procurement or Online-Marketing), sound knowledge of current and potential use (including actual and expected or target figures) of the relevant internet-based media is necessary, as an increasingly relevant strategic competition factor.

The information about usage intensity varies (on the demand side) regarding user behaviour and changes in user preferences, and, (on the supplier side), regarding the extent to which the firm already uses different internet-based media. For example, in the area of procurement with online auctions or in the area of marketing communication services with banner, video, search engine and affiliate advertising, or to which internet-based media, could be beneficial in the future.

Given the wide range of possible applications of this KPI, a generalized target for the value of indicators relating to "Usage intensity of internet-based media" is not definable. For orientation and benchmarking, internal comparisons (such as between different organizational units or actuals over time, or budget-actual comparisons) and corresponding external comparisons (such as branch-specific average values for the "best-practice" values), may be used as a guide.

In light of a very large number of generally accessible publications from a variety of sources on projected development, the methodical approach needs to be checked for validity, particularly in the case of results that are determined from surveys (e.g. on user behaviour). In order to facilitate major management decisions, it is desirable to draw upon a reliable and dependable database.

**!** **Useful Suggestions**

The practical multidimensional nature of the internet-based economy, as well as its growing influence on existing companies and their (electronically supported) business processes, offers numerous possibilities for activity-areas. The following are listed here as representative examples: eEducation, eEntertainment, eManufacturing, eShoping and eHealth.

Generally speaking, with regard to the corporate sustainability goals for economic benefits, social acceptance, and ecological viability, the range of services offered by a firm need to be designed more efficiently and be more customer-friendly.

With the possibility of using internet-based media, the focus lies in the choice of alternatives used for the digital processing of information, communication and transactions and the potential usage intensity of the alternatives.

Before executing the company specific strategies and programs for "management by internet", a systematized classification of the appropriate fields of activity can contribute to easier decision-making:

- type of participants (A – Administration; B – Business; C – Consumer) and the exchange of services (B2B, A2B, B2C, etc.) that result from a form of interaction pattern from the respective combination of provider or recipient positions. This could also apply to usage-intensity of internet-based media within one company, e.g. in the "intra business"
- type of business model (content, commerce, context, connection or rather eBusiness vs. mBusiness, where the latter indicates the merger of the Internet and mobile communication), and
- type of social media tools (e.g. blogs, wikis, social networking, application portals).

### Related Ratios/Additional Notes &

The peculiarities of the KPI "Usage intensity of internet-based media" can be combined in its absolute or relative versions depending on the chosen internet-based media, customer segment or functional area with various other controlling performance indicators, in order to obtain relevant information for any management decisions (e.g. Compound Annual Growth Rate (CAGR), Cost and Revenue Structure related, Contribution Margin KPIs, etc.)

### 3.2.5 Cost per Thousand

### Analytical Question ?

What is the cost of different communication media in relation to the realized number of contacts?

### Definition *

$$\frac{\text{Price of an Advertising Campaign} \cdot 1000}{\text{Number of Contacts (for example, as AdClicks)}}$$

Where:

The term AdClicks (Advertisement Clicks) implies the number of mouse-clicks on an advertising banner by an Internet user.

The Cost per Thousand (often referred to as CPM, where the letter M represents the Roman numeral for 1000) is measured in the unit of currency (for example in €).

## » Calculation/Derivation

The CPM can be taken from the media-data of the communication media. This data is made available in the Internet by various specialized market research institutes or directly by publishers, radio and television channels.

## # Interpretation and Typical Range

The CPM is a value measure for cost-based intra-media comparison in the framework of media planning. It shows how expensive a particular medium is for developing 1000 contacts. Thus, it might be more economical for a value-conscious firm to make a relatively more expensive advertisement in large national newspapers than to make several advertisements in cheaper regional newspaper. This is because the firm may be able to establish more media contacts with the same budget.

The CPM is always a positive amount, in the unit of currency in which it is applicable to a transaction. In inter-media comparison (for example, between television and newspaper), CPM can differ significantly. Thus, CPM should be considered additionally in intra-media comparisons (for example, which newspaper is cheaper). Thus, the lower the CPM, the better.

The Internet marketers also use CPM to price ad banners. Sites that sell advertising will guarantee an advertiser a certain number of impressions (number of times an ad banner is downloaded and presumably seen by visitors), then set a rate based on that guarantee, multiplied by the CPM rate. A Web site that has a CPM rate of $25 and, guarantees advertisers 600,000 impressions will charge $15,000 ($25 x 600) for an ad banner.

## ! Useful Suggestions

Since the use of communication media does not always fully correspond with the target group of the advertisement, it is desirable to use a weighted CPM. Thus, only such contacts that correspond with the target group are counted. The goal is to keep the "leakages" as low as possible. However, neither the weighted nor the simple CPM touches on the problems relating to advertising media contact probabilities and the quality of the contacts.

## & Related Ratios/Additional Notes

As a synonym for "Cost per Thousand", often a shorter version called "Thousand Price" is also used.

A measure closely related to CPM is called "Media Coverage".

### 3.2.6 Brand Awareness Level

**Analytical Question**  ?

What is the proportion of respondents who know an object (a product, a product group or a firm) or recognise it by its name, physical appearance or sound?

**Definition**  \*

$$\frac{\text{Number of Respondents, who know the Object} \cdot 100}{\text{Total Number of Respondents}}$$

The Brand Awareness Level is expressed as a percentage.

**Calculation/Derivation**  »

The required data for the purpose is usually drawn from market research through a survey, which is based on a representative sample of people. The persons interviewed should preferably be the potential clients. For example, in consumer goods markets, those consumers should be interviewed, who possess the purchasing power to buy the products.

There are two kinds of Brand Awareness Level:

– Unaided recall

In this case, the persons interviewed should name, without any help, the names of the products suited for a particular purpose; and

– Aided recall

Here persons interviewed receive a list of brand names, out of which they should name the products they know.

**Interpretation and Typical Range**  #

The Brand Awareness Level is a measure of its popularity. It indicates the so-called "conscious market share (share of mind)" and is a major indicator of the marketing communication policy; it is used to measure how efficient the advertising is.

The Brand Awareness Level is very significant for preference-oriented marketing strategies. The high profile of a brand is often understood as a prerequisite for the product image or acceptance. The product image or acceptance, in turn, is the prerequisite for the use or purchase of a product.

Theoretically, both the aided or unaided variants of this ratio could take a value anywhere between 0 % and 100 %. In the case of aided recall, however, the brand awareness is usually higher than in unaided recall; for major branded products, it is desirable to achieve an aided recall level of over 90 %, and unaided recall level of over 60 %.

**!** **Useful Suggestions**

Brand Awareness Level is the most tangible and easily measured ratio. It is also the most commonly used standard to determine the success of marketing efforts. Building brand awareness though, has become increasingly more challenging due to extensive media and market segmentation.

The interpretative power of this ratio, for developing precise marketing measures is derived from the following assumptions: the object (a product, a brand or a firm), under investigation, figures in the decision process of the potential customer only when the brand has sufficient acceptance and a positive image.

In practice, the threshold of the brand awareness level that is branch or product-specific is mostly defined with reference to empirical values. Below a particular threshold of brand awareness, the respondent has an incorrect association with the brand. When the level is above the threshold, the association of the product with the purpose is usually correct. To estimate the effects of the advertising campaigns, this information can be very valuable. In the case of lower brand awareness, the risk is that the respondents' association is incorrect, and any new advertising campaign could possibly lead to an association with another brand.

**&** **Related Ratios/Additional Notes**

The analysis of the Brand Awareness Level should be combined with other measures such as the customer coverage ratio and market penetration.

In highly competitive and saturated markets, brand acceptance and image is very important. However, brand awareness along with a good image may not be an indicator of brand success.

It is useful to check how far the brand awareness level translates into sales. If brand awareness is not transformed into sales, there is a need for a careful review for the reason(s) behind it.

## 3.3 Product Pricing

### 3.3.1 Profit Margin

**?** **Analytical Question**

- How much is the difference between the sales revenue and the costs? Or how much is the difference between gross margin and operating expenses, relating to a particular traded commodity (so-called absolute profit margin) or
- How big is the share of the absolute profit margin in the net sales price (termed as relative profit margin in the form of a mark down)? or
- How big is the share of the absolute profit margin in the acquisition price (the so-called relative profit margin in the form of a mark up)?

**Definition** ✱

Profit Margin (as an absolute variant):

> Net Sales Price (Gross sales price – rebates, discounts etc.)
> – Acquisition Price (Purchase price + acquisition or delivery costs)
> ─────
> = Gross Margin per Unit or per Period
> – Operating Expenses (for personnel, rent, energy, etc.)
> ─────
> = Profit Margin per Unit or per Period

Profit Margin (as a relative variant in the form of a profit mark down):

$$\frac{(\text{Gross Margin} - \text{Operating Expenses}) \cdot 100}{\text{Net Sales Price}}$$

Profit Margin (as a relative variant in the form of a profit mark up):

$$\frac{(\text{Gross Margin} - \text{Operating Expenses}) \cdot 100}{\text{Acquisition Price}}$$

The absolute profit margin is expressed in the form of monetary units (for example, in €) and the relative profit margin is expressed in %. It is important to note that the value added tax is not considered for calculating profit margin.

**Calculation/Derivation** »

The required data for calculating the profit margin of individual products or product groups (or further aggregated levels) is obtained from the detailed accounting and information system. The operating costs are computed from variable and fixed costs, and thus, make allocation of costs to different products or product-groups difficult.

**Interpretation and Typical Range** #

The Profit Margin is that part of the gross margin which covers the profit expectations of the firm.

The trade margin, as an absolute measure, is the branch-specific indicator for calculating the "contribution margin I" in those trading firms which use the direct costing method. The difference between unit sales price and unit variable costs should preferably be positive and, when added up for all the sold products for a specific period, should cover the fixed costs. If the periodic gross margin is above the fixed costs, a profit is created. Thus, the higher the periodic total for the gross margin, the quicker is the "over-compensation" for unchanged fixed costs, and the faster the creation of profit.

**!** **Useful Suggestions**

Along with the starting points for influencing the net sales price and the acquisition price, which should help in improving the gross margin, the concept of profit margin introduces operating expenses as a central factor influencing costs. The major cost-items for operating expenses are personnel costs, rent paid for space, transport costs, energy costs, depreciation and interest.

It is not just because of various information-technology supported instruments, which assist in coordination between suppliers and customers (in the form of upstream and downstream supply chains) that firms try to achieve a win-win situation for all participants in the supply chain.

For profit margins, a distinction is made between the expected profit margin (based on preliminary or standard costing) and the actual profit margin (based on final product costing). Such comparisons between expected and actual margins provide a hint concerning the achieved target levels. Depending upon the kind of reference base (net sales price or acquisition price), the relative profit margin can be a mark down or mark up.

**&** **Related Ratios/Additional Notes**

A common synonym for Profit Margin is "Operating Margin".

The absolute variant of profit margin is also known as "Net Margin" if a firm is using the full costing method, or "Contribution Margin" if the firm is using direct costing. Over and above the unit-based calculation, various aggregated reference points, such as product groups or business segments, can also be taken when calculating the profit margin.

**(S)** **3.3.2 Gross Margin**

**?** **Analytical Question**

- How much is the difference between the net sales price and the acquisition price for a traded commodity? (so-called Absolute Gross Margin) or
- How big is the share of the absolute gross margin in the net sales price (termed as relative gross margin in the form of a mark down)? or
- How big is the share of the absolute gross margin in the acquisition price (the so-called relative gross margin in the form of a mark up)?

**\*** **Definition**

Gross Margin (as an absolute variant):

|   | |
|---|---|
| | Net Sales Price (Gross sales price – rebates, discounts etc.) |
| – | Acquisition Price (Purchase price + acquisition or delivery costs) |
| = | Gross Margin per Unit or per Period |

Gross Margin (as a relative variant in the form of a mark down):

$$\frac{(\text{Net Sales Price} - \text{Acquisition Price}) \cdot 100}{\text{Net Sales Price}}$$

Gross Margin (as a relative variant in the form of a mark up):

$$\frac{(\text{Net Sales Price} - \text{Acquisition Price}) \cdot 100}{\text{Acquisition Price}}$$

The absolute gross margin is expressed in the form of monetary units (for example, in €) and the relative gross margin is expressed in %. It is important to note that value added tax is not considered in calculating the gross margin.

## Calculation/Derivation

The required data for calculating the gross margin of individual products or product groups (or further aggregated levels) is obtained from the detailed accounting and information system.

## Interpretation and Typical Range

The Gross Margin, as an absolute measure, is the branch-specific indicator for calculating contribution margin I in those trading firms which use the direct costing method.

The difference between unit sales price and unit variable costs should preferably be positive and, when added up for all the sold products for a specific period, should cover the fixed costs. If the periodic gross margin is above the fixed costs, a profit is created. Thus, the higher the gross margin periodic total, the quicker the "over-compensation" of unchanged fixed costs, and the faster the creation of profit.

## Useful Suggestions

The Gross Margin shows the computed value of how the bridging or transformation role of trade between a supplier and customer is rewarded.

Along with the efforts of the trading firm to increase the per unit gross margin, it has to consider the product range related economies of scope (both factual and seasonal), which often lead to a compensatory pricing policy.

With reference to the gross margin, a distinction is made between the expected gross margin (based on preliminary or standard costing) and actual gross margin (based on final product costing). Such comparisons between the expected and actual gross margin provide a hint as to the achieved levels for planned targets. Depending upon the kind of reference base (net sales price or acquisition price), the relative gross margin can be a mark down or mark up.

The Gross Margin (unit based or period based) is considered to be a major performance indicator for trading firms. Over and above its internal use in evaluating the performance of individual sales offices, branches etc., it is used as an important benchmark in comparing the gross margin of product groups or inter-firm comparisons within a branch.

## & Related Ratios/Additional Notes

The absolute variant of Gross Margin is also known as "Trade Margin" or "Unit Margin".

A very common synonym for acquisition price is the "Cost of Purchase".

The Gross Margin should not be confused with the term "Profit Margin", which is calculated by subtracting the operational costs (such as rent, energy and personnel costs) of the trading company.

### 3.3.3 Absolute Contribution Margin

## ? Analytical Question

By what amount does the price of a product or service exceed the per unit direct variable costs? Or, by what amount does the sales revenue, of a product or service, exceed the direct variable costs attributable to the quantity sold in a period?

## * Definition

Unit-based Perspective:

Contribution Margin per Unit = Sales Price per Unit – Direct Variable Costs per Unit

Time-based Perspective:

Contribution Margin per Period = Total Sales per Period
   – Direct Variable Costs relating to Goods sold in that Period

The Absolute Contribution Margin is expressed in currency units (such as in €).

## » Calculation/Derivation

To obtain the needed data, the direct or marginal costing system is required, which systematically classifies costs into variable and fixed components (activity-based classification) and direct and indirect components (object-based classification) in the category of marginal costing.

In activity-based classification, a distinction is made between quantity-dependent (variable) and quantity-independent (fixed) costs. In object-based classification, the distinction is drawn between costs directly attributable (prime) to the object, and overhead costs indirectly assigned to it.

## Interpretation and Typical Range                                    #

As the name suggests, contribution margin is a monetary indicator and is supposed to contribute towards covering another cost component. The difference between the unit price and the unit variable costs leads to the unit contribution margin that should preferably be positive. The sum total of the contribution margin of all sold items should cover the total fixed costs. If the total contribution margin is more than the total fixed costs, the emerging difference is called profit.

The contribution margin is a short-term, single-period performance measure: the greater the contribution margin, the quicker it is (in terms of time) to cover fixed costs and generate profits.

In order to obtain detailed information, the internal cost accounting is often organized to calculate multi-stage contribution margins. The total fixed costs are split into different levels with reference to where they arise (for example, product groups, departments, divisions or firm). This helps in avoiding the problems related to the full costing method, where the (fixed) overheads are allocated on the basis of some discretionary allocation-keys, or proportionately.

Depending upon the reference parameters adopted by a company, there could be various aggregation stages for splitting the fixed costs: for example, product-based: product type or group; region-based: sales area, country, or continent; client-based: Individual orders, customer, or customer segment. The contribution Margin (CM) calculated at each aggregation stage is often mentioned using the abbreviation CM I, II, III, IV and so on. The details about contribution margin at each stage should be clearly checked, since there are no specified definitions for each stage.

The contribution margin, which is shown here as an absolute value, can be used to obtain further insights; for example, for fixing the lowest price limit or for reshuffling the product range. For this purpose, other relevant factors need to be included in the analysis. (For details refer to other indicators, such as percentage contribution margin, contribution margin for each reference parameter, etc.)

## Useful Suggestions                                                   !

As the name suggests, the contribution margin represents a margin value. In the first step, unit price and variable costs are the two components which could be analysed for manoeuvring: unit price should be analysed with reference to whether it can be increased without ignoring the price-elasticity of demand. Costs should be analysed with reference to input factors, such as whether the costs could be reduced through lower input consumption or through cheaper procurement.

In the second move, in the step-wise calculation of the contribution margin, the fixed costs have to be assigned carefully to each stage. This can provide increased transparency and help in taking targeted action, towards reducing fixed costs and increasing the contribution margin at each stage.

**& Related Ratios/Additional Notes**

As a synonym for the Absolute Contribution Margin, the gross operating margin per unit is also used. Along with the absolute contribution margin, the percentage contribution margin and the contribution margin for each reference parameter should be considered.

By contrast with contribution margin, the "Net Profit per Unit" is often shown as the difference between price per unit and total cost per unit. However, in this case, a typical problem for full costing crops up. In the full-costing system, the fixed costs are assigned to the products or services proportionately.

As part of the breakeven analysis, the graphic presentation of the fixed costs, variable costs and contribution margin can provide visual information about the quantity at which the breakeven point is reached.

### 3.3.4 Percentage Contribution Margin

**? Analytical Question**

How profitable is a particular product or service? Or what is the percentage of the contribution margin in the unit price?

**\* Definition**

$$\frac{\text{Contribution Margin per Unit} \cdot 100}{\text{Unit Price}}$$

Where:
Contribution Margin per Unit = Sales Price per Unit – Direct Variable Costs per Unit

As the name suggests, this relative contribution margin is expressed as a percentage (%).

**» Calculation/Derivation**

To obtain the needed data, the use of the direct or marginal costing system is a prerequisite, which systematically classifies costs into variable and fixed components.

**# Interpretation and Typical Range**

The unit-based Percentage Contribution Margin is a short-term, single period performance measurement. The higher the percentage of the contribution margin in the unit price that is not consumed by variable costs, the more profitable a product or service is. It is a particularly important decision criterion for short-term product range optimization. Thus, the higher the Percentage Contribution Margin, the more attractive the offered individual product or service.

## Useful Suggestions

As the name suggests, the contribution margin represents a margin value. In the first step, unit price and variable costs are the two components which could be analysed for manoeuvring: unit price should be analysed with reference to whether it can be increased without ignoring the price-elasticity of demand. Costs should be analysed with reference to input factors, such as whether the costs could be reduced through lower input consumption or through cheaper procurement.

In general, a change in this ratio could be triggered by a disproportionate increase or decrease in the contribution margin (as numerator) and in the unit price (as denominator). *For further details and systematic explanations on this, refer to the information in Appendix I.*

## Related Ratios/Additional Notes

As a synonym for Percentage Contribution Margin, sometimes Contribution Margin Intensity is used. Another possible synonym is Percentage Gross Margin.

When the total contribution margin is compared with the net sales revenue, it is called contribution margin factor and is calculated as follows:

$$\frac{\text{Total Contribution Margin of a Product} \cdot 100}{\text{Total Net Sales}}$$

Where:
Net Sales = Gross Sales
       − Sales Returns
       + Allowances for Damaged or Lost Goods
       + Discounts Allowed

Along with the percentage contribution margin, the absolute contribution margin and the contribution margin has to be considered for each reference parameter.

### 3.3.5 Price Reduction Rate

**?** **Analytical Question**

How much is the average price reduction on the catalogue price, which the firm has offered in the form of rebates, bonuses and discounts?

**\*** **Definition**

$$\frac{\text{Sum Total of all Price Reductions} \cdot 100}{\text{Sales}}$$

The Price Reduction Rate is expressed in %.

**»** **Calculation/Derivation**

The required data for the volume of price reduction granted (numerator) and sales before price reduction (denominator) is obtained from the detailed internal accounting and information system. The information could be collected for each of the reference objects (products, customers and market segments) and for each reference subject (sales representative and sales person).

**#** **Interpretation and Typical Range**

The ratio Price Reduction Rate is an important measurement for judging whether the firm was successful in obtaining its catalogue price or whether the increase in sales volume was achieved by a disproportionate increase in the quantity sold (through price reduction).

In general, the average price reduction rate varies widely amongst different branches and customers. Therefore, it is difficult to provide a typical range. The Price Reduction Rate is often determined as part of the overall pricing policy adopted by the firm.

**!** **Useful Suggestions**

In the short-run, price reduction (through discounts and rebates) should be offered if the expected increase in sales provides an additional contribution margin. However, in the long-run, such a pricing policy should not lead to a sustained fall in price, creating a burden of a steady fall in profits. If the sales force is oriented towards a Price Reduction Policy, which does not lead to any improvement of the contribution margin, this may imply an expensive way of obtaining additional sales.

**&** **Related Ratios/Additional Notes**

"Sales-Deductions Rate" is often used as a synonym for the Price Reduction Rate.

The ratio "Rebate Rate" is but one part of the overall Price Reduction Rate. If the firm offers only price rebates and none or insignificant discounts or bonuses, then the rebate rate would be equal to the price reduction rate.

For further analysis of the offered price reduction, detailed ratios for each kind of rebate offered (such as quantity-based rebate, anniversary rebates, special rebates, etc.) can be computed.

### 3.3.6 Price Elasticity of Demand (PEoD)

**Analytical Question**

How sensitive is the demand change (measured in %) for a product or service to a price change (measured in %)?

**Definition**

$$\frac{\text{Relative Change in Quantity Demanded (in \%)}}{\text{Relative Change in Price (in \%)}}$$

The result of this measure is expressed in absolute numbers and does not have to be in whole numbers. The price elasticity, for example, could be 1.4.

**Calculation/Derivation**

To determine the empirical relationship between price (the independent variable) and demand (dependent variable), usually regression analysis is carried out. However, it is often difficult to establish this relationship precisely, because the price cannot be changed arbitrarily without causing serious loss in sales. An alternative instrument for collecting data on demand elasticity is to apply Conjoint Measurement Analysis.

**Interpretation and Typical Range**

The Price Elasticity of Demand (PEoD) sheds light on the impact of a percentage change in price on the quantity demanded. Thus, it is a measure used to find out the volume of demand change as a consequence of price-change decisions in the pricing policy of the firm.

As a rule, the PEoD is negative, meaning that buyers' reaction to a price increase is usually in the form of reduced demand and vice-versa. A price elasticity of -2 for example means that a 1% increase in price would lead to a 2% fall in the quantity demanded.

The price elasticity varies widely, depending upon the nature of the product or service. Products in the category of necessities have a PEoD (sometimes, perfectly inelastic) close to zero. The PEoD for substitute products is usually high (negative).

The price elasticity is often expressed in absolute numbers, so that three variations of PEoD are as follows:

1. A PEoD > 1 implies that the demand is sensitive to price changes; hence an increase of price leads to a more than proportional fall in total revenue (Elastic Demand).
2. A PEoD = 1 means the % change in demand is equal to % change in price; hence when the price is raised, the total revenue remains unchanged.
3. A PEoD between 0 and < 1 implies that the demand is insensitive to price changes; thus, when the price is raised, the total revenue rises more than proportionately (Inelastic Demand).

**! Useful Suggestions**

Often, PEoD is not linear. Instead it has a 3-phased correlation: A relatively highly elastic steep phase, a price-inelastic middle phase, and a relatively flat price-elastic end phase.

The following determinants have a tendency to influence the PEoD: availability of substitutes, proportion of income required to satisfy the need, permanence of price changes, the absolute level of price, degree of luxury or necessity, and time period considered.

**& Related Ratios/Additional Notes**

Sometimes, firms calculate "Cross Price Elasticity of Demand". In this case, the purpose is to find out the change in demand of product A (with unchanged prices) because of the change in the price of another product B:

$$\frac{\text{Relative Change in the Quantity Demand of Product A}}{\text{Relative Change in the Price of Product B}}$$

Income Elasticity of Demand:

This measure indicates the change in demand of a product (with unchanged prices) for a change in income.

$$\frac{\text{Relative Change in the Quantity Demand of a Product}}{\text{Relative Change in the Income of the Consumer}}$$

# 3.4 Cost-Profit-Volume Analysis

### 3.4.1 Breakeven Point (BEP)

**Analytical Question**

At what level of sales volume is the firm *just* able to cover its total costs? After what level of sales volume is the firm able to generate profit from its produced goods or services?

**Definition**

$$\frac{\text{Fixed Periodic Costs}}{\text{Contribution Margin per Unit}}$$

Where: Contribution Margin per Unit = Sales price per unit – Variable costs per unit

The Breakeven Point is measured and expressed in units of quantity (units of production, length, area, volume, weight and time).

**Calculation/Derivation**

To obtain the needed data to calculate BEP, the use of the direct or marginal costing system is required, which systematically classifies costs into variable and fixed components.

**Interpretation and Typical Range**

The BEP is the main ratio in the cost-profit-volume analysis. It helps in calculating the sales volume which should be achieved to cover all the costs or after which the product or service can start earning a profit. Depending upon total fixed costs on the one hand, and variable costs and sales price per unit on the other, the BEP can be achieved with under-utilized capacity or, in unfavourable situations, above the capacity limits.

It is desirable for a firm to cover its fixed costs as early as possible, in order to breakeven with normal capacity utilization.

**Useful Suggestions**

The instrument of Breakeven Point is part of the cost-profit-volume analysis. Although the basic version of BEP is strongly constrained by assumptions (for example, one product model or static costs), in practice, it is still intensively used because of its clarity in a short-term perspective.

The short-term time horizon for direct (or marginal costing) and the basic version of breakeven analysis allows only a limited spectrum of measures. Thus, there are only 3 parameters in the definition of BEP (price per unit and variable costs per unit which help in calculating the contribution margin per unit, and the fixed periodic costs) that can be manoeuvred. Through combined efforts in the pricing policy on the one hand, and cost management (by reducing variable costs per unit and sometimes total fixed costs) on the other, a firm can achieve a reduction of its BEP.

If this ratio is used as a decision factor for introducing a new product, it is important to consider only those fixed costs which relate to this new product/project and to include the likely change of sales price and the variable costs per unit.

A change in this ratio could be triggered by a disproportionate increase or decrease in fixed periodic costs (as numerator) and in the contribution margin per unit (as denominator). *For further details and systematic explanations on this, refer to the information in Appendix I.*

### & Related Ratios/Additional Notes

A synonym for BEP is Breakeven Sales or Cost-Volume-Profit (CVP) analysis.

The BEP belongs to the category of breakeven analysis. The other ratios in this category are Margin of Safety (measured in currency units), Margin of Safety Factor (measured in %) and Customer Significance Level. If these ratios/indicators are linked together with individual products, product groups or specific market segments, they offer significant insights into the short-term success or risk involved in the object under review.

When one or more input value changes, various interesting questions about the sensitivity of profit can be reviewed with the help of the "critical value" method or sensitivity analysis.

### 3.4.2 Margin of Safety

### ? Analytical Question

- How much decline in sales revenue would bring the firm to breakeven point, where profits are equal to zero?
- How far is a percentage decline in sales (or sales volume) tolerable (without incurring losses) for the firm?

### * Definition

|  Sales Revenue (Budgeted or Actual Values) |
| − Sales Revenue (Breakeven Sales) |
| = Margin of Safety |

The Margin of Safety is usually measured in monetary units (for example, in €) and also in units.

## Calculation/Derivation

To obtain the needed data to calculate the Margin of Safety, the use of the direct or marginal costing system is required which systematically classifies costs into variable and fixed components.

## Interpretation and Typical Range

The Margin of Safety is a measure of short-term immunity or security. It projects the absolute (quantity or value-based) amount of the safety margin which is available to a firm in the event of declining sales volumes, without going into the red. Thus, the higher the percentage value of the margin of safety, the further is the firm from its breakeven point (BEP) and consequently, better protected is its position (in terms of profits).

## Useful Suggestions

The instrument of the Margin of Safety is part of breakeven analysis. Although the basic version of breakeven analysis is strongly constrained by assumptions (for example, one product model or static costs), it is still intensively used in practice, because of its clarity in a short-term perspective.

The short-term time horizon for direct (or marginal) costing, and the basic version of breakeven analysis, allow only a limited spectrum of measures. Thus, there are only 3 parameters in the breakeven analysis that can be manoeuvred (price per unit, variable costs per unit which helps in calculating the contribution margin per unit and the fixed periodic costs). Through a combined effort in price policy on the one hand, and cost management (by reducing variable costs per unit and sometime total fixed costs) on the other, a firm can deduce the breakeven sales and, thus, stabilize or improve its margin of safety.

## Related Ratios/Additional Notes

The term Safety Margin is often used as a synonym for this ratio.

The Margin of Safety belongs to the category of breakeven analysis. The other ratios in this category are: Breakeven Point (BEP), Margin of Safety Factor, Customer Significance Level and the Cash Point. If these ratios/indicators are linked together with individual products, product groups or specific market segments, they offer significant insights into the short-term success, or risk, involved in the object under review.

The relative margin of safety, referred to as the margin of safety factor, provides the same explanation, though expressed as a percentage:

$$\left(1 - \frac{\text{Fixed Periodic Costs}}{\text{Periodic Contribution Margin}}\right) \cdot 100$$

When a scenario of declining sales is considered, with individual customers as a reference factor, a similar relative indicator, called the customer-significance-factor can also be calculated.

### 3.4.3 Margin of Safety Factor

**? Analytical Question**

What percentage in drop in sales brings the firm to the breakeven point, where profits are equal to zero?

What percentage decline in sales (or sales volume) is tolerable (without incurring losses) for the firm?

**✳ Definition**

$$\left(1 - \frac{\text{Fixed Periodic Costs}}{\text{Periodic Contribution Margin}}\right) \cdot 100$$

The Margin of Safety Factor is expressed as a percentage.

**» Calculation/Derivation**

To obtain the needed data to calculate the margin of safety factor, the use of the direct or marginal costing system is required, which systematically classifies costs into variable and fixed components.

**# Interpretation and Typical Range**

The Margin of Safety Factor is a measure of short-term immunity or security. It gives a projection for the percentage safety margin which is available to a firm in the event of declining sales volumes without going into the red. Thus, the higher the percentage value of the margin of safety, the further is the firm from its breakeven point (BEP) and consequently, the better protected is its position (in terms of profit).

**! Useful Suggestions**

The instrument of the Margin of Safety Factor is part of breakeven analysis. Although the basic version of breakeven analysis is strongly constrained by assumptions (such as one product model or static costs), it is still intensively used in practice because of its clarity in a short-term perspective.

The short-term time horizon of direct (or marginal) costing and the basic version of breakeven analysis allow only a limited spectrum of measures. Thus, there are only 3 parameters in the breakeven analysis (price per unit and variable costs per unit which help in calculating the contribution margin per unit, and the fixed periodic costs) that can be manoeuvred. Through a combined effort of price policy on the one hand and cost management (by reducing variable costs per unit and sometime total fixed costs) on the other, a firm can improve its margin of safety.

If this ratio is used as a decision factor for introducing a new product, it is important to consider only those fixed costs which relate to this new product/project and to include likely changes in sales price and the variable costs per unit.

A change in this ratio could be triggered by a disproportionate increase or decrease in fixed periodic costs (as numerator) and in the periodic contribution margin (as denominator). *For further details and systematic explanations on this, refer to the information in Appendix I.*

**Related Ratios/Additional Notes**                                                   &

Various terms, such as Safety Margin Factor or Factor of Safety Margin, are used as synonyms for this ratio.

The margin of safety factor belongs to the category of breakeven analysis. The other ratios in this category are: Breakeven Point (BEP), Safety Margin, Customer Significance Level and the Cash Point. If these ratios/indicators are linked together with individual products, product groups or specific market segments, they offer significant insights into the short-term success or risk involved in the object under review.

The absolute volume of the margin of safety (a measure of safety with the same name) provides the same explanation, though expressed in currency units.

When individual customers are taken as a reference factor, customer-significance-factor can also be calculated.

### 3.4.4  Cash Point

**Analytical Question**                                                               ?

At what level of sales volume is the cash received from sales able to cover all expenses and costs which involve a payment?

**Definition**                                                                        *

$$\frac{\text{Fixed Periodic Costs involving Cash Outflow}}{\text{Contribution Margin per Unit}}$$

Where:
Contribution Margin per Unit = Sales Price per Unit – Direct Variable Costs per Unit

The Cash Point is measured and expressed in units of quantity (units of production, length, area, volume, weight and time).

## » Calculation/Derivation

To obtain the needed data to calculate the cash point, a direct or marginal costing system is required which systematically classifies costs into variable and fixed components.

Depreciation is one of the most important expense items that are excluded from the numerator while calculating the fixed periodic costs involving cash outflows.

## # Interpretation and Typical Range

The Cash Point is one of the ratios in the cost-profit-volume analysis. It represents a measure of short-term liquidity risk, and refers to a special breakeven point (an output *or sales* volume), which must be achieved for covering all fixed expenses and costs, involving cash outflows. When this special breakeven point is achieved, the company does not need additional financial resources from other business divisions or external sources. In particular, during crisis situations, when the demand is lower (with consequent underutilized capacities) and liquidity is falling, cash point becomes an important operational threshold value.

The lower the threshold quantity, and the higher the positive variance to the sales quantity, the lower is the expected exposure of the firm to liquidity situation.

In general, it is desirable for a firm to cover its fixed costs as early as possible in order to breakeven, and to improve its overall profit.

## ! Useful Suggestions

The instrument by which cash point can be calculated, is part of breakeven analysis. Although the basic version of BEP and Cash Point is strongly constrained by assumptions (for example static and one product model), it is still intensively used in practice because of its clarity in a short-term perspective.

The short-term time horizon of direct (or marginal) costing and the basic version of breakeven analysis, allow only a limited spectrum of measures. Thus, there are only 3 parameters in the definition of cash point that can be manoeuvred (price per unit and variable costs per unit which help in calculating the contribution margin per unit, and the cash outflow related fixed periodic costs). Through combined efforts of price policy on the one hand, and cash flow related cost management (by reducing variable costs per unit and sometime total fixed costs) on the other, a firm can achieve a reduction of its cash point.

If this ratio is used as a decision factor for introducing a new product, it is important to consider only the cash impact of those fixed costs which relate to this new product/project and to include the likely change in sales price and the variable costs per unit.

A change in this ratio could be triggered by a disproportionate increase or decrease in cash outflow related periodic fixed costs (as numerator) and in contribution margin per unit (as denominator). *For further details and systematic explanations on this, refer to the information in Appendix I.*

## Related Ratios/Additional Notes

Two related ratios in this family for cash point are Breakeven Sales or Cost-Volume-Profit (CVP) analysis.

The Cash Point belongs to the category of breakeven analysis. The other ratios in this category are Breakeven Point, Safety Margin (measured in currency units), Safety Margin Factor (measured in %), and Customer Significance Level. If these ratios/indicators are linked together with individual products, product groups or specific market segments, they offer significant insight into the short-term success or risk involved in the object under review.

## 3.5 Market Coverage Indicators

### 3.5.1 Internationalization Level

### Analytical Question

- What is the scale of a firm's involvement in foreign markets?
- To what extent has a firm diversified its business opportunities and risks in different regions?
- What is the magnitude of a firm's activities in more than one country?

### Definition

$$\frac{\text{Size of Different Stock or Flow Volumes Abroad}}{\text{Total of Different Stock or Flow Volumes of the Whole Firm}}$$

The quotient shown above is also known as "Foreign to Total Operations (FTO) Ratio".

Typical stock volumes, which are economically relevant in this quotient, could be "Employees", "Number of Branches", "Assets", or "Equity Capital". Similarly, for flow volumes, the relevant variables could be "Sales", "(operating or net) Profits" or "expenditures/costs".

The Internationalization Level is expressed as a percentage since both numerator and denominator are in identical quantities or monetary units.

### Calculation/Derivation

The required data for this ratio could be obtained from the accounting department, or in certain cases, from the computer-based information and reporting system (such as, statistics and data banks) classified separately for each functional department, division, and/or country. For the external analysts, only a part of the needed information is directly available in the form of annual report or other voluntary publications of the firm.

In the case of stock volumes, typically end of the year or annual average values are taken. For the flow volumes, which per definition relate to a period, mostly annual values are utilized.

### # Interpretation and Typical Range

The "Internationalization Level" shows the relative magnitude of the economic connection of a firm with countries abroad. The linkage could be represented by a concrete attribute such as "Sales" or "Employees". The measurement of internationalization level could be based on varying indicators that are considered to be economically relevant and meaningful:

– *Stock-volume indicators*
   for example, number of employees, customers, suppliers, shareholders or number of affiliates, production locations or branches, asset-size or accumulated foreign direct investment.
– *Flow-volume indicators*
   for example, sales, expenditures/costs, profits, orders received, investments made over a period or value added.

Thus, there is no "single" measure for Internationalization Level. Instead, it is measurable in a variety of ways. The business value and relevance of each indicator should be viewed from the perspective of each company individually. Nevertheless, the stock-volume indicator of "asset-size" and flow-volume indicators of "sales" and "profits" are the most common measures of Internationalization Level.

It is not possible to suggest a general target for the desired level of internationalization. For orientation, particularly for individual business segments, the firm could make comparisons between budgeted and realized levels of internationalization. The branch-specific averages or "best-practice examples" could also be used as desired directions.

### ! Useful Suggestions

An ever-increasing number of firms, which participate in the internationalization process, continuously ask themselves the question about the level of their international involvement. They not only try to develop strategies towards a "better" or "optimum" internationalization level, but are also sensitive about how they can measure their international involvement.

In addition to the appropriate strategies and measures which individual departments have to implement, monitoring the internationalization level as an important quotient helps in detecting some basic problem issues:

- Domestic versus Foreign Domain.

  For example, whether the domestic base of the firm is treated as the "country-of-origin" or what would happen if the firm were to have two headquarters in the wake of fast external growth.
- Small Domestic Base.

  The ratio may be biased because the firms from small "countries of origin" could arithmetically achieve a higher internationalization level than the firms from large "countries of origin".
- Exchange Rate Fluctuations.

  If flow-volumes are used for estimating this ratio, the effects of exchange rate fluctuations could be of noticeable significance.
- Transfer Price Determination.

  When a firm draws on its balance sheet or income statement for stock or flow-volumes, it would have the possibility of using transfer pricing, depending upon the accounting standards used. So, transfer pricing could be applied to reduce the total tax liability of the firm.

The real-life experience and the results of research on the subject do not provide any empirically tested relationship between the individual indicators of internationalization level and the operational success of a firm. As a matter of fact, for a proper interpretation of this ratio, the position of the firm in the situational context of its markets and competition conditions has to be considered. Therefore, a comparison of this ratio over time, and with relevant (and potential) competitors, is more useful than a single period ratio.

On the one hand, this is good for recognizing own strengths and weaknesses and, on the other hand, helps in implementing concrete business strategies in terms of products offered, and regional markets covered. This, in turn, allows for targeted exploiting of the opportunities in growth-markets abroad, as well as spreading the risks through regional diversification.

**Related Ratios/Additional Notes**                                              &

As a synonym for the "Internationalization Level", "Foreign Operations Level" is used as a specific indicator.

A variant of "Internationalization Level" is the "Foreign to Domestic Operations (FDO) Ratio". In a specific example of this ratio, the numerator is the foreign market share and the denominator, the domestic market share. The resultant ratio shows a firm's position in two markets.

In the category of related indicators, we measure the "Internationalization Profile" and the "Internationalization Index". In the first case, an internationalization profile (with graphic support) could be created with the help of several indicators for the internationalization level. This could be compared, internally over time, or externally with other firms (in particular with competitors). In the case of

"Internationalization Index", a weighted average of various indicators for the internationalization level is calculated. A separate index for stock-volume indicators, and another for flow-volume indicators, or a combination of the two can be considered. However, this approach to the internationalization index is not standardized and its interpretation is not without problems.

### 3.5.2 Distribution Coverage Level

**?** **Analytical Question**

What is the density of market presence, for a given product or a brand, within a given market area?

**\*** **Definition**

Quantitative Variant:

$$\frac{\text{Number of Outlets which sell a Particular Product or Brand} \cdot 100}{\text{Total Number of Outlets which (are needed to) sell this Product Group}}$$

Value Variant:

$$\frac{\text{Sales Volume of Outlets which sell a Particular Product or Brand} \cdot 100}{\text{Sales Volume of all Outlets which (are needed to) sell this Product Group}}$$

The Distribution Coverage Level is expressed as a percentage.

**»** **Calculation/Derivation**

The required data for the distribution coverage (at least at the level of some product groups) is regularly collected in the framework of trade-panel research by various market research groups.

**#** **Interpretation and Typical Range**

The Distribution Coverage Level is a measure of the distribution channel policy adopted by a firm. It shows the market penetration of a product or a brand at the end consumer level. It is typically a classification ratio, where the numerator is a sub-set of the denominator.

The distribution coverage is an important prerequisite for the successful implementation of a brand in the market, particularly for branded products. This is because ubiquity (availability everywhere) for a product is viewed as a significant success factor. However, it is relevant to note that this ratio provides only a quantitative interpretation of the market presence. The qualitative aspects of market presence, which could reflect upon the special position in the market, are not shown in this ratio. In some cases, despite good market coverage, there can be a discrepancy between "listed items" and "items available in stock".

Basically, the higher this ratio, the better it is. Theoretically, this ratio could take a value anywhere between 0 % (no market presence) to 100 % (full ubiquity).

### Useful Suggestions

The ratio has to be interpreted with reference to the market coverage strategy followed by the firm: the strategy could range from exclusive distribution to selective distribution, and further to intensive distribution.

The market coverage strategy, based on this ratio, can help in evaluating and deciding the distribution (outlets) of a particular product. In this case, the market coverage would be the percentage of outlets where the product is available, compared with the number of possible outlets where the product could be available.

### Related Ratios/Additional Notes

If the markets in which the product is to be sold vary significantly in size, another ratio called "weighted distribution coverage" gains prominence. Through weighted distribution coverage, the size or the sales strength of the outlets is included in the analysis. Thus, a large consumer market carries a larger weight, because its sales volume is larger than that of other comparable markets. For example, a numerical distribution coverage level of 50 % and a weighted distribution coverage ratio of 75 % clearly hint at the market presence in large sales units.

If a particular product demands a special counselling service, which may be offered only in small specialty stores, the interpretation power of this ratio should be reviewed carefully.

Like other similar ratios, it is important to analyse this ratio in the context of relevant market conditions, if the ratio is used as the basis for operative and strategic decisions.

### 3.5.3 Customer Coverage Ratio

### Analytical Question

What percentage of the target group bought the product (or the brand) under consideration, during the survey period?

### Definition

$$\frac{\text{Number of Customers of the Particular Product or Brand} \cdot 100}{\text{Total Number of Customers in the Target Group}}$$

The Customer Coverage Ratio is expressed as a percentage.

## » Calculation/Derivation

The required data for this purpose is usually collected through market research, which is based on a representative sample of consumers. Various market research groups sometimes also collect the data through a consumer-panel survey.

## # Interpretation and Typical Range

The Customer Coverage Ratio is the basic target value in strategic market planning. The size of this ratio depends upon the level of competition as well as the number of substitutes available in the market. It is also dependent upon the duration of market-presence. The customer coverage ratio for newly introduced products is lower than that of products that have been available for a long-time. Therefore, mostly customer-accumulation over a period of time is considered useful.

Basically, the higher this ratio, the better it is. Theoretically, this ratio could take a value anywhere between 0 % (no market presence) to 100 % (monopoly). With customer coverage at 100 %, nearly everybody in the target group uses the product under consideration.

## ! Useful Suggestions

The Customer Coverage Ratio does not say anything about the frequency of purchases by the customer in the target group. All kinds of buyers are covered in the survey, independent of whether they are frequent or one-time buyers. Therefore, it is desirable that the customer coverage ratio is viewed in the context of buying-intensity, where the frequency of purchases and the quantity of each purchase could be included in the analysis. This can also help in making differential analysis of first-time and frequent-buyers.

## & Related Ratios/Additional Notes

A close synonym for the Customer Coverage Ratio is the Brand Coverage Ratio.

The concept of penetration is related to the measure of the customer coverage ratio. In market penetration, the focus is on customer accumulation in a particular brand in relation to the customer accumulation for the total product group.

### 3.5.4 Market Saturation Level

**Analytical Question**

What kind of growth potential does the market have? Has the sold quantity of the product reached a peak?

**Definition**

$$\frac{\text{Realized Market Volume} \cdot 100}{\text{Potential Size of the Market}}$$

The Market Saturation Level is expressed in percentage terms.

**Calculation/Derivation**

To calculate the Market Saturation Level, it is important to have approximate estimates for the market volume (sum total of all realized sales quantities) and the potential size (total saleable quantity) of the market. The market volume can be determined relatively precisely by adding up sales volumes for all vendors in the market. However, the experts can make the estimation of market potential, only through multi-staged forecasting methods and complex market research. The estimation of the potential size of the market can vary substantially, and would be subject to various economic growth related variables, changes in customer and user behaviour, fashion trends and other changes in the economic environment.

**Interpretation and Typical Range**

The Market Saturation Level, as the name suggests, indicates how far the market under consideration is already satiated. This ratio is of particular significance in the framework of market development strategies. A high saturation level (such as long-lasting consumer assets in industrially developed countries) implies that, over and above normal replacement demand, there is very little growth potential in the market. Thus, the growth potential for individual sellers can only come through (price-based and margin-cutting) displacement of competitors.

Basically, the ratio can be between 0 and 100 %; the lower the ratio, the more attractive is the market and the higher is the potential for selling in this market.

**Useful Suggestions**

The Market Saturation Level should not be used in isolation to judge the attractiveness of the market. The number of competitors in the market and the competitive pressures should also be considered in the analysis.

Even if a market has a lower saturation level, its development may be gripped by strong price competition and, therefore, may not be very promising from the point of view of profitability.

It should also be noted that the saturation level of the whole market may differ from the saturation level of its segments. Thus, within the cosmetic branch, the male and female market segments should be analysed separately.

**& Related Ratios/Additional Notes**
Business practices have shown many examples in all branches, how innovative developments lead to the creation of new market segments. It is also possible to create new consumer demand through advertising and, thus, additional demand can help to delay the onset of market saturation. Good advertising campaigns can help to increase buying frequency or to reach new buyer segments which were not included in the forecast.

## 3.6 Market Position Indicators

### 3.6.1 Absolute Market Share

**? Analytical Question**
What is the market position of the firm (or a business unit) in terms of its share in the total relevant market?

**\* Definition**
Variant I (Value-Based Market Share):

$$\frac{\text{Total Sales of the Firm} \cdot 100}{\text{Total Sales of all Suppliers (or Bidders)}}$$

Variant II (Quantity-Based Market Share):

$$\frac{\text{Total Quantity Sold by the Firm} \cdot 100}{\text{Total Quantity Sold by all Suppliers (or Bidders)}}$$

The result of this measure in expressed as a percentage.

**» Calculation/Derivation**
The market share is calculated mostly through systematic market research, and it is usually the primary research (panel research). Sometimes, secondary research can also be used if the quantity and value related data is available for the product or the branch.

**# Interpretation and Typical Range**
The Absolute Market Share is significant in strategic and operative marketing and is used for planning business goals and action plans. It specifies the share of one firm

in the total turnover (value based) and volume (quantity based) of all suppliers in a market segment or branch. It is used as a measure of success, or as a symbol of the market position achieved by a firm or a product in a market.

In general, the higher the market share, the better it is. It is based on the assumption that, through economies of scale, a high market share helps in achieving a decisive (cost-oriented) competitive advantage. However, the impact of market share on profitability is not clear. Sometimes, firms with a small market share are able to achieve very high ROI as specialists.

Basically, the possible range of market share could be anywhere between 0 % (no participation in a market) to 100 % (monopoly position). To judge the market position of the firm, it is desirable to calculate both value and quantity-based market shares. Thus, a quantity-based market share of 25 % and a value-based market share of 18 % may hint at below-average sales revenue per unit of product sold.

## Useful Suggestions

The market share alone does not give sufficient information about the real competitive situation in the market (except of course in the case of a 100 % market share). For example, the ratio does not give information about the number of competitors, their strengths and weaknesses, and the market situation (growth potential or coverage perspective). Therefore, this indicator should be collected on a regular basis and should be placed in the overall category of competitors (in the category of so-called relative market share calculation). A comparison of the past market share of the firm, with present and forecasted developments in it, could provide a good base for analysis.

An increase of the market share through an aggressive pricing policy may be at the expense of the profitability and therefore, should be viewed as problematic. Such a policy may only be good when it helps in eliminating the competitors, which in turn may help the firm to achieve a higher profit margin later on. Similarly, a fall in the market share should not be seen as negative, if the profit levels can be maintained and resources are invested in growing or more profitable areas.

The market share should not necessarily be seen as an indicator of market power. If, for example, entry barriers are low and the rate of innovation is high, the firm with a high market share may not be able to market the product well above its marginal cost.

## Related Ratios/Additional Notes

It is often useful to calculate the Relative Market Share, which shows the relationship between one firm vis-à-vis the strongest firm in the market, or even the average of the 3 strongest in the market.

Ⓢ **3.6.2 Relative Market Share**

❓ **Analytical Question**

How is the firm or one of its (strategic) business unit positioned when compared with its competitors?

✳ **Definition**

The following two formulae for calculating market share can be used both for value-based and quantity-based calculations:

$$\frac{\text{Market Share of the Firm} \cdot 100}{\text{Market Share of the Strongest Firm in the Market}}$$

or

$$\frac{\text{Market Share of the Firm} \cdot 100}{\text{Average Market Share of the 3 Strongest Firms in the Market}}$$

The result of this measure in expressed in decimal numbers. Thus, a firm having a relative market share of 0.8, with reference to the strongest or the average of the 3 strongest competitors, has achieved 80 per cent of the benchmark.

» **Calculation/Derivation**

Market share is calculated mostly through systematic market research, and it is usually the primary research (panel research). Sometimes, secondary research can also be used if the quantity and value related data is available for the product or the branch.

\# **Interpretation and Typical Range**

Within the portfolio-planning framework for strategic management, the Relative Market Share is the main focus of analysis. In a 2x2 matrix of market share and growth portfolio, the relative market share shows how the firm under consideration is positioned vis-à-vis its competitors. It shows whether the firm has market leadership in a product segment.

When the relative market share ratio is above 1, the firm under consideration is the market leader; when it is below 1, the firm is a follower. Considering the past and forecasted values of the relative market share, its current value could provide interesting insight for strategic and operative management decisions (2 meaning that the firm is twice and 0.5 meaning the firm is half the size of the next strongest).

Some empirical studies have led to the finding that the experience-curve based cost advantages are distinctive and noticeable, in many cases, only beyond a relative market share of 1.5.

## Useful Suggestions !

The core idea of portfolio planning is that it is only in above-average growth markets, where the suppliers with a volume-based strong position, gain the advantage of the experience curve. Given this idea, it would be desirable for firms to seek a relative market share larger than 1 in those markets where the products are relatively homogeneous. Thus, market leadership position will reduce the unit production cost, offering an attractive margin and lastly high profitability.

## Related Ratios/Additional Notes &

Dividing the value-based market share by the quantity-based market share, the price level co-efficient can be calculated. For firms with a product differentiation strategy, the price level coefficient usually lies above 1. For a cost-leadership strategy, because of a below average price level, the price level coefficient usually lies below 1.

In the framework for the Profit Impact of Market Strategies (PIMS), one of the empirical studies (in which data of 2000 strategic business divisions has been collected and analysed for many years), revealed that the absolute and relative market share are two major success factors in achieving an above-average ROI and cash flow.

### 3.6.3 Bid Acceptance Rate

## Analytical Question ?

What is the percentage of bids which the customers confirm through an order?

## Definition *

$$\frac{\text{Number of Orders Received} \cdot 100}{\text{Number of Bids Made}}$$

The "Bid Acceptance Rate" is expressed as a percentage.

## Calculation/Derivation »

The required data for this quotient is derived from the information system (which is upstream of external accounting) for marketing, sales, or distribution departments. The information is compiled in sales statistics, customer and order databases. It might be useful to collect the information for various reference points, such as market segments, products, sales representative, customer-groups, etc.). Some large companies increasingly make use of a special controlling section called "Request-for-Quotation-Controlling".

## # Interpretation and Typical Range

The "Bid Acceptance Rate" is a ratio in the category of sales related measures. It is particularly important for firms which produce-to-order. It has its special relevance in the context of early warning and early diagnosis indicators. On the market side, a high bid acceptance rate implies that customers find the firm attractive in fulfilling their demand.

A time-series analysis of this ratio (increasing, stable or falling tendencies) should firstly be analysed internally with reference to various groupings, such as product, customer, and region-based analysis. Externally, it should be analysed with reference to general developments and the competition structure in the market. In a monopolistic market, the bid acceptance rate should in general be higher than in other markets.

However, the order volume does not give any immediate indication about the profit-potential of the orders received.

## ! Useful Suggestions

In addition to the number of orders (the numerical variant), the Bid Acceptance Rate should also be shown in monetary terms. This can help in analysing whether the firm primarily got small or large orders. Moreover, a series of other differentiations are possible; for example, what part of orders was based on bids made in trade-fairs, advertising campaigns or from enquiries.

Similarly, the unsuccessful bids and their rejection rate should be analysed. The knowledge derived from such analysis could help in improving the success rate of future projects.

As an early indicator in profit forecasting, it might be useful to calculate the profitability of the acquired orders (when needed, classified into major categories).

## & Related Ratios/Additional Notes

In order to make reliable comparisons over time, it would be good to supplement the contextual analysis with the help of market position indicators. Thus, for example, the Relative Market Share could be included in the analysis, to track the relative position of the firm.

# 3.7 Sales Efficiency Indicators

## 3.7.1 Sales per Reference Parameter

**Analytical Question**

How good is the economic yield of a particular input factor or reference parameter (measured in quantity) with respect to sales (measured in currency units)?

**Definition**

$$\frac{\text{Sales}}{\text{Total Quantity of Input Factor or Reference Parameter}}$$

As the quantity for the denominator, the total production volume, the total number of (production) employees, the number of clients, total length, total area, total weight, or total time span can be used as a reference parameter. For each of these parameters, the appropriate dimension of this ratio would be: € per unit of production, € per employee, € per customer, € per square metre, € per cubic metre, € per kg, € per foot, € per minute, € per hour, or € per year.

**Calculation/Derivation**

Most of the information needed for this ratio can be taken from cost and activity accounting. The information should be:
- Organized in detail with reference to cost-types, cost-centres, and cost-objects,
- supplemented with multi-stage sales-performance accounting, which could be further classified with reference to employees, customers, distribution channel, regions and orders reported to the responsible decision makers.

If the denominator in the ratio were the total quantity sold, the resultant figure would be the product price. However, if the denominator happens to be "time", the resultant number would act like a "wild card" and would separate the sales only into different time periods. Contrary to this, if the denominator is a production input factor, such as "human resource" or "sales area", the ratio would deliver a measure of input efficiency, which may be used as a planning and steering instrument.

**Interpretation and Typical Range**

Because of its ease of calculation, many firms use this ratio for steering and coordinating various business units within the firm. It is often used as an incentive system for deciding the compensation paid to employees.

A general target range for this ratio cannot be determined. For orientation and benchmarking, internal (such as the ratio in different organizational units or plan-actual values) or external comparisons (such as branch-specific average period or the "best-practice" value), may be used as a guide.

Assuming that comparable firms have a similar structure of products, processes or potentials, any variance from the average values provides a clear indication for serious review. These should help in analysing the positive and negative consequences and steer them in the context of corporate goals.

Through a comparison of the changing value of this ratio over time, a trend analysis can be carried out, which could show a converging or diverging trend. This helps in drawing inferences about an intended convergence to a better competitor, or a desired distancing from a bad comparative value.

### ! Useful Suggestions

Often, the ratios in the category of "Sales per Reference Parameter" are used as measures of efficiency. These are seen as target values for aligning the performance of various sub-parts of the business to overall business goals. Thus, in many cases a profitability measure dominates and a particular relationship between sales and profits is simply taken for granted, which does not always have to be true. In fact, such target values often lead to conflicting goals. For example, if the sales force of the firm is managed on the basis of sales volume and contribution margin is ignored, it often leads to less profitable decisions.

Thus, it is desirable to check whether the targets for sales per employee, sales per square metre, or even sales per client/order/region could (or should) preferably be replaced by stronger business targets, having a better alliance with result-oriented goals (for example, in the form of contribution margin per reference parameter).

A change in this ratio could be triggered by a disproportionate increase or decrease in sales (in numerator) and reference parameters (in denominator). *For further details and systematic explanations on this, refer to the information in Appendix I.*

### & Related Ratios/Additional Notes

Basically, "Sales per Reference Parameter" is an indicator similar to productivity, and is used, in practice, in a similar way to "Contribution Margin per Reference Parameter". It is sometimes explained under the heading "Efficiency".

## 3.7.2 Contribution Margin per Reference Parameter

**Analytical Question**

How much is the economic efficiency of a particular input factor or reference parameter (measured in quantity) with respect to its short-term performance? How much is the contribution margin per input or reference factor?

**Definition**

$$\frac{\text{Contribution Margin}}{\text{Quantity of Input Factor}}$$

As the quantity for the denominator, the total production volume, the total number of (production) employees, the number of clients, total length, area or volume, total weight, and total time span can be taken as a reference parameter.

For each of these parameters, the appropriate dimension of this ratio could be: € per unit of production, € per employee, € per customer, € per square metre, € per cubic metre, € per kg, € per foot, € per minute, € per hour, or € per year.

Some specific examples could be: the contribution margin per sales person, or per customer, the contribution margin per consultation hour or per customer visit, the contribution margin per order or per region.

**Calculation/Derivation**

Most of the information needed for this ratio can be taken from the cost and activity accounting, which has to be based on direct or marginal costing. The information should be:
- Organized in detail with reference to cost-types, cost-centres, and cost-objects,
- supplemented with multi-stage sales-performance accounting reported to the responsible decision makers.

**Interpretation and Typical Range**

For decisions extending into short-term horizons, an accounting system based on direct costing provides the relevant performance indicators. Often, the contribution margin is used as an incentive system for deciding on the compensation paid to employees.

Though the contribution margin has become very popular, it is not always interpreted correctly. Along with its known advantages, it is important to be aware of the main limitations of its interpretations which may be considered when using it (for example, the contribution margin is used by sales representatives as a negotiation range with clients, whereas it is important for covering the fixed costs).

In the following, it would be desirable to distinguish between some variants of the contribution margin per input factor:

- The contribution margin per sales object (product or service in the above mentioned quantities): In this case, we refer to "absolute contribution margin" per unit (refer to the details of the measure with this name).
- The contribution margin per input unit of a technical production factor (particularly machines, storage space, transport): In this case, we refer to a situation that is called a "bottleneck contribution margin" (refer to the details of the measure with this name).
- The contribution margin per employee (with human resource as a production factor): This so-called "per head" ratio is primarily used in sales and distribution related areas, such as contribution margin per sales person or per sales representative.
- The contribution margin per client-visit, per order, per client, per distribution channel, per branch, per region: In this case, the short-term performance is related to a special object, where the result is used for various purposes.

Whereas the first two of the variants are explained in the book, the following details will focus on the last two variants.

It is difficult to provide a generalized target for this ratio because of the heterogeneity of the business areas. As a typical range, internal benchmarks between and amongst various units in the firm or budget-actual comparison could be used. External benchmarks could be the average for the industry or the best-practice value.

Assuming that the comparable firms have a similar structure of products, processes or potentials, any variance from the average values provides important guidelines for influencing the negative or positive difference, depending upon corporate goals.

**❗ Useful Suggestions**

Irrespective of the reference factor, the contribution margin is a short-term, single-period performance measure. Effects (in respect to product- or customer life cycle with changing contribution margin) which extend over many periods, cannot be illustrated through this method. The same is true for all synergies in respect to product-range.

A decisive factor for the interpretive power of this ratio is the careful and precise assignment of the fixed costs (reference to customers, orders or branch fixed costs) in a multi-stage contribution margin system.

If the contribution margin is used for employee compensation plans, it is important to carefully integrate the above-mentioned aspects. Thus, based on low contribution margin, a customer may be ignored because the employee is more interested in maximizing his total contribution margin (for compensation purposes). However, it is likely that the business relationship with this customer is in the initial stages and the customer could have remarkable growth potential. This, unfortunately, cannot be captured by the contribution margin analysis and may have to be supplemented with other indicators, such as Customer Lifetime Value.

**Related Ratios/Additional Notes**                                          &

Basically, the Contribution Margin per Reference Parameter is an indicator similar to productivity and is used, in practice, as similar to "sales per reference parameter" and sometimes explained under the heading "efficiency".

Similar to other ratios, it is desirable to check the integral components of a particular parameter and whether the ratio, based on this parameter, would be of assistance in resolving the problem at hand.

### 3.7.3 Sales Space Productivity

**Analytical Question**                                                      ?

How efficiently is the (bottleneck of) sales area used?

**Definition**                                                               *

The terminology of sales space productivity is defined in two different variants: the sales-oriented variant (Type I) and the profit or contribution margin variant (Type II). The second one is often referred to as "sales space profitability".

Type I:

$$\frac{\text{Sales Volume}}{\text{Sales Area}}$$

Type II:

$$\frac{\text{Total Contribution Margin}}{\text{Sales Area}}$$

The Sales Space Productivity is expressed in the "currency units per square metre" (such as € per square metre).

**Calculation/Derivation**                                                   »

Through the use of modern materials management technologies, such as scanner-cash terminals, bar-coded product movements, detailed shelf-data and Radio Frequency Identification (RFID), it is possible to aggregate and analyse the required data (in the case of need, precisely for each item) in different ways.

**Interpretation and Typical Range**                                         #

The Sales Space Productivity is a typical ratio for evaluating the performance of the retail trading firms. It is a significant decision factor for the operational product display system. As a comparative measure for evaluating the efficiency of the area-under-use, other products (competing for space), other locations, and other competitors can also be taken. As a reference point, along with the total sales location, individual sales departments or product segments can also be taken.

The optimization for allocating the products to available (shelf) area should be analysed and interpreted with additional information about the value of various shelf levels. Thus, in retail trade, the so-called impulsively-purchased products are often displayed at eye level or in prominent areas. In contrast, the necessities are usually displayed at lower shelf levels. Similar display rules are applied to products which have higher or lower contribution margins.

### ❗ Useful Suggestions
With the help of computer-based shelf-optimization systems (so-called shelf-management systems), the layout and the optimum display-width (so-called facings) based on economic considerations can be determined. However, the technical aspects (for example, shelf heights), logistical aspects (for example, refill-frequency), and marketing aspects (for example, expected demand) should also be considered.

In general, a change in this ratio could be triggered by a disproportionate increase or decrease in the sales or contribution margin (as numerator) and sales space (as denominator). *For further details and systematic explanations on this, refer to the information in Appendix I.*

Since the space used for sales cannot be enlarged significantly at short-notice, the focus lies primarily in influencing the business results through measures relating to a better price or volume strategy on the sales side, and measures towards a more efficient use of the factors of production (other than sales space) on the expense side.

### & Related Ratios/Additional Notes
Often, the space-productivity is used without the word "sales". In such cases, when making inter-firm comparisons, special care should be taken in ensuring the clarity of terminology and definitions.

In Type II sales space productivity, other than "sales space profitability", sometimes "space earnings" is also used.

## 3.7.4 Capacity Coverage Ratio

**Analytical Question**  ?
Given the present orders, how long can the firm operate at full capacity?

**Definition**  *

$$\frac{\text{Orders at Hand (in €)} \cdot 360 \text{ Days}}{\text{Sales (in €) per Year}}$$

The Capacity Coverage Ratio is calculated in the units of time. The resultant quotient is expressed in days, when working with (as in the above formula) the 360 days factor, in weeks with the factor "52", and in months, when working with the factor "12".

**Calculation/Derivation**  »
The required data for this quotient is derived from the information system (which is upstream of external accounting) of marketing, sales, or distribution departments. The information is compiled in sales statistics, customer and order databases.

**Interpretation and Typical Range**  #
The Capacity Coverage Ratio is a combined ratio in the category of sales and production-related measures. It has its special relevance in the context of early warning and early diagnosis indicators. On the market side, a high capacity coverage ratio implies that customers find the firm attractive in fulfilling the demand. On the production side, a high ratio signals stability in the capacity utilization.

It is assumed for the sake of simplicity, that the volume of sales and capacity utilization are related proportionately. Out of an order volume at hand, for example, of €525,000 and an annual sales volume of €800,000, the derived capacity coverage is 7 months or 30.3 weeks, or 210 days, depending upon the time factor of "12", "52" or "360" respectively.

A general target for this ratio is not possible. For benchmarking, and for orientation purposes, the branch-specific average values could be taken or the "best-practice" value, if published information is available. One could also check the demand-fluctuation-rate in the industry, to find out whether the firm is strong or weak when compared to the rest of the market. The smaller the ratio value, the thinner is the so-called "order-cover" and the bigger is the danger that production capacities will be under-utilized or that the production may even have to stop.

However, the order volume does not give any immediate indication about the profit-potential of the orders received.

**!** **Useful Suggestions**

A time-series analysis of this ratio (increasing, stable or falling tendencies) should firstly be analysed internally with reference to various groupings, such as a product, customer, and region-based analysis. Externally, it should be analysed with reference to the general developments and the competition structure in the market.

Thus, in a highly competitive environment and in times of weaker growth, orders can often only be obtained through price-concessions. In such situations, the volume and value are not proportionate.

On the other hand, comparably longer delivery lead-times could lead to loss of orders. Keeping in mind the special branch-specific competition and customer conditions, the management should focus its attention on stable profit developments.

**&** **Related Ratios/Additional Notes**

Continuous updating of the product and service programs (with customer-oriented innovations), high quality and reliable delivery timing are some of the major factors which contribute to the strengthening of the market position and ensure stable customer demand.

The name "Capacity Coverage Ratio" hints a strong production-oriented perspective for this ratio. From a marketing perspective, the ratio is called "Order Range Ratio".

### 3.7.5 Book-to-Bill Ratio

**?** **Analytical Question**

What is the ratio between the current periodic incoming orders, and the current periodic sales? Or, when compared with current sales, whether the incoming orders are rising or falling?

**\*** **Definition**

$$\frac{\text{Incoming Orders for a Period} \cdot 100}{\text{Sales for a Period}}$$

As a matter of rule, internally, most companies choose a month as the reference period. However, for external reporting, annual numbers are more common. The Book-to-Bill Ratio is expressed in percentage.

**»** **Calculation/Derivation**

The required data for this quotient is derived from the information system (which is upstream of the external accounting) of marketing, sales, or distribution departments. The information is compiled in sales statistics, customer and order databases.

**Interpretation and Typical Range**

The Book-to-Bill Ratio is of special relevance in the context of early warning and early diagnosis indicators. It provides a base for future demand, which is allocated to the firm under consideration.

In order to maintain current sales (as a comparison base), the value of this ratio should be noticeably above 100 % of current sales to offset the (branch-specific volume of) order-cancellations. A ratio well above 100 % could also be an indicator of the fact that the firm has more orders than its installed capacity for a period. Assuming that all customers may not accept delays, it may eventually mean that the firm has to expand its capacity to meet increased demand.

**Useful Suggestions**

Usually, seasonal fluctuations (which can be statistically corrected) should be considered in interpreting this ratio. The fundamental changes in the ordering behaviour (preference for ordering at short-notice) should also be included in the analysis.

Depending upon the usual branch-specific peculiarities, arrangements such as annual supply agreements or target-costing based quotations (with discount offers for early-ordering) may be used to ensure stable order book (and regular capacity utilization) without neglecting a reasonable profit margin.

**Related Ratios/Additional Notes**

To get a detailed insight into the firm's developments, it may be useful to combine the Book-to-Bill Ratio together with the Capacity Coverage Ratio, the Breakeven Point and the Margin of Safety Factor.

In the framework for external reporting, sometimes only the percentage change in the book-to-bill ratio is reported.

### 3.7.6 Finished Goods Turnover Period

**Analytical Question**

In which time span is the finished goods inventory replaced once? Or, for how long will the inventory holding of finished goods last on average?

**Definition**

Variant A (Based on Sales Price)
with n = 30, 60, 90 and so forth, depending upon period length:

$$\frac{\text{Average Inventory of Finished Goods (Valued at Sales Price)} \cdot \text{n Days}}{\text{Gross Sales of the Period under Consideration}}$$

Variant B (Based on Production Costs)
with n = 30, 60, 90 and so forth, depending upon period length:

$$\frac{\text{Average Inventory of Finished Goods (Valued at Production Costs)} \cdot \text{n Days}}{\text{Production Costs of Gross Sales of the Period under Consideration}}$$

The ratio is expressed in terms of number of days. Thus, with a stock of 50 Million Euros and a sales volume of 100 Million Euros in a 30-day period, the turnover period will be 15 days.

## » Calculation/Derivation

The required data, depending upon the level of aggregation for the chosen products, can be obtained from the accounting information system (internal and external). For example, the data can be based on an ERP (Enterprise Resource Planning) system with a module-based structure.

For an inter-firm or time-series comparison, it is important to check the consistency of the valuation base for the inventory amount. The valuation could be based on the acquisition price or sales price, the current price or average price, or appropriate production costs.

## # Interpretation and Typical Range

On the one hand, this ratio delivers information about the average lock-up period of the capital blocked in the inventory and, on the other hand, it provides information about the supply situation of the product in question. The higher the ratio value, the more stable and longer the supply secured for the market. However, the longer the turnover period, the higher the capital commitment and consequently, the higher are various direct and indirect costs for managing the warehouse.

A general target range for this ratio cannot be determined. For orientation and benchmarking, internal (such as the ratio in different organisational units or plan-actual values) or external comparisons (such as the branch-specific average period or the "best-practice" value), may be used as a guide.

## ! Useful Suggestions

Assuming that firms in the same branch usually have similar production and asset structures, the ratio values differ significantly from the appropriate averages and offer clear indications for serious reviews. These should help in analysing the positive and negative consequences, and steer them in the context of corporate goals.

Along with the cost-oriented analysis, it is important not to ignore the market-oriented perspective. A sizable reduction in the turnover period could jeopardize the expected delivery plan of the customer. In such cases, however, it is good to consider the pros and cons of all business aspects.

A change in this ratio could be triggered by a disproportionate increase or decrease in the inventory amount (in numerator) and the sales volume (in denominator). *For further details and systematic explanations on this, refer to the information in Appendix I.*

### Related Ratios/Additional Notes &
The word "turnover period" is sometimes substituted by the synonym "coverage period".

If the numerator and denominator are turned upside down, the resultant coefficient is called "turnover-coefficient" or simply "turnover".

## 3.8 Customer-related Ecological Indicators

### 3.8.1 Product Carbon Footprint

### Analytical Question ?
–  To what extent are environmentally harmful carbon dioxide ($CO_2$) emissions linked to the existence or production of a reference object (for example, a particular product or service)?
–  How large is the amount of $CO_2$ emissions throughout the entire life cycle of a product (known as the Product Carbon Footprint)?

### Definition ✱
The Sum of the Quantity of $CO_2$ Emissions (attributed to a Product or Object)

In the comprehensive version of life-cycle perspective, the indicator includes emissions from all phases of raw material acquisition, product creation, product use/consumption, product-disposal and all associated transport processes.

The indicator "product carbon footprint" is expressed in terms of "mass" or "weight", namely in gram or kilogram per reference unit.

If the area of analysis also contains other relevant, environmentally harmful gases, known as Kyoto-gases, then a carbon footprint can also be calculated in an analogous way using the $CO_2$e dimension (e stands for equivalent). For further explanation, refer to the section "related ratios" below.

### Calculation/Derivation »
Acquiring the needed data, poses a special challenge for the use of this methodology and, as a result, for the calculation of this KPI. In principle, the job lies in

collecting and adding the $CO_2$ values from the emissions linked to the corresponding material and energy flows over the individual lifecycle phases.

The diverse nature of international production implies that, apart from the user, multiple companies participate along the value chain and they all need to be integrated into the data gathering process. Moreover, due to the presence of various alternative approaches towards data collection and environmental accounting, there has so far, been a lack of a universally accepted standardisation in the process. The standardisations being strived for need to either overcome current divergent methods through a sense of harmonisation or at least, determine reasonable rules for their interpretation. The aim is to define the unified system limits for the observed (life cycle) phases, to agree upon harmonised qualification methodologies for the emissions and thus to achieve comparable data quality for the carbon footprint.

## # Interpretation and Typical Range

The measurement of ecologically relevant facts is one of the key tasks for sustainability accounting and management. The aim is to use this information as a basis for making responsible business decisions, and to be able to place oneself in an advantageous position compared with the competition.

At the centre of the calculation of the Product Carbon Footprint is the task of tracing and determining the so-called greenhouse gas potential of a product or service. On the one hand, the vivid nature of the notion of a footprint has the advantage of being able to spread awareness about the climate impact of emissions in a visually and uncomplicated way to a large global audience. On the other hand, the apparently simple terminology runs the risk of underestimating the complexity and costs of data gathering, as well as its systematic, accountable (and complete) compilation. Despite multiple approaches and generally accepted process regulations, a large part of the collected emission data is based on particular assumptions and individual estimations. Even if one assumes the best of intentions from those involved, the data may not pass the validity tests of an inter-subjective and verifiable measurement method.

Though a whole series of pilot projects have been successfully completed in the current phase of development, the KPI carbon footprint is still waiting for its comprehensive implementation, not in the least due to insufficiently standardised processes worldwide.

Keeping in mind the number of various objects being analysed, a general guideline or target for the level of each carbon footprint cannot be determined. However, one can use not only comparison possibilities over a period of time (given sufficient data) but also the respective information from competitors, the industry averages or best practice values as an orientation for the scale of Product Carbon Footprint.

**Useful Suggestions**

The "$CO_2$e-Footprint" is an indicator for sustainable business practices. It allows a targeted, realistic saving on environmentally relevant materials and energy in production, as well as consumption processes taking place on the basis of a critical parameter and its evolution over time.

Within the framework of a business strategy based on sustainability, the following areas of activity can be emphasized, which include the need to improve their respective carbon footprints:

- Creating more transparency with regard to the participants and their production and consumption behaviour, along the entire chain of product lifecycles.
- Increasing awareness about $CO_2$ emissions amongst all stakeholders at different phases of a product lifecycle, such as raw materials acquisition, product creation, product use or consumption, product-disposal and all associated transport processes.
- Internal and external communication of the calculated key indicator "Product Carbon Footprint", in order to position itself as an environmentally conscious company with regard to its specific reference, product or transport service.
- Identifying the potential for $CO_2$ emission reduction, especially in emission-intensive phases, along with the respective cost (reduction) impact or $CO_2$-compensation schemes.
- Thinking and acting across phases, in order to achieve overcompensation effects. For example, increased emissions during the assembly of a fuel-efficient motor can be compensated manifold by reduced emissions during its use in a normal product lifespan. Certainly, the opposite situation is also likely. For example, lowered energy consumption per usage hour of a product can lead to a longer use of the product or an increase in the number of users.

**Related Ratios/Additional Notes**

The concept carbon footprint finds its primary area of application in those concrete cases where products and services are sales objects. Similarly, the carbon footprint of a company or a significant division thereof, such as an assembly location, or of a multi-levelled, procedural segment of the value-chain can be the object of the indicator. It can also be used to categorically personalise the emission behaviour of a person or a group of persons over a definite timespan. In order to achieve valuable results for varying objects, the system parameters of the field of analysis have to be appropriately modified.

If necessary, to determine a comprehensive $CO_2$e-footprint, there are published lists, for example, from the International Panel for Climate Change (IPCC), of important environmentally-relevant gases, which generally include the 6 so-called "Kyoto-gases": $CO_2$ (carbon dioxide); $CH_4$ (methane); $N_2O$ (nitrous oxide); HFCs (Hydro fluorocarbons; $NF_3$ (nitrogen trifluoride); $SF_6$ (sulphur hexafluoride). These lists summarise the mentioned greenhouse gases in a category of effect (the so-called $CO_2$-equivalences) and simultaneously specify the conversion factors that are in accordance with the most recent findings on climate-related research.

Considering the increasing global scarcity of fresh water resources, an analogous key indicator called "water footprint" can be observed. This encompasses the total amount of water consumed, polluted or evaporated during all stages and processes of production in a term known as "virtual water". In this way, companies can also determine a product-specific water footprint (Product Water Footprint; PWF), which possibly covers the entire value-chain and could point towards a sustained reduction in the consumption of water over a period of time.

### (S) 3.8.2 Emission Volume of Usage-related Pollutants

**?** **Analytical Question**

What is the volume of pollutants released in the environment through usage of a product, or through a particular usage-intensity (for example, part or full-load) or through individual phases of usage (start, acceleration, or braking phase)?

- As a life-cycle based variant, the ratio can be classified into various emitted pollutants (for example, as exit air, dust, noise, etc.), which can be further classified into sub-groups (exit air can be classified into $CO_2$ or $NO_x$).
- As a usage-phase based variant, the ratio can be classified into various pollutants for different usage-intensities (for example, part- or full-load) or for individual phases (for example, start, acceleration, or braking phase).

**\*** **Definition**

Life-cycle based Variant:

Average Quantity of Emitted Pollutants per Product-Life-Cycle

As a measured value for the quantity of solid, liquid or gaseous resources consumed, one could use the number of units, length, area and volume units, as well as weight specifications. An example could be $SO_2$ or $CO_2$ in tonnes per year.

Usage-phase based Variant:

$$\frac{\text{Quantity of Emitted Pollutants}}{\text{Duration of Phase under Analysis}}$$

For the denominator, the scale could be in terms of time units (such as seconds, minutes or hours).

Out of each combination for input and output, the ratio could be expressed in the form of the emission quantity per unit of time (for example, $CO_2$ per hour).

## Calculation/Derivation

A prerequisite for obtaining the required data for this emission-oriented ratio is the existence of a detailed (computerised) business environment information system. A business environment information system is responsible for collecting, processing and reporting of all environment related data, in particular:
- Compilation of quantity and value-based information about resources consumed,
- Documentation of information for external legal reporting, and
- Calculation of meaningful ratios for presenting complex details, and showing trends in internal and external changes over time.

## Interpretation and Typical Range

The main message of sustainability management is the idea of offering a development process which satisfies the needs of the present generation without jeopardizing the aspirations of future generations. The application of the sustainability principle, at the firm level implies, as far as possible, avoiding unnecessary pollution of the natural environment. Thus, both variants show the emission volume problem from two different perspectives.

Because of a strongly diversified product spectrum of firms, comparable data about typical range is possible only for firms which have similar product groups – internal with actual-actual or budget-actual comparisons. External benchmarks could be taken from the branch-specific averages or the best-practice values.

Because of strong campaigning against global warming and climate change, $CO_2$ emission is considered to be a lead-indicator in general.

## Useful Suggestions

Assuming that most firms are increasingly guided by the basic performance idea of conserving natural resources both on the input and output side, there are a large number of measures which are not only applied to the consumption efficiency of resources, but also help in producing environmentally-friendly products.

Through careful, systematic and foresighted management, a firm can use a life cycle assessment approach where alternative materials and supplies are analysed for their environmental impact, from raw-material extraction to consumption and final recycling or disposal. Through environmental targets, a firm can develop specifications towards material consumption efficiency, recycling capability, energy saving, emission standards and noise-reduction. Thus, an optimal recycling concept begins with the design and conceptual phase of new products.

**& Related Ratios/Additional Notes**

The scope, data-collection frequency, and level of detail in measuring and reporting on the sustainability indicators are largely at the discretion of firms and their environmental consciousness. Sometimes, however, there are legal directives which require regular information from firms.

The external reporting towards sustainability is much less regulated than classical reporting, according to national and international reporting standards. As a good orientation, reference is often made of the lists of indicators published in the directives of Global Reporting Initiative (GRI). As an independent institution, GRI took upon itself the job of developing formal guidelines for improving the comparability of sustainability reporting.

### 3.8.3 Product-related Recyclability Rate

**? Analytical Question**

To what extent have raw materials used in a certain product (components etc.) been purchased with a clear perspective that these can be returned back into a reasonable recycling materials loop?

**\* Definition**

$$\frac{\text{Recyclable Quantity (or Value) of Materials of an Output Unit} \cdot 100}{\text{Total Quantity (or Value) of Material of an Output Unit}}$$

The material can be further differentiated by specific types (e.g. by metals, plastics) or by certain modules (e.g. components, assemblies).

Usually, the information about the amount of material is measured by weight, and sometimes also in monetary units. The extent of the parameter "Product-related Recyclability Rate" is ultimately indicated by the dimension "%", by multiplying by the factor "100".

**» Calculation/Derivation**

The necessary information for this KPI is usually prepared internally and, in particular, gathered from the product design (on the basis of bills for material and work plans). The responsibility for the preparation and maintenance of this kind of information rests with research and development, and also the production department. The external parties or stakeholders are basically dependent on the publication and credibility of manufacturer information, unless additional audit certificates, from a neutral third party, are added or supplied.

**Interpretation and Typical Range**                                            `#`

In the light of increasing regulations, firstly on a national level, in the form of laws on recycling economy and waste management, or secondly, on a supranational level e.g. through the European Union, with appropriate EU directives or EU regulations, the indicator "Product-related Recyclability Rate" is an indicator for the proactive sense of responsibility for product designers and manufacturers on the "output-side" of their decisions.

In the early phases of product design, and the conceptual stage of the applicable manufacturing process, the ease with which the severability of product parts, decomposability of assemblies, their exchange or further use or their disposal, should be checked.

In general, at first, the focus of analysis for this KPI should be on selected expensive or rather scarce primary material types (e.g. rare earths in the field of electronic engineering) or products (parts) with a correspondingly high intrinsic value.

One should notice that the amount of already achieved product-related recyclability ratio differs significantly from, for example, the specifically pursued recyclability targets for the next-generation of products. The next generation recyclability targets are usually higher, due to numerous technical, physical, chemical and economic improvements and also differ between individual branches and companies.

For orientation and benchmarking, internal (such as between different products or programs or budget-actual comparisons) and corresponding external comparisons (such as the data from the competitors, branch-specific average values or the "best-practice" values), may be used as a guide.

**Useful Suggestions**                                                          `!`

Besides the pursuit of company's internal sustainability goals, the driving forces for companies to think and act stronger in overall sustainability terms, during the product life cycle, are governmental and regulative interventions, e.g. statutory "take-back" requirements. The internalisation of intermittent external environmental costs has convinced companies not only to carry out a targeted preparation for a reasonable product recycling concept, but also to ensure a corresponding implementation of this concept. Various forms of cooperation could run across corporate boundaries to increase recyclability (e.g. the development and collaborative use of retro-distribution systems, as well as the coordinated reprocessing of solid, liquid or gaseous substances).

Meaningful product documentation, with bills for materials, graphically supported by so-called blow-up drawings, and special references to suitable dismantling techniques, reinforce the economic efficiency of material recycling (e.g. in the sense of overall decrease in recycling costs, savings effects through the use of secondary materials or potentially higher revenues from selling preferably pure recycled material under specific types).

With a dominant reference to recyclability, given the output-related ability to ensure a subsequent return into a recyclable materials loop, this KPI can be further classified in order to provide meaningful insights and interpretation, as follows:

– Product components recyclability:

Reutilization-variant I: After recycling, the product component should be reused for the same purpose as it was originally used. For example, after overhauling, a motor is used as a power unit again.

Reutilization-variant II: An unwanted by-product is not disposed of immediately and cost-intensively, but serves another purpose, other than what it was originally used for. For example, drinking water contaminated during the production process is used for cooling purposes after primary waste water treatment.

– Product material recyclability:

Recycling-variant I: The material is used as input again in the same (or identical) production process, though the shape and form of material may have changed partly or completely. For example, recycled aluminium as a secondary raw material.

Recycling-variant II: The material is utilized in production processes to extract new substances or products. For example, use of wooden pallets, which were initially and intentionally untreated, as natural fuel (small wooden pellets) used in private households

## & Related Ratios/Additional Notes

When we take the input perspective of the indicator, the "Recycling Ratio (see KPI No. 4.6.4)" in the sense of a "reuse rate" it is counted among the related key figures.

Beyond legal regulations, the explicit reference to the key figure "Product-Related Recyclability Rate" represents an argument that is fast becoming ecologically significant, considering marketing aspects which could generate comparative competitive advantages in winning certain customer groups.

# 4 Process Perspective

## 4.1 Project Controlling

### 4.1.1 Schedule Performance Index (SPI)

**Analytical Question**     `?`

How good is the time-efficiency of the project so far? What is the ratio (at a milestone or review deadline) between the value of work completed and the value of work planned on a project, as an indicator of the progress achieved?

**Definition**     `*`

$$\frac{\text{Earned Value} \cdot 100}{\text{Planned Value}}$$

Where:

Earned Value   = Budgeted Cost of the Work Performed (BCWP)
Planned Value = Budgeted Cost of the Work Scheduled (BCWS)

The SPI is expressed as a percentage. When the numerator is not multiplied by 100, the resultant quotient is expressed in decimal points.

**Calculation/Derivation**     `»`

In the framework for Earned Value Approach (EVA), a prerequisite for the computation of SPI is that a detailed (computerised) information system is in place for a structural display of all project activities (for example, in the form of a network plan). The information system should provide for regular updating of the project's progress report, in terms of costs, performance and work schedule (both budgeted and actual).

**Interpretation and Typical Range**     `#`

A major dimension for project controlling is to ensure informational transparency in the design and successful execution of each planned activity. The Earned Value Approach (implying what is completed is also earned, as shown by sales revenue) offers an efficient and methodical instrument of SPI for measuring the schedule (time) efficiency of a project at a particular point in time. It is an interesting "early-diagnosis" indicator towards continuous monitoring of developments in a project. An SPI equal to or greater than 100 % (or 1) indicates a favourable condition, and a value of less than 100 % (or 1) indicates an unfavourable condition. Thus, an SPI of 80 % (or 0.8) implies that only 80 % of the scheduled work has been completed so far.

https://doi.org/10.1515/9783110598094-005

**❗ Useful Suggestions**

The whole field of project management, along with project controlling, offers a broad spectrum of possible managerial and operational measures towards efficient completion of the project work. As a matter of principle, the instruments used for managing a project should focus on the simultaneous achievement of output, time, quality and input goals. This helps in avoiding or reducing the cost over-runs, schedule-over-runs, performance deficits and/or resource shortages.

**& Related Ratios/Additional Notes**

In the framework for project controlling, the family of Earned Value Approach offers various ratios for evaluating the project performance, such as "Cost Performance Index (CPI)", "To Complete Performance Index (TCPI)", "Estimate at Completion (EAC)", and "Time Estimate at Completion (TEAC)".

### 4.1.2 Cost Performance Index (CPI)

**❓ Analytical Question**

How cost efficient has the project been so far? What is the ratio between the budgeted and actual cost of the work completed, at a milestone or a particular point in time in the life of a project?

**✱**

$$\frac{\text{Earned Value} \cdot 100}{\text{Actual Cost}}$$

Where:

Earned Value = Budgeted Cost of Work Performed (BCWP)

Actual Cost = Actual Cost of Work Performed (ACWP)

The CPI is expressed as a percentage. When the numerator is not multiplied by 100, the resultant quotient is expressed in decimal points.

**» Calculation/Derivation**

In the framework for Earned Value Approach (EVA), a prerequisite for the computation of CPI is that a detailed (computerised) information system is in place for a structural display of all project activities (for example, in the form of a network plan). The information system should provide for regular updating of the project's progress report, in terms of costs, performance and work schedule (both budgeted and actual).

The numerator in the definition represents the budgeted cost of the work already performed, and the denominator shows the actual cost of the work already performed.

### Interpretation and Typical Range        `#`

A major dimension for project controlling is to ensure informational transparency in the design and successful execution of each planned activity. The Earned Value Approach (implying what is completed is also earned, as shown by sales revenue) offers an efficient and methodical instrument in the form of the CPI.

The CPI provides information about the conformance of actual costs of the work performed to the budget of the project, at a particular point in time. Whereas TCPI shows the cost effectiveness to be achieved *in the future* in order to finish the work within budget estimates, the CPI is an indicator of the *historical cost performance* of the project. The CPI is an interesting "early-diagnosis" indicator, towards continuous monitoring of developments in a project. If the CPI value is below 100 % (say at 90 %), it implies that the actual costs exceed the budgeted costs.

### Useful Suggestions        `!`

The whole field of project management, along with project controlling, offers a broad spectrum of possible managerial and operational measures towards efficient completion of the project work. As a matter of principle, the instruments used for managing a project should focus on the simultaneous achievement of output, time, quality and input goals. This helps in avoiding or reducing the cost over-runs, schedule over-runs, performance deficits and/or resource shortages.

### Related Ratios/Additional Notes        `&`

In the framework for project controlling, the family of Earned Value Approach offers various ratios for evaluating the project performance, such as "Schedule Performance Index (SPI)", "To Complete Performance Index (TCPI)", "Estimate at Completion (EAC)", and "Time Estimate at Completion (TEAC)".

It is interesting to note that when we multiply SPI with CPI, the resultant number is called Critical Ratio (CR), which is a combined measure, both in terms of time schedule and cost budget. With an SPI of 80 % (0.8) and CPI of 67 % (0.67), the CR of 0.536, which represents the overall status of the project, is achieved. If CR is equal to 1, then the project is being managed perfectly.

### 4.1.3 Time Estimation at Completion (TEAC)

**?  Analytical Question**

What is the revised completion time for an activity, a work package, or a project based on the work completed, at a particular milestone or status date, after starting the project? Which completion date is to be expected as an early-warning?

**✳  Definition**

$$\frac{\text{Time at Completion}}{\text{Schedule Performance Index}}$$

Where:

| | | |
|---|---|---|
| Time at Completion | = | Original Schedule at Completion (SAC) |
| Schedule Performance Index | = | Budgeted Cost of the Work Performed (BCWP) *Divided by* Budgeted Cost of the Work Schedule (BCWS) |

The TEAC is expressed in terms of time units, such as hours, days, weeks, etc.

**»  Calculation/Derivation**

In the framework for Earned Value Approach (EVA), a prerequisite for the computation of TEAC is that a detailed (computerised) information system is in place for a structural display of all project activities (for example, in form of a network plan). The information system should provide for regular updating of the project's progress report, in terms of costs, performance and work schedule (both budgeted and actual).

SPI mentioned in the denominator, as an "early-diagnosis" indicator, shows the time efficiency of the project.

**#  Interpretation and Typical Range**

A major dimension for project controlling is to ensure informational transparency in the design and successful execution of each planned activity. The Earned Value Approach (implying what is completed is also earned, as shown in sales revenue) offers an efficient and methodical instrument for *revised* time estimate for completion in the form of TEAC. The TEAC provides information about the updated schedule for the expected time on completion. It is an interesting "early-diagnosis" indicator towards the continuous monitoring of developments in a project.

If the SPI is below 100 % (say at 80 %, which is true of many projects in real life), it indicates that only 80 % of the scheduled work was completed. This would mean that the revised time at completion will have to be adjusted upwards. Thus, with an original schedule at completion (SAC) of 40 weeks and the latest SPI of 80 % (0.8), the revised estimate of the completion time should now be 50 weeks. However, in this case it is assumed for the sake of simplicity, that the SPI will remain constant during the rest of the project period.

## Useful Suggestions

The whole field of project management along with project controlling offers a broad spectrum of possible managerial and operational measures towards an efficient completion of project work. As a matter of principle, the instruments used for managing a project should focus on the simultaneous achievement of output, time, quality and input goals. This helps in avoiding or reducing the cost over-runs, schedule over-runs, performance deficits and/or resource shortages.

## Related Ratios/Additional Notes

In the framework for project controlling, the family of Earned Value Approach offers various ratios for evaluating the project performance, such as "Schedule Performance Index (SPI)", "Cost Performance Index (CPI)", and "To Complete Performance Index (TCPI)".

## 4.1.4 Estimate at Completion (EAC)

### Analytical Question

What is the revised estimation of costs at completion of an activity, a work package or a project, based on the cost performance at a milestone or a particular status date after starting the project?

### Definition

$$\frac{\text{Budget at Completion}}{\text{Cost Performance Index}}$$

Where:

Budget at Completion = Original Budgeted Costs at Completion
Cost Performance Index = Budgeted Cost of the Work Performed (BCWP) *Divided by* Actual Cost of the Work Performed (ACWP)

The EAC is expressed in terms of currency units, such as €.

### Calculation/Derivation

In the framework for Earned Value Approach (EVA), a prerequisite for the computation of EAC is that a detailed (computerised) information system is in place for a structural display of all project activities (for example, in the form of a network plan). The information system should provide for regular updating of the project's progress report, in terms of costs, performance and work schedule (both budgeted and actual).

## # Interpretation and Typical Range

A major dimension for project controlling is to ensure informational transparency in the design and successful execution of each planned activity. The Earned Value Approach (implying what is completed is also earned, as shown in sales revenue) offers an efficient and methodical instrument for a *revised* cost estimation at completion, in the form of EAC. The updated expected cost at completion is based on an assessment of cost performance from the most recent status date. It is an interesting "early-diagnosis" indicator towards continuous monitoring of developments in a project.

If the CPI is below 100 % (say at 90 %, which is true of many projects in real life), it indicates that actual costs exceed budgeted costs and, as a consequence, the revised estimates of the costs will have to be adjusted upwards. EAC is a linear projection of the past cost performance into the future because it assumes, for the sake of simplicity, that the CPI will remain constant during the rest of the project work. Thus, with an original budget at completion (BAC) of 100 Euro, the latest CPI of 80 % (0.8) implies that the revised estimate of the cost at completion will now be 125 Euro. Again, it is assumed that the CPI will remain constant during the rest of the project period.

## ! Useful Suggestions

The whole field of project management, along with project controlling, offers a broad spectrum of possible managerial and operational measures towards an efficient completion of the project work. As a matter of principle, the instruments used for managing a project should focus on the simultaneous achievement of output, time, quality and input goals. This helps in avoiding or reducing the cost over-runs, schedule over-runs, performance deficits and/or resource shortages.

If because of specific project management measures, the cost effectiveness of inputs is improved, the condition of constant CPI can be maintained. Assuming that CPI is changeable during the remaining project period, the revised value of EAC will be as follows:

$$\text{Actual Costs} + \frac{(\text{Budget at Completion} - \text{Earned Value})}{\text{Cost Performance Index}}$$

The actual costs represent the actual costs of the work performed (ACWP), the earned value shows the budgeted costs of the work performed (BCWP), and the information contained within brackets is the value of remaining work.

**Related Ratios/Additional Notes** &

In the framework for project controlling, the family of Earned Value Approach offers various ratios for evaluating the project performance, such as "Schedule Performance Index (SPI)", "Cost Performance Index (CPI)", "Time Estimate at Completion (TEAC)", and "To Complete Performance Index (TCPI)".

## 4.1.5 To-Complete-Performance Index (TCPI)

**Analytical Question** ?

What is the future projection of the average productivity needed to complete the project within the estimated budget, based on the work completed, at a milestone or a particular status date after starting the project? What is the ratio between the value of the work completed and the value of the work planned in a project?

**Definition** *

$$\frac{(\text{Budget at Completion} - \text{Earned Value}) \cdot 100}{\text{Budget at Completion} - \text{Actual Cost}}$$

Where:

| | | |
|---|---|---|
| Budget at Completion (BAC) | = | Total Planned Value (at Baseline) |
| Earned Value | = | Budgeted Cost of the Work Performed (BCWP) |
| Actual Cost | = | Actual Cost of Work Performed (ACWP) |

The TCPI is expressed as a percentage. When the numerator is not multiplied by 100, the resultant quotient is expressed in decimal points.

**Calculation/Derivation** »

In the framework for Earned Value Approach (EVA), a prerequisite for the computation of TCPI is that a detailed (computerised) information system is in place for a structural display of all project activities (for example, in the form of a network plan). The information system should provide for regular updating of the project's progress report, in terms of costs, performance and work schedule (both budgeted and actual).

The numerator in the definition represents the value of the remaining work and the denominator shows the amount of the remaining budget.

**Interpretation and Typical Range** #

A major dimension for project controlling is to ensure informational transparency in the design and successful execution of each planned activity. The Earned Value

Approach (implying what is completed is also earned, as shown in sales revenue) offers an efficient and methodical instrument in the form of the TCPI.

The TCPI provides information about cost efficiency or productivity which must be achieved in order to finish the work within the original budget estimates (BAC). The TCPI is an interesting "early-diagnosis" indicator towards a continuous monitoring of developments in a project.

The TCPI must be used in conjunction with the Cost Performance Index (CPI), which, in effect, reflects upon the historical cost efficiency or productivity of the project. If the TCPI is well above the latest CPI value, the efficiency of the project must be improved; otherwise it is more likely that the project will have a cost over-run.

**!** **Useful Suggestions**

The whole field of project management, along with project controlling, offers a broad spectrum of possible managerial and operational measures towards an efficient completion of the project work. As a matter of principle, the instruments used for managing a project should focus on the simultaneous achievement of output, time, quality and input goals. This helps in avoiding or reducing the cost over-runs, schedule-over-runs, performance deficits and/or resource shortages.

**&** **Related Ratios/Additional Notes**

In the framework for project controlling, the family of Earned Value Approach offers various ratios for evaluating the project performance, such as "Schedule Performance Index (SPI)", "Cost Performance Index (CPI)", "Estimate at Completion (EAC)", and "Time Estimate at Completion (TEAC)".

### 4.1.6 Process Acceleration Costs

**?** **Analytical Question**

Which additional costs have to be incurred in order to accelerate the completion of a (critical) project activity or to reduce the time planned for it by one time-unit?

**\*** **Definition**

$$\frac{\text{Process Costs for Shortened Period} - \text{Process Costs for Normal Period}}{\text{Normal Period} - \text{Shortened Period}}$$

A commonly used unit base for time is "one day". The ratio Process Acceleration Costs are measured in terms of monetary units (for example, in € or as "Euros per day").

## Calculation/Derivation

A prerequisite for obtaining the required cost and time data for this ratio is a detailed (computerised) documentation of all project activities, with the appropriate cost and time data. This could be based on the foundations of a project network plan. In this context, the acceleration costs not only have a linear movement, but also change abruptly at intervals (the so-called step-fixed costs) or increase progressively.

## Interpretation and Typical Range

The ratio is an important element of project-controlling and information systems. It is used for planning, manoeuvring and controlling complex, one-off and limited-period projects or transactions which are often made up of many small activities. The ratio provides a measure of how expensive a planned reduction in the project completion period is. A reduction in the project period may have been necessitated:
- to make up for the lost time, or
- to gain a competitive advantage in a market, where a prime-mover advantage is expected, or
- to avoid any disadvantages (such as penalties for time over-runs).

## Useful Suggestions

The reduction in the project completion period is often applied to those activities which demand a (so-called) critical path analysis. The analysis begins with a search for those activities which show the lowest process acceleration costs. Depending upon the required time-savings, the search for the lowest cost option is repeated many times. However, any such search may lead to a change of activities or workflow and, eventually, may create new critical paths. It often leads to an increase in the lowest acceleration costs at a faster pace, so that one has to match the target time with the target costs. Moreover, such an analysis needs to be conducted with reference to the availability of the needed machine and human-resource capacities.

## Related Ratios/Additional Notes

For those projects which involve introducing a new product into the market, a timely completion of the project is of extreme importance. In many practice situations, it was clearly evident that delays and, as a consequence, the loss of innovation-leadership (which is anyway for limited periods) often led to considerably lowered profits (because of lower prices).

In the framework for project controlling, there are related ratios in the family of Earned Value Approach which offer other measures for evaluating the project performance, such as "Scheduled Performance Index" (SPI), "Cost Performance Index" (CPI), "To Complete Performance Index" (TCPI), "Estimate at Completion" (EAC), and "Time Estimate at Completion" (TEAC).

## 4.2 Quality Controlling

(S) ### 4.2.1 Quality Rate

**?** **Analytical Question**

What proportion of the production is qualitatively faultless at different levels of work, cost centres, production stages, etc.? How big is the share of products which is free from defects and will be processed further?

**\*** **Definition**

$$\frac{\text{Defect-free Quantity (of a given centre) in a Period} \cdot 100}{\text{Total Quantity Produced (of a given centre) in a Period}}$$

The Quality Rate is expressed as a percentage.

**»** **Calculation/Derivation**

The required data for this quotient is prepared from the (computerised) information system of production planning and controlling, in particular, the one related to quality controlling. The data could be classified according to the nature of defects, the production location or production stage.

**#** **Interpretation and Typical Range**

The Quality Rate is an important measure in the area of operational quality management. It quantifies that part of total production which was faultless, when measured in terms of specified quality requirements.

In individual cases, the typical range for this ratio can differ significantly, depending upon the product-type and production method. Since eliminating every single defect is associated with heavy follow-up costs, it is desirable to strive for a high quality rate. Even time plays an important role in deciding an acceptable quality rate: thus, at the time of production start or in the start-up phase, one expects a lower quality rate than later on. The quality rate can, however, be targeted from the beginning, or improved rapidly through appropriate quality-management techniques.

**!** **Useful Suggestions**

There is a broad spectrum of possible measures which can be applied for improving Quality Rate or stabilizing it at a high level. From a holistic perspective, not only production processes need to be analysed carefully, but also all the upstream (product development, design engineering) and downstream (sales and customer service) business processes have to be included in the analysis. A systematic and coordinated concurrence of all processes, with active involvement of suppliers and consumers during the total product life cycle, can help to improve information flow and fulfil quality requirements.

There are various quality management techniques which are used for obtaining the so-called "zero-defect quality" (or a high quality rate from the very beginning). Some known techniques are: Quality Function Deployment (QFD), Failure Method Effective Analysis (FMEA), Statistical Process Control (SPC) and Six Sigma. However, there is no substitute for quality conscious employees who should undergo intensive training in quality management.

**Related Ratios/Additional Notes**                                  `&`

Quality Level, Quality Co-efficient, and Zero-defect Rate are common synonyms for Quality Rate.

The so-called "First Pass Yield" (FPY), is a similar ratio which represents that part of the products (processes or work-packages) in the total production that did not need any reworking.

In the large family of quality-related indicators, there are other measures such as conformity and non-conformity costs, defect follow-up costs, defective supply and defective delivery costs, etc. Depending upon the production processes and the collaboration between partners in a supply or demand chain, various other measures could be conceived.

## 4.2.2 Rejection Rate

**Analytical Question**                                               `?`

– What proportion of the production is defective and has to be scrapped?
– How big is the share of defective units that will not be processed further?

**Definition**                                                        `*`

$$\frac{\text{Rejected Quantity (of a given centre) in a Period} \cdot 100}{\text{Total Quantity Produced (of a given centre) in a Period}}$$

The Rejection Rate is expressed as a percentage.

**Calculation/Derivation**                                           `»`

The required data for this quotient is prepared from the (computerised) information system for production planning and controlling, in particular the one related to quality controlling. The data could be classified according to the nature of defects, the production location or production stage.

**#** **Interpretation and Typical Range**

The Rejection Rate is an important measure in the area of quality management. However, what is considered as rejected depends on how rejection is defined internally: An item can be treated as rejected when it is seriously damaged or spoiled so that any reworking on it may not be possible, or may not be worthwhile.

In individual cases, the typical range for this ratio can differ significantly, depending upon the product-type and production method. Even time plays an important role in deciding the acceptable Rejection Rate: thus, at the time of the start of production or in the start-up phase, one expects a higher Rejection Rate than later on. The rejection rate can be kept to a minimum from the beginning or reduced speedily through appropriate quality-management techniques.

The unique character of the production process makes it very difficult to draw inter-firm comparisons for the Rejection Rate; the possibility of using external benchmarks is thus not easy here. A firm can compare its own performance in Rejection Rate over time, or between different business units (with the standard terminology for what constitutes a rejection). An easy method, for example, is to compare the budgeted rate with the actual Rejection Rate. Another method is to graph the rejection rate development over time.

**!** **Useful Suggestions**

In the framework for a modern corporate quality management, a holistic view of linkages between product planning, production process, capacity-utilisation and control phases is important from a strategic perspective. In this all-embracing framework, it is necessary that the product and/or service creation process is accompanied by measurable indicators, so that the competitiveness of the firm is not only maintained but also strengthened.

There are various quality management techniques which are used for obtaining the so-called "zero-defect quality" (or a minimum Rejection Rate from the very beginning). Some known techniques are: Quality Function Deployment (QFD), Failure Method Effective Analysis (FMEA), Statistical Process Control (SPC) and Six Sigma. However, there is no substitute for quality conscious employees who should undergo intensive training in quality management.

In order to respond faster, it is always good to measure the Rejection Rate at shorter intervals, through timely data collection.

**&** **Related Ratios/Additional Notes**

The terms Scrap Rate, Defect Rate and Spoilage Rate are often used as synonyms for the Rejection Rate.

In the large family of quality-related indicators, there are other measures, such as conformity and non-conformity costs, quality rate, defect follow-up costs, defective incoming delivery and defective outgoing delivery costs, etc. Depending upon the production processes and the collaboration between partners in a supply or demand chain, various other measures could be conceived.

### 4.2.3 Follow-up Costs Ratio

**Analytical Question**
- What is the relative share of the follow-up costs which are incurred for managing the *unintentional* non-compliance in the firm with the quality requirements of the customer?
- What is the share of follow-up costs for eliminating the quality variance or the consequences thereof?

**Definition**

$$\frac{\text{Product specific or Customer specific Follow-up Costs} \cdot 100}{\text{Total Production Cost for a Product (or Product Group)}}$$

The Follow-up Costs Ratio is expressed as a percentage.

**Calculation/Derivation**
The data for this ratio is not directly available in the cost accounting information system because most companies do not make explicit segregation of various quality costs. Thus, the required data has to be individually collected and analysed for product specific or customer specific requirements. As a base, however, the (computerised) information system of production process planning and controlling can be drawn upon. Furthermore, special records for complaints management (statistics, order-book, after-sales reports, etc.) in the sales department, could also be drawn on for additional information.

For this purpose, it is also essential that the company collects costing data, based on the direct costing system (where costs are classified into variable and fixed components) and can aggregate the costing data for various cost-centres.

Follow-up costs are part of "Non-conformity costs", both focused on the economic consequences of quality variance. In the category of operative follow-up costs, we include costs relating to warranty costs, guarantee costs and product recall costs. In the category of strategic follow-up costs, we include loss of future contribution margin and additional sales promotion costs. If the direct costs of non-compliance were to be added, such as variance-testing, rework costs, or scrap costs, the total would be the non-conformity costs.

**Interpretation and Typical Range**
The Follow-up Costs Ratio constitutes a central element in cost management for implementing the quality targets in all the processes of a value chain. However,

follow-up costs focus on the consumption of resources which arise after the sale because of some defect in the product or service. The operative elements of follow-up costs can be measured directly. However, the strategic elements of follow-up costs are perceived as opportunity costs from non-compliance.

The unique character of the production process makes it very difficult to draw inter-firm comparisons of follow-up costs; the possibility of using external benchmarks is thus not easy here. However, a firm can compare its own performance in follow-up costs over time, or between different business units (with the standard terminology of what should be included in it). An easy method, for example, is to compare the budgeted with the actual Follow-up Costs Ratio. Another method is to graph the development of follow-up costs over time.

**!  Useful Suggestions**

In the framework for modern corporate quality management, it is not enough to categorize the costs into conformity and non-conformity costs. What matters is a holistic view of linkages between product planning, production process, utilization, and control phases. The last two phases are the focus of operative and strategic follow-up costs.

In this all-embracing framework, it is necessary that the product and/or service creation process is accompanied by measurable indicators, so that the competitiveness of the firm is not only maintained but also strengthened. When planning a systematic catalogue of measures for eliminating quality variance, it is particularly important to consider that the costs of repairing a defect or variance, increases with every delay in detecting it. This is true both for internal development and production processes, as well as for exponential costs when the follow-up costs extend to the customer.

**&  Related Ratios/Additional Notes**

Related ratios are: Conformity Costs Ratio or the Non-Conformity Costs Ratio.

### 4.2.4 Conformity Costs Ratio

**?  Analytical Question**

What are the costs involved in complying with the quality requirements of the customer?

***  Definition**

$$\frac{\text{Product specific or Customer specific Conformity Costs} \cdot 100}{\text{Total Production Cost for a Product (or a Product Group)}}$$

The Conformity Costs Ratio is expressed as a percentage.

**Calculation/Derivation**                                                    »

The data for this ratio is not directly available in the cost accounting information system because most companies do not make explicit segregation of various quality costs. Thus, the required data has to be collected and individually analysed for product or customer specific requirements. As a base, however, the (computerised) information system for production process planning and controlling can be drawn upon.

For this purpose, it is also essential that the company collects costing data, based on the direct costing system (where costs are classified into variable and fixed components) and can aggregate the costing data for various cost-centres.

In the category of conformity costs, the first most important element relates to the preventive (error-reduction) costs, such as costs for installing quality management techniques. Some common techniques are: Quality Function Deployment (QFD), Failure Method Effective Analysis (FMEA), Statistical Process Control (SPC) and Six Sigma. The second important element relates to conformity costs which ensure that quality requirements (both in-process and final requirements) have been complied with. In certain industries, such as pharmaceuticals and foods, conformity costs have a third element of costs when complying with legal requirements imposed by the state, towards quality-controls, such as trial costs and documentation costs.

**Interpretation and Typical Range**                                          #

The Conformity Costs Ratio constitutes a central element in cost management for implementing quality targets in all processes in a value chain. From a marketing perspective, all the requirements, agreed with the customer, constitute the yardstick towards the quality of the product or service provided. The costs involved in fulfilling and complying with those requirements need to be managed carefully.

A conceptual counterpart of conformity costs is the "Non-conformity costs" which comes into focus when the quality requirements are not complied with, or there is a variance from the agreed requirements, for example, non-compliance costs related to variance-testing, rework costs, or scrap costs. Other operative or strategic costs can relate to warranty costs, guarantee costs, product recall costs, loss of future contribution margins and sales promotion costs.

The unique character of the production process makes it very difficult to draw inter-firm comparisons for conformity costs; the possibility of using external benchmarks is thus not easy here. However, a firm can compare its own performance, in conformity costs over time or between different business units (with the standard terminology of what should be included in it). An easy method, for example, is to compare the budgeted with the actual Conformity Costs Ratio. Another method is to graph the development of conformity costs over time.

## ! Useful Suggestions

In the framework for a modern corporate quality management, it is not enough to categorise the costs into conformity and non-conformity costs. What matters is a holistic view of linkages between product planning, production process, capacity utilisation and control phases, which is important from a strategic perspective. Costs, as a quantified image of the resource consumption, have to be managed across the board, starting from the quality rating of the suppliers, down to the questions of costs involved in recycling and disposal of waste.

In this all-embracing framework it is necessary that the product and/or service creation process is accompanied by measurable indicators, so that the competitiveness of the firm is not only maintained but also strengthened.

## & Related Ratios/Additional Notes

Compliance Cost Ratio is a common synonym for Conformity Costs Ratio.

The related ratios are: Non-Conformity Costs Ratio, or Variance Costs Ratio.

### 4.2.5 Non-Conformity Costs Ratio

## ? Analytical Question

What is the relative share of costs which are incurred from managing the *unintentional* non-compliance (in the firm) with the quality requirements of the customer? What is the share of costs for eliminating the quality variance, or the consequences thereof?

## * Definition

$$\frac{\text{Product specific or Customer specific Non-Conformity Costs} \cdot 100}{\text{Total Production Cost for a Product (or a Product Group)}}$$

The Non-Conformity Costs Ratio is expressed as a percentage.

## » Calculation/Derivation

The data for this ratio is not directly available in the cost accounting information system because most companies do not make an explicit segregation of the various quality costs. Thus, the required data has to be collected and analysed for product specific or customer specific requirements individually. As a base, however, one could draw upon the (computerised) information system of production process planning and controlling.

For this purpose, it is also essential that the company collects costing data, based on the direct costing system (where costs are classified into variable and fixed components) and can aggregate the costing data, for various cost-centres.

In the category of "Non-conformity costs", those costs which are included come into focus because of non-compliance with the quality requirements, or because of a variance from the agreed requirements, for example, non-compliance costs related to variance-testing, rework costs, or scrap costs. Other operative or strategic costs could relate to warranty costs, guarantee costs, product recall costs, loss of future contribution margin and sales promotion costs.

## Interpretation and Typical Range

The Non-Conformity Costs Ratio constitutes a central element in cost management for implementing the quality targets in all the processes of a value chain. From a marketing perspective, all the requirements agreed with the customer, constitute the yardstick towards the quality of the product or service provided. The costs involved in fulfilling and complying with those requirements need to be managed carefully.

A conceptual counterpart of non-conformity costs is "Conformity Costs". The primary element in conformity costs relates to the preventive (error-reduction) costs, such as costs for installing quality management techniques. Some common techniques are: Quality Function Deployment (QFD), Failure Method Effective Analysis (FMEA), Statistical Process Control (SPC) and Six Sigma. The second most important element relates to conformity costs which ensure that quality requirements (both in-process and final requirements) have been complied with. In certain industries, such as pharmaceutical and food, conformity costs have a third costs element in complying with the legal requirements imposed by the state, towards quality-controls, such as trial costs and documentation costs.

The unique character of the production process makes it very difficult to draw inter-firm comparisons for non-conformity costs; the possibility of using external benchmarks is thus not easy here. However, a firm can compare its own performance in non-conformity costs (with the standard terminology of what should be included in it) over time, or between different business units. An easy method, for example, is to compare the budgeted with the actual Non-Conformity Costs Ratio. Another method is to graph the development of non-conformity costs over time.

## Useful Suggestions

In the framework for a modern corporate quality management, it is not enough to categorize the costs into conformity and non-conformity costs. What matters is a holistic view of linkages between product planning, production process, capacity utilization and control phases. This is important from a strategic perspective. Costs, as a quantified image of the resource consumption, have to be managed across the board and should include:
- The quality rating of the suppliers;
- Production processes geared towards fulfilling customer requirements and expectations; and
- Costs involved in recycling and disposal of waste.

In this all-embracing framework, it is necessary that the product and/or service creation process is accompanied by measurable indicators, so that the competitiveness of the firm is not only maintained but also strengthened. When planning a systematic catalogue of measures for eliminating the quality variance, it is particularly important to consider that the costs of repairing a defect or variance increases with every delay in detecting it. This is true both for internal development and production processes, as well as for exponential costs when the follow-up costs extend to the customer.

### & Related Ratios/Additional Notes

Non-Compliance Costs Ratio and Variance Costs Ratio are common synonyms for Non-Conformity Costs Ratio.

A related ratio is: Conformity Costs Ratio or Compliance Costs Ratio.

## 4.3 Supply Chain Management

### 4.3.1 Procurement Efficiency Ratio

### ? Analytical Question

How much are the procurement costs in relation to the total procured volume? How efficient is the purchasing department in terms of volume managed and costs generated?

### * Definition

$$\frac{\text{Costs of the Purchasing Department per Period} \cdot 100}{\text{Volume Procured per Period}}$$

Where:

Volume Procured = Ordered Quantity × Acquisition Price
Costs of Purchasing Department = Proxy for Resources Consumed by Purchasing Department (e.g. Salaries, Office Occupancy Costs, Telecommunication Costs, Depreciation of Assets used in Purchasing Department, Insurance Costs, Travel and General Administrative Costs)

The Procurement Efficiency Ratio is expressed as a percentage.

### » Calculation/Derivation

The required information for this ratio is to be obtained primarily through internal cost accounting data. The information is aggregated, typically for various cost centres and cost types.

### Interpretation and Typical Range

Procurement Efficiency Ratio is a widespread measure for the cost-effectiveness of the purchasing department. The ratio primarily compares the fixed costs of the purchasing department with the changing volume of the quantity procured. In this respect, the task lies in allocating the indirect costs, associated with the procurement activities, which is not an easy task. Depending upon how strongly the procured volume varies in a particular period (linked to the changing capacity utilization level or discount offers for large volume purchases), the computed ratio also varies accordingly.

Therefore, it is difficult to recommend a meaningful target for this ratio. As orientation and for comparison purposes, internal benchmarks between various units within the firm can be used. The performance over time can be analysed with the help of budget-actual comparisons. External benchmarks can be taken from the branch-specific averages or the best-practice values.

### Useful Suggestions

Process costing is usually applied to those business processes which are repetitive in nature; it helps in calculating a process cost rate which is a promising method for allocating at least part of the fixed costs, on the basis of actual consumption. When prices are constant, the Procurement Efficiency Ratio shows strong similarities with the quantity-oriented process cost rate.

With appropriate differentiation of various costs, one can get detailed information on how efficiently A, B, and C categories (or even X, Y, Z categories) of goods are procured through diverse procurement channels (for example, eProcurement) or through a range of legal contracts (for example, annual supply agreements). This information can be of immense value for strategic and operational decisions.

A change in this ratio, in the context of desired corporate goals, can be achieved by a disproportionate increase or decrease in the cost of procurement (as numerator) and procured volume (as denominator). *For further details and systematic explanations on this, refer to the information in Appendix I.*

Along with direct efforts at influencing the operational costs through organizational structure, process-flow planning, price based and/or quantity based policy measures in the purchasing department, one can improve procurement efficiency, and also by a careful (price and quantity based) optimization of the required goods and services that are procured over time.

### Related Ratios/Additional Notes

In addition to this period based ratio, procurement efficiency is also calculated "per purchaser." However, this number has to be interpreted carefully because of the above-mentioned limitations.

(S) **4.3.2 Supplier-Audit Ratio**

**?** **Analytical Question**

To what extent are the purchased products and services of a firm acquired from audited suppliers (in the sense of a successfully completed explicit screening process)?

**\*** **Definition**

Indicator variant based on the number of suppliers:

$$\frac{\text{Number of Audited Suppliers per Period} \cdot 100}{\text{Total Number of Suppliers per Period}}$$

Indicator variant based on the value of purchased volume:

$$\frac{\text{Value of Purchased Volume from Audited Suppliers per Period} \cdot 100}{\text{Total Value of Purchased Volume per Period}}$$

Both indicator variants have the dimension %.

**»** **Calculation/Derivation**

The required data for this KPI can be obtained from (computerised) information systems devoted to purchase or procurement planning, management and monitoring. The data can be organized in cooperation with the legal department because of its involvement in the supplier audit process. A well-developed and decision-facilitating supplier databank should be regularly maintained. Due to the variety of testing items, the testing methods and screening procedures, the details of suppliers' audit and the level of certification may differ amongst suppliers, leading to huge complexities in calculating the KPI.

**#** **Interpretation and Typical Range**

Within the framework for supplier's auditing, whether the selected objects, such as individual processes, functional areas or the entire company meet the requirements set by the auditor or fulfil certain generally accepted guidelines should be checked.

According to the organisational position of the auditor(s), the following three basic forms of auditors can be differentiated:

1. Internal auditing (so-called 1st Party Auditing), where auditors are employees of the audited organization.
2. External business partner auditing (so-called 2nd Party Auditing), where auditors are employees of a direct customer, supplier, etc.
3. External independent auditing (so-called 3rd Party Auditing), where auditors represent a neutral "third" organisation that is not related in business terms, for example TÜV or similar agencies which typically carry out certification audits.

The typology of criteria-catalogues for suppliers' audit is characterised by different points of focus, and can range from firm and/or industrial branch guidelines all the way to international guidelines that align themselves with UN standards.

The validity of an audit is significantly influenced by stipulation of, and compliance with, an appropriate frequency of repetition over time, often supplemented by intermittent and independent internal audits, as well as by unannounced and new external audits.

A general corporate target for the extent of each Supplier-Audit Ratio cannot be meaningfully determined. For orientation and benchmarking, internal comparisons (such as the ratio in different organizational units or budget-actual comparisons or actuals over time) and corresponding external comparisons (where the information about the competitors, branch-specific average values or the "best-practice" values) may be used as a guide.

## Useful Suggestions

In a globally interconnected economy, based on division of labour and varied vertical depths of manufacturing, the importance of supply and demand-chain performance indicators has increased significantly. The mutual dependencies in the multi-levelled supply chain often make it imperative to check the reliability of partners through auditing mechanisms and to ensure reliability through contractual obligations.

Alongside the analysis of an initial condition for the company being checked, an audit can also help bring to light, through due-diligence tests, the current deficits with respect to each criteria-catalogue. This can help uncover weaknesses and, with appropriate suggestions, improve and maintain the performance of suppliers in line with auditor's expectations. If necessary, this could lead to purchasing practices of the firm being changed or standing contracts with suppliers terminated.

Keeping in mind the increasingly widespread concept of Corporate Social Responsibility (CSR) and three-dimensional sustainability in terms of economic benefits, social responsibility and environmental viability, audits must specially or comprehensively contribute towards avoiding, reducing and rectifying the negative consequences of business activity. Typically, the following points of focus have to be worked upon:

- Quality management
- IT-security management
- Environmental management
- Risk management
- Health and safety management.

## Related Ratios/Additional Notes

The corresponding reporting indicator for the Global Reporting Initiative (GRI) is based upon the percentage-threshold of only new suppliers, which are checked according to environmental criteria (disclosure 308-1). Other related ratios for GRI are labour practices criteria (disclosure 407-1: freedom of association and collective bargaining) or social impact criteria (disclosure 414-1).

In comparison with auditing (especially 1st Party and 2nd Party), the 3rd Party certification is generally a systematic procedure or a confirmation of a successfully completed process of acquiring, for example, an ISO-Certificate by a recognised certification organisation. The certification is often granted on the basis of, amongst others, the DIN EN ISO 19011 which provides the guidelines for audits on quality and environmental management systems of the supplier.

Ⓢ **4.3.3 Supply Chain Cycle Time**

**❓ Analytical Question**

How long does it take, in the inter-organizational supply chain, to procure the raw material, produce the product and deliver it to the customer? What is the longest time required in the supply chain to satisfy a customer order, if all inventory levels were extremely low or zero, for example in the just-in-time (JIT) model?

**✳ Definition**

Procurement Time
+ Production Time
+ Internal Inventory Time
+ Packaging and Shipment Time

The KPI "Supply Chain Cycle Time" is computed in number of days, and can also be in weeks or months.

**» Calculation/Derivation**

The required data for this performance indicator is derived from the (computerised) information system of procurement planning, production planning, sales planning and actual time consumed in the processes. The budgeted and realised data should preferably be compiled for each product or customer order in a period.

In most cases today, the basic data for this purpose is drawn from an ERP (Enterprise Resource Planning) system with a module-based structure.

**# Interpretation and Typical Range**

Supply Chain Cycle Time (SCCT) begins with the purchase order, placed on supplier and ends with the final placement of the finished product, on the shelf or delivery to the customer's warehouse. It includes the time consumed in the upstream supply chain processes (including order placement at supplier, inbound logistics and inspection) to manufacturing, inventorying and further on to all the downstream supply chain processes (including packaging, outbound logistics, delivery to the customer). It could also be interpreted as the sum total of the procurement lead-time and order-fulfilment time.

An underlining assumption for the indicator is that the firm has zero inventory levels. Therefore, SCCT refers to the maximum (not minimum or average) time required in the procurement and delivery. The budgeted maximum SCCT has to be compared with the realized SCCT for locating the variance at each process-component for remedial actions.

Because of the individual profiles of the companies (product complexity or capital-intensive production process), it is difficult to recommend a meaningful target. As orientation and for comparison purposes, internal benchmarks between various units within the firm can be used. The performance over time can be analysed with the help of budget-actual comparisons. External benchmarks could be taken from the branch-specific averages or the best-practice values.

Assuming that firms in the same branch usually have similar production and asset structures, the ratio values, differing significantly from the averages, are clear candidates for serious reviews. This should help in analysing the positive and negative developments or consequences, and in manoeuvring them in the context of corporate goals.

It should, however, be said that minimizing the SCCT should not be an efficiency-target because it often leads to sub-standard and less optimal solutions. The challenge lies in optimizing the SCCT without sacrificing the parameters of quality and costs.

## Useful Suggestions

Given the fact that we live in an era of speed competition, a major key to success is time compression. Fast movement of information and products is essential for survival. Thus, efforts at optimizing the SCCT mean decreasing the inventory-holding days and reducing the cash conversion cycle, both of which release the capital tied by these processes.

Managing the SCCT requires concerted efforts at all levels. It not only involves cross-functional process, re-engineering within the company, but also inter-organizational integration in the upstream and downstream supply chain. Suppliers, at the supply chain source, are considered to have an incredible impact on the supply chain as to time, inventory, quality and logistic costs, impact that goes far beyond pricing and placing purchase orders. Visibility of purchase orders, at suppliers, in-transit and at each step in the chain, from vendor's plant to delivery at the warehouse, store or customer can be important factors for optimizing SCCT.

It is relevant to note that effective supplier management is based on technology, process and people. More importantly, it is how purchase orders and suppliers' relationship are managed. The technology enables the revising of orders, their priorities, their style and other mixes, their timing, quantities and more. Technology gives visibility to directing and controlling supplier performance and what is in the supply chain, including what is happening with transport and other logistics service providers.

**&** **Related Ratios/Additional Notes**

A closely related and equally important ratio is Cash-to-Cash Cycle which measures the length of time during which liquidity is tied to the operational cycle. Whereas, the focus of SCCT is on the time consumed in the operational cycle, it shifts to capital blocked in the Cash-to-Cash Cycle.

When attention switches from the time efficiency to cost efficiency of the procurement cycle, the resultant ratio to focus on is the Procurement Efficiency Ratio. It is not good to ignore the fact that too much focus on SCCT often results in Faulty Incoming and/or Faulty Outgoing Delivery Rates which may create high inspection costs.

The two ratios having a strong impact on SCCT are Throughput Time (TPT) and Days Inventory Outstanding (DIO). A good management of these components of SCCT is entirely within the internal operations of the company.

### 4.3.4 Faulty Incoming Delivery Rate

**?** **Analytical Question**

How big is the share of faulty incoming deliveries in total, or from each of the suppliers?

**\*** **Definition**

$$\frac{\text{Number of Faulty Incoming Deliveries} \cdot 100}{\text{Total Number of Incoming Deliveries (in a Period or per Supplier)}}$$

The Faulty Incoming Delivery Rate is expressed as a percentage.

**»** **Calculation/Derivation**

The required data for this quotient is prepared from the (computerised) information system for procurement planning and controlling. The data could be compiled for all the suppliers in a period, or separately for each supplier.

**#** **Interpretation and Typical Range**

The Faulty Incoming Delivery Rate is an important measure for the suppliers' quality rating system. It provides an indicator for judging a supplier's performance in terms of guaranteeing supplies to the firm, in the right quality, and in time. (See in connection with this, another indicator of supplier's readiness to deliver under the heading "Supplier's Service Level".)

Given the individual inventory holding policy of a firm, and the cost involved in managing the faulty incoming deliveries, it is desirable to optimize both and keep the faulty deliveries to a minimum. This is important for ensuring an uninterrupted supply of needed input in the operational processes.

**Useful Suggestions**

In our networked business world, companies often outsource their operations to external parties which leads to a decline in the in-house production intensity. In consequence, there is an increasing need to measure the performance of the parties involved in the supply chain. Thus, ratios for measuring quality, costs or time of incoming deliveries have become more relevant today than before.

Accordingly, the need to coordinate supply chains has increased and, in extreme cases of just-in-time supply systems, the relationship with suppliers is often based on precise planning of the preparatory and simultaneous flow of information in both directions.

**Related Ratios/Additional Notes**

If only the quantity of the faulty incoming deliveries is taken as the numerator in the ratio, the resultant "Quantity-based Complaint Rate" can be shown as follows (calculated separately for A, B, and C category items):

$$\frac{\text{Quantity of Complained Units} \cdot 100}{\text{Total Number of Acquired Units (in a Period or per Supplier)}}$$

In contrast, if the value of the incoming deliveries is taken as the numerator in the ratio, the resultant "Value-based Complaint Rate" can be shown as follows:

$$\frac{\text{Value of the Complained Units} \cdot 100}{\text{Total Value of Incoming Deliveries (in a Period or per Supplier)}}$$

## 4.3.5 Faulty Outgoing Delivery Rate

**Analytical Question**

How big is the share of faulty outgoing deliveries of the total deliveries, or of total deliveries to each of the customers separately?

**Definition**

$$\frac{\text{Number of Faulty Outgoing Deliveries} \cdot 100}{\text{Total Number of Outgoing Deliveries (in a Period or per Customer)}}$$

The Faulty Outgoing Delivery Rate is expressed as a percentage.

**» Calculation/Derivation**

The required data for this quotient is prepared from the (computerised) information system for sales planning and controlling. The data can be compiled for all the customers in a period, or separately for each customer.

**# Interpretation and Typical Range**

The Faulty Outgoing Delivery Rate is an important measure of the quality of the delivery and distribution system, organized by the firm. From a customer's perspective, it is also a useful criterion towards the suppliers' quality rating system. It provides an indicator for judging performance in terms of guaranteeing supplies to the customers at the right quality, and in time. (See in connection with this, another indicator for supplier's readiness to deliver, under the heading "Supplier's Service Level".)

Given the individual inventory holding policy of a firm, and the cost involved in managing the faulty outgoing deliveries, it is desirable to optimize both, and keep the faulty deliveries to a minimum. This is important to ensure an uninterrupted supply of needed input to customers.

**! Useful Suggestions**

In our networked business world, companies often outsource their operations to external parties, which leads to a decline in the in-house production intensity. In consequence, there is an increasing need to measure the performance of the parties involved in the supply chain. Thus, ratios for measuring quality, costs or time of outgoing deliveries, have become more relevant today than before.

Accordingly, the need for coordination of supply chains has increased and, in the extreme cases of just-in-time supply systems, the relationship with suppliers is often based on a precise planning of preparatory and simultaneous flow of information in both directions.

The basic element of all measures towards reducing faulty deliveries (or stabilizing the lower level of faults) is a systematic analysis of the causes of such problems and their permanent elimination through intensive quality management and controlling.

**& Related Ratios/Additional Notes**

If only the quantity of the faulty outgoing deliveries is taken as the numerator in the ratio, the resultant "Quantity-based Complaint Rate" can be (calculated separately for A, B, and C category items) shown as follows:

$$\frac{\text{Quantity of Complained Units} \cdot 100}{\text{Total Number of Delivered Units (in a Period or per Customer)}}$$

In contrast, if the value of the outgoing deliveries is taken as the numerator in the ratio, the resultant "Value-based Complaint Rate" can be shown as follows:

$$\frac{\text{Value of the Complained Units} \cdot 100}{\text{Total Value of Outgoing Deliveries (in a Period or per Customer)}}$$

### 4.3.6 Vertical Integration Level

**Analytical Question**

- What proportion of the total production is carried out within the company? Or
- When measured in terms of relative value added, what is the level of vertical integration within the firm?

**Definition**

$$\frac{\text{Value Added} \cdot 100}{\text{Total Output}}$$

The gross value added is the difference between the output and input. In business terminology, it is determined by subtracting the value of goods and services purchased from the total production value for the current period. If depreciation is also subtracted, the resultant amount is called net value added.

The Vertical Integration Level is expressed as a percentage.

**Calculation/Derivation**

The required data for this quotient is prepared from the information system relating to internal cost accounting and external financial accounting. In the case of external financial accounting based on the annual report, value added is derived by subtracting the cost of goods sold from net sales.

**Interpretation and Typical Range**

The gross value added is considered as a better measure for fixing the firm's size than sales revenue, because:

- Value added takes into account not only the vertical integration level but also the total output.
- A price based or quantity based increase in the value of purchased goods and services which is passed through to the customer shows a numeric growth (in sales) for the firm. However, other factors remaining the same, it does not contain any *real* increase in value added.

For comparison between or amongst firms with varying levels of absolute value added (which may create a biased judgment), the explicit consideration of the Vertical Integration Level, as a relative ratio, can provide more transparency.

The higher the Vertical Integration Level, the higher the share of internally generated value in the total output of the firm. If the ratio is falling over time, it could be an indicator of increased outsourcing of the business processes. However, a lower or higher Vertical Integration Level does not, in principle, indicate a negative or positive state of affairs. A firm with lower vertical integration could be as profitable as (more profitable than) its competitor who has, relatively speaking, a higher value added. The level of vertical integration is strongly influenced by the situation of the firm in the market, its competitive position, and the branch specific environment.

## ! Useful Suggestions

From a strategic perspective, the configuration of the firm's supply chain is of primary importance. Which of the processes should be carried out internally by the firm because of the competitive advantages gained over time? Which of the processes can be carried out more cost effectively by suppliers and partners in the production network? The qualitative and quantitative advantages and disadvantages of strong vertical integration should be compared carefully with the advantages and disadvantages of focusing on core-competence (and as a consequence of lower vertical integration).

If a firm is experiencing problems due to continuous bottlenecks or shortages, its value chain should be reviewed carefully. It should examine the economic benefits of shifting the squeezed activities, through external procurement or outsourcing. The firm can also conduct capital budgeting analysis on the benefits of a targeted capacity expansion.

## & Related Ratios/Additional Notes

The term vertical integration has its origins in the area of industrial organization. However, it has become very popular in the last decade, primarily in the context of supply chain management. The ratio can also be used by all other kinds of firms as "Value Added Level" or "Value-Added Quota".

Depending upon the need for taking action on a strategic level (in the case of enduring bottlenecks) or on the operative level (from temporary overloaded capacity), the management is confronted with the problem of choosing an appropriate level of vertical integration (which is often summed up as "Make or buy decision", or "Out versus In-sourcing") or just tolerating the bottleneck related additional costs of internal production.

### 4.3.7 Supplier's Service Level

**Analytical Question**

- In the context of sales, how far is the firm able to make timely supplies to *external customers*? Or
- In the context of procurement, how far is an external supplier able to make timely supplies to *us*? Or
- In the context of internal logistics, how far is an internal supplier able to make timely supplies to an *internal recipient*?

**Definition**

$$\frac{\text{Number of Scheduled Deliveries (in a Period)} \cdot 100}{\text{Total Number of all Deliveries (in a Period)}}$$

The Supplier's Service Level is expressed as a percentage.

**Calculation/Derivation**

If the focus is on external customers (or external suppliers) the required data for this quotient is prepared from the (computerised) information system for sales (procurement) planning and controlling.

In the case of an internal supplier, the needed data could be provided by the internal logistic information system, particularly, the warehouse and transportation data.

**Interpretation and Typical Range**

Depending upon the focus, on sales or external (or internal) procurement, this ratio measures whether the outgoing or incoming deliveries were carried out in time or as per the given schedule. The ratio is one of the performance evaluation criteria for measuring the internal or external delivery and availability, in terms of time, assuming that the quality of the delivered object is good.

Given the individual inventory holding policy of a firm, and the cost involved in managing the faulty outgoing deliveries, it is desirable to optimize on both and keep the delivery-delays to a minimum. This is important for ensuring an uninterrupted supply of needed input.

**Useful Suggestions**

In the modern business world with strong emphasis on networking, companies often outsource their operations to external parties, which leads to a decline in the in-house production intensity. In consequence, there is an increasing need to measure the performance of the parties involved in the supply chain. Thus, ratios for measuring quality, costs or time of deliveries have become more relevant today than before.

Accordingly, the need for coordination of supply chains has increased and, in extreme cases of a just-in-time supply system, the relationship with suppliers is often based on a precise planning of preparatory and simultaneous flow of information in both directions.

The basic element of all measures towards reducing delays in deliveries (or stabilizing scheduled deliveries) is a systematic analysis of the causes of such problems, and their permanent elimination through an intensive quality management and controlling.

### & Related Ratios/Additional Notes

If the value of the deliveries is taken as the numerator in the ratio, the resultant "Value-based Complaint Rate" could be shown as follows:

$$\frac{\text{Value of the Complained Deliveries (in a Period)} \cdot 100}{\text{Total Value of all Deliveries (in a Period)}}$$

The ratio can be shown separately for complaints relating to delays, and complaints relating to quality problems. These could be further classified into outgoing deliveries and incoming deliveries.

As synonyms for the Supplier's Service Level, "On-time Delivery Rate" or "Scheduled Adherence Rate" could be used.

### 4.3.8 Cooperation Index

### ? Analytical Question

Are the net benefits, derived from internal and/or external cooperative processes, higher or lower over time? To what extent has the company gained from higher levels of cooperation in the inter- and intra-organizational processes?

### * Definition

$$\frac{\text{Net Benefits from Cooperative Processes in Period t}}{\text{Net Benefits from Cooperative Processes in Period t-1}}$$

Cooperation Index could be in multiples or (when multiplied by 100) as a percentage.

### » Calculation/Derivation

The calculation of the benefits from cooperative processes requires monetary estimation of all the synergies and savings which the firm has achieved through inter-and intra-organizational cooperative processes. The costs incurred (for technical or human resources) in implementing cooperative processes, must be subtracted from the value of all synergies and savings to calculate the net benefits.

For better results, it is desirable to systematically pool all the costs in a separate cost-centre.

## Interpretation and Typical Range

The Cooperation Index provides a pragmatic and quantifiable measure of the cooperative processes (for example, new methods of communication) introduced by the firm across functional, business and organizational boundaries. It is a useful tool for managers to measure the impact of various strategic and process options implemented over time to improve the cooperative capacity of the organization.

If a company adopts new cooperative strategies and processes in inter- and intra-organizational activities over time, it commits higher amounts of technical and human resources towards the realization of an improved cooperative environment. The efficiency gains achieved through such initiatives must be measured in monetary terms to justify such moves.

It is not possible to give a desired target ratio for this ratio. If the index is successively higher over time, it should be interpreted as positive and effective.

However, since the benefits of various cooperative strategies and processes may lag for some periods, the initial higher costs may create confusion when comparing results. Thus, for long-term impact analysis, time-series results over several periods should be compared.

## Useful Suggestions

In a world where value must be created through innovation, where ubiquitous communication technology has levelled the playing field, where resources are coupled flexibly as needed, cooperation becomes *the* most critical organization capability. Today, across the world, organizations struggle to reap the benefits of processes that are dependent on purposeful cooperation – innovation, flexible sourcing, customer sensing, workforce deployment, resource allocation, and many others. The ability to cooperate is a critical success factor in mergers, partnerships, and joint ventures, which, more than ever before, are fundamental elements in most organization's strategic plans.

The resource commitment for cooperative processes can often be very expensive and demands clear homework on cost-benefit analysis for such actions. For example, asking a supplier to adopt a particular technical system for faster communication may require financing such an initiative. This would demand a serious analysis of the long-term efficiency gains which must surpass the investment involved in it. Often, it would demand a capital budgeting exercise, where the monetary benefits of such a decision have to be discounted over the effective period.

For improving the Cooperation Index, mutual resource dependence and congruent goals are considered to be the two most important pre-requisites. In a situation of mutual dependence, organizations will cooperate in order to exchange resources that make it possible to achieve organizational goals, whereas shared interests and a similar commitment to a policy make it easier to get along and reduce costs. Needless to say, mutual trust also reduces various costs and increases cooperation.

A change in this ratio could be triggered by a disproportionate increase or decrease in synergies and/or costs involved in new cooperative initiatives. The benefits may often lag behind the costs involved in cooperative projects.

### & Related Ratios/Additional Notes

Sometimes, in an inter-organizational context, Cooperation Index is viewed as the number of strategic alliances made (minority and majority stakes, license agreements, R&D projects, joint-ventures, mergers and acquisitions, etc.) and network-memberships obtained by a firm. In this case, the index would refer to the percentage change in the total number of such alliances and memberships between two periods.

A related ratio is considered to be the Coordination Index. This, however, would be a non-monetary measure of, for example, how frequently different departments (involved in a collective process) communicate or meet with each other.

The monetary quantification of the synergies generated by inter- and intra-organizational processes is not an easy job. Similarly, the subjective separation of estimated costs and savings of cooperation projects, from the rest of the costs and savings, may make the application of this indicator somewhat difficult.

## 4.4 Production Capacity Management

### 4.4.1 Plant Availability

### ? Analytical Question

What is the effective availability of the plant and machinery for direct production? What is the proportionate time, out of the total operational time, during which a plant is ready for use in production?

### * Definition

$$\frac{\text{Production Time} \cdot 100}{\text{Total Operation Time}}$$

The term "Total Operation Time" is made of three time components:
- production time (maximum possible production hours)
- setup and change-over time (non-productive time)
- servicing, maintenance and repairing time (idle time)

The Plant Availability is expressed as a percentage.

## Calculation/Derivation  »

The required data for this quotient is prepared from the (computerised) information system of production planning and controlling.

## Interpretation and Typical Range  #

The Plant Availability is viewed as one of the main ratios in process-controlling in the area of fixed-asset management. It is based on the competitive factor of time, and provides a percentage value about the availability of a particular machine, a set of machines or a multi-layered production plant for use in the production process. The higher the actual production time, and the lower the unplanned interruptions, the better the capacity utilization of the machine.

## Useful Suggestions  !

The high capital intensity involved in modern production processes makes it imperative that the production capacities, and their availability, are managed systematically. An increase in machine running-time is not only possible through an extension of the total operation time (for example, through increase in the number of shifts in a day) but also through a reduction of the non-productive and idle time. This can be achieved with the help of strategic measures relating to organizational structures in production management, or through measures aimed at operative production planning and controlling.

Therefore, in investment and maintenance controlling, the discovery and removal of the wasteful activities is considered a central issue. The sources of wasteful activities could be in operational time and availability loss, shift-starting times or setup times, as well as intensity and quality problems.

## Related Ratios/Additional Notes  &

Two synonyms for Plant Availability are Plant Utilization Rate or Machine Running Time Ratio.

### 4.4.2 Plant Downtime Rate

## Analytical Question  ?

What is the proportionate time, out of the total operational time, during which a plant is (unplanned) *not* available for production because of a breakdown or interruption?

## Definition  *

$$\frac{\text{Downtime} \cdot 100}{\text{Total Operation Time}}$$

The term "Total Operation Time" is made up of three *time* components:
- production time (maximum possible production hours)
- setup and change-over time (non-productive time)
- servicing, maintenance and repairing time (idle time)

The Plant Downtime Rate is expressed as a percentage.

### » Calculation/Derivation

The required data for this quotient is prepared from the (computerised) information system, relating production planning and controlling. In particular, the data which contains the operational time records has to be considered. It is important to mention that downtime is a part of the total idle time.

### # Interpretation and Typical Range

The Plant Downtime Rate is viewed as one of the main ratios for process-controlling in the area of fixed-asset management. It is based on the competitive factor of time, and provides a percentage value about the non-availability of a particular machine, a set of machines or a multi-layered production plant for use in the production process. The lower the unplanned interruptions, i.e. downtime, the better the capacity utilization of the machine.

### ! Useful Suggestions

The high capital intensity involved in modern production processes makes it imperative that the production capacities and their availability are managed systematically. An increase in machine running-time is not only possible through an extension of the total operation time (for example, through increase in the number of shifts in a day) but also through a reduction of non-productive and idle time. This can be achieved with the help of strategic measures, relating to organizational structures in production management, or through measures aimed at operative production planning and controlling.

Efforts made at reducing or avoiding downtime is a major aspect in maintenance, proactive servicing and repair management systems.

### & Related Ratios/Additional Notes

Sometimes, Idle Plant Time Ratio or Plant Breakdown Rate, are mentioned as synonyms for Plant Downtime Rate.

### 4.4.3 Maintenance Cost Intensity

**Analytical Question**

What is the ratio between the annual maintenance costs and the imputed depreciation of the asset being maintained?

**Definition**

$$\frac{\text{Maintenance Costs in a Period} \cdot 100}{\text{Imputed Depreciation of the Asset in a Period}}$$

The Maintenance Cost Intensity is expressed as a percentage.

**Calculation/Derivation**

The required data for this quotient is prepared from the (computerised) information system used for asset-controlling, in particular from data relating to production planning and controlling.

The maintenance costs are composed of two components which, as a matter of rule, behave in opposite directions:
- Inspection and preventive maintenance costs for checking the existing condition of the machine. This entails early fault-diagnosis as well as regular care to prevent wear and tear; and
- Repair costs for removing any problem and, in some situations, the costs of managing breakdowns and malfunctioning.

**Interpretation and Typical Range**

The Maintenance Cost Intensity is a widely used ratio which shows the periodic relation between cost of maintaining the performance of an asset, and its imputed depreciation.

Depending upon the strategy chosen for the maintenance of assets, the numerator in this ratio may show consistently similar values. This would be particularly true if the maintenance strategy is primarily focused on preventive maintenance. However, with the increasing age of the machines, this cost item should show an upward trend. On the other hand, the value in the denominator may be constant or change over different periods, depending upon whether the imputed depreciation is time-based or activity-based. Therefore, any specific target benchmark for this ratio is hard to recommend.

However, it is important to review the variance between the planned and unplanned developments in this ratio. It is also important to check when the target for taking corrective measures misses the mark. In extreme cases, it is better to replace the asset earlier than planned.

**❗ Useful Suggestions**

The high capital intensity involved in modern production processes makes it imperative that expected profitability be achieved. This can be ensured by making maximum use of available production capacities. This, in turn, has to be obtained by high reliability and quality in utilizing plant capacities.

With its broad spectrum of measures, maintenance (both preventive and non-preventive) occupies a major role in guaranteeing reliability and quality. Included in the list of measures are various strategic and operative options for internal or external services for inspection, upkeep and repair of machines. The timely integration of maintenance in the production cycles, in the form of periodic or sequential work, is equally important. Similarly, clear emphasis on the maintenance strategy (whether it is mainly managing breakdowns or a clear preventive strategy) should constitute a major parameter in the action plan.

**& Related Ratios/Additional Notes**

The terminology used in the academic and industrial world for maintenance (with its many variants, such as inspection, upkeep, servicing, and repair) is not uniform; as a result, identical ratios are sometimes defined differently. Therefore, it is important to check how the ratio is calculated or derived.

It is common to use the term "Maintenance Intensity" as a shorter variant of Maintenance Cost Intensity.

A related ratio which is commonly calculated for gaining more insight into maintenance costs, is called "Maintenance Rate" or "Maintenance Cost Rate". It is calculated by dividing maintenance costs by the acquisition cost of the asset.

**Ⓢ 4.4.4 Capacity Utilization Level**

**❓ Analytical Question**

How much of the installed capacity was used or is being used?

**✳ Definition**

Variant A:

$$\frac{\text{Effective Production Hours} \cdot 100}{\text{Maximum Possible Production Hours}}$$

Variant B:

$$\frac{\text{Actual Output Quantity} \cdot 100}{\text{Planned Output Quantity}}$$

The values in both numerator and denominator are either time units or quantities.

The Capacity Utilization Level is expressed as a percentage.

## Calculation/Derivation

`»`

The required data for this quotient is prepared from the (computerised) information system relating to production planning and controlling. Depending upon needs, the data could be classified for individual work-stations, cost-centres or production levels.

In variant A, the value "effective production hours" represents the actual hours spent in production. The denominator "maximum possible production hours" refers to technical, legal, normal, or cost-optimum-operational maximum.

In variant B, the quantity of output produced is compared with the planned operational level.

The terminology used for this ratio is neither consistent in the literature, nor in practice. Therefore, it is very important to ensure the consistency of data in drawing inter-firm and intra-firm comparisons.

## Interpretation and Typical Range

`#`

The Capacity Utilization Level is viewed as one of the main ratios in process-controlling in the area of fixed-asset management. It is based on the competitive need for maximum utilization of the production potential, and provides a percentage value about the actual deployment of available capabilities. From a technical point of view, the reference base for available capacity could be a particular machine, a set of machines or a multi-layered production plant for use in the production process. From the organizational perspective, the reference point for available capacity could be a particular work-station, a cost-centre, a plant or a firm.

The higher the Capacity Utilization Level, the lower the costs that should be shouldered by the individual production item. The explanation lies in the regressive behaviour of fixed costs; where per unit fixed costs fall for every increase in production, until maximum capacity is reached. In the case of multi-layered production processes, it is important to check that the capacities at each level of production are matched; otherwise unused capacities may be visible in the operational efficiency of produced goods and services.

In general, a capacity utilization level of 85 to 90% is considered desirable; however, such a goal, at the same time, may be viewed as challenging.

## Useful Suggestions

`!`

The high capital intensity involved in modern production processes makes it imperative that the production capacities and their availabilities are managed systematically. An increase in machine running-time is not only possible through an extension of the total operation time (for example, through increase in the number of shifts in a day) but also through a reduction of the non-productive and idle time.

This can be achieved with the help of strategic measures relating to organizational structures in production management, or through measures aimed at operative production planning and controlling.

If the capacity utilization is continuously below the target planned, at the time of capital investment, the fixed costs must be allocated to a lowered production volume, leading to higher product costs, and as a consequence, to lower profits or even loss. Therefore, it is important to plan plant capacities and manpower requirements very carefully, in alignment with strategic orientation. A good capacity plan should also include various flexible options, such as outsourcing alternatives and external production networks.

**&** **Related Ratios/Additional Notes**

Capacity Utilization is often used as a short expression for Capacity Utilization Level. "Activity Level" and "Operational Level" are other synonyms used, particularly, when time-capacities of the employees are a reference point.

However, the word "Capacity Level" is used only for a special capacity utilization level, where the breakeven point is achieved.

### 4.4.5 Contribution Margin per Unit of the Constrained Resource

**?** **Analytical Question**

In the case of short term resource constraints (for example, capacity bottlenecks), what is the criterion for selecting the products and services that will contribute to greater profitability?

**✳** **Definition**

$$\frac{\text{Contribution Margin per Unit}}{\text{Constrained Factor Consumption per Unit}}$$

Where:

| | | |
|---|---|---|
| Contribution Margin per Unit | = | Price per unit – variable costs per unit |
| Constrained Factor Consumption per Unit | = | The capacity or consumption per unit of the constrained factor. The unit of the constrained factor could be in square meter, cubic meter, weight, or time. |

The ratio is measured in monetary value per unit of the constrained factor, for example, € per machine minute or € per hour.

## Calculation/Derivation

The information needed for this ratio can be taken from cost and activity accounting, which has to be based on direct or marginal costing. For additional information, one has to depend on the computerised information collection systems for production planning and control. Basically, the constrained factor can be any production input, creating the need for different kinds of information.

## Interpretation and Typical Range

The "Contribution Margin per Unit of the Constrained Resource" is an operative indicator which derives its relevance during periods of operational bottlenecks. Typical bottlenecks in machine capacities, but also shortages in any of the business inputs (warehouse space or volume, raw material or energy supply, transport capacities, or human resources) can be overcome with such profitable solutions and ideas.

The contribution margin per unit, in the numerator, shows the short-term performance indicator for products and services. This advantage per unit is related to the capacity needed per unit, to draw a comparative number on all such products and services which compete for the constrained factor.

## Useful Suggestions

Assuming that it is not easy to increase or change the capacities of production inputs in the short-run, the decision rule should be to prefer production of objects with the highest contribution margin per unit. In this context, the minimum quantities (contractual commitment to customers) for products with a "weaker contribution margin" should be taken from the available capacities, and the rest of the capacity should be distributed stepwise to products based on the rule of higher contribution margin.

With a given contribution margin per unit, this ratio will help in maximizing the profits (or reducing the loss of non-recovered fixed costs) because the constrained capacity is distributed optimally with reference to the contribution margin per unit.

In case of a continuing problem with bottlenecks, one should consider redesigning the supply chain, deciding to outsource the constrained activity and/or check the benefit of strategic options such as capacity expansion, through the discounted cash flow method.

## Related Ratios/Additional Notes

This ratio is sometimes also referred to as "Specific Contribution Margin" or "Relative Contribution Margin".

Depending upon whether the corrective measures are strategic (for enduring bottlenecks) or operative (for transition bottlenecks), the management is confronted with serious decisions about production intensity or vertical integration (Make or buy and also outsourcing/off-shoring). In this context, the added costs involved in checking whether in-house production would be better than contracting an external supplier should be considered.

## 4.5 Process Controlling

### 4.5.1 Throughput Time (TPT)

**? Analytical Question**
- What is the *average* total (planned or realized) time that elapses in producing a product or service, from the first work-operation to the last work-operation?
- What is the average time that a unit requires to flow through the process of completion, from the entry point to the exit point?

**\* Definition**
Depending upon a narrow or broad concept design, there are various time components which are included in the definition of TPT. In general, the following are always counted in a minimum version of TPT:

> Process Occupancy Time + Transition Time + Idle Time

Where:

| | |
|---|---|
| Process Occupancy Time | = Processing, Set-up, and Testing Periods |
| Transition Time | = Transportation Time |
| Idle Time | = Interim Storage Idle Time, Work-flow related Idle Time, Breakdown related Idle Time, and Worker Idle Time |

However, in different technical and practical situations, a multitude of proposals are made for calculating the TPT. Thus, if the TPT is defined as the total order-processing time, there are other time components which are added to the above three. These are upstream time components (for example, between order-receipt and production-begin) and downstream time components (for example, between production-termination and delivery to the customer).

As the name suggests, the TPT is expressed in time units, such as minutes, hours and days, etc.

**» Calculation/Derivation**
The required data for this quotient is prepared from the (computerised) information system, related to production planning and controlling. If the concept of TPT is understood as order processing time, the information about the upstream time components (order-receiving and materials management related activities) and downstream time components (invoicing, documentation, and delivery related activities) have to be derived from various operational time records. In most cases today, the basic data

for this purpose is drawn from an ERP (Enterprise Resource Planning) system with a module-based structure.

## Interpretation and Typical Range

The conceptual confines of TPT, with a clear determination of starting- and finishing point, often depends strongly on the type of business, or the operational conditions. If TPT is viewed from a customers' perspective, it would be more appropriate to take the period between order-receipt and delivery of the product. Mostly, however, TPT is used in manufacturing for production planning and operational performance evaluation.

A general target for this ratio cannot be given without considering production process complexities and applied labour intensive or capital intensive manufacturing methods. As orientation and for comparison purposes, internal benchmarks between various units within the firm can be used. The performance over time can be analysed with the help of budget-actual comparisons. External benchmarks could be taken from branch-specific averages or best-practice values.

Assuming that firms in the same branch usually have similar production and asset structures, the ratio values, differing significantly from the averages, are clear candidates for serious review. This should help in analysing positive and negative developments or consequences, and in manoeuvring them in the context of corporate goals.

## Useful Suggestions

The main issue involved in designing an appropriate TPT is always the question of how to reduce or minimize it. If market perspective is taken into consideration, the customer is always interested in obtaining fast delivery of the ordered product or service. Thus, when firms are interested in reducing capital tied-up in the production process (with additional warehousing and financial costs), the significance of lean production (mostly in real time and after the order is received) and shorter TPT, has increased considerably.

Various surveys of the ratio between idle time (non value generating activities, sometimes accounting for over 80 % of total TPT) and processing time (value generating activities, often accounting for less than 20 % of total TPT) have made "process-reengineering" as an important issue to be managed. Counted in this is a broad spectrum of measures, such as minimization of idle time, modularization of production processes and simultaneous completion of different work flows to achieve a reduction in the TPT.

## Related Ratios/Additional Notes

TPT is also known as "Flow Time". However, TPT should not be confused with "Cycle Time" which implies the time required for a task to repeat itself. Furthermore, TPT is not equal to "Process Time" which can be measured by subtracting transition and idle time from TPT.

A related term for TPT is the "Throughput Rate" (also known as "Flow Rate"). It represents the average rate at which production units' flow past a specific point in the process. An example could be the units that pass through a scanner per hour in a quality check.

It is interesting to notice that the work-in-process (WIP) inventory is related to TPT and throughput rate. Thus,

WIP Inventory = Throughput Rate · TPT

This relation is known as *Little's Law*, named after John D.C. Little, who proved it mathematically in 1961.

### 4.5.2 Days Inventory Outstanding (DIO)

**?** **Analytical Question**

How long is the available inventory going to last? How long does it take to turn, for example, the finished goods inventory into sales?

**\*** **Definition**

Basic Variant:

$$\frac{\text{Average (Daily) Inventory Level} \cdot 360 \text{ Days}}{\text{Average (Daily) Need}}$$

or

Special Variant for Finished Product Inventory:

$$\frac{\text{Average Value of Inventory} \cdot 360 \text{ Days}}{\text{Net Sales or Cost of Goods Sold}}$$

This ratio is expressed in terms of time, depending upon the multiplier. Thus, with the 360 days' multiplier, it is expressed in days; with the 52, it is expressed in weeks; and with the 12, it is expressed in months.

Though some practitioners use average sales as the denominator, it is the cost of goods sold which is more appropriate for calculating this ratio. Cost of goods sold is the proxy for "consumption" or "inventory issued".

The above formula is a value-based variant of DIO. The ratio can also be calculated with reference to the quantity of goods sold, in which case the formula is as follows:

$$\frac{\text{Average Quantity of Inventory} \cdot 360 \text{ Days}}{\text{Quantity of Goods Sold}}$$

The computation of DIO can be carried out for various categories of inventoried objects, independent of their physical condition as solid, liquid or gaseous goods. Thus, the objects may be grouped:

- according to their position in the value chain. For example, there could be a separate inventory turnover ratio for raw-materials, utilities and supplies, work in process (modules and components, etc.) and finished products; or
- according to their value in A, B, and C categories, or according to their consumption-volume prediction accuracy in X, Y, or Z categories.

### Calculation/Derivation

The data for the (value based variant of) DIO of finished products can be obtained from published external accounting reports. Thus, sales and/or cost of goods sold is available in the income statement, and the average inventory can be computed from the balance sheet values from the beginning inventory and ending inventory. For all other inventory objects or types of stocks, the needed data will have to be based on the internal computer-based information system for inventory management (This information, however, may not be accessible to external analysts). The data will also be linked with production planning and internal cost accounting. Thus, for example, the information could be drawn from various statements of stock and consumption. In certain circumstances, the goods in transit may have to be included in the calculation.

### Interpretation and Typical Range

The DIO can be grouped in the category of process controlling as well as in the category of operational efficiency. It is also often used as a measure of liquidity. In the case of trading companies, DIO shows the average time it takes to sell the inventory. Another interpretation of this ratio is that it provides information about the supply situation of the stored item; the ratio indicates the duration, for which the inventory is available. The ratio is considered both as a cost driver as well as a value driver.

Depending upon the level at which this ratio is computed, the insight gained may be related to a macro aggregated level (such as a production plant) or may be related to various detailed micro levels (such as individual products or product groups).

With the established inclusion of supply chain management in business processes (also outside the firm's boundaries), holding of inventories is viewed as an alleged symbol for "not well-coordinated production planning". However, the envisaged reduction of inventory levels often conflicts with the value-generating functions (such as smoothing, transformation, and the transfer function) of inventory holding. Thus, in each individual case, the needed inventory levels should be calculated with reference to the operational specifics.

A higher value of DIO may be viewed as stable provisioning of needed supplies; however, it also implies a higher commitment to capital in inventory holding. In addition, one has to consider the cost of capital linked with the variable and fixed costs in maintaining and using the warehouse facilities.

Because of diverse operational constellations, a generalized target for the inventory turnover ratio cannot be determined. Nevertheless, achieving a successively lower DIO is usually considered favourable; it indicates that the inventory moves more quickly through the production process to the ultimate customer, reducing storage and obsolescence costs, and releasing the tied up capital for other purposes. However, in order to reduce the risk of production interruptions, it is not only important to maintain safety stock levels, but also to ensure that DIO is able to bridge the lead time needed for the future deliveries.

As orientation and for comparison purposes, internal benchmarks between various units within the firm (such as locations and plants) can be used. The performance over time can be analysed with the help of budget-actual comparisons. External benchmarks could be taken from the branch-specific averages or best-practice values.

Along with quantity-based measures, this ratio can also be calculated with monetary-values. For such value-based comparisons, it is important to ensure the consistency of the price component used to calculate the inventory value (acquisition price, sales price, current price, average price or production costs).

### ❗ Useful Suggestions

Assuming that firms in the same branch usually have similar production and asset structures, the ratio values, differing significantly from the averages, are clear candidates for serious reviews. This should help in analysing positive and negative developments or consequences and in manoeuvring them in the context of corporate goals.

In principle, a fall or rise in the profitability of the firm may be analysed with reference to a change in return on sales or in the inventory turnover ratio (including DIO) and corrective measures could be applied. More efficient purchasing and production techniques, such as the just-in-time inventory, help in improving the DIO.

A change in DIO could be triggered by a disproportionate increase or decrease in the average inventory (as numerator) and net sales/cost of goods sold (as denominator). *For further details and systematic explanations on this, refer to the information in Appendix I.*

When deciding on the appropriate DIO, a cost-based review is obviously important. However, over and above that, the market perspective should be carefully analysed. A considerable reduction in the DIO for finished products may jeopardize the delivery schedule expected by the client. One should, therefore, compare and contrast all operational issues across various functional departments. Above all, whether the customers accept the changed delivery schedules and whether the tight delivery schedules are viewed by clients as a positive signal, as is the case in the luxury goods market, should be checked.

**Related Ratios/Additional Notes**
DIO is also known as "Inventory Holding Period", "Average Days to Sell Inventory", "Inventory on Hand", "Days Stock on Hand" and "Inventory Coverage Period".

The mathematical reciprocal (Cost of Goods Sold /Average Inventory) of DIO, without multiplication by days in a year, is termed as "Inventory Turnover Ratio" or "Stock Turnover Ratio".

## 4.5.3 Inventory Turnover Ratio

**Analytical Question**
How efficient are inventory management activities? How often is the average inventory level turned over in the period under consideration?

**Definition**
Basic Variant:

$$\frac{\text{Average (Daily) Need}}{\text{Average (Daily) Inventory Level}}$$

or
Special Variant for Finished Product Inventory:

$$\frac{\text{Net Sales or Cost of Goods Sold}}{\text{Average Value of Inventory}}$$

This ratio is expressed in terms of multiples.

In the special variant, though some practitioners use average sales as the numerator, it is the cost of goods sold which is more appropriate for calculating this ratio. Cost of goods sold is the proxy for "consumption" or "inventory issued". The special variant is a value-based variant of the Inventory Turnover Ratio.

The Inventory Turnover Ratio can also be calculated with reference to the quantity of goods sold, in which case the formula is as follows:

$$\frac{\text{Quantity of Goods Sold}}{\text{Average Quantity of Inventory}}$$

In the basic variant, the "need" is often replaced with "consumption" or "issued". Along with the quantity-based definition of numerator and denominator, a value-based variant of this ratio is often used in practice. However, for an inter-firm or time-series comparison of value based results, it is important to check the consistency and choice of the price component for the inventory valuation. The valuation could be based on acquisition price or sales price, current price or average price, or appropriate production costs.

The computation of the Inventory Turnover Ratio could be made for various categories of inventoriable objects, independent of their physical condition as solid, liquid or gaseous goods. Thus, the objects may be grouped:
- according to their position in the value chain. For example, there could be a separate inventory turnover ratio for raw-materials, utilities and supplies, work in process (modules and components, etc.) and finished products; or
- according to their value in A, B, and C categories, or according to their consumption-volume prediction accuracy in X, Y, or Z categories.

**» Calculation/Derivation**

The data for (value based variant of) the Inventory Turnover Ratio of finished products can be obtained from published external accounting reports. Thus, sales and/ or cost of goods sold is available in the income statement, and the average inventory can be computed from the balance sheet values of the beginning inventory and the ending inventory. For all other inventory objects or types of stocks, the needed data will have to be based on the internal computer-based information system for inventory management (which, however, may not be accessible to external analysts). The data will also be linked with production planning and internal cost accounting. For example, the information could be drawn from various statements of stock and consumption. In certain circumstances, the goods in transit may have to be included in the calculation.

**# Interpretation and Typical Range**

The Inventory Turnover Ratio can be grouped in the category of "process controlling" as well as in the category of operational efficiency. It is often used as a measure of liquidity as well. The ratio reflects the relationship of the inventory to the volume of goods sold during a period. It communicates the intensity with which a particular stocked item is utilized (or turned over) in the operational production process. The ratio is considered both as a cost driver as well as a value driver.

Depending upon the level at which this ratio is computed, the insight gained may be related to a macro-aggregated level (such as a production plant) or may be related to various detailed micro levels (such as individual products or product groups).

Because of diverse operational constellations, a generalized target for the Inventory Turnover Ratio cannot be determined. Nevertheless, achieving a successively higher inventory turnover is usually considered favourable because it indicates that the inventory moves more quickly through the production process to the ultimate customer, reducing storage and obsolescence costs, releasing tied up capital for other purposes.

For orientation and comparison purposes, internal benchmarks between various units within the firm can be used. The performance over time can be analysed with the help of budget-actual comparisons. External benchmarks could be taken from the branch-specific averages or the best-practice values. Whenever comparisons are made, it is important to ensure the consistency of the price component used to calculate the inventory value (acquisition price, sales price, current price, average price or production costs).

**Useful Suggestions**                                                            !

Assuming that firms in the same branch usually have similar production and asset structures, the ratio values, differing significantly from the averages, are clear candidates for serious reviews. This should help in analysing positive and negative developments or consequences, and in manoeuvring them in the context of corporate goals.

In trading companies, the Inventory Turnover Ratio constitutes a central measure for steering supply chain management. This is primarily because trading companies do not have production of their own.

The significance of the Inventory Turnover Ratio is evident when we view inventory as "asset", particularly in the context of the ROI framework (*for the details on the so-called DuPont System, see details in Appendix II*). The profitability (Net Income/Average Capital) as a key ratio is extended into two ratios where return on sales is based on EBIT/Sales and asset turnover is based on Sales/Average Assets. The multiplicative link between "Return on Sales" and "Asset Turnover" ratios in ROI shows that a firm can maintain its profitability despite a fall in the return on sales, if it is able to improve its inventory turnover ratio. For this, one should carefully evaluate the short, medium, and long-term impact of all the measures which reduce the inventory base without negatively influencing the sales-generating capacity. The Inventory Turnover Ratio can be increased by focusing on the "fast-selling" products. If there are many "slow-moving-items" in the inventory, the ROI can be influenced primarily by increasing the return on sales.

In principle, a fall or rise in the profitability of the firm could be analysed with reference to a change in return on sales, or the Inventory Turnover Ratio, and corrective measures could be applied. More efficient purchasing and production techniques, such as just-in-time inventory, cause the Inventory Turnover Ratio to be high.

A change in the Inventory Turnover Ratio could be triggered by a disproportionate increase or decrease in the net sales or cost of goods sold (as numerator) and average inventory (as denominator). *For further details and systematic explanations on this, refer to the information in Appendix I.*

If the Inventory Turnover Ratio is too high, it may indicate that sales were lost because the desired item was not in stock. The cost of a lost sale is much higher than the lost profit; it may impact on all future profits on lost sales from a lost customer.

**&** **Related Ratios/Additional Notes**
The Inventory Turnover Ratio is known variously as "Rate of Inventory Turnover" or "Stock Turnover Ratio".

The mathematical reciprocal (Average Inventory/Cost of Goods Sold) of the Inventory Turnover Ratio, when multiplied by days in a year, is called "Inventory Holding Period", "Average Days to Sell Inventory" or "Days Stock on Hand"

### 4.5.4 Material Coverage Period

**?** **Analytical Question**
How long is the available inventory of material going to last?

**\*** **Definition**
Basic Quantity Variant:

$$\frac{\text{Average (Daily) Material Inventory Level} \cdot 360 \text{ Days}}{\text{Average (Daily) Need}}$$

or
Value Based Variant:

$$\frac{\text{Average Value of Material Inventory} \cdot 360 \text{ Days}}{\text{Average Value of Need or Consumption}}$$

This ratio is expressed in terms of time, depending upon the multiplier. Thus, with the 360 days' multiplier, it is expressed in days; with 52, it is expressed in weeks; and with 12, it is expressed in months.

Along with the quantity-based definition of numerator and denominator, the value-based variant of this ratio is often used in practice. However, for an inter-firm or time-series comparison of value based results, it is important to check the consistency and choice of the price component for the inventory valuation. The valuation could be based on acquisition price, sales price, current price, average price, or appropriate production costs.

The computation of the Material Coverage Period could be made for various categories of inventoried objects, independent of their physical condition as solid, liquid or gaseous goods. Thus, the objects may be grouped:
– according to their position in the value chain. For example, there could be a separate Material Coverage Period for raw-materials, utilities and supplies, work in process (modules and components, etc.) and finished products; or
– according to their value in A, B, and C categories or according to their consumption-volume prediction accuracy in X, Y, or Z categories.

## Calculation/Derivation

The needed data can be derived from the internal computer-based information system for inventory management (This information, however, may not be accessible to external analysts). The data will also be linked with production planning and internal cost accounting. For example, the information could be drawn from various statements of stock and consumption. In certain circumstances, the goods in transit may have to be included in the calculation.

## Interpretation and Typical Range

The Material Coverage Period can be grouped in the category of "process controlling", as well as in the category of operational efficiency. It is often used as a measure of liquidity as well. In the case of trading companies, the Material Coverage Period shows the average time it takes to sell the inventory. Another interpretation of the ratio is in providing information about the supply situation of the stored item; the ratio indicates the duration, for which the inventory is available. The ratio is considered both as a cost driver, and as a value driver.

Depending upon the level at which this ratio is computed, the insight gained may be related to a macro aggregated level (such as a production plant) or may be related to various detailed micro levels (such as individual products or product groups).

With the established inclusion of supply chain management (also outside the firm's boundaries) in business processes, the holding of inventories is viewed as an alleged indication of not well-coordinated production planning. However, the envisaged reduction of inventory levels often conflicts with the value-generating functions (such as smoothing, transformation, and transfer function) of inventory holding. Thus, in each individual case, the needed inventory levels with reference to operational specifics has to be calculated.

A higher value in Material Ccoverage Period may be viewed as a stable provisioning of the needed supplies; however, it also implies a higher commitment to capital in inventory holding. In addition, cost of capital linked with the variable and fixed costs, in maintaining and using warehouse facilities has to be considered.

Because of diverse operational constellations, a generalized target for the Material Coverage Period cannot be determined. Nevertheless, achieving a successively lower Material Coverage Period is usually considered favourable; it indicates that the inventory moves more quickly through the production process to the ultimate customer, reducing storage and obsolescence costs, and releasing tied up capital for other purposes. However, in order to reduce the risk of production interruptions, it is not only important to maintain safety stock levels, but also to ensure that the Material Coverage Period is able to bridge the lead time needed for the future deliveries.

For orientation and comparison purposes, internal benchmarks between various units within the firm can be used. The performance over time can be analysed with the help of budget-actual comparisons. External benchmarks could be taken from the branch-specific averages or the best-practice values. Whenever comparisons are made, it is important to ensure the consistency of the price component used to calculate the inventory value (acquisition price or sales price, current price or average price or production costs).

## ! Useful Suggestions

Assuming that firms in the same branch usually have similar production and asset structures, the ratio values, differing significantly from the averages, are clear candidates for serious review. This should help in analysing positive and negative developments or consequences, and in manoeuvring them in the context of corporate goals.

In principle, a fall or rise in the profitability of the firm may be analysed with reference to a change in the Return On Sales or the Inventory Turnover Ratio (including the Material Coverage Period) and corrective measures can be applied. More efficient purchasing and production techniques, such as just-in-time inventory, can help in improving the Material Coverage Period.

A change in the Material Coverage Period could be triggered by a disproportionate increase or decrease in the average inventory (as numerator) and net sales/cost of goods sold (as denominator). *For further details and systematic explanations on this, refer to the information in Appendix I.*

When deciding on the appropriate Material Coverage Period, a cost-based review is obviously important. However, over and above that, the market perspective has to be carefully analysed. A considerable reduction in the Material Coverage Period for finished products may jeopardize the delivery schedule expected by the client. One should, therefore, compare and contrast all operational issues across various functional departments. Above all, whether the customers accept the changed delivery schedules and whether tight delivery schedules are viewed by clients as positive signal, as is the case in the luxury goods market should be checked.

## & Related Ratios/Additional Notes

The Material Coverage Period is also known as "Inventory Holding Period", "Average Days to Sell Inventory", "Inventory on Hand", "Days Stock on Hand" and "Inventory Coverage Period".

The mathematical reciprocal (Average Consumption/Average Inventory) of the Material Coverage Period, without multiplication by days in a year, is called the "Inventory Turnover Ratio" or the "Stock Turnover Ratio".

## 4.5.5 Process Cost Rate

**Analytical Question** ?

How much does it cost to accomplish (or execute) a particular process?

**Definition** ✱

| Process Costs per Period |
| --- |
| Process Quantity per Period |

The process costs represent the value of resources consumed relating to a particular process. The process quantity shows the number of times a process was accomplished in a period, and is often labelled as the cost-driver. Example: Costs of order-processing in relation to the number of orders processed.

    The Process Cost Rate is expressed in currency units per process (for example € per process completion).

**Calculation/Derivation** »

The required information for this ratio is to be obtained primarily through internal data, collected upstream of the cost accounting system, which is then supplemented through business process reengineering (vertical and horizontal). The information is aggregated mostly for various cost centres, so that the interfaces in information and production flow can be made transparent.

**Interpretation and Typical Range** #

The Process Cost Rate is the main measure in the product costing system. It fulfils two main objectives in cost accounting: Firstly, it serves as a yardstick for careful allocation of indirect costs to the relevant cost objects. Mostly those cost objects are focused here which are supporting services, such as planned activities in different functional departments or in the administration. Secondly, the process cost rate provides important costing information for pricing policy decisions, based on the full-costing method. For example, it can help in fixing a long-term price ceiling on the procurement side, and a long-term price floor on the sales side.

    The Process Cost Rate as a measure is usually applied to those business processes which are repetitive in nature, are independent of hierarchy levels, or functional areas. A Process Cost Rate can be calculated for any process within a cost-centre; however, it can also be calculated for several cost-centres, if the process is accomplished by several cost-centres collectively.

    Which processes should be investigated in a firm is so firm-specific that no generalized opinion can be given about the typical range of process cost rates. For comparable process-definitions and identical activities, one could take internal benchmarks as orientation values. If information is available, the best-practice values from external sources can also be used.

## ! Useful Suggestions

The foundation for a sound analysis of process costing is a comprehensive structuring of all the indirect services, in vertical and horizontal linked processes, with varying complexities. The processes could be classified from "business-processes" into "main-processes" and further on into "sub-processes". These business activity flows, depending upon their utilization, have to be assigned to all costs which are cost-driver dependent, and, to make it more transparent, also to all other costs which are independent of cost drivers.

By comparison with other classical forms for calculating the overhead rate (mostly a value-based percentage), the Process Cost Rate is cost-driver-based, i.e., a quantity-based overhead rate, and it offers an accurate allocation of indirect costs. Since indirect costs constitute an increasing portion of total costs, it is important to pay careful attention to its allocation and control.

## & Related Ratios/Additional Notes

When a firm conducts business process analysis, the vertical and horizontal process classification often reveals many interfaces in informational and real terms. Many of these interfaces show a "point of rupture" which often appear as "data disruptions" in the information system. In real terms, a firm often tries to cover such ruptures or disruptions employing various protective measures, such as keeping higher levels of safety stock. With the help of process costing, an attempt is made to simplify the work flow, which helps in improving the operational efficiency and strengthening the competitive position of the firm.

### 4.5.6 Expected Process-based Loss

## ? Analytical Question

What is the expected loss that a firm is likely to incur, due to a process or event? What is the likely monetary impact of an operational risk or failure?

## ✳ Definition

$$\frac{\text{Key Risk Indicator (KRI) of the Firm} \cdot \text{Average Industry Loss}}{\text{Key Risk Indicator (KRI) of the Industry}}$$

Where:

KRI = Quantifiable measure of the performance of a firm's processes which has an impact on its operational risks.

Some examples of KRIs are number of failed transactions/trades, staff turnover rate, number of IT-systems failures, average hours of overtime per employee, and number of customer complaints, etc.

The Expected Process-based Loss is expressed in monetary terms.

## Calculation/Derivation

The data relating to various KRIs can be obtained from the firm's internal reporting system. The quality of the KRI depends upon the accuracy and detail of the information collected by various functional departments within the firm. For external analysts, this kind of information may not be accessible.

The availability of branch-specific information for KRIs depends upon published or unpublished research or survey reports. In the absence of good quality data, branch-specific benchmarks, or best-practice examples could be used.

## Interpretation and Typical Range

Expected Process-based Loss shows the monetary impact of a firm's operational risks. It illustrates a direct linkage between operational risks created by various business processes/events, and the future loss it might create. With such a linkage, KRIs are potentially the most useful matrices for measuring the required operational-risk capital. The Basel Committee for operational-risk capital suggests a similar approach to the internal measurement of risks; therefore, the indicator is of particular relevance for banks and other financial institutions.

Depending upon the types (and completeness) of operational KRIs, a firm would include in its analysis, the sum total of their monetary impact could help in calculating the overall Expected Process-based Loss. Such an expected loss will have to be set against the other profits of the firm to gain an overall assessment of the changing profile of the firm's profitability.

It is not possible to suggest a typical range for this ratio. A desired target would obviously be to keep the expected process-based losses to a minimum, through an efficient process-controlling system. A well-defined management information system may help in making budget versus actual comparison, and providing internal benchmarking over time. The use of external benchmarks and best-practice examples is also desirable.

## Useful Suggestions

In the present uncertain business world, building effective indicators to monitor operational risks is absolutely imperative. Expected loss provides a quantifiable and forward looking measure for risk impact analysis; KRIs provide an intermediate scale to relate the experienced loss in a pool of firms (branch average) to the anticipated loss in a firm. Thus, the KRI matrices do not lag, but lead operational risk assessment and management.

If a firm is able to improve its business processes and improve upon the KRIs, it can minimize the economic capital that needs to be set aside for such purposes. The amount of Expected Process-based Loss, the duration of such loss, the financial strength and need for economic capital have a strong impact on the solvency of the firm and its reputation. An ongoing assessment of the expected losses may also impact on the pricing of the underlying financial assets, and the way firms manage their business.

The suggested measures for reducing expected loss, relate to operational efficiency and control systems within a firm. An ex-ante assessment of the business environment and processes/events may require hedging of some of the operational risks, such as increases in raw-material prices or energy costs.

**&** **Related Ratios/Additional Notes**

A related variant of "Expected Process-based Loss" is "Unexpected Loss". It means estimating the impact of unforeseeable events on the operational performance of the firm.

Sometimes, expected loss is defined as the mean average of the expectations of what one could lose. For operational risk purposes, the expected loss generated is expressed over a one-year time horizon, based on the business profile today. To make this indicator forward-looking, the expected loss could be adjusted for known or likely business changes. Another variant of this definition is to take the worst aggregated loss which the firm could expect in any one year out of 10 years.

The calculation of Expected Process-based Loss with the formula proposed above is not without problems. The main problem could be the availability of data both at firm and branch level. Secondly, it is difficult to map external experience to a firm's internal processes. Despite these limitations, it is one of the best ways of quantifying operational risk.

### 4.5.7 Machine Hour Rate

**?** **Analytical Question**

What are the various costs attributable to running a machine for one hour?

**\*** **Definition**

$$\frac{\text{Machine-related Costs}}{\text{Total Machine Runtime}}$$

The Machine Hour Rate is expressed in currency units per hour (for example, € per hour).

## Calculation/Derivation

The required information about machine costs and runtime is available primarily in the internal cost accounting system, supported by asset and production controlling data. The costs attributable to running a machine may include light, heating, repair/maintenance, depreciation and overheads.

## Interpretation and Typical Range

The Machine Hour Rate is one of the main components in product costing, based on activity drivers. It shows the proportionate machine-related indirect costs per unit of time (mostly per hour and sometimes also per minute). For a fair calculation of the costs involved in producing goods and services, it is important that the resource consumption is assigned accurately to the products (as far as possible).

The Machine Hour Rate is an important decision parameter for comparative purposes, particularly in those cases where production methods vary (because of different automation levels or capital-intensity), or where production locations vary (because of decentralized production in different countries).

## Useful Suggestions

In cost accounting, the allocation rates for indirect costs are usually calculated on a cost-centre basis. An additional differentiation, based on individual work-stations (machine or work area), is desirable in all those cases where different products or services use the work-stations of a cost-centre in distinctly varying time cycles.

To obtain a valuable economic insight into the costing information, one should put more emphasis on splitting the machine or planned costs into activity-driven (controllable) and activity-neutral (uncontrollable or idle time) costs.

The high capital intensity involved in modern production processes makes it imperative that production capacities, and their availabilities, are managed systematically. This can be achieved with the help of strategic measures, relating to organizational structures in production management, or through measures aimed at operative production planning and controlling. Efforts made at reducing or avoiding downtime is a major aspect in maintenance, proactive servicing and repair management systems.

## Related Ratios/Additional Notes

Various synonyms, such as "Reference Rate", "Allocation Rate", and "Activity Rate" are used for Machine Hour Rate or Work-Station Rate.

If a group of machines are allocated to a cell (or an isle), where a complete operation is carried out, the Machine Hour Rate is calculated by aggregating the costs attributable to this group of machines. This is becoming popular in many high-tech production methods where team based cell-operations are common.

### 4.5.8 Bottleneck-induced Incremental Costs

**? Analytical Question**

What is the economic criterion for managing an operational bottleneck through internal (to another production unit within the firm) or external (outsourcing/bought-in supply) relocation of production?

**\* Definition**

$$\frac{\text{Incremental Costs per Unit}}{\text{Release of Constrained Factor per Unit}}$$

Where:

Incremental Costs per Unit     =   Variable costs per unit in the new relocated alternative *Less* Variable costs per unit in the existing bottleneck situation

Release of Constrained Factor     =   The capacity released through relocation per unit.
per Unit

The unit of released factor could be in square metres, cubic metres, weight, or time, depending upon the unit of measurement applicable to the constrained factor.

The ratio is measured in monetary value per unit of the constrained factor, for example, € per machine minute or € per hour.

**» Calculation/Derivation**

The information needed for this ratio can be taken from cost and activity accounting, which has to be based on direct or marginal costing. For additional information, one has to depend on the computerised information collection systems for production planning and control. For bought-in supplies, one has to obtain the price quotations (cost of purchase) of potential suppliers from the purchasing department.

Basically, the constrained factor can be any production input and the bottleneck can arise in any operational area. Thus, the appropriate information needs may vary significantly.

**# Interpretation and Typical Range**

The ratio "Bottleneck-induced Incremental Costs" is an operative indicator which derives its relevance during periods of operational bottlenecks. A typical bottleneck in practice is linked to machine capacity, but shortage in any of the business inputs (warehouse space or volume, raw materials or energy supply, transport capacities, or human resources) can be overcome with careful economic solutions and ideas.

The incremental costs per unit in the numerator correspond to the "cost-disadvantage" arising out of the decision to relocate production. This is matched with respective released capacities in the denominator. That is why this ratio is labelled as "Bottleneck-induced Incremental Costs".

For the application of this operational decision method, it is not essential to focus on the absolute differential in term of the incremental costs. Instead, the focus has to be on the (step-by-step) sequence of relocating or outsourcing to those alternatives which have the lowest cost-disadvantage, in terms of incremental costs. The process of step-wise relocation has to be repeated till the constrained resource is no longer in a bottleneck.

However, because of increasing variable costs, the absolute contribution margin should be falling. If the falling contribution margin is no longer able to cover the periodic fixed costs, it is important to check whether there are compelling reasons (such as the contractual obligation to deliver a particular quantity) for continuing the production program in its present form.

**Useful Suggestions**
Generally, assuming that it is not easy to increase or change the capacities of production inputs (particularly that of machinery and human resource) in the short-run, the rule should be to prefer the production of objects with the lowest variable costs (or the highest contribution margin, with constant prices) per unit. With a given contribution margin per unit, this ratio will help in maximizing the profits (or reducing the loss of non-recovered fixed costs) because the constrained capacity is distributed optimally with reference to the contribution margin per unit.

In additional to the bottleneck-induced incremental cost-disadvantage, one must ensure that outsourcing (particularly to external parties) guarantees compliance with the qualitative, quantitative and schedule expectation. In the case of long-term outsourcing decisions, one has to consider the strategic aspects of losing technical know-how. The outsourcing decision may also lead to image or reputation losses in the market because the external supplier may not be looking after expected core activities, such as customer-loyalties.

In the case of continuing problematic bottlenecks, one should think of redesigning the supply chain or check the benefit of strategic options such as capacity expansion through the discounted cash flow method.

**Related Ratios/Additional Notes**
Depending upon whether the corrective measures are strategic (for enduring bottlenecks) or operative (for transition bottlenecks), the management is confronted with serious decisions about production intensity or vertical integration (Make or buy and also outsourcing/off-shoring). In this context, one should also consider the added costs of checking whether in-house production would be better than using an external supplier.

### (S) 4.5.9 Cost Effectiveness of Risk Management

### [?] Analytical Question

How cost effective (in monetary terms) is the internal risk management function with reference to the monetary value of risk exposure?

### [*] Definition

$$\frac{\text{Total Cost of Risk Management (in monetary terms)} \cdot 100}{\text{Total Value of the Risk Exposure ( in monetary terms)}}$$

Where:

Total cost of risk management is the cost of all risk managing processes and techniques adopted by the company in a particular period. The common elements of risk management costs include risk-administration costs (incurred in risk management), risk-mitigation costs (incurred for reducing risks, such as new software to reduce IT security risks), risk-control costs (incurred for operational processes designed to reduce risk, such as due diligence costs) and risk-transfer costs (incurred in using insurance or financial hedging techniques).

Any estimation of exposure demands a quantification of the risk impact. A basic calculation of the total value of risk exposure is based on an estimate of the probability of a risk, and its impact. Thus, for example, if there is a 20 percent chance of a new product failing on the market, and if the impact of product failing will result in a $1000,000 loss, the risk exposure is $200,000 (0.20*$1000,000).

The Cost Effectiveness of Risk Management is expressed as a percentage.

### [»] Calculation/Derivation

The Cost Effectiveness of Risk Management demands identification and quantification of several types of risks associated with the business. Therefore, the creation of a risk profile through, say, an impact probability matrix is helpful. A pooling of the cost of risk under its various elements such as mitigation costs, transfer costs, control costs and administration costs can be useful to compare total costs over time.

Timeliness and accuracy of information to the required level of materiality is of utmost importance for proper quantification of the monetary value of probable impact. A strong key risk indicator (KRI) aggregation, and reporting program, should be in place for effective monitoring.

The data for this ratio can be lagged (ex-post) based on the actual or historical numbers of a period, or leading (ex-ante) based on the budgeted numbers for a particular period in the future.

### [#] Interpretation and Typical Range

If the Cost Effectiveness of Risk Management is measured with the help of actual or historical data, it shall allow for a better control of the risk management function and can help improve in strategic and operational decision-making. However, a pro-active instance of measuring cost effectiveness is achieved if the reporting system is geared towards budgeting various elements of risk costs, with reference to assumed scenarios (such as risk costs estimation for best, normal and worst case scenarios).

A generalized specification for the Cost Effectiveness of Risk Management is not possible. With changing business-related circumstances, the periodic targets fixed by the company serve as an important yardstick. However, if the costs are agreed with the contractual partners for transferring risks, such as in an insurance contract, the changing pattern of costs over time can be compared for improving effectiveness, or changing the insurance provider.

## Useful Suggestions

Successful risk management creates a framework that allows a firm to handle risk and uncertainty. There are several types of risks a company has to face: pure risk, market risk, default risk, operational risk and liquidity risk. As a result, risk management consists of a set of financial and operational activities, maximizing the value of a company or portfolio.[1]

Cost Effectiveness of Risk Management is a powerful ratio guiding the senior staff in gauging the overall performance of the risk function.

This KRI can also be used in project-based risk management. Project managers often estimate (ex-ante) the cost of risks inherent in the project phases, and share them with their clients to provision for various contingencies.

Projects are often exposed to time-overruns which become the main source of risk. The cost effectiveness of managing such exposures, in the event of actual time-overruns (ex-post), helps in ensuring the viability of a project. Various methods can be developed for the concurrent evaluation of the risk management effectiveness during the project execution.

The cost of managing a risk can help prioritize risks into rank-order, so that the costliest of the risk gets maximum attention.

## Related Ratios/Additional Notes

There are various techniques and tools that can guide calculation and chasing subsections for cost effectiveness in various functional departments, such as IT, HR, Finance and procurement. If agreed, each department can have its own cost-effectiveness as a sub-classification. Thus, cost of hedging or cost of insurance can be computed as related yet independent ratios.

Whereas, risk transfer and risk mitigation may be two important KRIs, it is no less significant to chase the risk management from the point of reporting practices. Thus, various KRIs need to be appropriately shared for decision making in various

---

1 (Dionne, 2013)

organizational units within the company, depending upon their relevance to individual decision-makers.

## 4.6 Process-related Ecological Indicators

### 4.6.1 Internally Generated $CO_2e$ Emissions (Scope 1)

**? Analytical Question**

What quantity of greenhouse gases are released, due to internal processes of a company, in a given time period? The emissions are measured in $CO_2$-equivalent values.

**❋ Definition**

> Sum of the Weighted Quantities of Emissions per Period

When there are greenhouse gases, (GHGs) other than $CO_2$ constituting emissions, the company is required to thoroughly disclose them. The information has to be shown in gross volumes, independent of other GHG trading activities and transfer of compensation payments or other licenses.

The indicator "Internally Generated $CO_2e$ Emissions" (Scope 1)[2] is presented in terms of "mass" or "weight" with the appropriate units, such as tonnes.

**» Calculation/Derivation**

The prerequisite for obtaining the data for the emissions related indicator is a detailed, computerised Environment Information System (EIS). The primary task of an EIS, in this context, is the compilation, processing and preparation of ecologically relevant data, especially for

- Quantitative data collection (for various types of emission)
- Documentation for compulsory external reporting (determined by laws and regulations, etc.)
- Developing meaningful key indicators, so that complex inter-linkages can be presented in a concise form.
- Comparing the internal and external situations/developments over time.

The underlying overview of the Global Reporting Initiative (henceforth GRI) takes into account the climate relevant gases in the Kyoto-Protocol from the United Nations, also known as the "Kyoto-Gases". These include the following: $CO_2$ (Carbon

---

2 The definition of this KPI is based on the Disclosure 305-1 from the GRI-framework.

dioxide); $CH_4$ (Methane); $N_2O$ (Nitrous oxide); HFCs (Hydro fluorocarbons); HPFCs (Hydroperfluorocarbon); $SF_6$ (Sulphur hexafluoride); $NF_3$ (Nitrogen trifluoride).

The greenhouse gases, listed above, can be calculated as a $CO_2$ equivalents ($CO_2$e) by using emission factors that are in accordance with the current state of climate research. This information is available from publications from the Intergovernmental Panel on Climate Change (IPCC), for example.

According to the GRI, "Scope 1" focuses on all sources of emission that are under the ownership of the company, as well as those under its operational or financial control. This does not include any $CO_2$e emissions that are caused by externally sourced energy (included in the category "Scope 2") and emissions caused upstream, along the value-chain, emissions caused by own employees' activities with external companies (business trips with independent airlines) or by external processing, usage and disposal of products (included in the category "Scope 3").

## Interpretation and Typical Range

The focal point for the concept of sustainability is the idea that development should be possible in a way such that the needs of the present are fulfilled without endangering the ability of future generations to fulfil their own needs.

The implementation of this fundamental principle, at the level of individual companies means that, amongst other things, the natural environment should be burdened only within reasonable limits, and as little as possible. In view of strong climate protection activities, $CO_2$ emissions are generally considered as the lead-indicator on both the micro- as well as on macroeconomic levels.

The comparability of values related to coverage over time can always be problematic. For example, if all locations of a company have not been covered in the survey data before, this will cause the basic size of coverage to change. During the current development of sustainability reporting, comparability over time is a widespread problem. The numbers presented by companies in their reports are not always accurately comparable, due to continuous refinement and development of methods for recording and compiling of data as well as the sale and acquisition of business units.

A general guideline or target for the scale of the indicator "Internally Generated $CO_2$e Emissions" (Scope 1) cannot be determined. Alongside the usual internal possibilities for comparison (between organizational departments in the form of actual-actual over time or plan-actual relations), corresponding external comparisons, with the branch-specific average values or the "best-practice" values, may be used as a guide.

## Useful Suggestions

Using the basic idea of a business model that not only tries to minimize the consumption of natural resources on the input side but, above all, increasingly during the value creation processes, the following spectrum of possibilities is available to the firms for the purpose. It is important that the company has the ability to analyse and, if need be, change the planning, controlling and monitoring of processes stretching across material, energy and water management. To this end, the following measures could be suggested:

- Identifying technical and organizational weak points or possibilities to reduce the consumption of energy and material, including their respective $CO_2e$ effects. If need be, this is possible through the creation of systems of circular recycling-loops.
- Sensitizing and promoting environmental awareness amongst employees and increasing incentives within the parameters of the remuneration system to motivate them to take action.
- Savings while paying for necessary $CO_2$ emission certificates, environmental taxes and fees.
- Increasing revenue through improved public image and special labelling and positioning of products, such as with $CO_2$-labels.

The complex physical, chemical and biological links as well as the diverse interdependencies of the environmental impact, often make it difficult to find quick and easy solutions but, as in all other fields of business management, the journey always begins with the first step.

### & Related Ratios/Additional Notes

The external reporting on sustainability is markedly less standardized than the "classical" reporting of companies according to national or international standards of financial reporting. The system of guidelines in the GRI is, however, increasingly being taken into account for orientation. As an independent organization, the GRI has taken upon itself the task of developing comprehensive guidelines to facilitate comparability of sustainability reporting for companies worldwide.

The distinctive GRI categories of Scope 1, 2 and 3 should facilitate the compilation of the necessary data on $CO_2$ emissions. Reference is made here to the independent presentation of the KPI No. 4.6.2 on "Indirect $CO_2e$ Emissions caused by Energy Usage" (Scope 2).

Depending on the business model, for example in the service sector, business trips could make up a large part of the $CO_2$ emissions of a company. These are however, according to the strict definitions, categorized as "Other Indirect Emissions" (Scope 3).[3] In the case of companies which use their own cars, as opposed to an airline for business trips, comparability is not always accurately possible, and depends largely on additional explanations provided by the reporting company.

---

**3** The definition of this KPI is based on the Disclosure 305-3 from the GRI-framework.

## 4.6.2 Indirect $CO_2$e Emissions caused by Energy Usage (Scope 2)

**Analytical Question**  ?
What amount of greenhouse gases are released, due to energy generation, by other companies when a company procures and consumes that energy in a time period? The emissions are measured in $CO_2$-equivalent values.

**Definition**  *

  Sum of the Weighted Quantities of Emissions per Period

In the case where there is greenhouse gases (GHGs) other than $CO_2$ as part of the emissions, the company is required to thoroughly disclose them. The information has to be shown in gross volumes, independent of other GHG trading activities, and transfer of compensation payments or other licenses.

The indicator "Indirect $CO_2$e Emissions caused by Energy Usage" (Scope 2)[4] is presented in terms of "mass" or "weight" with the appropriate units, such as tonnes.

**Calculation/Derivation**  »
The acquisition of the necessary data presents a challenge for this methodology and subsequently for the calculation of this indicator. In principle, the energy consuming company has to collect and compile the verifiable information regarding the $CO_2$e emissions of the appropriate quantities of energy supplied by the energy provider. For example, information has to be compiled about the type of fuel sources, processes used, efficiency-levels and transmission losses.

Because of the environmental impact of the utilization of each type of energy source (for example, the various levels of emissions during the extraction of raw materials and their conversion to a usable form of energy and its consumption), designing a suitable composition of energy sources used by companies is becoming increasingly relevant for strategic management.

The underlying overview of the Global Reporting Initiative (henceforth GRI) takes into account the climate relevant gases in the United Nations Kyoto-Protocol, also known as the "Kyoto-Gases". These include the following: $CO_2$ (Carbon dioxide); $CH_4$ (Methane); N2O (Nitrous oxide); HFCs (Hydro-fluorocarbons); HPFCs (Hydroperfluorocarbon); $SF_6$ (Sulphur hexafluoride); $NF_3$ (Nitrogen trifluoride). The greenhouse gases listed above can be calculated as a $CO_2$ equivalent ($CO_2$e) using emission factors that are in accordance with the current state of climate research. This information is available from publications by the Intergovernmental Panel on Climate Change (IPCC), for example.

---

**4** The definition of this KPI is based on the Disclosure 305-2 from the GRI-framework.

**#** **Interpretation and Typical Range**

The focal point for the concept of sustainability is the idea that development should be possible in a way such that the needs of the present are fulfilled without endangering the needs of future generations.

The implementation of this fundamental principle, at the level of individual companies, means that, amongst other things, the natural environmental should be burdened only within reasonable limits, and as little as possible. In view of strong climate protection activities, $CO_2$ emissions are generally considered as the lead-indicator on both the micro- as well as on macroeconomic level.

Usable energy for each operational purpose of the company can be categorized in the following forms: electricity, fuel oils for power or combustion, heating, cooling, steam and pressurised air.

The comparability of values related to coverage over time can always be problematic. For example, if all locations in a company have not been covered in the survey data before, this will cause the basic size of coverage to change. During the current development of sustainability reporting, comparability over time is a widespread problem. The numbers presented by companies in their reports are not always accurately comparable, due to the continuous refinement and development of methods of recording, and compiling of data, as well as the sale and acquisition of business units.

A general guideline or target for the scale of the indicator "Indirect $CO_2e$ Emissions caused by Energy Usage" (Scope 2), cannot be determined. Alongside the usual internal possibilities for comparison (between organizational departments in the form of actual-actual over time or plan-actual relations), corresponding external comparisons, where the branch-specific average values or the "best-practice" values may be used as a guide.

**!** **Useful Suggestions**

The basic principle of a corporate energy management system, namely that resource consumption has to be minimised already on the input side and not later during the value creation processes, opens up a wide spectrum of plausible sets of measures. On the one hand, it is important to systematically analyse and, thus, try to reduce total energy usage and internal energy needs. At the very least, the specific energy use per unit of output should be reduced as much as possible. The exception is if an increase in internal energy consumption is overcompensated for, by energy efficient products, and reduced consumption during their usual lifespans.

On the other hand, inevitable energy needs should be covered from sources with least $CO_2e$ emissions while keeping in mind the results and reliability of the supply source. When choosing the sources, it is especially important to focus on a balanced energy composition.

Within the energy-consuming company, it is important that the company has the ability, keeping in mind the energy-saving measures, to analyse and, if need be, change the planning, controlling and monitoring of processes stretching across the

material, energy and water management. To this end, the following measures are suggested:
- Identifying technical and organizational weak points or improvements to reduce the consumption of needed energy flows, including their respective $CO_2$e effects. If need be, this is possible through the creation of systems of circular recycling-loops.
- Sensitizing and promoting environmental awareness amongst employees and increasing incentives within the parameters of the remuneration system to motivate them to take action.

The complex physical, chemical and biological links as well as the diverse interdependencies of environmental impacts often make it difficult to find quick and easy energy-saving solutions but, as in all other fields of business management, the journey always begins with the first step.

### Related Ratios/Additional Notes

The external reporting on sustainability is markedly less standardized than the "classical" reporting of companies, according to national or international standards of financial reporting. The system of guidelines in the GRI is, however, increasingly being taken into account for orientation. As an independent organization, the GRI has taken upon itself the task of developing comprehensive guidelines to facilitate comparability for the sustainability reporting of companies worldwide.

The distinctive GRI categories of Scope 1, 2 and 3 should facilitate the compilation of the necessary data on $CO_2$ emissions. According to the GRI, "Scope 1" focuses on all the sources of emissions that are under the ownership of the company, as well as those under its operational or financial control. Reference is made here to the separate presentation of the KPI No. 4.6.1 on "Internally Generated $CO_2$e Emissions" (Scope 1).

As mentioned here, the data compiled in "Scope 2" includes all $CO_2$e emissions that are caused by consuming externally sourced energy. Meanwhile, the data in "Scope 3"[5] covers emissions caused upstream along the value-chain, as well as those by employees' activities with external companies (business trips with independent airlines) or by external processing, usage and disposal of products.

---

5 The definition of this KPI is based on the Disclosure 305-3 from the GRI-framework.

### 4.6.3 Emission Volume of Production-related Pollutants

**?** **Analytical Question**

What is the volume of pollutants released into the environment per period (mostly per year) or per unit of output (for example, per ton of steel) which are emitted during the production process?

- As a period-relevant measure, the ratio can be classified into various pollutants (for example, waste material, waste water, exit-air, heat, dust or noise), which can be further classified into sub-groups (for example, waste material can be classified into plastic, paper, glass and special garbage, etc.)
- As a volume-driven measure, the ratio can be classified into various output units (units of finished products, distance covered in kilometres, tons of steel produced, etc.)

**✳** **Definition**

Period-relevant Usage:

> Quantity of Emitted Pollutants per Period

As a measured value for the quantity of solid, liquid or gaseous resources consumed, one could use number of units, length, area and volume units, and also weight-specifications. Examples could be $SO_2$ or $CO_2$ in tons per year.

Volume-driven Usage:

$$\frac{\text{Quantity of Emitted Pollutants per Period}}{\text{Quantity of Produced Output Units per Period}}$$

As a measured value for the quantity of solid, liquid or gaseous resources consumed or output produced, one could use number of units, length, area and volume units, as well as the weight-specifications.

Out of each combination of input and output, the ratio could be expressed, for example, as waste water emission per unit of finished product.

**»** **Calculation/Derivation**

A prerequisite for obtaining the required data for this emission-oriented ratio is the existence of a detailed (computerized) business environment information system. A business environment information system is responsible for collecting, processing and reporting of all environment related data, in particular:

- compilation of quantity and value-based information about the resources consumed;
- documentation of information for external legal reporting; and

- calculation of meaningful ratios for presenting complex details, and for showing the trend of internal and external changes over time.

## Interpretation and Typical Range
The main message of sustainability management is the idea of offering a development
process which satisfies the needs of the present generation without jeopardizing the
aspirations of future generations. The application of the sustainability principle, at
the firm level, implies avoiding, as far as possible, unnecessary pollution of the natural environment. Thus, both period-relevant and volume-driven measures show the
units of resources consumed, from two different perspectives.

Because of a strongly diversified product spectrum of firms, comparable data
about typical range is possible only for firms which have similar product groups.
The comparability of only period-relevant measures (such as consumed megawatts
or cubic meters per year) could prove complicated if data was not complied for all
locations of the firm, and the total number of location changes. This is a common
problem in the development of sustainability reporting.

Presenting the measure as a volume-driven ratio provides a relative number
where the absolute quantity of resource consumed is compared with the unit of output produced, such as waste water produced per unit of finished product.

As orientation and for comparison purposes, internal benchmarks between various
units within the firm (such as locations/plants) can be used. The performance over
time can be analysed with the help of budget-actual comparisons. External benchmarks could be taken from the branch-specific averages or the best-practice values.

Because of advancements or continuous (definitional) improvements in data
collection methods, as well as because of the frequent buying and selling of firms,
the numbers reported by large firms may not be comparable over time.

Because of a strong campaign against global warming and climate change, $CO_2$
emission is considered to be a lead-indicator in general.

## Useful Suggestions
On the supposition that firms in the same branch usually have similar production
structures, the ratio values, differing significantly from the averages, are clear candidates for serious reviews. This should help in analysing positive and negative developments, or consequences, and in manoeuvring them in the context of corporate
goals.

In general, assuming that most firms are increasingly guided by the basic performance idea of conserving natural resources, both on the input and output side,
there are a large number of measures which can be applied for the efficient consumption of resources. It is always beneficial to plan, steer and control the flow of
resource, such as raw-material, energy and water. Analysing and, if needed, changing the flow of these resources can be a useful exercise. Included in the list of measures are:

- identification of technical or organizational weaknesses;
- initiating improvements for reducing the energy and material flows (if possible, by implementing a circular flow or recycling system);
- developing ideas for improving the environmental impact of the production processes;
- saving on environment related taxes and payments;
- improving sales through image-campaigning and labelling/positioning of products (ecological label or energy-saving label), and
- encouraging the environmental conscious behaviour of the employees, and rewarding them for such behaviour in the framework of a compensation system.

Since most of the emissions have a (mostly increasing) price, a reduction in the volume-driven emission should, in general, lead to (assuming constant environment protection costs) a cost reduction.

The complex character of physical, chemical and biological processes, and the multitude of their interdependent effects, makes it very difficult to find good ecological solutions. However, as in all other business activities, a humble beginning can be a good start.

### & Related Ratios/Additional Notes

The scope, data-collection frequency and the level of detail in measuring and reporting of the sustainability indicators is largely at the discretion of the firms and their environmental consciousness. Sometimes, however, there are legal directives which require regular information from firms. Although, in external reporting, such information is usually required annually, for internal controlling, it is desirable to use half-yearly or even monthly information.

The external reporting towards sustainability is much less regulated than the classical reporting, according to national and international reporting standards. As a good orientation, reference is often made to the lists of indicators published in the directives of Global Reporting Initiative (GRI). As an independent institution, the GRI has taken upon itself the job of developing formal guidelines for improving the comparability of sustainability reporting.

## 4.6.4 Recycling Ratio ⓢ

**Analytical Question** [?]

How high is the proportion of operational materials (energy) which is reused in the production cycle?

**Definition** [*]

$$\frac{\text{Reused Input (Consumed) Quantity for an Object} \cdot 100}{\text{Actual Total Input (Consumption) for an Object}}$$

The Recycling Ratio is expressed as a percentage.

**Calculation/Derivation** [»]

The required information for this ratio is to be obtained, primarily through production data which is collected upstream of the cost accounting system and is classified according to the types of materials.

**Interpretation and Typical Range** [#]

The Recycling Ratio has gained in prominence, due to an increasing environmental consciousness in the business world, both at the macro and micro level. It is used as an indicator for sustainable management in which materials and energies created in the production- and consumption processes are reused in production. In general, the focus of analysis is initially on a selected number of basic materials (mostly expensive and scarce), or products where high recoverable (or intrinsic) value and purity is most important.

The volume of the achieved or targeted recycling ratio differs significantly between different branches and firms due to technical, physical and economic reasons. For orientation and benchmarking this ratio, one could take internal comparisons (such as the ratio in different organizational units or plan-actual values) or external comparisons where the branch-specific average period or the "best-practice" value may be used as a guide.

**Useful Suggestions** [!]

What kind of approach a firm adopts for recycling reflects on its internal system (for example, avoiding the disposal of unwanted sub-products through reutilization) or could be guided by collaboration amongst firms, such as the creation and collective use of the retro-distribution system, or the coordinated reprocessing of hard, liquid or gaseous materials.

To gain useful insights, the Recycling Ratio can be further classified into the following categories:

- Product-recycling ratio

  Reutilization-variant I: After return, the product is reused in the same way as it was originally used, i.e. refund bottle.

  Reutilization-variant II: After return, the product is reused for a purpose other than its first use. For example, railroad ties for garden fencing.

- Material-recycling ratio

  Recycling-variant I: The material is used as input in the same production process, though the shape and form of material may have changed partly or completely (for example, recycled glass).

  Recycling-variant II: The material is used for creating new materials or products. For example, the plastic chairs in a stadium made out of drinks packaging, often labelled as "down-cycling" or "up-cycling".

The range of activities available to a firm are increasingly being influenced by a variety of national and international (legal or regulatory) directives.

**&** **Related Ratios/Additional Notes**

Along with the quantity-based measures for recycling, several value-based ratios, which are possible in the area of environment-controlling could also be used. The purpose of value-based ratios could be in analysing the cost of recycling, or the saving effects from using the recycled material, or revenues from the sale of recycled materials.

# 5 Human Resource and Innovation Perspective

## 5.1 Personnel Cost Management

### 5.1.1 Personnel Costs Ratio

**Analytical Question**

What is the relative significance of gross personnel costs of a period in the total costs of a firm in that period?

**Definition**

$$\frac{\text{Gross Personnel Costs in a Period} \cdot 100}{\text{Total Costs in a Period}}$$

Where:

Gross Personnel Costs = Gross Wages + Gross Salaries + Supplementary Personnel Costs (Employer's Contribution to Retirement Benefits. etc.)

The Personnel Costs Ratio is expressed as a percentage mostly combined with a particular calendar or business year as a time reference.

**Calculation/Derivation**

The required data for this ratio could be obtained from the (computer-based) information system for accounting. External analysts can obtain the values for this ratio from the income statement which is based on the full-costing system.

For the sake of simplicity, no conceptual difference should be made between costs and expenses. In case there are special circumstances (such as restructuring) where sizable sums have been spent as extraordinary, non-operating, or unrelated to the accounting period personnel costs, this should be shown separately for several years to ensure transparency. Similar treatment should be mandated to the imputed costs in terms of employer's salary in partnerships.

**Interpretation and Typical Range**

In many firms, the personnel costs represent a major cost pool. Thus, for maintaining and improving competitiveness, it is important to chase the volume and trend of the personnel costs ratio and manage it actively. A generalised target for a typical range cannot be defined. For orientation about a typical range, one could take internal comparisons (such as the ratio in different organisational units or plan-actual values) or external comparisons where the branch-specific average or the "best-practice" value may be used as a guide.

https://doi.org/10.1515/9783110598094-006

However, the interpretative power of the Personnel Costs Ratio is limited. For example, when a firm reduces vertical integration, the costs of buying products and services increases, and the weight of personnel costs falls in the total. In the case of higher vertical integration, the impact is accordingly reversed.

**! Useful Suggestions**

Assuming that firms in the same branch usually have similar production and cost structures, the ratio values, differing significantly from the averages, are clear candidates for serious review. This should help in analysing the positive and negative developments or consequences, and manoeuvring them in the context of corporate goals. Thus, if for example, the firm has hired employees with special qualifications (with consequently higher salaries) in order to maintain or improve competitive advantages, an intentionally higher Personnel Costs Ratio may be desirable.

A change in this ratio may be triggered by a disproportionate increase or decrease in the gross personnel costs (as numerator) and total costs (as denominator). *For further details and systematic explanations on this, refer to the information in Appendix I.*

Along with direct methods for influencing personnel costs, through measures relating to a better price or volume strategy on the sales side, this ratio can be improved by measures towards a more efficient use of the factors of production on the total costs side.

**& Related Ratios/Additional Notes**

"Payroll Costs" and "Staff Costs" (not to be confused with staffing costs which means the cost of recruiting) are two synonyms for personnel costs. Several extensions of personnel costs are available for deeper analysis, such as "Labour Costs Ratio" and "Salaries Ratio", etc.

"Personnel Costs Intensity" is a related term which shows the relationship between personnel costs and sales. The above description for the personnel costs ratio is also valid for the personnel costs intensity, with the additional complication that sales price and profit margin changes have to be included in the analysis.

### 5.1.2 Supplementary Personnel Costs Ratio

**? Analytical Question**

What is the share of supplementary personnel costs in relation to the gross personnel costs in a period?

**\* Definition**

$$\frac{\text{Supplementary Personnel Costs in a Period} \cdot 100}{\text{Gross Wages} + \text{Gross Salaries}}$$

The Supplementary Personnel Costs Ratio is expressed as a percentage.

**Calculation/Derivation**
The required data for this ratio could be obtained from the (computer-based) information system of the human resource department. For extended analysis, the supplementary personnel costs can be further classified into the following categories:
- Required by law: employer's contribution to pension, unemployment, health, and long-term care insurances;
- Required by collective wage agreement: holiday and Christmas payments, professional development costs, and retirement benefits;
- Required by voluntary agreement: various benefits given to employees such as working clothes, subsidisation of travel costs, profit-sharing, and construction loans, etc.

The classification of supplementary personnel costs into the above three categories is not always warranted. It is often based on national labour laws, agreements between parties and arrangements at the firm level. It could vary significantly within the same country (between large and small-sized firms) or even in an international context.

**Interpretation and Typical Range**
The Supplementary Personnel Costs Ratio represents a measure of the relationship between "all other" personnel costs to the gross payment made to employees (legal, collective wage agreement based and voluntary payments).

Along with some components of supplementary personnel costs which move proportionately (for example, the employer's contribution to the retirement benefits fund) to the gross payment made to the employees, there are other components which also move disproportionately (for example, subsidization of travel costs). Therefore, for any target configuration of supplementary personnel costs (in respect of any selective upgrading, reorganising or downsizing of benefits), a systematic analysis of the direct and indirect effects of individual measures must be made.

In many companies, along with the absolute volume of supplementary personnel costs, the development of the ratio over time is also carefully analysed.

The typical range for the supplementary personnel costs ratio varies substantially. In Germany, for example, this ratio lies in the majority of cases, between 70% and 90%. Depending upon how supplementary personnel costs are defined, in some branches, this ratio exceeds the 100% limit as well. In recent years, the proportion amongst the three types of supplementary personnel costs (legal, collective wage agreement based and voluntary payments) has moved away from a uniform distribution (a third for each) to the detriment of voluntary payments. The share of voluntary payments in the total is now about 10%. In general, the Supplementary Personnel Costs Ratio has shown a downward trend.

Depending upon the collective agreements and the legal arrangements, there are substantial differences in practice, so that any judgment based on the average ratio of supplementary personnel costs may not be free from bias.

### ! Useful Suggestions

Basically, from an operational perspective, costs incurred in a firm are the business-related consumption of resources which generate or deliver some output. In the same way, supplementary personnel costs have to be seen in reference to the specific performance-potential of employees, which is rewarded through agreements and arrangements. When designing its plan for such agreements (through collective agreements or voluntary arrangements), a firm must consider the targets it wants to achieve. Maintaining or improving motivation, welfare and security of employees (and of family members), appreciation of performance, facilitating capital formation and retirement benefits are some examples of this.

Whereas legally binding supplementary personnel costs cannot be influenced, an employer can withdraw himself from a collective agreement. In the case of voluntary payments to employees, the employers have maximum freedom. However, it must be considered carefully because the supplementary personnel costs determine the attractiveness of the employer. Therefore, in times of tense economic situations, a firm should strive towards maintaining a portfolio of social and supplementary benefits for its employees and, when necessary, think of economising only on such benefits which were perceived as "not so important" by the employees.

### & Related Ratios/Additional Notes

As a synonym for supplementary personnel costs, it is also common to use the term "Fringe Benefits".

In general, this ratio is calculated annually; however, if there are significant legal changes, the ratio could be calculated during the year as well.

When making international comparisons, supplementary personnel costs are viewed as a "location-parameter". It is an economic factor which can be influenced by governments at an economic level to make the country an attractive location.

### 5.1.3 Personnel Costs per Employee

**Analytical Question**

What is the average gross personnel cost per employee? What is the sum of gross wage, gross salaries and supplementary personnel costs per employee to the firm?

**Definition**

$$\frac{\text{Gross Personnel Costs per Period}}{\text{Number of Employees (Normalised to Full-Time Employees)}}$$

Where:

Gross Personnel Costs = Gross Wages + Gross Salaries + Supplementary Personnel Costs (Employer's Contribution to Retirement Benefits, etc.)

In order to avoid any statistical bias (the quota might appear to be falling when the number of part-time staff increases), and to ensure comparability over time as well as amongst firms, the formula proposes that the value shown in the denominator should be normalised to full-time employees, e.g., two part time employees, each working on a 50% job, make one full-time employee.

The Personnel Costs per Employee are expressed in monetary terms; for example, € per employee.

**Calculation/Derivation**

The required data for this ratio could be obtained from the (computer-based) information system of the human resource department, particularly the deployment data. For additional analysis, the information could be further classified into functional activity groups, or for national and international locations within the corporate group.

**Interpretation and Typical Range**

The Personnel Costs per Employee provide a measure of the personnel cost burden. For international competition analysis, this indicator (often normalised into personnel cost or labour cost per hour) is often compared, to analyse the location advantage. More relevant for the location comparisons is, however, the labour cost per unit which considers the proportional time consumed per unit.

In many companies, along with the absolute volume of personnel costs per employee, the development of the ratio over time is also carefully analysed.

The typical range of Personnel Costs per Employee varies substantially. Drawing inter-firm comparisons, based on this number, may not be very helpful because firms usually have a very heterogeneous composition of employees (both in terms of numbers, and as well as in terms of qualifications). However, an inter-firm comparison can offer more insights, if the ratio is calculated for pre-defined segments (for example, classified according to job-area).

Over and above the national differences, legally binding fringe benefits, collective agreements and the arrangements for voluntary payments introduce substantial differences in practice, so that any judgment based on the average ratio for personnel costs per employee may not be free from bias.

**❗ Useful Suggestions**

Basically, from an operational perspective, costs incurred in a firm are the business-related consumption of resources which generates or delivers some output. In the same way, personnel costs have to be seen with reference to the specific performance-potential of employees which is rewarded through agreements and arrangements. When designing its plan for such agreements (through collective agreements or voluntary arrangements), a firm must consider the targets it wants to achieve. Maintaining or improving the motivation, welfare and security of employees (and of family members), the appreciation of performance, facilitating capital formation and retirement benefits are some examples of this.

In all business areas, financial remuneration represents a major factor in determining the attractiveness of the employer. When attempting to hire and win-over a more qualified candidate, it is considered as an important competitive factor.

As orientation for the annual development of the direct personnel costs, the magnitude of productivity-increase is often taken as a guiding factor.

**& Related Ratios/Additional Notes**

"Wage-hour Rate" and "Unit Labour Costs" are two important related ratios of Personnel Costs per Employee.

The amount of Personnel Costs per Employee is strongly influenced by developments in the area of fringe benefits, which is known as the "Supplementary Personnel Cost Ratio". This ratio is often used for comparisons, both nationally and internationally.

**Ⓢ 5.1.4 Unit Labour Cost**

**❓ Analytical Question**

What are the average direct-labour (gross personnel) costs per unit of manufactured output (for example, per unit or per ton)?

**✳ Definition**

$$\frac{\text{Gross Personnel Costs of Direct Labour in a Period}}{\text{Total Units of Output manufactured in a Period}}$$

Where:
Gross Personnel Costs = Gross Wages + Gross Salaries + Supplementary Personnel
Costs (Employer's Contribution to Retirement Benefits. etc.)

The Unit Labour Cost is expressed in monetary terms, for example in € per unit. Other measures used in the denominator could be the length, area, volume or weight.

## Calculation/Derivation

The required data for total labour costs can be obtained from the record of the human resource department, or from the accounting and/or the controlling department. Details about the volume of output manufactured in a period can be derived from the production department records.

It is important to note that, as a quotient, the Unit Labour Cost is applied primarily in the context of direct labour, i.e. labour directly engaged in the manufacturing process. Therefore, when calculating the total labour cost, a careful distinction has to be made between direct and indirect labour, and only costs relating to direct labour have to be taken in the denominator.

## Interpretation and Typical Range

The Unit Labour Cost is a central and straightforward measure for analysing the trends in production costs, particularly in those manufacturing firms where labour cost is the single largest component of production costs. It is often used for comparing the competitive position of firms in a particular branch or location.

Being a relative quotient, the Unit Labour Cost is always viewed in relation to productivity. If productivity is measured as the quantity of output produced for a given time of labour input, the unit labour cost rises when the gross personnel costs rise faster than labour productivity. Thus, if labour productivity improves by 2 per cent and workers' gross personnel costs remain the same; the unit labour cost will decline. Conversely, when productivity remains unchanged but workers' gross personnel costs increased by 2 per cent, the unit labour cost would rise. Therefore, the changes in Unit Labour Cost reflect the net effect of changes in workers' compensation and changes in worker productivity.

A generalised target for Unit Labour Cost is not easy to define. If other things (including quality) remain the same, the lower the unit labour cost, the more competitive the firm shall be in terms of its total production costs. For orientation about a typical range, often internal comparisons of unit labour costs are made (such as the ratio in different organisational units or plan-actual values). The interpretative power of this ratio is increased if the developments in the unit labour cost are compared over time, and a trend is analysed. The Unit Labour Cost can also be taken for external comparisons, where the branch-specific average or the "best-practice" value may be used as a guide. When making external comparisons, it is important to ensure the consistency of definitions.

**❗ Useful Suggestions**

The Unit Labour Cost is an important indicator of the trend in production costs, particularly for manufacturing firms with labour intensive technology or in those cases where labour costs are a major component in total production costs. A sustained increase in the unit labour cost will cause an upward shift in its average and marginal total curves. This has the immediate effect of negatively influencing profits.

A sustained increase in the unit labour cost can affect the competitiveness of a firm in its market. Whether a firm, confronted with rising unit labour cost, is able to increase price depends upon the price-related competitive pressures in the market. In a monopoly or oligopoly market, the ability to transfer increases in the unit labour cost to the market is easier than in other kinds of markets. Many firms react to unit labour cost disadvantage by shifting production to locations where unit labour costs are lower and/or have a slower upward trend.

**& Related Ratios/Additional Notes**

There are three ratios in the category of "personnel costs" which may be considered as related ratios for Unit Labour Cost. Firstly, "Personnel Costs per Employee" is derived from gross personnel costs divided by the total number of employees. Secondly, "Personnel Costs Ratio" refers to the relative significance of gross personnel costs in the total costs of a firm. Thirdly, "Supplementary Personnel Costs Ratio" shows supplementary personnel costs in relation to gross wages and salaries.

In order to clearly appreciate the meaning of Unit Labour Cost, it is important to understand the difference between productivity and efficiency. *The reader is advised to refer to the basic indicators to check the differences between these terms in the book.*

## 5.2 Human Resource Controlling

### 5.2.1 Labour Productivity

**❓ Analytical Question**

How large is the yield from labour, as an input factor (measured in quantity), as shown in terms of a particular output volume (measured in quantity or monetary value)?

**✳ Definition**

$$\frac{\text{Output (measured in Produced Quantity or Value Added)} \cdot 100}{\text{Input (Number of Employees or Time at Work)}}$$

Various measures of quantity in the numerator are: units produced, length, area in square meters, weight and time-duration. The value added is measured in monetary units (for example, in €).

For the denominator, basically either the deployed manpower (per head rate, where the part-time contracts have to be converted into appropriate full-time manpower) or the operational work-time (in hours or days) is taken.

The measured value of labour productivity may be expressed in: "units per head", "Kg per head", "units per hour", "square meter per hour" or "€ per hour", etc.

**Calculation/Derivation**                                                          »
The required data for this quotient is prepared from the internal cost accounting system which is then processed and made available to decision makers in different cost types, cost-centres, and product costing.

**Interpretation and Typical Range**                                                #
With the help of Labour Productivity, a measure of yield for labour as a production factor is derived. Labour Productivity is a central measure for labour efficiency. It is treated as the most important duty of the manager.

Since various combinations of production factors (each one measured differently) are used for a particular output, the data for measuring economic productivity has to be collected and valued for each factor separately. Often the measured value shows partial efficiency only.

It is not easy to recommend a typical range for this ratio. A useful interpretation of this ratio is possible over time when intra-firm or inter-firm comparisons are made over several periods. Since the deployed factors of production are usually scarce, managers always seek to achieve, in the framework of social and legal norms, the highest possible Labour Productivity. An important, though simplified, assumption made for calculating this quotient is that the input and output factors have a linear cause-and-effect relationship with each other. It should be emphasised that this assumption of linearity is not always true.

**Useful Suggestions**                                                              !
A change in this ratio, in the context of desired corporate goals, can be achieved by a disproportionate increase or decrease in the achieved output (as numerator) and deployed input (as denominator). *For further details and systematic explanations on this, refer to the information in Appendix I.*

The demand for targeted productivity increases in firms is often grounded in the need to improve future competitiveness. Through an improved (monetary value-based) output-input relationship, the firm should make maximum use of the scarce production factors. Improvements in productivity are focused at increasing the monetary yield of the deployed resource input. Thus, measuring productivity over time is an important step in process-optimization; this is often achieved through skilfulness in avoiding wasted time or wasted energy. Lean manufacturing is an interesting example of process improvement which supports the business benefits of rapid execution.

It is relevant to note that gains in Labour Productivity have to be compared constantly with the quality indicators. The improvements in Labour Productivity have to be achieved under the conditions of upholding or maintaining quality standards.

There is one more aspect which needs to be considered. If the input factors of production have substitutes, a part-improvement in productivity may not lead necessarily to total improvement in productivity. Moreover, an improvement in the productivity of a particular factor may well be due to increased consumption in another input factor.

### & Related Ratios/Additional Notes

Sometimes, "Personnel Productivity", "Personnel Efficiency" and "Work-Efficiency" are used as synonyms for Labour Productivity. A closely related ratio is "Technical Productivity" where the performance of a particular input is measured in physical terms and not in monetary terms.

In order to make better judgments about the performance of a particular process, it is desirable to measure the outputs (the numerator) in monetary terms. This leads to the calculation of "economic productivity". If both output and various input factors are measured in monetary units, the resultant value is called "operational efficiency". In process reengineering, for example, any change that increases economic productivity is considered an economically efficient change.

### 5.2.2 Overtime Quota

### ? Analytical Question

Is the relative amount of regular working-time that had to be exceeded to complete a job in producing products and services in the given schedule?

### * Definition

$$\frac{\text{Number of Overtime Hours in a Period} \cdot 100}{\text{Total Number of Regular Working Hours in a Period}}$$

The Overtime Quota is expressed as a percentage.

### » Calculation/Derivation

The required data for this ratio could be obtained from the (computerised) information system relating to time-records for employees. The data could also be available from the Human Resource software module of any ERP system. It is desirable to classify the overtime-related information into cost-centres, or into different business processes. Moreover, the information could be collected on a weekly or monthly basis.

## Interpretation and Typical Range     `#`

The Overtime Quota is the main measure for checking the even distribution of the normal volume of work in a firm. Except for special circumstances demanding overtime, a continuous excess workload is reflected in the Overtime Quota and thus shows the work-peaks which cannot (or could not) be accomplished in the normal (agreed) work timings. Since the employees have to be paid more for the overtime, this extra work time is more expensive than the normal work time. Therefore, usually a comparably lower Overtime Quota is considered desirable.

## Useful Suggestions     `!`

From a firm's perspective, additional manpower requirements can be covered either through fresh hiring or overtime. If the strong demand for a firm's products is likely to be perpetual, it would be desirable, along with increasing capital-intensity or rationalization measures to increase the headcount. The increase in work force could also be achieved by converting part-time jobs into full-time contracts, which obviously requires the consent of part-time employees.

However, if the future prospects are uncertain and the additional need for manpower appears to be temporary, in most cases, it would lead to an increase in the hours of overtime worked. In the case of fluctuating (or seasonal) capacity-utilization, many firms have resorted to short-term (or limited period) contracts. In the recent past, a flexible working-hours system has also been introduced by many firms which allows the staff to be compensated for the fluctuation in the workload through a compensatory mechanism or account. This is beneficial for the firm because it leads to a general reduction in the Overtime Quota, and most of the overtime is managed without additional payment for it.

Within organisational aspects, in particular, through detailed analysis of available data related to critical business processes or special bottlenecks within the firm, a "root-cause-analysis" of the situation can be made, so that appropriate short-term human resource policy responses can be developed.

If the employees are exposed to additional work permanently through overtime, it often leads to an increase in physical and psychological stress. Consequently, employees may make more mistakes at work, leading to a loss in quality and increases in follow-up costs.

## Related Ratios/Additional Notes     `&`

From a macroeconomic perspective, trends in the Overtime Quota are viewed as an indicator of the expected number of people employed; though with a lag of time, an increasing trend in the Overtime Quota leads to positive expectations about an increase in the number of job-positions offered.

### 5.2.3 Workforce Composition Ratios

**? Analytical Question**

Over the last few decades, in academic literature as well as in practice, a large number of ratios have cropped up for analysing human resource related problems and searching for new solutions. These ratios group employees into different categories and, through an analysis of their number and development over time, offer insights into the changing significance and impact of each group in the firm.

Without claiming to be exhaustive, the following categories for employees could be taken as specific groupings for creating an analytical question:

What is the share of the following in the total staff of the firm?

- Trainees
- Skilled Workers
- Unskilled Workers
- Executives
- Employees with International Experience
- Employees in a particular age group (e.g. employees over 50)
- Employees in Home country or Overseas
- Employees with Disabilities
- Part-time Employees
- Female or Male Employees

The list can be extended and refined depending upon the needs of each firm.

**\* Definition**

$$\frac{\text{Number of Employees in a Particular Group} \cdot 100}{\text{Total Number of Employees in the Firm (or a Sub-total)}}$$

An example of a sub-total in the denominator would be: The ratio of female trainees, equal to the number of female trainees divided by the total number of trainees in the firm.

All the ratios in the human resource composition are expressed as a percentage.

**» Calculation/Derivation**

The required data for these ratios could be obtained from the (computer-based) information system of the human resource department, particularly the master files about different categories of employees. For additional analysis, the information could be further classified into functional activity groups or for national and international locations within the corporate group.

The data-collection frequency for these ratios depends upon the information needs of the decision-makers. Often the data is collected annually or semi-annually, and sometimes also between two standard periods for specific needs.

## Interpretation and Typical Range

The comparative change in one category of employees with the change in total employees provides a snap shot on a cut-off deadline. Along with this relative value, it is often better to know the absolute number of employees in each group for a correct interpretation of ratios. This is more likely in groups with a small absolute number, where a small increase in the denominator or decrease in the numerator may show a significant change in the ratio.

To estimate the desirability of a particular ratio (for a group, such as trainees), it is important to keep in mind the size of the firm and its branch-specific features. Furthermore, along with the absolute volume of change in a particular category, the development of the ratio over time has to be analysed as well.

A generalised target for the typical range cannot be defined. For orientation about a typical range, internal comparisons (such as the ratio in different organisational units or plan-actual values) or external comparisons (where the branch-specific average or the "best-practice" value) may be used as a guide.

## Useful Suggestions

Assuming that firms in the same branch usually have similar production and cost structures, the ratio values, differing significantly from the averages, are clear candidates for a serious review. This should help in analysing the positive and negative developments or consequences and manoeuvring them in the context of corporate goals:

- Working at achieving a competitive advantage (for example, through an extensive build-up of a highly qualified service-team); or
- Working at reducing a competitive disadvantage (for example, firms expanding overseas could train their domestic employees through a careful placement overseas).

A change in this ratio could be triggered by a disproportionate increase or decrease in the number in a group (as numerator) and the total number of employees in the firm (as denominator). *For further details and a systematic explanation on this, refer to the information in Appendix I.*

## Related Ratios/Additional Notes

To choose ratios for human resource composition which should be regularly compiled and reported to the decision makers for their strategic and operative decisions, it is important to check the following:

- Whose information needs have to be covered through these ratios?
- What the resource consumption (in terms of time and cost) for data-compilation and reporting of these ratios is?

### 5.2.4 Internally-staffed Executive Positions Ratio

**?** **Analytical Question**

To what extent is it possible for employees within the firm to be promoted to executive or leading positions?

**\*** **Definition**

$$\frac{\text{Number of New Executive Positions Filled Internally in a Period} \cdot 100}{\text{Total Number of New Executive Positions in a Period}}$$

This ratio is expressed as a percentage.

**»** **Calculation/Derivation**

The required data for this ratio could be obtained from the information system in the human resource department, particularly from human resource master files. The employee record could be classified further for additional analysis; for example, position in the hierarchy, functional area, gender or qualification.

**#** **Interpretation and Typical Range**

The Internally-staffed Executive Positions Ratio is an indicator that can be grouped in the category of human resource development and recruitment.

This ratio is gaining in significance, from different perspectives in international competition. From the employees' perspective, it is an indicator of the potential for career development within the firm, showing the extent to which promotion possibilities are available in senior positions. From the firm's perspective, promotion opportunities offer a chance to hire competent employees, who can create synergies through their existing knowledge about the firm. For the firm, the internal staffing has the additional advantage of reducing orientation time in a new position and the costs related to it.

It is very difficult to recommend any specific target range. The ratio depends strongly on the corporate culture within the firm. For example, a firm may prefer to staff senior positions from within its own ranks which is often reflected in institutionalised career planning, and requires intensive and individual professional training of employees. The external recruitment of employees may be equally advantageous for the firm. This is particularly useful in those cases where the firm wants to acquire knowledge about a new product, market, technology or country, innovative processes, or special management experience (for example, in starting new businesses or restructuring), etc.

Last but not least, because of a general shortage in highly qualified people, many companies strive for a ratio of 60 to 70% for internally staffed senior positions.

## Useful Suggestions

The spectrum of possible measures for the human resource development could have both a strategic and an operative component. Strategically, one could consider targeted professional development of senior executives, through a combination of "on-the-job" and "off-the-job" training phases. Operationally, professional development could be fostered through various measures of the classical human resource policy, such as temporary assignments in new responsibilities (example: project-related responsibilities with varying degrees of complexity).

## Related Ratios/Additional Notes

An important factor, influencing meaningful interpretation of the internal executive-staffing ratio, is the size of the firm. Thus, if the senior positions in a firm are limited, the attractiveness of the position can be increased, despite limited promotion chances, through a participative leadership style and a meaningful delegation of responsibility and authority.

## 5.2.5 Staff Recruitment Period

## Analytical Question

What is the average time consumed between the staff requirement notification by a department, and recruitment? How long does the firm's average hiring process take?

## Definition

The Staff Recruitment Period could be sub-divided in several phases. The following example provides a sub-division into five phases:

- Phase A: Internal Preparation Period
  (The time span needed to approve a vacancy, and the internal and/or external advertisement of the vacancy)
- Phase B: Application Period
  (The time span between the advertisement and the deadline for submitting applications)
- Phase C: Selection Process Period
  (The time span needed for the multi-level selection of suitable candidates, the decision process and issuing of an employment contract. The phase is coupled

with evaluating the applications, selecting the candidates through a personal interview or assessment centre and so on)
- Phase D: Contract Completion Period
  (The time span between the issuing and final signing of the contract)
- Phase E: Transition Period
  (The time span between the contract signing and joining of the selected person).

The number of phases in the staff recruitment process, as well as the name of each phase, varies both in literature and in practice. However, irrespective of the number and name, what matters is the operative significance of each phase and how it is organised.

The Staff Recruitment Period is expressed in terms of time (such as days, weeks or months).

### » Calculation/Derivation
The required data for these indicators could be obtained from the information system of the human resource department, particularly from the projects relating to staff-recruitment. In order to draw meaningful operational conclusions, the information may be classified with reference to different categories of positions, such as trainees, skilled workers, executive staff, specialists and top management positions. This classification will allow for additional analytical differences, and help justify the individual requirements of each category.

### # Interpretation and Typical Range
In the framework of human-resource controlling, the Staff Recruitment Period (with its individual phases) is an important indicator of the total time it takes to fill a vacancy.

In practice, depending upon the (legal) formalities or the purpose of individual positions, the typical recruitment period varies substantially. A generalised target is, therefore, not easy to define. For orientation about a typical range, internal comparisons (such as the ratio in different organisational units or plan-actual values) or external comparisons (where the branch-specific average or the "best-practice" value) may be used as a guide.

### ! Useful Suggestions
Without denying the branch-specific peculiarities, it may be a good approach to benchmark the Staff Recruitment Period beyond the limits of one's own branch. Thus, if one's own ratio-values differ significantly from the averages or best values, these would be clear candidates for serious review. This should help in analysing the positive and negative developments or consequences, and manoeuvring them in the context of corporate goals. The available spectrum of possible measures is strongly influenced by the type of vacancy to be filled. Thus, the recruitment focus for filling trainee positions is different from that for filling specialist positions.

In the following, measures towards reducing the recruitment period are shown for each phase:
- Phase A:
  Internal preparation period could be reduced with the help of well-defined vacancy description. Standardization of the needed coordination amongst various departments (including the involvement of works-council), choice of advertisement media could be equally helpful here.
- Phase B:
  Positioning the schedule with reference to the calendar and giving adequate time for applicants to react could reduce application period.
- Phase C:
  Avoiding the "idle time" after the application deadline is over could reduce selection process period. It is good to treat the selection process as a project, where all aspects of the selection criteria are already defined and prepared.
- Phase D:
  Contract completion period is reduced through clear terms in the contract and concrete communication with the selected candidates.
- Phase E:
  Transition Period depends primarily on the need of the firm to fill the vacant position in time.

It is important to note that there is a strong linkage amongst all the five phases in the recruitment process. Thus, if the vacancy details have been clearly defined and the advertisement media is carefully selected, this would reduce the number of non-qualified applicants and, as a consequence, may make the selection process a lot easier.

**Related Ratios/Additional Notes**

"Time-to-Fill" and "Recruitment Duration" are two common synonyms for the Staff Recruitment Period.

Along with time-related measures of staffing, cost-related measures could also be used. For example, Cost per Applicant or Cost per Recruitment could help in evaluating the efficiency of the recruitment process.

## 5.3 Human Resource Development Indicators

### 5.3.1 Professional Development Training Time per Employee

**?** **Analytical Question**

What is the average time-span that the employees spend for professional training in a period?

**✱** **Definition**

$$\frac{\text{Number of Total Professional Training Days}}{\text{Average Number of Employees}}$$

If because of part-time contracts, the annual working days of some employees differ significantly, the denominator should be normalised to reflect full-time employees.

The Professional Development Training Time per Employee is expressed in days.

**»** **Calculation/Derivation**

The required data for this ratio could be obtained from the information system in the human resource department, particularly relating to human resource development. For further analysis, the information may be collected for each type of professional training (such as on-the-job or off-the-job, preparatory training or regular training, departmental focus of training, etc.).

**#** **Interpretation and Typical Range**

The ratio "Professional Development Training Time per Employee" is viewed as an indicator of the targeted skill-building intensity of the employees. As is the case with many other ratios, varying organisational frameworks can hamper the comparability of this indicator, particularly in inter-firm comparisons. Thus, for example, there are firms that integrate professional training potential, in the normal on-the-job time, through a clear "job-rotation" strategy. However, the professional development of an employee can also be achieved without job rotation which is clearly an "off-the-job" variant of training. The ratio may vary substantially, depending upon what kind of approach is adopted by a firm.

It is very difficult to derive any specific target range for the needs of a firm in respect of reasonable or meaningful professional training time. Primarily, the need for training is influenced by the knowledge level of the employees and the speed with which existing technical or operational knowledge becomes out-dated.

**!** **Useful Suggestions**

Conceptualizing and implementing professional training programs for employees is a collective effort between those responsible for human resource development and those who manage various departments. Both parties have to consider the strategic aspirations of the firm, so that the professional development helps in ensuring the sustained competitiveness of the firm. It is important to note that this ratio is a general indicator of how much time is devoted to professional training, but does not give any clue about the content of training or its effectiveness.

The willingness and commitment of a firm to allocate resources for the professional training of employees is often correlated with the current and/or future expected profitability, growth potential and macroeconomic cycles. Thus, in times of general thriving business, companies tend to commit more resources to employees' training.

## Related Ratios/Additional Notes &

Other related measures for professional training include "Training Budget per Period", "After-Training Cost Savings", and "Employees Satisfaction Index".

## 5.3.2 Professional Development Training Costs Ratio Ⓢ

### Analytical Question ?
What is the share of professional training costs in total personnel costs? What is the financial impact of the professional training programs in the framework of the human resource development policy of the firm?

### Definition *

$$\frac{\text{Professional Training Costs} \cdot 100}{\text{Gross Wages} + \text{Salaries}}$$

The "Professional Development Training Costs Ratio" is expressed as a percentage, and the measurement frequency is usually annual.

### Calculation/Derivation »
The required data for this ratio could be obtained from the (computer-based) information system (particularly relating to human resource development) of the human resource department. For extended analysis, the information could be further classified into the following categories:
- Introductory training of employees,
- Functional responsibility of employees, and
- Internal or external training.

In the case of professional training costs, it is important for comparison purposes, to ensure the consistency of definitions: whether only direct costs of training are included in the definition or the traveling, boarding and lodging costs are also part of the total.

**#** **Interpretation and Typical Range**

The ratio is a financial indicator of the targeted skill-building intensity of the employees. As is the case with many other ratios, varying organisational frameworks can hamper the comparability of this indicator, particularly in inter-firm comparisons. Thus, for example, there are firms that integrate the professional training potential in the normal on-the-job time through a clear "job-rotation" strategy. However, the professional development of an employee can also be achieved without job rotation which is clearly an "off-the-job" variant of training. The ratio may vary substantially, depending upon what kind of approach is adopted by a firm.

It is very difficult to derive any specific target range for the needs of a firm with respect to reasonable or meaningful professional training times. Primarily, the need for training is influenced by the knowledge level of the employees and the speed with which the existing technical or operational knowledge becomes out-dated.

**!** **Useful Suggestions**

Conceptualizing and implementing professional training programs for employees is a collective effort between those responsible for human resource development and those who manage various departments. Both parties have to consider the strategic aspirations of the firm, so that professional development helps in ensuring the sustained competitiveness of the firm. It is important to note that this ratio is a general indicator of how much time was devoted to professional training, but does not give any clue about the content of training or its effectiveness.

The willingness and commitment of a firm to allocate resources for the professional training of employees is often correlated with the current and/or future expected profitability, growth potential and macroeconomic cycles. Thus, in times of general thriving business, companies tend to commit more resources to employees' training.

**&** **Related Ratios/Additional Notes**

As a related ratio, we could refer to "Professional Training Time per Employee" which is an indicator of the time spent in training, and does not refer to its economic value.

### 5.3.3 Human Resource Internationality Index

**?** **Analytical Question**

To what extent can individual employees, or specific employee groups (e.g. on selected management levels), be grouped under the characteristic category "international"?

## Definition

The indicator "Human Resource (henceforth HR) Internationality Index"[1] is composed of indices linking several single components. Following the concept of Schmid/Dauch, the index depends upon four individual dimensions:

$$\frac{1}{n} \cdot \sum_{i=1}^{n} \left( \frac{1}{4} \cdot \left( F_i + \left(1 - \frac{1}{E_i+1}\right) + \left(1 - \frac{1}{W_i+1}\right) + \left(1 - \frac{1}{A_i+1}\right) \right) \right)$$

Wherein:

n = total number of employees included in the survey

$F_i$ = nationality refers to the country, where the person i spent their childhood/
    school days (homeland: "0"; foreign country: "1")

$E_i$ = number of educational years person i spent abroad (education)

$W_i$= number of years of professional experience person i gained abroad (work)

$A_i$ = number of external supervisory mandates person i had at companies abroad

The mathematical result is a decimal number that is multiplied with the factor "100" and then indicated as a "%".

For example, for a person who grew up in the company's homeland (F=0), studied abroad for 4 years (E=4), worked 7 years of his or her professional life abroad (W=7) and held accordingly 3 supervisory mandates (A=3), an individual "HR Internationality Index" shall have a value of 0.606 or 60.6%.

## Calculation/Derivation

The necessary data can be extracted from the company's computer-based HR information systems (HR master data). While calculating this index, the legal provisions of the data protection law applicable in the country should be carefully studied and observed.

The survey frequency, for calculating the internationality index, depends on the decision-makers' and the external stakeholders' need for information. Usually, the calculation is made on an annual basis, e.g. on the occasion of external reporting to emphasize the aspired international diversity of executive and supervisory boards.

## Interpretation and Typical Range

In contrast to the goods market level, where for example, the proportion of foreign sales in total turnover makes it easy to calculate the level of internationality, a decently acceptable investigation of the "internationality" on a personnel management level can only be made with the help of suitable auxiliary indicators.

---

**1** The definition is drawn from the concept proposed by Schmid/Dauch, zfbf, (2012), pp. 772 ff.

Any attempt at operationalizing the HR Internationality Index in the present conceptual version not only happens on the basis of individual characteristics (unidimensional on the basis of nationality), but also with the help of four characteristics whose peculiarity is added with equal weights, as mentioned in the formula above. The framework of this comprehensive approach tries to integrate, both the defining impressions of childhood, an apprenticeship and/or a university study, as well as professional experience and external senior management positions held abroad. The chosen indicators, therefore, refer primarily to the specific acquisition of knowledge and the experience of particular norms/values, as well as to behaviour patterns and attitude in other countries and cultures.

As with any other forms of indirect derivation of a statement about a complex situation in the form of a key indicator, the choice of characteristics for internationality index, its mathematical description and its linkage can also be questioned. The same applies to the implicit assumption (along with the quality of its empirical verification) that managers can potentially handle the challenge of cross-border business better when they themselves have a high level of personal internationality imbibed in their personality.

An economically generalized target for the level of HR Internationality Index of an employee group (e.g. on the 1st, 2nd or 3rd top-management level or in specific specialist departments or in project teams) is not determinable. Typically, multinational companies from the U.S.A. and other Anglo-Saxon countries tend to have a higher internationality index amongst their board of directors than multinational companies from continental Europe, Japan or China.

For orientation and benchmarking this key indicator, depending upon the size of employees' groups included in the survey, one could make internal comparisons (such as the ratio in different organizational units or budget-actual comparisons). Of particular relevance in this context could be corresponding external comparisons, where the branch-specific average values or the "best-practice" values may be used as a guide.

### ⚠ Useful Suggestions

Before developing suitable strategies and programs for international HR management, two central and formal problem areas have to be considered:
- National vs. International Classification
  If the country of origin counts as "national", what happens when a fast-growing company has more than one head office or shifts its country-of-origin headquarter over time?
- Small home country
  For companies from small countries of origin, the results may be distorted because mathematically, with all other factors being equal, its HR internationalization index may be comparatively higher in relation to companies from big countries of origin.

Under the premise that increasing international personnel diversity is beneficial and desirable for a company, the question for the HR development managers is how to sensibly achieve this goal. A possibly increasing HR Internationality Index would be an advantage factor for the attractiveness of a potential location. However, it should never be viewed as an end in itself.

Besides the recruitment of new employees with an international experience profile, the instrument of job-rotation should be reviewed by the international HR management, because of its possibly stronger intensity and practical use than hiring persons with international experience. This systematic change would, from the perspective of nationality, affect three groups of persons:

- Host Country Nationals (HCNs): company employees that have the citizenship of the host country where the respective subsidiary is located
- Parent Country Nationals (PCNs): company employees that have the citizenship of the country where the parent company is located.
- Third Country Nationals (TCNs): company employees that have the citizenship of a third country.

For an internationally oriented staffing strategy, in many cases, a typical central goal is to ensure:

- A more intensive, task-based, mutual know-how transfer,
- Reduced conflicts in the coordination of business units, and
- Better development of top-management through an on-the-job approach.

**Related Ratios/Additional Notes**

Related key indicators are, among others, the "Level of Internationality" and the "International Profile".

The first case deals with several characteristics, in which the extent of internationality is measured individually, with the help of an indicator (for further details, refer to KPI No. 3.5.1.)

The second case deals with a graphical illustration from several levels of internationality – like HR Internationality Index – that can help to develop appropriate "company profiles" and can, over time, be compared internally as well as externally, particularly with reference to competitors.

## 5.3.4 Ratio of Employees with Risk-aligned Remuneration Packages

**Analytical Question**

What is the relative percentage of the employees of the company who have their compensation or remuneration package aligned to prudent risk taking and risk management? What is the share of employees, of the total staff of the company who have variable salary components connected with risk-based performance management?

**✱ Definition**

$$\frac{\text{Number of Employees with Variable Salary Components} \cdot 100}{\text{Total Number of Professionals (or a Sub-group) in the Firm}}$$

This ratio of number of employees with risk-aligned remuneration packages or variable salary components is expressed as a percentage.

**» Calculation/ Derivation**

The required data for this key risk indicator (KRI) can be derived from the HR department's information system. The data can be further classified for finer evaluation, e.g., according to hierarchy levels of the employees and/or professional fields of their activity. Sometimes, it may be meaningful to make comparisons between domestic and various foreign locations within a group, to find out how significant the "risk-based variable component" remuneration policy of a particular location is.

**# Interpretation and Typical Range**

Most large firms have performance measurement frameworks in place, to assess the achievements of the firm as a whole, its business units, organizational units as well as individual employees. In order to maximize the incentives, to deliver adequate performance and to take into account any risks of the business activities, some firms closely link remuneration outcomes (so-called variable component) with performance and risk outcomes.

This KRI explains the significance of risk alignment in the remuneration package. The increasing ratio of employees with variable salary contracts may suggest a new remuneration policy where fresh recruitments for certain types of professional roles are all based on contracts which are performance-risk-aligned remuneration packages. It could also mean that old employment contracts have been changed or upgraded into remuneration packages with a larger responsibility for performance and risk management.

The key indicator "Ratio of Employees with Risk-aligned Remuneration Packages" can be calculated with the denominator of "total professional staff" or a particular sub-group. Thus, it may be interesting to check, over time, how many employees in an organizational unit, a location, a project team, or a professional sub-group (for example, procurement professionals) have variable salary components in their salary with a variable part linked to some performance-risk indices.

The question of an ideal ratio for this indicator depends upon the risk-management framework of the firm. It also has a strong linkage with the corporate governance framework established by the firm for compliance with national regulations and directives. The size of the firm, complexity of the firm's business, type of business model (e.g., local, national or international) and risk tolerance capacity of the firm are other factors that may influence how the HR department develops a variable remuneration system and recruits more people with performance and risk aligned packages.

As with many other key indicators, the interpretation and comparison of concrete values may not be easy, particularly in certain kinds of companies, where noticeably extensive content relating to external legal standards has to be implemented. Nevertheless, to begin with, the collection and reporting of this indicator makes it clear that the firm is pursuing a preventive strategy of securing risk management and corporate compliance in a world full of uncertainties and regulatory regimes. However, for orientation and benchmarking this ratio, one could take internal comparisons (such as the ratio in different organizational units or budget-actual comparisons) and corresponding external comparisons, where the branch-specific practices or the risk-management frameworks adopted by competitors may be used as a guide.

**Useful Suggestions**

There are three categories of staff whose professional activities or roles have a material impact on the risk management of the firm:

- The senior executive/top management. Includes all persons who, because of their roles, have the capacity to make decisions that materially affect the interests of all stakeholders of an institution.
- Risk and financial control executives. Includes all persons who have a critical role in maintaining the financial soundness of the firm. They act as "gatekeepers" to ensure that the business is in line with the risk-appetite of the firm. Employees working in legal and corporate governance roles are often also included in this category.
- Material risk takers. This category captures those persons who receive a significant portion of pay as performance-based remuneration. For example, a trader in a bank who engages in the operational task of executing or settling transactions on a daily basis. Often, a middle-level manager, with relatively low salary, may also be in this category because their variable salary component depends, for example, on a commission or fee-based performance. The ratio of staff in this category has considerable importance for risk-aligned remuneration policies.

It is often not easy to identify the impact of a particular employee's role in risky business decisions and, even more difficult, in risk-mitigation. Given that many business activities are "pool decisions", where a project team or a cross-functional-team (CFT) is involved, it is important that remuneration contracts clearly specify the variables used to measure risk and performance, and relate these, as far as possible, to the decisions made by an employee. Conversely, it may be good to develop award processes where all the members of project team or CFT have a pool-bonus and individual allocation is articulated based on the position of the employee and his contract stipulations.

**&** **Related Ratios/ Additional Notes**

It is important that the HR department collaborates with the managers of the specialist departments (such as the legal department) and the company's top management, to develop suitable risk-aligned remuneration packages. The legal restrictions, applicable locally for variable component contracts, should be carefully studied before pursuing performance-risk based remuneration policies. This is particularly important if the HR department wants to introduce claw backs (provisions withdrawing a payment already made to an executive) in the employment contract.

The "Ratio of Employees with Risk-aligned Remuneration Packages" is more a general indicator that is based on the headcount of the professional considered eligible for a variable salary incentive system, but does not provide a reliable statement about the complexity of the content. The subject of remuneration policies is an intricate one, particularly when the risk-impact can often be assessed only ex-post (over several years after the decision) and not in the year in which the decision was made.

The budgeting process is more complex for those companies which have to estimate the financial impact of variable salary contracts. It is recommended that the financial modelling of different scenarios, of performance-risk outcomes, be compiled to develop related KPI, such as budget actual comparisons of the "Cost Effectiveness of Risk Management" (*refer to KPI No. 4.5.9 for more details on the subject*) over time, to convey the (increasing) strategic significance of preventive measures.

### 5.3.5 Compliance Training Hours per Employee

**?** **Analytical Question**

What is the total duration of training, or participation hours, spent by a company's employees in programs on compliance related standards and guidelines, in a particular period?

**\*** **Definition**

$$\frac{\text{Amount of Compliance Training Hours in a Particular Period}}{\text{Average Amount of Employees in a Particular Period}}$$

The dimension of the KPI is calculated as "average training hours per person in a period".

**»** **Calculation/ Derivation**

The required data for this key indicator can be derived from the information system of the HR department. The data can be further classified for finer evaluation, e.g., according to hierarchy levels of the employees, and/or professional fields of their activity. Sometimes, it may be meaningful to make comparison between domestic and various foreign locations within a group, to find out how significant compliance related issues are.

**Interpretation and Typical Range**                                    #

The task areas, grouped under the terminology "Corporate Compliance", are intended to ensure permanently that the employees' actions, at all levels, are always in accordance with external and internal requirements for proper and responsible corporate management. Often, the obligation to comply with such requirements and standards are drawn in writing in so-called "Codes of Conduct". The obligation to comply with the rules should be clearly documented in a top-down process in a company, with appropriate consequences in the event of non-compliance.

With this background in mind, the KPI "Compliance Training Hours per Employee" is regarded as a rough but vivid indicator of the intensity of focused further training of the workforce in a particular subject area. In view of the increasing complexity and sheer number of external regulations, not least because of the increasing activities of companies in countries of the most diverse legal systems and socio-cultural customs, compliance with many external legal requirements, and existing internal standards of conduct, have gained considerable importance over time.

As with many other key indicators, the interpretation and comparison of concrete values may not be easy, particularly in certain kinds of companies where noticeably extensive content, relating to external legal standards, has to be conveyed. Nevertheless, to begin with, the collection and reporting of this indicator makes it clear that a preventive strategy of securing corporate compliance through targeted topic-related training is being pursued over time.

It is not easy to suggest target standards (e.g. minimum) or duration of time required for the compliance related training for each type of company. Among other factors, it is significantly influenced by the employees' current level of knowledge and the rate of change with which e.g. legal or administrative knowledge (very different depending on the business area and country) becomes obsolete. In individual cases, internal company comparisons of actual to actual values over time, or the budgeted to actual ratio, and external comparisons within a particular location or industry (if possible) can be helpful as orientation, by including corresponding information from individual competitors or industry averages.

**Useful Suggestions**                                                  !

So far, in technical literature and business practice, no clear definition of "corporate compliance" or "compliance" has been established. In general, the external norms, particularly, the respective national-legal obligations and prohibitions, as well as other regulatory standards, are included in the scope of compliance. In order to differentiate the internal rules and requirements, compliance can be extended to include internally generated stipulations. In addition to that, the adoption of further voluntary codes of conduct is also considered as part of compliance.

It is difficult for external parties to estimate and appreciate the significance and scope of the time on training for compliance. In most cases, explicit reference is made in external reporting about the "voluntary adoption of branch-specific accepted codes of conduct in the corporate compliance framework".

### & Related Ratios/ Additional Notes
It is important that the responsible persons in the human resource development collaborate, together with the managers of the specialist departments (such as the legal department) and the company's top management, to develop suitable further-training programmes. These programmes should be implemented systematically, so that the company's competitiveness is not jeopardised or damaged by violations against rule-based behaviours.

The "Compliance Training Hours per Employee" is a general indicator that is based on the amount of time, but does not provide a reliable statement about the complexity of content.

Very much like in quality-related training, a related ratio could be a budget to actual comparison of the "Cost of Compliance Training" over time, to convey the (increasing) strategic significance of preventive measures.

## 5.4 Organisational Behaviour Indicators

### ⓢ 5.4.1 Labour Turnover Rate

### ? Analytical Question
What is the proportion of employees who quit the firm in the period under consideration?

### * Definition

$$\frac{\text{Number of Employees Quitting in a Period} \cdot 100}{\text{Average Number of Employees in a Period}}$$

The Labour Turnover Rate is expressed as a percentage. Thus, if 150 employees of a firm leave within a year, and the firm has 2000 employees, the labour turnover rate is 7.5 % (150 · 100/2000).

### » Calculation/Derivation
The required data for this quotient can be obtained from the (computerised) information system of the human resource department. The data about the employees who leave the firm, can be further classified into the following categories:

- Employees who left the firm voluntarily.
- Employees who were given notice by the firm, and
- Employees who retired normally.

These finer differentiations can be of great significance for human resource policy purposes.

There is another variant of the Labour Turnover Rate, where the number of departures is compared with the number of new arrivals in a period. Though this variant may provide valuable information, it has to be interpreted carefully. When comparing the Labour Turnover Rate across different firms, it is important to check the consistency of the definition.

## Interpretation and Typical Range `#`

Labour turnover refers to the movement of employees in (entrants) and out (leavers) of a firm. However, the term is commonly used to refer only to those who leave the firm. Thus, the Labour Turnover Rate measures the percentage of employees who leave the firm for whatever reason.

Some labour turnover is considered unavoidable. Labour turnover, due to retirement or non-job related reasons, does not pose any problem for human resource managers. However, it is the voluntary departure of experienced and (potentially) important employees that represents "wastage" for the firm, has a cost, and is a cause for concern.

A generalised target for a desirable Labour Turnover Rate is not easy to define. Again, a lower or higher turnover may be good or bad in different situations. Sometimes, organisations encourage employees to leave, particularly when the objective is to shrink the size of the firm. In "normal circumstances", often, internal comparisons (such as the ratio in different organisational units or plan-actual values) of labour turnover rate over time may provide information for trend analysis. External comparisons of labour turnover rate have to be done carefully; two firms may not be strictly comparable from a human resource perspective.

## Useful Suggestions `!`

The Labour Turnover Rate is a major issue for most employers because it imposes various avoidable costs on them. The main costs of high rates of labour turnover are:
- Replacement costs (i.e. recruiting and interviewing new employees),
- Transition costs (including induction programs and training costs), and
- Indirect costs (involving a loss of customer service whilst new workers are trained and gain relevant work experience).

Therefore, it is important for the human resource department to analyse the reasons for the high labour turnover. A high level of voluntary labour turnover could be caused by many factors:

- Inadequate wage levels leading to employees moving to competitors;
- Poor morale and low levels of motivation within the workforce;
- Recruiting and selecting the wrong employees in the first place, those who may leave to seek more suitable employment; and
- A buoyant local labour market offering more (and perhaps more lucrative) opportunities to employees.

The highest Labour Turnover Rate often tends to be among those who joined the firm recently. If the longer-serving employees choose to leave, it is considered more damaging for the firm because of their experience and knowledge about the firm.

By understanding the nature and reasons for labour turnover, a firm can develop appropriate human resource practices that address employees' concerns and, thereby, keep the turnover ratio under control.

**&  Related Ratios/Additional Notes**

A pre-emptive method for avoiding a high Labour Turnover Rate is a regular survey of employee satisfaction and motivation. As a related ratio, "Employee Satisfaction Index" provides a clear indication to the firm about which aspects of the work environment are important for employees, and which ones have to be improved to retain the employees on a long-term basis.

**Ⓢ 5.4.2 Employee Satisfaction Index**

**?  Analytical Question**

To what extent are the employees of the firm satisfied with their place of work? Do existing employees view the firm as an attractive employer?

**✳  Definition**

Employee satisfaction is the result of a comparative process between the (explicit) expectations of the employees in the period under consideration, and the individual's experience during this period.

As an indicator of employee satisfaction, the employee's assessment of an individual parameter is estimated, or a global measure based on the average value of a large number of factors, criteria or attributes is taken.

As a global measure, the "Employee Satisfaction Index" is calculated as follows:

$$\frac{\Sigma\,(\text{Employee Satisfaction Assessment per Parameter}\,\cdot\,\text{Weight})}{\text{Sum Total of all Weight Factors}}$$

The Employee Satisfaction Index is measured as a percentage.

## Calculation/Derivation

»

The employee satisfaction assessment data is collected at regular intervals through special anonymous (mostly in the form of written standard) surveys of practically all employees. In the majority of the cases, such an exercise is conducted (by the human resource department or external agencies), with a list of questions containing various work-attributes in the following ways:

- How satisfied are you personally with the compliance or implementation of the given factors in the firm? Or
- Mention, on a given scale, how important these factors are for you?

Both of the above questions could be answered on a 5-level scale, such as:

- Very satisfied – Satisfied – Neutral – Dissatisfied – Very dissatisfied
- Very important – Important – Neutral – Irrelevant – Absolutely Irrelevant.

When the employees' assessment is transformed into a numbered scale (such as 1–2–3–4–5, or 5–4–3–2–1), it is possible to calculate the average value, and to add the values in case of several attributes.

The assumption behind a more common use of the global measure, based on several attributes, is that the satisfaction level on individual attributes can be aggregated to see the total picture.

As factors or attributes, the following are frequently used:

- Basic salary (or salary grade), additional remuneration (performance-related bonus), social welfare schemes (during employment or after retirement)
- Interaction with seniors or with the boss, cooperation (or teamwork) with peers and colleagues, participation in decision making, organisation of work-processes and work-units
- Nature of work, job-security, chances of promotion, professional development possibilities
- Working conditions, work schedules, workload, convenience in obtaining tools and supplies for work.

This list of factors or attributes can be extended in order to fit the requirement of a firm. Both in theory and practice, the applied methods for measuring employee satisfaction show a high level of diversity, particularly in terms of the complexity of surveys.

## Interpretation and Typical Range

#

The Employee Satisfaction Index is a measure of the ability of a firm to fulfil the explicit and implicit expectation of its employees. Though the measure is based on the average of individual and subjective assessment of employees, the result provides a clear indication of how employees perceive the strengths and weaknesses of the employer.

In the framework of good leadership concepts (for example, in a balance score-card model), employee satisfaction is viewed as an important value driver and is an important prerequisite for the high performance capability of the firm. It reflects itself in the appreciation of the customers where customer satisfaction is seen as a consequence of quality conscious and friendly employees.

A generalised target for the Employee Satisfaction Index is not easy to define. The higher the index, the better the employee satisfaction. For orientation about a typical range, one could take internal comparisons (such as the ratio in different organisational units or plan-actual values) or external comparisons where the branch-specific average or the "best-practice" value may be used as a guide. The results of regular (or periodic) surveys are often communicated within the firm as "Satisfaction Barometer".

## ! Useful Suggestions

The employees of a firm contribute decisively to the creation and realisation of its competitive advantage through their expertise, personal motivation and positive behaviour. Under the assumption that highly satisfied employees, as a matter of rule, are also high performing people, it is very important for a firm's leadership to achieve and maintain high employee's satisfaction.

In general, the factors and attributes in the survey constitute the starting point for improving Employee Satisfaction Index. If a significant variance or continuous decline is noticeable between expected and actual levels of satisfaction, it is important to examine (in the framework of business or human resource strategies) the areas where there is an immediate need for action. If it becomes evident, for example, that the social welfare schemes are viewed by employees as "important" and "unsatisfactory", even when the firm has a comparatively above-average level, it is obviously a communication problem. Such a situation can be managed easily through an active information policy within the firm.

Methodically, there are several ways in which the results obtained from the surveys can be utilised. Thus, the ranking of the important factors by employees allows the firm to gain a clear picture of the factors that should be on the "hit list". If employees are asked to assess the importance of, and their satisfaction with, each factor, then it is good to combine the information and see whether they are "satisfied" with "important" factors, or whether similar correlations exist.

## & Related Ratios/Additional Notes

Along with the satisfaction indices which are based on the subjective assessment of the employees in different surveys, there are also indices that provide (sometimes indirectly) objective assessment of employee satisfaction. Good examples of such objective factors are the "Sickness-Absenteeism Rate" and "Labour Turnover Rate".

### 5.4.3 Sickness-Absenteeism Rate

**Analytical Question**  ?

How big is the sickness-related absenteeism share of the total number of workdays in the period under consideration?

**Definition**  *

$$\frac{\text{Number of Sickness-Absenteeism Days in a Period} \cdot 100}{\text{Total Number of Budgeted Work Days in a Period}}$$

This ratio is expressed in terms of percentages, and is usually for one period (for example, one year, a quarter or a month).

**Calculation/Derivation**  »

The required data for this ratio could be taken from the information and reporting system in the human resource department. The needed data could be further classified into departments, cost-centres, etc.

**Interpretation and Typical Range**  #

This ratio sheds light on the magnitude of absenteeism, created by the sickness of employees. In order to gain more insight into this ratio, reasons for sickness-related absenteeism, as far as permitted by data protection laws should be analysed. In the case of "on-the-job" accidents, the necessity of removing probable security-related deficits should be reviewed.

Empirical studies have shown that sickness absenteeism not only depends upon the nature of work, but also has branch-specific or firm's size related variations. Often, the macroeconomic situation is also seen as one of the factors influencing this ratio.

**Useful Suggestions**  !

In order to ensure and foster the good health of the employees, a wide variety of measures are available. Some examples are mentioned below:

- Measures towards avoiding physical damage (safety-at-work, in terms of protecting employees from hazardous physical strains at work);
- Measures towards avoiding psychic strains (safety-at-work, in terms of protecting employees from hazardous mental strains at work); and
- Measures towards improving employees' awareness about a health-conscious life-style. For example, preventive measures (immunization), measures towards early-diagnosis (regular medical care), measures towards increased awareness about risk factors (offer for treating addictions), and measures towards healthy diets (balanced diets and drinks in daily life).

**&** **Related Ratios/Additional Notes**

A common synonym for Sickness-Absenteeism Rate is "Sickness Rate".

There are two more ratios which help analyse sickness-related information:

– Absence Rate

This relates to a comprehensive concept for total time-related absence from work (due to sickness, annual-leave, training, and/or absence without permission) compared with the budgeted work-time. The Sickness-Absenteeism Rate is, thus, a part of the total absence rate. The absence rate can be further classified into the "paid-absence" and "unpaid absence" rate.

– Sick-Employees Quota

This ratio relates to the number of employees who are sick at any point of time, in relation to the total staff. It is a snapshot about what percentage of employees are missing at a particular point in time.

### 5.4.4 Accident Occurrence Rate

**?** **Analytical Question**

In relation to the workload, how often do accidents occur in the firm? How secure or insecure is the work process?

**\*** **Definition**

$$\frac{\text{Number of Reportable Work Accidents in the Period under Consideration} \cdot 1 \text{ Million}}{\text{Total Number of Hours Worked in the Period under Consideration}}$$

The ratio "Accident Occurrence Rate" is reported in decimals in the form of "Accidents per Million Hours Worked". In general, the ratio is compiled for each business or calendar year.

Usually, an industrial or work-related accident is reportable to authorities, when the injured person is unable to work for more than three days or dies because of the after-effects of the accident.

**»** **Calculation/Derivation**

The required data (classified separately for each division, cost centre, etc.) for this ratio could be obtained from the computer-based information system of the human resource department.

**#** **Interpretation and Typical Range**

The ratio "Accident Occurrence Rate" hints at a relative measure of the risk-exposure for the employees at work, and is reflected in the attribute "accident". It is an indicator of the security and responsibility consciousness of the top management towards the physical protection of its employees.

All work-related temporary events which have an external-physical impact on the employees leading to health problems or death, may be classified as occupational accidents. In developed service economies where blue colour jobs are being replaced by white colour jobs, this ratio has a tendency to fall. However, various branch-specific variations are still observed. For example, the Accident Occurrence Rate is higher in construction, agriculture and forestry sectors, and in transport and manufacturing industry, than in the banking/insurance, public administration and private service sectors.

As a general guide, the ideal goal of zero could be viewed as desirable for this indicator. The typical range for this ratio could be based on branch-specific characteristics. The benchmark could be drawn from the past performance of the firm (as a whole or in parts), or the branch-specific averages or best-practice examples.

**Useful Suggestions**
In order to provide a healthy work environment for the employees, and to protect them from work-related hazards, a large spectrum of measures is available. As illustrative examples, some measures are:
- Avoiding direct physical damage; for example, work protection and accident prevention in terms of a clear concept for not exposing the employees to physically dangerous work.
- Proper organisational design of the work processes; for example, planning of production processes with sufficient breaks in order to prevent accidents caused by loss of concentration, or developing security-leaflets/checklists and ensuring their compliance.
- Strengthening the individual capacity of the employees towards security consciousness at work; for example, using protective-wear, such as helmets, glasses, shoes, etc. Appointment of a security officer could be another such measure.

National rules for occupational safety play a major role in providing protection at the workplace and preventing excessive demands on employees. In addition to the local legal framework and the *de facto* inspection by public authorities and independent experts, the direct responsibility of the company is particularly significant in the form of "compliance management". Some companies have voluntary accident and health protection measures for the benefit of its employees that are over and above mandatory minimum requirements.

**& Related Ratios/Additional Notes**

Accident Occurrence Rate is also known as "Accident Occurrence Quota" or "Accident Occurrence Index".

As a related indicator, in terms of "Accident-Severity Rate", the "Accident Burden Index" shows the time-related impact of accidents. This is calculated by comparing the sum total of work-hours lost by accidents with the sum total of accomplished work-hours in the period under consideration:

$$\frac{\text{Number of Work-hours Lost by Accident} \cdot 1 \text{ Million}}{\text{Total Number of Hours Worked} \cdot 10}$$

### 5.4.5 Participation Rate in Ideas Management

**? Analytical Question**

How big is the share of employees who participate in the internal ideas management system initiated by the firm?

**\* Definition**

$$\frac{\text{Number of Employees making Suggestions in a Period} \cdot 100}{\text{Average Number of Employees in a Period}}$$

This ratio is expressed as a percentage.

**» Calculation/Derivation**

The required data for this ratio could be obtained from the information system in the human resource department which is linked to the internal ideas management. The number mentioned in the numerator will have to be adjusted if there are several suggestions made by one employee during the period under consideration. For further analysis of the participation rate, in respect of which kind of employees submit suggestions, additional information about their departments, qualifications and hierarchy levels may also be collected.

**# Interpretation and Typical Range**

The employees' ideas management system is a widespread institutional tool for encouraging employees to contribute to organisational development, to put forward ideas for improvement and to act responsibly. The higher the participation rate of employees in the internal ideas management system, the stronger the benefit to the firm from knowledge and expertise of employees is. A higher participation rate also indicates that the firm is able to draw on the voluntary participation of the employees in generating various improvements. These improvements could eventually contribute to the sustained development of the firm's position.

The comparability of the participation rate, particularly the inter-firm comparison, is significantly influenced by how the suggestions for improvements are classified (separating the routine suggestions from the rest) and how they are integrated into the employee's performance evaluation and reward system.

### Useful Suggestions

Employee suggestion programs can offer any organisation a distinct competitive advantage with their many benefits, including: cost savings, increased revenues, decreased waste, improved quality, improved safety, better customer service, improved corporate culture, employee motivation and employee satisfaction.

It is always desirable to explicitly link the employee suggestion program with some reward or bonus system. However, the process of evaluating employees' suggestions should be carried out by an independent committee which has expertise in the area, and can provide an unbiased opinion of the value generated by a particular suggestion.

### Related Ratios/Additional Notes

In the family of indicators for managing employee suggestion programs, other measures, such as "Suggestions Rate (per Period)", "Implementation Rate", "Average Reward Rate per Suggestion", and measures toward analysing the characteristics of employees who file suggestions (divisional origins, qualifications and hierarchy levels) are also included.

## 5.5 Innovativeness

### 5.5.1 Innovation Rate

### Analytical Question

How large is the share of sales relating to new products and services, of the total sales of the firm?

### Definition

$$\frac{\text{Periodic Sales of New Products and Services} \cdot 100}{\text{Total Periodic Sales}}$$

The Innovation Rate is expressed as a percentage.

**» Calculation/Derivation**

The required data for this ratio can be obtained from the information system which is upstream of the external accounting system. Included in this information system could be statistics, clients and other data banks of the marketing, and/or sales department.

**# Interpretation and Typical Range**

The Innovation Rate is a typical indicator of the modernity of the products and services offered by a firm. However, the calculated value depends considerably on the defined duration (how long a product should be considered "new"?) and on the extent of novelty.

A generalised target for typical range cannot be defined; the length of typical product-cycles essentially affects it. For orientation about typical range, internal comparisons (such as the ratio in different organisational units or plan-actual values) or external comparisons (such as the branch-specific average or the "best-practice" value) may be used as a guide.

**! Useful Suggestions**

In many markets which show noticeable tendencies of glut, and even in growth markets which are strongly influenced by technology, many firms view a faster change in product generations as a distinctive instrument for increasing competitiveness. For such firms, the Innovation Rate is an important indicator; it represents the potential to introduce new products and services into the market, in order to win new customer-groups, or to arouse the existing customers' replacement-need. Any conscious decision by the manufacturer to shorten the product or service cycle is, however, not without risk. Often, fast-track product development is at the cost of quality; the product-recall activities of many reputed companies have shown that quality cannot be taken for granted and managed by itself.

In addition to this, the "leapfrogging-effect" should be carefully considered. It represents the consumer behaviour in which customers choose to jump over many generations of fast changing products. The customers prefer to wait for the following product-generation after the next innovation, instead of buying each of the innovations. In this respect, it could lead to the occurrence of the so-called "speed-trap" where the innovative firm is forced to innovate faster and faster, in a vicious circle of falling sales.

A general strategy towards a desirable dimension for the Innovation Rate does not exist. Similarly, it is not easy to transform an innovation into a value-generating proposition. It is also relevant to note that the conscious strategy of "moving-a-step-behind" the competitor gets lower appreciation from the customers than the strategy of "prime-mover".

## Related Ratios/Additional Notes

&

Though not very common, "Innovation Quota" and "New Product Sales" can be used as synonyms for Innovation Rate.

### 5.5.2 Research and Development Intensity (R&D Intensity)

#### Analytical Question

?

How active is a firm in R&D, in terms of the relative share of R&D expenditure in sales? What is the ratio of a firm's R&D in relation to its periodic sales?

#### Definition

*

$$\frac{\text{R\&D Expenditure per Period} \cdot 100}{\text{Sales Revenue per Period}}$$

The R&D Intensity is measured in terms of percentages. Both the numerator and the denominator relate to the same period values (mostly, one financial year). However, this definition does not make any distinction between "expenses" and "costs".

#### Calculation/Derivation

»

The figure for the denominator (which is also available to the external analyst) can be obtained directly from the income statement. However, the R&D expenditure is not published by all companies and therefore, may not be available to the external analyst. For internal analysis, the accuracy of R&D expenditure depends primarily upon the details available in the cost accounting and internal cost allocation system.

#### Interpretation and Typical Range

#

The R&D Intensity is a widely used ratio which shows the significance of R&D activities in a firm. It is an important indicator of extra efforts made by the firm for ensuring future success of its products and services in the market. The implied forecasting value of this ratio lies in the assumption that higher R&D expenditure tends to produce strong innovative results which translate into higher sales revenue and profits. However, this line of argument is neither qualitatively nor quantitatively determinable. Thus, it should be viewed primarily as an indicator of future potential.

The published R&D ratios differ widely in practice, both within the same industry and within the same economic sector. This could be due to varying cost accounting practices adopted by firms, and different ways of capitalizing development costs. The ratio could also be influenced by how much R&D is carried out in-house, or outsourced, and how these costs are recorded in financial accounting.

Furthermore, the R&D Intensity is calculated with the values for the same period for the numerator and the denominator, which may be biased, depending upon the changing pattern of sales or R&D expenditure. The following two examples explain this bias:

- If the firm is enjoying market success (reflected in increasing sales volume) based on products developed earlier, then a constant volume of R&D expenditure will show a falling calculated value for R&D Intensity. This may be interpreted wrongly as a reduced focus on R&D.
- Conversely, in times of reduced market success (reflected in the falling sales volumes) based on products developed earlier, a constant volume in R&D expenditure will show an increasing R&D value. Thus it would appear that the firm has increased its R&D activity.

The above-mentioned arguments show the problems in interpreting R&D Intensity as an indicator.

In general, it is assumed that there is a time lag between the R&D expenditure, the products and services created from R&D, and realised sales and profits. The "future-impact" aspect of R&D expenditure is not displayed in the ratio. A better approach would be to only compare the increase in sales for the current period with the R&D expenditure of previous periods (for example, branch-specific or business-specific, between 1 and 5 years).

**!** **Useful Suggestions**

The R&D activities provide an interesting example for the fact that accounting practices are not able to deliver the true economic value of such business processes.

Assuming that the comparable firms have similar structures for products, processes or potentials, any variance from the average values provides a clear indication for serious review. These should help in analysing positive and negative developments in the ratio, and steer them in the context of corporate goals.

An interesting limitation of R&D Intensity is that it does not allow for the inclusion of delayed success from earlier innovative activities. To this end, one can depend upon other measures, such as "Innovation Rate", or "R&D Productivity" which help in making inter-firm comparisons.

In practice, changes in the R&D expenditure have to be reviewed alongside other relevant facts. For example, whether the increase in R&D expenditure is due to new R&D projects in promising areas or whether a fall in R&D expenditure is due to a changed strategy with increased focus on licensed technology in the value chain.

**&** **Related Ratios/Additional Notes**

As synonym for R&D Intensity, "Research Intensity" is also used.

Related ratios which touch upon the topic of R&D Intensity, are as follows:

- R&D-Employee Intensity: it shows the ratio of R&D staff to the total number of employees.

- R&D Costs Ratio: it shows the ratio of the R&D costs to the total costs per period.
- R&D Productivity: it shows the ratio between the period-specific contribution margin of new products and R&D costs for the same period.

### 5.5.3 Research and Development Costs Ratio (R&D Costs Ratio)

**Analytical Question**

How active is a firm in R&D, in terms of the relative share of R&D costs from the total costs for the period under consideration?

**Definition**

$$\frac{\text{R\&D Costs per Period} \cdot 100}{\text{Total Costs per Period}}$$

The R&D Costs Ratio is measured in terms of percentages. Both the numerator and the denominator relate to the same period (mostly, one financial year) values.

**Calculation/Derivation**

For external analysts, the value for the denominator can be obtained directly from the income statement. However, the R&D costs are not published by all companies and therefore, may not be available to external analysts without additional information support.

For an internal analysis, the accuracy of R&D costs depends primarily upon the details available in the cost accounting and internal cost allocation system. To this end, it is important to check whether the costs of product innovation and process innovation, which are equally important for their success, are marked and assigned separately.

**Interpretation and Typical Range**

The R&D Costs Ratio shows, in a general and compact form, the impact of R&D activities in a firm. It is an important indicator of extra innovative efforts made by the firm, particularly for technologically driven companies, to ensure future success of products and services in the market.

When interpreting the significance of this ratio over time, either internally amongst various parts of the firm, or externally with reference to the branch-specific averages (or best-practice examples of the market leader), often an implicit assumption is that higher R&D costs, or a higher R&D Costs Ratio is advantageous. It is believed that the costs incurred in R&D provide proportionally increasing economic efficiency. However, this line of argument is not necessarily true; the success rate of R&D projects is equally dependent upon effective project management and controlling.

The published values from R&D ratios differ widely in practice, both within the same industry and within the same economic sector. This could be due to varying cost accounting practices adopted by firms, and different ways of capitalising development costs. The ratio could also be influenced by how much of the R&D is carried out in-house, or outsourced, and how these costs are recorded in the financial accounting.

Furthermore, the R&D Costs Ratio is calculated with the values of the same period for the numerator and the denominator, which may be biased, depending upon the changing pattern of values. The following two examples explain this bias:

- If the total costs are increasing (because of increases in the underlying prices and/or consumed quantity) and R&D fixed costs are constant, the R&D Costs Ratio will show a falling calculated value. This may be wrongly interpreted as a reduced focus on R&D.
- Conversely, if total costs are falling (because of a decrease in the underlying prices and/or quantity produced), and R&D costs are constant, the R&D Costs Ratio will show a rising calculated value. This may appear to suggest that the firm has increased its R&D activity.

The above-mentioned arguments show the problems in interpreting R&D Costs Ratio as an indicator.

### ❗ Useful Suggestions

Since in most cases, no direct market-impact of the commercial research and development is measurable, an indicator based purely on the accounting number is not without problems. In such cases, the typical limitations of performance measurement which are based on internal and external accounting, should be clearly reviewed.

Assuming that comparable firms have similar structures in their products, processes or potentials, any variance from the average values provides a clear input for serious review. The positive and negative developments in the ratio should be given due attention and influenced in the right direction with the help of effective project management and controlling.

In practice, changes in the R&D costs have to be reviewed alongside other relevant facts. For example, whether the increase in R&D costs is due to new R&D projects, in promising areas, or whether a fall in R&D costs is due to a changed strategy, such as an increased focus on licensed technology in the value chain.

### & Related Ratios/Additional Notes

So far, the terminology in the literature and in practice is not uniform. Particularly, when inter-company comparisons are made, the parameters that have been used for calculating the ratio should be carefully checked.

Related ratios, which touch upon the topic of R&D Intensity, are as follows:
- R&D-Employee Intensity: it shows the ratio of R&D staff to the total number of employees.
- R&D Cost Ratio: it shows the ratio of the R&D costs to the total costs per period.
- R&D Productivity: it shows the ratio between the period-specific contribution margin of new products and R&D costs for the same period.

## 5.5.4 Breakeven Time

### Analytical Question
How long is the estimated time needed to recover the investment made in researching and developing (R&D) a product, through to cash inflow from its sale?

### Definition
Basically, Breakeven Time is a special usage of the financial measure "Payback Period", where the payback period for the product or service related R&D process is estimated.

The exact value of this ratio is understood as time elapses when the total cash inflow from sales equals (or exceeds) the R&D (costs/expenditure) investment made in a particular product. The ratio can also be calculated with discounted cash flows.

The Breakeven Time, as the name suggests, is expressed in terms of "time-duration" (which is typically in years or months).

### Calculation/Derivation
The data for this ratio should be recorded (preferably project-specific) in the form of cash inflows and outflows, and can be derived from the firm's investment and financial plan. The data could also be derived from a project accounting system established for research and development processes.

In practice, for the sake of simplicity, a simple payback period is often calculated with the help of projected sales and costs, or with projected cash inflows and outflows. If the cash outflows and inflows for a project occur at different points in time, and the time aspect is neutralised by discounting for cash flows, this "time-adjusted" payback period provides a better insight than a simple payback period. This is particularly true for R&D projects that are managed over longer periods.

### Interpretation and Typical Range
In addition to the measures for the economic profitability of the planned investment in absolute and relative terms (for example, profit contribution or return on investment), the payback period covers a special risk-factor (i.e. time) which should be used as supplementary to other performance measures.

The calculation of the Breakeven Time draws its strength from providing increasing competitiveness in business. Here, the product life span is often shorter than the breakeven time for recovering R&D costs. The risk involved should be explained through careful analysis of all processes (and the integrated design of individual phases of product development, production and marketing). Sometimes there may be a risk that the capital invested in R&D and the targeted return may not be recovered. However, as a time-based perspective on risk, the Breakeven Time offers a very general valuation criterion, and ignores various strategic factors that may have a delayed positive impact on the project's success.

Because of the complexity and diversity of firm-specific R&D processes, it is not possible to determine a target period for Breakeven Time. A general orientation could be given by stating that, from a market perspective, the breakeven time should not exceed the product life-cycle.

Assuming that comparable firms have similar structures of products, processes or potentials, any variance from the average values provides clear indication for serious review. This should help in analysing the positive and negative developments in the ratio, and steer them in the context of corporate goals.

## ! Useful Suggestions

The focal point of various measures that may be implemented to improve the Breakeven Time, lies in boosting the effectiveness and efficiency of R&D projects. Along with a systematic choice (which is aligned with the strategic orientation of the firm), continuous monitoring of R&D projects is of paramount importance. From the operational point of view, the success factor "time" is of equal significance.

There are various organisational and technical possibilities for shortening the product-development time, and the "time-to-market". Some examples are: acceleration of project work, and parallel-integrated project management (for example, through simulations). These techniques can help to bring down the Breakeven Time to competitive levels or to strengthen one's competitive advantage.

## & Related Ratios/Additional Notes

The Breakeven Time is also known as "Payback Period", "Pay-off Time", and "Payout Time".

## 5.6 Resource-related Ecological Indicators

### 5.6.1 Resource Consumption Level

**Analytical Question**

How much is the period-relevant (mostly for a year) or volume-driven (per unit of output) usage of particular (primarily environmentally important) resources in the firm?
- As a period-relevant measure, the ratio can be classified into various resource-types (for example, energy, water or raw-materials), which can be further classified into sub-groups (for example, the energy could be gas, electricity, oil, etc.)
- As a volume-driven measure, the ratio can be classified into various output units (units of finished products, distance covered in kilometres, tons of steel produced, etc.)

**Definition**

Period-relevant Usage:

Quantity of Resource Consumed per Period

As a measured value for the quantity of solid, liquid or gaseous resources consumed, one could use the number of units, length, area and volume, as well as weight-specifications.

Volume-driven Usage:

$$\frac{\text{Quantity of Resource Consumed per Period}}{\text{Quantity of Output Units per Period}}$$

As a measured value for the quantity of solid, liquid or gaseous resources consumed or output produced, one could use the number of units, length, area and volume, as well as weight-specifications.

Out of each combination of input and output, the ratio could be expressed, for example, as energy consumed per ton of steel produced, or water consumed per unit of finished product.

**Calculation/Derivation**

A prerequisite for obtaining the required data for this resource-oriented ratio is the existence of a detailed (computerised) business environment information system. A business environment information system is responsible for collecting, processing and reporting of all environment related data, in particular:
- compilation of quantity and value-based information about resources consumed;
- documentation of information for external legal reporting; and

– calculation of meaningful ratios for presenting complex details and for showing the trend of internal and external changes over time.

# Interpretation and Typical Range

The main message of sustainability management is the idea of offering a development process that satisfies the needs of the present generation without jeopardizing the aspirations of future generations. The application of the sustainability principle, at the firm level, implies an efficient consumption of scare resources. Thus, both period-relevant and volume-driven measures show the units of resources consumed from two different perspectives. The period-relevant measure is useful for resources having an indirect cost character, but can also be used for directly consumed resources. The volume-driven measure is more suitable for resources that have a direct-cost character.

Because of a strongly diversified product spectrum of firms, comparable data about typical range is possible only for firms that have similar product groups. The comparability of only period-relevant measures (such as consumed megawatts or cubic meters per year) could prove complicated if data is not complied for all locations of the firm and the total number of location changes. This is a common problem in the development of sustainability reporting.

Presenting the measure as a volume-driven ratio provides a relative number where the absolute quantity of resource consumed is compared with the unit of output produced, such as energy consumption per ton of steel produced, or water consumed per unit of finished product.

As orientation and for comparison purposes, internal benchmarks between various units within the firm (such as locations/plants) can be used. The performance over time can be analysed with the help of budget-actual comparisons. External benchmarks could be taken from the branch-specific averages or best-practice values.

Because of advancements or continuous (definitional) improvements in data collection methods, and also because of the frequent buying and selling of firms, the number reported by large firms may not be comparable over time.

# Useful Suggestions

On the supposition that firms in the same branch usually have similar production structures, the ratio values, differing significantly from the averages, are clear candidates for serious review. This should help in analysing the positive and negative developments or consequences, and in manoeuvring them in the context of corporate goals.

In general, assuming that most firms are increasingly guided by the basic performance idea of conserving natural resources both on the input and output side, there is a large number of measures which could be applied to reduce the resource consumption. In particular, it plans, steers and controls the flow of resources, such as raw-materials, energy and water. Analysing and, if needed, changing the flow of these resources can be a useful exercise.

Included in the list of measures are:
- identification of technical or organizational weaknesses;
- initiating improvements for reducing the energy and material flows (if possible by implementing a circular flow or recycling system);
- developing ideas for improving the environmental impact of the production processes; and
- encouraging the environmental conscious behaviour of employees and rewarding employees for such behaviour in the framework of a compensation system.

Since most of the resources have a (mostly increasing) price, a reduction in the volume-driven consumption should, in general, lead to a cost reduction (assuming constant environment protection costs).

In addition to the development and implementation of specific environmental protection measures, it is desirable to put into practice appropriate organizational structures (with centralised and decentralised responsibilities) for establishing a regular environment management system. A clear reference is made here to certification of environment management systems under ISO 14001 or under Eco-Management and Audit Scheme (EMAS II) that is a European Union standard.

**Related Ratios/Additional Notes**                                                                    &

The scope, the data-collection frequency and the level of details in measuring and reporting of sustainability indicators is largely at the discretion of firms and their environmental consciousness. Sometimes however, there are legal directives that require regular information from firms. Although, in external reporting, such information is usually required annually, for internal controlling, it is desirable to use half-yearly or even monthly information. The external reporting towards sustainability is much less regulated than classical reporting, according to national and international reporting standards. As a good orientation, reference is often made to the lists of indicators published in the directives of Global Reporting Initiative (GRI). As an independent institution, GRI took upon itself the job of developing formal guidelines for improving the comparability of sustainability reporting.

It is interesting to note that a new branch for cost accounting has emerged recently which draws upon resource consumption as its base. It is known as Resource Consumption Accounting (RCA). A main feature of RCA is that it does not allocate resource *costs* to products. It traces resource *usage*, in units of resource consumed, and not in monetary terms. This obviously helps managers to segregate resource consumptions into those that are avoidable, and those that are unavoidable.

Ⓢ **5.6.2 Resource Consumption Reduction Rate**

❓ **Analytical Question**

How did the consumption quantity of a particular (primarily environmentally important) resource in the firm change in comparison with the previous period?

- As a period-relevant measure, the ratio can be classified into various resource-types (for example, energy, water or raw-materials) which can be further classified into sub-groups (for example, the energy could be gas, electricity, oil, etc.).
- As a volume-driven measure, the ratio can be classified into various output units (units of finished products, distance covered in kilometres, tons of steel produced, etc.).

✱ **Definition**

Period-relevant Usage:

$$1 - \frac{\text{Quantity of Resource Consumed in Period t}}{\text{Quantity of Resource Consumed in Period t-1}}$$

Volume-driven Usage:

$$1 - \frac{\text{Quantity of Resource Consumed per Unit of Output in Period t}}{\text{Quantity of Resources Consumed per Unit of Output in Period t-1}}$$

Both variants are expressed in multiples (for example, 0.8) or, when multiplied by 100, in percentages (for example, 80%).

If the actual consumption of a resource, in the current period t is 10 kg, and in the previous period t-1 was 50 kg, then consumption reduction rate (1 – 10/50) is 0.8 or 80%. Similarly, a current period consumption of 80 kg and a previous period consumption of 40 kg, the calculated value (1 – 80/40) is –1, which implies negative resource consumption efficiency. A negative value implies increased consumption. The volume-driven ratio can also be interpreted in a similar fashion.

The resource consumption reduction goals need not necessarily be compared over a single period. Sometimes, a larger time horizon is also taken for comparison purposes.

» **Calculation/Derivation**

A prerequisite for obtaining the required data for this resource-oriented ratio is the existence of a detailed (computerised) business environment information system. A business environment information system is responsible for collecting, processing and reporting of all environment related data, in particular:

- compilation of quantity and value-based information concerning the resources consumed;
- documentation of information for external legal reporting; and
- calculation of meaningful ratios for presenting complex details, and for show-ing the trend of internal and external changes over time.

**Interpretation and Typical Range**                                          #

The main message of sustainability management is the idea of offering a develop-ment process which satisfies the needs of the present generation without jeopardiz-ing the aspirations of future generations. The application of the sustainability principle, at the firm level, implies an efficient consumption of scare resources. Thus, both period-relevant and volume-driven measures show the units of resour-ces consumed, from two different perspectives. The period-relevant measure is use-ful for resources having an indirect cost character, but can also be used for directly consumed resources. The volume-driven measure would be more suitable for re-sources which have a direct-cost character.

Because of a strongly diversified product spectrum of firms, comparable data about typical range is possible only for firms that have similar product groups. The comparability of only period-relevant measures (such as consumed megawatts or $CO_2$ emissions in tons per year) could prove complicated if data is not complied for all locations of the firm, and the total number of locations changes. This is a com-mon problem in the development of sustainability reporting.

Presenting the measure, as a volume-driven ratio, provides a relative number where the absolute quantity of resource consumed is compared with the unit of out-put produced, such as energy consumption per ton of steel produced or water con-sumed per unit of finished product.

As orientation and for comparison purposes, internal benchmarks between var-ious units within the firm (such as locations/plants) can be used. The performance over time can be analysed with the help of budget-actual comparisons. External benchmarks could be taken from branch-specific averages or best-practice values.

Because of advancements or continuous (definitional) improvements in data collection methods, as well as the frequent buying and selling of firms, the numbers reported by large firms may not be comparable over time.

**Useful Suggestions**                                          !

On the supposition that firms in the same branch usually have similar production structures, the ratio values, differing significantly from the averages, are clear candi-dates for serious review. This should help in analysing the positive and negative devel-opments or consequences, and in manoeuvring them in the context of corporate goals.

In general, assuming that most firms are increasingly guided by the basic per-formance idea of conserving natural resources, both on the input and output side, there are a large number of measures which can be applied to the consumption reduction of resources. It is always beneficial to plan, steer and control the flow of resources, such as raw-material, energy and water. Analysing and, if needed, changing the flow of these resources can be a useful exercise. Included in the list of measures are:

- identification of technical or organizational weaknesses;
- initiating improvements for reducing the energy and material flows (if possible by implementing a circular flow or recycling system);
- developing ideas for improving the environmental impact of the production processes; and
- encouraging environmental conscious behaviour in employees, and rewarding the employees for such behaviour in the framework of a compensation system.

Since most of the resources have a (mostly increasing) price, a reduction in the volume-driven consumption should, in general, lead to (assuming constant environment protection costs) a cost reduction.

### & Related Ratios/Additional Notes

The Resource Consumption Reduction Rate is mostly applied to the input side of the production process. However, the ratio can also be applied to the output side, as well as to the application phase of a product where resource efficiency can be measured, for example, as emission related efficiency.

The scope, data-collection frequency and the level of detail in measuring and reporting of sustainability indicators is largely at the discretion of firms, and their environmental consciousness. Sometimes, however, there are legal directives which require regular information from firms. Although in external reporting, such information is required annually for internal controlling, it is desirable to use half-yearly or even monthly information. The external reporting towards sustainability is much less regulated than the classical reporting according to national and international reporting standards. As a good orientation, reference is often made to the lists of indicators published in the directives of Global Reporting Initiative (GRI). As an independent institution, GRI took upon itself the job of developing formal guidelines for improving the comparability of sustainability reporting.

It is interesting to note that a new branch of cost accounting has emerged recently which draws upon resource consumption as its base. It is known as Resource Consumption Accounting (RCA). A main feature of RCA is that it does not allocate resource *costs* to products. It traces resource usage, in units of resource consumed, and not in monetary terms. This obviously helps managers to segregate resource consumption into those that are avoidable, and those that are unavoidable.

### 5.6.3 Energy Source Ratio

**Analytical Question**  ⟦?⟧

What is the proportion of a specific energy source used in the total energy mix of the company under consideration?

**Definition**  ⟦*⟧

Version I:

$$\frac{\text{Consumed Quantity from one (or a Sub-group) Energy Source per Period} \cdot 100}{\text{Consumed Quantity from (a Sub-group or) all Energy Source(s) per Period}}$$

- As a period-based variant, this key performance Indicator (KPI) is usable for either an analysis of the entire company or specific locations.
- If need be, it can be further classified by energy source (coal, wind, etc.) and further into appropriate sub-categories (for coal into bituminous or lignite, and for wind-energy into offshore or onshore wind-energy.)

Version II:

$$\frac{\text{Proportional Consumed Quantity from one (or more) Energy Source}}{\text{Products, Processes or Organizational Units as Reference-Objects}}$$

- As a variant based on reference-objects, this KPI is usable for the analysis of various relevant value drivers and reporting-parameters.
- If needed, it can be further classified as per various output units (for example, quantity of finished products or number of transport-kilometres completed).

Depending on the nature of the analysis, the numerator could consist of a single or multiple energy sources that have been put together in meaningful groups. Similarly, the denominator could contain meaningful aggregates (partial ones as well), such as power-supply groups or product groups.

The measuring dimensions for each of the analysed energy sources could be Volume, Weight, Joules and Watts. By converting them into relevant energy units, all variants of Version I will result in a percentage. In the case of Version II, the numerator is a percentage, such as 24% of energy from renewable sources, whereas the denominator will have the units of the reference objects, such as the produced quantity of a product category.

**Calculation/Derivation**  ⟦»⟧

The prerequisite for obtaining the required data for these energy-optimization KPI types is the existence of an appropriate and detailed, computer-based corporate Environmental Information System (EIS). The prime tasks of an EIS in this context include the collection, processing and preparation of ecologically relevant data, especially the quantity and value-based collection of energy consumption, its sources and its classification according to the relevant reference objects.

### # Interpretation and Typical Range

The focal point of the concept of sustainability is the idea that development should be possible in a way such that the needs of the present generation are fulfilled without endangering the ability of future generations to fulfil their own needs.

Based on their general concern to create products and services with minimal usage of resources, companies plan, control and monitor their total energy usage as part of their energy-optimization system. Because of the environmental impact of the utilization of each type of energy source (for example, the various levels of emissions during the extraction of raw materials, and their conversion to a usable form of energy and its consumption), design of a suitable composition of energy sources used by the companies is becoming an increasingly relevant topic for strategic management.

The implementation of this fundamental principle at the level of individual companies means that, amongst other things, the natural environmental should be burdened only within reasonable limits and as little as possible. The usable energy for each operational purpose of the company can be categorised in following forms: electricity, fuel oils for power or combustion, heating, cooling, steam and pressurised air.

Due to numerous and specific contexts, and connections within individual functional areas as well as between various levels of the organization, a generalised target for the proportional use of each energy-source is obviously not possible. Most companies, however, strive to increase the share of energy-sources that are based on renewables rather than non-renewables.

Alongside the usual internal possibilities for comparison (between organizational departments in the form of actual-actual over time or plan-actual relations), corresponding external comparisons, where the branch-specific average values or the "best-practice" values may be used as a guide.

### ! Useful Suggestions

Using the idea of a business model that not only tries to minimise the consumption of natural resources on the input side, but also during the value creation processes, a broad spectrum of alternatives are available for energy optimization. An analysis and, if necessary, an improvement in the planning, controlling and monitoring of the production and administrative processes would help reduce the level of energy needed is the first step.

Since the energy sources for each company location vary often in their pricing, and price trends may also be affected by state support (subsidies) or tax-burdens, the management of the energy-mix is increasingly important, both from pricing and supply reliability (risk-minimization) perspectives.

A company should strive for a mix of energy sources, bearing in mind the middle and long-term development plans of the company. The energy strategy should also be in accordance with the economic, social and environmental goals of the company.

**Related Indicators/Additional Notes**

In order to get a first impression of the fundamental energy strategy of the company, the indicator "proportion of energy sources" and its change over time should be carefully looked into. The linkage between the absolute level of energy consumption, and its development, is completed only when an analysis of the related amounts of $CO_2$ emissions is made. In-depth insights allow for the analysis of "Internally Generated $CO_2e$ Emissions (Scope 1)" and "Indirect $CO_2e$ Emissions caused by Energy Usage (Scope 2)".

Currently, attention is shifting to the ratio of non-renewable to renewable energy. The non-renewable energy sources include: Bituminous and lignite coal, natural gas, oil and nuclear energy. Renewable energy sources include the following: Wind power, solar energy, hydroelectric power, biomass/biofuel, geothermal.

In sustainability reporting, the values of the energy consumption, as a function of time, (as well as its distribution over various sources) are given in Joules and decimal multiples thereof. The first letter in each case is the abbreviation, for example k for kilo Watt-hours or kWh:

- "K" for Kilo: thousands
- "M" for Mega: millions
- "G" for Giga: billions
- "T" for Tera: trillions
- "P" for Peta: quadrillions.

# Appendix I:  Systematic Analysis of Possible Changes in Relative Ratios

The calculation of the key performance indicators helps, in the first instance, in mapping the state of affairs of a business. Using these indicators to derive measures for achieving corporate goals more effectively is the ultimate goal of every manager. In order to develop possible actions or alternatives, it is important to proceed systematically. For this purpose, the basic changes that are possible in a relative ratio are shown here. Later, these changes are explained with the help of the ratio called "Return On Sales":

The elementary alternatives of numerator and denominator could be described as:
- Increase ($\uparrow$),
- Constant ($\leftrightarrow$) and / or
- Decrease ($\downarrow$)

If the relation between the numerator and the denominator increases or falls disproportionately, these are shown graphically with double arrows ($\uparrow\uparrow$ and $\downarrow\downarrow$).

From the 5 possible changes in the numerator and the denominator, 25 possible permutations and combinations can be conceived. These can be grouped, avoiding double counting, into 3 clusters (henceforth, labelled as C1, C2 and C3):

## C1:
The calculated value of the relative ratio remains unchanged if:
a    both numerator and denominator remain constant
b    both numerator and denominator show identical percentage increase
c    both numerator and denominator show identical percentage decline

## C2:
The calculated value of the relative ratio grows if:
a    the numerator increases and the denominator remains constant
b    the denominator decreases and the numerator remains constant
c    the numerator increases faster than the denominator
d    the denominator decreases faster than the numerator
e    the numerator increases with a simultaneous fall in denominator

https://doi.org/10.1515/9783110598094-007

**C3:**

The calculated value of the relative ratio falls, if:

a    the numerator decreases and the denominator remains constant

b    the denominator increases and the numerator remains constant

c    the numerator decreases faster than the denominator

d    the denominator increases faster than the numerator

e    the numerator decreases with a simultaneous increase in denominator

The following table provides a graphical view of all the constellations once again:

| | D ↑↑ | D ↑ | D ↔ | D ↓ | D ↓↓ |
|---|---|---|---|---|---|
| **N ↑↑** | R ↔ | R ↑ | R ↑ | R ↑ | R ↑ |
| **N ↑** | R ↓ | R ↔ | R ↑ | R ↑ | R ↑ |
| **N ↔** | R ↓ | R ↓ | R ↔ | R ↑ | R ↑ |
| **N ↓** | R ↓ | R ↓ | R ↓ | R ↔ | R ↑ |
| **N ↓↓** | R ↓ | R ↓ | R ↓ | R ↓ | R ↔ |

Legend: N = Numerator; D = Denominator; and R = Relative Ratio

Thus, changes in relative ratios could be achieved through a disproportionate impact on the size of the numerator and the size of the denominator, both of which are related to each other.

In order to consciously influence the relative performance indicators towards corporate goals, it is useful to have clarity about all possible actions that lead to achieving the target increase or decrease in the value of a ratio. In business practice, it is additionally important to know whether the changes in numerator or denominator are easier to achieve; if one of the two is externally determined, the chances of influencing its value is constrained.

In the following, the process of influencing a relative ratio is explained with the help of practical examples relating to a widespread ratio called "Return On Sales".

A step-wise derivation of Return On Sales:

$$\frac{\text{Profit}}{\text{Sales}} = \frac{\text{Sales} - \text{Costs}}{\text{Sales}}$$

$$\frac{\text{Sales} - (\text{Variable Costs} + \text{Fixed Costs})}{\text{Sales}}$$

$$\frac{\text{Sales} - (\text{Variable Unit Cost} \cdot \text{Quantity Sold} + \text{Fixed Costs})}{\text{Sales Price} \cdot \text{Quantity Sold}}$$

The 13 possibilities mentioned in clusters C1, C2 and C3, are now explained with practical examples for influencing the relative ratio of return on sales:

## C1:

The calculated value of the relative ratio remains unchanged if

a   both numerator and denominator remain constant

Example: In an urban water supply company, the profits and sales remain constant, if the period under consideration is very short and the terms and conditions remain unchanged (for example, in long-term contracts).

b   both show identical percentage increase

Example: A newspaper publisher can increase the circulation of its newspaper with constant prices and sales increases (say for example) of 3 per cent. If, however, the costs also increase (because of increased paper consumption, etc.) by 3 per cent, the Return On Sales will remain unchanged.

c   both show identical percentage decreases

Example: A manufacturer of shavers must reduce his sales price by 7 percent in order to keep the sales volume constant. Thus, the sales value falls by 7 per cent. If the firm succeeds in reducing its costs by 7 per cent, the Return On Sales remains constant, despite the unfavourable market situation.

**C2:**

The calculated value of the relative ratio grows if:

a   the numerator increases and the denominator remains constant

Example: A firm in the machine-building industry is hoping for stable market conditions in the period under consideration. However, because of intensive contract negotiation with the suppliers, it succeeds in reducing its material costs by 5 per cent. As a result, the variable costs fall and the profit increases.

b   the denominator decreases and the numerator remains constant

Example: A consumer goods manufacturer has to accept a fall in sales quantity, despite a small reduction in the sales price. Thus, its sales decrease. However, the savings in variable and fixed costs partly compensate for the decrease in sales. As a consequence, the profits remain stable.

c   the numerator increases faster than the denominator

Example: A public transport company which has been operating below capacity until now, succeeds in attracting 8 per cent more customers, without increasing its price. This helps in increasing the passenger-kilometres (sales quantity) leading to an increase in sales. Under conditions of no change in fixed costs, until full-capacity utilization, and very small variable costs per unit, the profits increase over-proportionately.

d   the denominator decreases faster than the numerator

Example: Because of weak demand for cosmetic products, the quantity sold falls (say for example) by 6 per cent. Parallel to that, the firm decides to reduce its capacities, so that the major fixed costs, such as depreciation and human resource costs, decrease. Thus, the profits decline by only 4 per cent.

e   the numerator increases with a simultaneous fall in denominator

Example: A trading company decided to remove loss-making products from its product range. With other factors remaining the same, it leads to a fall in sales. However, this brings an increase in profits, because the products having a negative impact on profits have been removed.

**C3:**

The calculated value of the relative ratio falls, if:

a   the numerator decreases and the denominator remains constant

Example: The increase in raw-material prices, which are not directly rolled-over to the customer through price-increases, leads to an increase in variable costs for an energy supply company. With other factors remaining the same, it means a fall in profits.

b   the denominator increases and the numerator remains constant

Example: The demand for the services of a craftsman increases under the conditions of constant prices. Simultaneously, the variable costs increase, so that the profits can only be maintained at this present level.

c   the numerator decreases faster than the denominator

Example: In the automotive industry, because of the competitors' offer of price-aggressive products, the firm is forced to cut its prices (say for example) by 5 per cent to avoid a fall in sales. Since the costs (because of the constant sales quantity) remain unchanged, the profits fall over-proportionately.

d   the denominator increases faster than the numerator

Example: In an insurance company, a new type of contract for private customers offers very favourable conditions, which leads to a strong increase in sales. The new marketing campaign, in magazines and television-spots, leads to a considerable increase in fixed costs, so that the profits increase only by a smaller proportion.

e   the numerator decreases with a simultaneous increase in denominator

Example: A pharmaceutical company could increase its sales by adding innovative products to its product rage. Simultaneously, it has to incur considerably higher research and development costs, so that the profits fall.

In the above-mentioned examples of 13 constellations, changes in maximum two relevant factors were considered to prove the direct effect due to didactical reasons. In real life, in addition to the dominating impact of one factor, there could be many other relevant factors which appear simultaneously or with a lag. Similarly, there could be factors which move in the same direction and increase their effect or move in opposite directions and neutralize each other's effect.

The selected examples above are purposefully taken from firms in different branches in order to underline the universality of the systematic approach. The constellations can, however, be applied equally well to a single firm.

# Appendix II: DuPont Ratio System

For a large number of companies, it has long been a tradition to focus on a financial goal for managing the firm. In order to achieve this main goal, it was often classified into various drivers or sub-goals. This led to a pyramid-type structure of performance indicators. The DuPont ratio system is a major representative of such a pyramid-type system. It is named after the US American firm that pioneered the introduction of this hierarchical method. The success of the DuPont system is attributed to its ability to help in developing operational arguments and analytical thinking which assists the management in realizing its corporate goals.

In this appendix, the "Return On Equity" is taken as the main corporate goal, and its sub-classifications are shown as multiplicatively linked. The operational arguments related to DuPont analysis, and some useful suggestions, are explained below. The starting point in the DuPont analysis of a firm is the following analytical question:

What are the sources of a firm's profitability? What are the three ways in which management can improve profitability? Conversely, which factors could damage the profitability of a firm?

The "Return On Equity" as the main goal, and its three drivers, are classified as follows:

Return On Equity (ROE) =

Return On Sales ·        Asset Turnover        ·        Financial Leverage

$$\frac{\text{Net Income}}{\text{Net Sales}} \cdot \frac{\text{Net Sales}}{\text{Average Total Assets}} \cdot \frac{\text{Average Total Assets}}{\text{Average Stockholders' Equity}}$$

It is important to note that Return On Equity and Return On Sales are expressed as a percentage. Asset Turnover and Financial Leverage are expressed as multiples.

The data for net income and sales is available from the income statement. The average of total assets and average stockholder's equity can be calculated by taking the beginning and ending balances from the balance sheet.

The DuPont system helps the analysts to examine the sources of a firm's profitability. The three ratios report on the effectiveness of the firm's operating, investing and financing activities/strategies, respectively.

Since the Return On Sales (or net profit margin) is an income statement ratio, a high return on sales is equally an indication of good cost and price-management. A high Asset Turnover Ratio demonstrates efficient use of the assets on the balance sheet. A high Financial Leverage Ratio (as the inverse of Equity Ratio) shows the proportion of assets financed by debt. Whereas Return On Sales reflects upon the operating efficiency, Asset Turnover Ratio indicates asset-utilization efficiency. A high

https://doi.org/10.1515/9783110598094-008

Financial Leverage Ratio represents additional use of debt for improving Return On Equity.

Since DuPont analysis offers three explanations about the profit drivers or levers, each of these can be individually benchmarked. For orientation and comparison purposes, it is advisable to use the ratios of competitors within the same branch, or of listed (inter)national firms, as a benchmark.

The three drivers of Return On Equity provide, individually and collectively, explanations for its rise and fall. The Return On Sales can be improved, for example, by increasing sales volume, increasing sales price or decreasing expenses. Asset turnover efficiency can be achieved, among others, by increasing sales volume or disposing of less productive assets. Financial leverage can be improved by increased borrowing or repurchasing (decreasing) outstanding volume of stock. The firms following a low-cost strategy, such as Dell Computers, usually produce high ROE with higher asset turnover and higher leverage, to make up for their lower net profit margin.

The multiplicative link between "Return On Sales" and "Asset Turnover" ratios is reflected in Return On Investment (ROI). It shows that a firm can maintain its profitability despite a fall in the Return On Sales, if it is able to improve its Asset Turnover Ratio. For this, it is necessary to carefully evaluate the short, medium, and long-term impact of all the measures which reduce the asset base without negatively influencing sales-generating capacity. Similarly, a rise or fall in the profitability of the firm could be analysed with reference to return on sales and/or asset-turnover, and so measures for improvement can be developed.

In the same manner, a reduction in ROE can be analysed through these three drivers. In particular, careful consideration should be given to the dangers involved in the high burden of debt which is reflected in the high leverage ratio.

# Appendix III:   Alphabetical Overview of Key Performance Indicators

**Legend**

| Key Performance Indicator Name (KPI) | KPI Number | Perspective Category | Page |
|---|---|---|---|
| Absolute Contribution Margin | 3.3.3 | C | 178 |
| Absolute Market Share | 3.6.1 | C | 198 |
| Accident Occurrence Rate | 5.4.4 | HRI | 324 |
| Accumulated Depreciation to Fixed Assets Ratio | 2.8.6 | F | 112 |
| Asset Coverage Period | 2.8.5 | F | 111 |
| Asset Turnover Ratio | 2.8.4 | F | 109 |
| Average Collection Period | 2.8.1 | F | 104 |
| Average Payment Period | 2.8.2 | F | 106 |
| Bankruptcy Prediction Score | 2.4.5 | F | 68 |
| Bid Acceptance Rate | 3.6.3 | C | 201 |
| Book-to-Bill Ratio | 3.7.5 | C | 210 |
| Bottleneck-induced Incremental Costs | 4.5.8 | P | 276 |
| Brand Awareness Level | 3.2.6 | C | 173 |
| Breakeven Point (BEP) | 3.4.1 | C | 185 |
| Breakeven Time | 5.5.4 | HRI | 333 |
| Capacity Coverage Ratio | 3.7.4 | C | 209 |
| Capacity Utilization Level | 4.4.4 | P | 256 |
| Cash Flow | 2.5.1 | F | 71 |
| Cash Flow at Risk (CFaR) | 2.5.5 | F | 79 |
| Cash Flow Margin | 2.6.1 | F | 84 |
| Cash Flow per Share | 2.10.6 | F | 131 |
| Cash Flow Return On Equity (CFROE) | 2.6.3 | F | 87 |
| Cash Flow Return On Investment (CFROI) | 2.6.2 | F | 85 |
| Cash Point | 3.4.4 | C | 189 |

https://doi.org/10.1515/9783110598094-009

Appendix III (continued)

Appendix III (continued)

| Key Performance Indicator Name (KPI) | KPI Number | Perspective Category | Page |
|---|---|---|---|
| Dividend Yield | 2.10.3 | F | 126 |
| Earnings before Interest and Taxes (EBIT) | 2.1.2 | F | 23 |
| Earnings before Interest, Taxes and Amortization (EBITA) | 2.1.3 | F | 25 |
| Earnings before Interest, Taxes, Depreciation and Amortization (EBITDA) | 2.5.6 | F | 81 |
| Earnings before Taxes (EBT) | 2.1.1 | F | 21 |
| Earnings Per Share (EPS) | 2.2.5 | F | 41 |
| EBIT-Turnover-Yield | 2.2.1 | F | 34 |
| EBITDA-Turnover-Yield | 2.6.4 | F | 88 |
| Economic Efficiency | 1.3 | B | 9 |
| Economic Profit (EP) | 2.9.2 | F | 116 |
| Economic Value Added (EVA) | 2.9.3 | F | 117 |
| Efficiency | 1.2 | B | 7 |
| Elasticity | 1.6 | B | 14 |
| Emission Volume of Production-related Pollutants | 4.6.3 | P | 286 |
| Emission Volume of Usage-related Pollutants | 3.8.2 | C | 216 |
| Employee Satisfaction Index | 5.4.2 | HRI | 320 |
| Energy Source Ratio | 5.6.3 | HRI | 341 |
| Equity Ratio | 2.7.4 | F | 95 |
| Equity-To-Fixed-Assets Ratio (Level I) | 2.7.1 | F | 90 |
| Equity-To-Fixed-Assets Ratio (Level II) | 2.7.2 | F | 92 |
| Equity-To-Fixed-Assets Ratio (Level III) | 2.7.3 | F | 93 |
| Estimate at Completion (EAC) | 4.1.4 | P | 225 |
| Expected Process-based Loss | 4.5.6 | P | 272 |
| Faulty Incoming Delivery Rate | 4.3.4 | P | 244 |
| Faulty Outgoing Delivery Rate | 4.3.5 | P | 245 |
| Financial Leverage Index | 2.7.5 | F | 97 |
| Finished Goods Turnover Period | 3.7.6 | C | 211 |
| Flop Rate | 3.1.9 | C | 163 |
| Follow-up Costs Ratio | 4.2.3 | P | 233 |
| Free Cash Flow (FCF) | 2.5.3 | F | 76 |
| Gross Margin | 3.3.2 | C | 176 |
| Gross or Net Cash Flow | 2.5.2 | F | 74 |

Appendix III (continued)

| Key Performance Indicator Name (KPI) | KPI Number | Perspective Category | Page |
|---|---|---|---|
| Human Resource Internationality Index | 5.3.3 | HRI | 310 |
| Indirect $CO_2e$ Emissions caused by Energy Usage (Scope 2) | 4.6.2 | P | 283 |
| Innovation Rate | 5.5.1 | HRI | 327 |
| Interest Coverage Ratio | 2.4.3 | F | 64 |
| Internally Generated $CO_2e$ Emissions (Scope 1) | 4.6.1 | P | 280 |
| Internally-staffed Executive Positions Ratio | 5.2.4 | HRI | 304 |
| Internationalization Level | 3.5.1 | C | 191 |
| Inventory Turnover Ratio | 4.5.3 | P | 265 |
| Labour Productivity | 5.2.1 | HRI | 298 |
| Labour Turnover Rate | 5.4.1 | HRI | 318 |
| Machine Hour Rate | 4.5.7 | P | 274 |
| Maintenance Cost Intensity | 4.4.3 | P | 255 |
| Margin of Safety | 3.4.2 | C | 186 |
| Margin of Safety Factor | 3.4.3 | C | 188 |
| Market Saturation Level | 3.5.4 | C | 197 |
| Market-to-Book Ratio | 2.10.1 | F | 123 |
| Material Coverage Period | 4.5.4 | P | 268 |
| Media Coverage Level | 3.2.1 | C | 165 |
| Net Operating Profit After Taxes (NOPAT) | 2.1.7 | F | 33 |
| Net Present Value | 2.11.3 | F | 136 |
| Non-Conformity Costs Ratio | 4.2.5 | P | 236 |
| Non-periodic Income | 2.1.6 | F | 31 |
| Operating Cash Flow (OCF) | 2.5.4 | F | 77 |
| Overtime Quota | 5.2.2 | HRI | 300 |
| Participation Rate in Ideas Management | 5.4.5 | HRI | 326 |
| Payback Period | 2.11.1 | F | 133 |
| Percentage Contribution Margin | 3.3.4 | C | 180 |
| Personnel Costs per Employee | 5.1.3 | HRI | 295 |
| Personnel Costs Ratio | 5.1.1 | HRI | 291 |
| Plant Availability | 4.4.1 | P | 252 |
| Plant Downtime Rate | 4.4.2 | P | 253 |
| Price Elasticity of Demand (PEoD) | 3.3.6 | C | 183 |
| Price Reduction Rate | 3.3.5 | C | 182 |

Appendix III (continued)

| Key Performance Indicator Name (KPI) | KPI Number | Perspective Category | Page |
|---|---|---|---|
| Price-Earnings Ratio (P/E Ratio) | 2.10.4 | F | 128 |
| Price-To-Cash Flow Ratio | 2.10.5 | F | 129 |
| Process Acceleration Costs | 4.1.6 | P | 228 |
| Process Cost Rate | 4.5.5 | P | 271 |
| Procurement Efficiency Ratio | 4.3.1 | P | 238 |
| Product Carbon Footprint | 3.8.1 | C | 213 |
| Product-related Recyclability Rate | 3.8.3 | C | 218 |
| Professional Development Training Costs Ratio | 5.3.2 | HRI | 309 |
| Professional Development Training Time per Employee | 5.3.1 | HRI | 308 |
| Profit Margin | 3.3.1 | C | 174 |
| Profitability | 1.4 | B | 10 |
| Profitability Index | 2.11.4 | F | 138 |
| Provisions Rate | 2.7.7 | F | 101 |
| Quality Rate | 4.2.1 | P | 230 |
| Quick Ratio | 2.3.2 | F | 56 |
| Ratio of Employees with Risk-aligned Remuneration Packages | 5.3.4 | HRI | 313 |
| Recycling Ratio | 4.6.4 | P | 289 |
| Rejection Rate | 4.2.2 | P | 231 |
| Relative Market Share | 3.6.2 | C | 200 |
| Research and Development Costs Ratio (R&D Costs Ratio) | 5.5.3 | HRI | 331 |
| Research and Development Intensity (R&D Intensity) | 5.5.2 | HRI | 329 |
| Resource Consumption Level | 5.6.1 | HRI | 335 |
| Resource Consumption Reduction Rate | 5.6.2 | HRI | 338 |
| Resource Efficiency | 2.12.1 | F | 140 |
| Result from Continued Operations | 2.1.4 | F | 28 |
| Result from Discontinued Operations | 2.1.5 | F | 30 |
| Return On Assets (ROA) | 2.2.4 | F | 40 |
| Return On Capital Employed (ROCE) | 2.2.8 | F | 48 |
| Return On Equity (ROE) | 2.2.3 | F | 38 |
| Return On Invested Capital (ROIC) | 2.2.7 | F | 46 |
| Return On Investment (ROI) | 2.2.6 | F | 43 |

Appendix III (continued)

| Key Performance Indicator Name (KPI) | KPI Number | Perspective Category | Page |
|---|---|---|---|
| Return On Net Assets (RONA) | 2.2.9 | F | 50 |
| Return On Sales (ROS) | 2.2.2 | F | 36 |
| Risk Adjusted Return On Capital (RAROC) | 2.2.10 | F | 52 |
| Sales per Reference Parameter | 3.7.1 | C | 203 |
| Sales Space Productivity | 3.7.3 | C | 207 |
| Schedule Performance Index (SPI) | 4.1.1 | P | 221 |
| Sickness-Absenteeism Rate | 5.4.3 | HRI | 323 |
| Staff Recruitment Period | 5.2.5 | HRI | 305 |
| Stock Yield | 2.10.2 | F | 125 |
| Supplementary Personnel Costs Ratio | 5.1.2 | HRI | 292 |
| Supplier-Audit Ratio | 4.3.2 | P | 240 |
| Supplier's Service Level | 4.3.7 | P | 249 |
| Supply Chain Cycle Time | 4.3.3 | P | 242 |
| Sustainable Value | 2.12.2 | F | 142 |
| Technical Productivity | 1.1 | B | 5 |
| Throughput Time (TPT) | 4.5.1 | P | 260 |
| Time Adjusted or Discounted Payback Period | 2.11.2 | F | 134 |
| Time Estimation at Completion (TEAC) | 4.1.3 | P | 224 |
| To-Complete-Performance Index (TCPI) | 4.1.5 | P | 227 |
| Turnover Rate | 1.5 | B | 12 |
| Unit Labour Cost | 5.1.4 | HRI | 296 |
| Usage Intensity of Internet-based Media | 3.2.4 | C | 169 |
| Value at Risk (VaR) | 2.9.5 | F | 121 |
| Vertical Integration Level | 4.3.6 | P | 247 |
| Weighted Average Cost of Capital (WACC) | 2.9.4 | F | 119 |
| Workforce Composition Ratios | 5.2.3 | HRI | 302 |
| Working Capital | 2.3.4 | F | 58 |

# Appendix IV:   Smart Key Performance Indicators at a Glance

## Financial Perspective

| KPI No. | KPI Name | Formula/Computations | Page No. |
|---|---|---|---|
| 2.1.2 | Earnings before Interest and Taxes (EBIT) | Net Income + Taxes on Income + Interest Expense | 23 |
| 2.2.6 | Return On Investment (ROI) | $\dfrac{(\text{Net Income} + \text{Interest Expense}) \cdot 100}{\text{Average Total Asset 'or' Average Total Capital}}$ | 43 |
| 2.3.3 | Current Ratio | $\dfrac{\text{Current Assets}}{\text{Current Liabilities}}$ | 57 |
| 2.4.4 | Debt Service Coverage Ratio (DSCR) | $\dfrac{\text{Cash Flow per Period} \cdot 100}{\text{Interest} + \text{Principal Payments on Debt per Period}}$ | 66 |
| 2.7.4 | Equity Ratio | $\dfrac{\text{Total Owners' Equity} \cdot 100}{\text{Total Capital}}$ | 95 |
| 2.8.3 | Cash-to-Cash Cycle | Days Inventory Outstanding + Days Sales Outstanding − Days Payable Outstanding | 108 |
| 2.9.5 | Value at Risk (VaR) | VaR (at 95% confidence level) = Expected Daily Returns − (1.96 · Standard Deviation) | 121 |
| 2.12.1 | Resource Efficiency | $\dfrac{\text{Monetary Value of the Output (measured in Revenue 'or' Yield)}}{\text{Amount of the Ecological Input (measured in Quantity Units)}}$ | 140 |

https://doi.org/10.1515/9783110598094-010

## Customer Perspective

| KPI No. | KPI Name | Formula/Computations | Page No |
|---|---|---|---|
| 3.1.7 | Customer Satisfaction Index | $\dfrac{\sum(\text{Average Satisfaction Score for each Parameter} \cdot \text{Relative Weight})}{\text{Total of all Relative Weights}}$ | 158 |
| 3.2.4 | Usage Intensity of Internet-based Media | $\dfrac{\text{Number or Value of monitored Objects in one specific Type of Internet-based Media within one Period}}{\text{Target Indicator per Period from a carefully selected Population Basis}}$ | 169 |
| 3.3.2 | Gross Margin | $\dfrac{(\text{Net Sales Price} - \text{Acquisition Price}) \cdot 100}{\text{Net Sales Price 'or' Acquisition Price}}$ | 176 |
| 3.4.1 | Breakeven Point (BEP) | $\dfrac{\text{Fixed Periodic Costs}}{\text{Contribution Margin per Unit}}$ | 185 |
| 3.6.2 | Relative Market Share | $\dfrac{\text{Market Share of the Firm} \cdot 100}{\text{Market Share of the Strongest Firm in the Market}}$ | 200 |
| 3.8.2 | Emission Volume of Usage-related Pollutants | $\dfrac{\text{Quantity of Emitted Pollutants}}{\text{Duration of Phase under Analysis}}$ | 216 |

# Process Perspective

| KPI No. | KPI Name | Formula/Computations | Page No. |
|---|---|---|---|
| 4.2.1 | Quality Rate | $\dfrac{\text{Defect Free Quantity (of a given Centre) in a Period} \cdot 100}{\text{Total Quantity Produced (of a given Centre) in a Period}}$ | 230 |
| 4.3.2 | Supplier-Audit Ratio | $\dfrac{\text{Number of Audited Suppliers per Period} \cdot 100}{\text{Total Number of Suppliers per Period}}$ | 240 |
| 4.3.3 | Supply Chain Cycle Time | Procurement Time + Production Time + Internal Inventory Time + Packaging and Shipment Time | 242 |
| 4.4.4 | Capacity Utilization Level | $\dfrac{\text{Effective Production Hours} \cdot 100}{\text{Maximum Possible Production Hours}}$ 'or' $\dfrac{\text{Actual Output Quantity} \cdot 100}{\text{Planned Output Quantity}}$ | 256 |
| 4.5.3 | Inventory Turnover Ratio | $\dfrac{\text{Average (Daily) Need}}{\text{Average (Daily) Inventory Level}}$ 'or' $\dfrac{\text{Net Sales or Cost of Goods Sold}}{\text{Average Value of Inventory}}$ | 265 |
| 4.5.9 | Cost Effectiveness of Risk Management | $\dfrac{\text{Total Cost of Risk Management (in monetary Terms)} \cdot 100}{\text{Total Value of the Risk Exposure (in monetary Terms)}}$ | 278 |
| 4.6.4 | Recycling Ratio | $\dfrac{\text{Reused Input (Consumed) Quantity for an Object} \cdot 100}{\text{Actual Total Input (Consumption) for an Object}}$ | 289 |

## HR/Innovation Perspective

| KPI No. | KPI Name | Formula/Computations | Page No |
|---|---|---|---|
| 5.1.4 | Unit Labour Cost | $\dfrac{\text{Gross Personnel Costs of Direct Labour in a Period}}{\text{Total Units of Output manufactured in a Period}}$ | 296 |
| 5.3.2 | Professional Development Training Costs Ratio | $\dfrac{\text{Professional Training Costs} \cdot 100}{\text{Gross Wages} + \text{Salaries}}$ | 309 |
| 5.3.4 | Ratio of Employees with Risk-aligned Remuneration Packages | $\dfrac{\text{Number of Employees with Variable Salary Components} \cdot 100}{\text{Total Number of Professionals (or a Sub-group) in the Firm}}$ | 313 |
| 5.4.1 | Labour Turnover Rate | $\dfrac{\text{Number of Employees Quitting in a Period} \cdot 100}{\text{Average Number of Employees in a Period}}$ | 318 |
| 5.4.2 | Employee Satisfaction Index | $\dfrac{\Sigma\,(\text{Employees Satisfaction Assessment per Parameter} \cdot \text{Weight})}{\text{Sum Total of all Weight Factors}}$ | 320 |
| 5.5.1 | Innovation Rate | $\dfrac{\text{Periodic Sales of New Products and Services} \cdot 100}{\text{Total Periodic Sales}}$ | 327 |
| 5.6.2 | Resource Consumption Reduction Rate | $1 - \dfrac{\text{Quantity of Resource Consumed in Period t}}{\text{Quantity of Resource Consumed in Period t-1}}$ | 338 |

# Selected Bibliography (For Balanced Scorecard Approach)

## Financial Perspective

Berk, J. B. *Corporate Finance*, 3. Edition, Pearson Education Limited, London, 2014.

Brealey, R. A., Myers, S. C. and Marcus, A. J. *Fundamentals of Corporate Finance*, 10. Edition, McGraw-Hill Education, New York, 2020.

Brooks, R. *Financial Management: Core Business*, 4. Edition, Pearson Education, London, 2018.

Brignall, T. J. S. A Financial Perspective on Performance Management. *Irish Accounting Review*, 14(1), 2007, pp. 15–29.

Davis, S. and Albright, T. An investigation of the effect of Balanced Scorecard implementation on financial performance. *Management Accounting Research*, June, 2004, pp. 135–153.

Diederichs, M. *Risikomanagement und Risikoncontrolling*. 3. Edition, Munich, 2012.

Dionne, G. *Risk Management: History, Definition and Critique*. Montreal, Canada, 2013.

Figge, F. and Hahn, T. *Nachhaltig Erfolgreich Wirtschaften*, September 9, 2009, http://www.new-projekt.de/downloads/newstudielangversion.pdf.

Madura, J. and Fox, R. *International Financial Management*, 4. Edition, Cengage Learning EMEA, Boston, 2017.

Romeike, F. and Hager, P. *Erfolgsfaktor Risiko-Management 3.0*, 3. Edition. Wiesbaden 2013.

Vanini, U. *Risikomanagement*, Stuttgart, 2012.

Wu, C. R., Lin, C. T. and Tsai, P. H. Analysing Alternatives in Financial Services for Wealth Management Banks: The Analytic Network Process and the Balanced Scorecard Approach. *IMA Journal of Management Mathematics*, 20(3), 2009, pp. 303–321.

## Customer Perspective

Bijmolt, T. *Advanced Methods for Modeling Markets*, Springer International Publishing, Cham, 2018.

Cavallone, M. *Marketing and Customer Loyalty*, Springer, Cham, 2017.

Ip, Y. K. and Koo, L. C. BSQ strategic formulation Framework: A Hybrid of Balanced Scorecard, SWOT Analysis and Quality Function Deployment. *Emarald Insight*, 19(4), 2004, pp. 533–543.

Kaplan, R. S. and Norton, D. N. *The Balanced Scorecard. Translating Strategy into Action*. Harvard, 1996.

Kotler, P. and Armstrong, G. *Principles of Marketing*, 7. Edition, Pearson, Boston 2014.

Kuß, A. *Strategic Marketing: Market-Oriented Corporate and Business Unit Planning*, Springer Gabler, Wiesbaden, 2018.

Li, Y. L., Chin, K. S. and Luo, X. G. Determining the Final Priority Ratings of Customer Requirements in Product Planning by MDBM and BSC. *Expert Systems with Applications*, 39(1), 2012, pp. 1243–1255.

Stieler, M. *Creating Marketing Magic and Innovative Future Marketing Trends: Proceedings of the 2016 Academy of Marketing Science (AMS) Annual Conference*, Springer, Cham, 2017.

Wise, R. I. The Balanced Scorecard Approach to Strategy Management. *The Public Manager: The New Bureaucrat*, 1997.

Worapon T. B. P. Supplier Evaluation Framework Based on Balanced Scorecard with Integrated Corporate Social Responsibility Perspective. Hong Kong, *IMECS*, 2009.

https://doi.org/10.1515/9783110598094-011

## Process Perspective

Amaratunga, D., Baldry, D. and Sarshar, M. Process Improvement Through Performance Measurement: The Balanced Scorecard Methodology. *Work Study*, 50(5), 2001, pp. 197–189.

Andersen, P. *Operations Management and Sustainability: New Research Perspectives*, Springer International Publishing, Cham, 2018.

Camilleri, M. A. *Corporate Sustainability, Social Responsibility and Environmental Management: An Introduction to Theory and Practice with Case Studies*, Springer, Heidelberg, 2017.

Chiwoon C. S. L. A Study on Process Evaluation and Selection Model for Business Process Management. *Expert Systems with Applications*, 38 (5),Elsevier, 2011, pp. 6339–6350.

Chopra, S. *Supply Chain Management: Strategy, Planning, and Operation*, Global, 6. Edition, Pearson, London, 2015.

Christopher, M. Logistics and Supply Chain Management, 5. Edition, *Financial Times Prent.*, London, 2016.

D'heur, M. *Sustainable Value Chain Management: Delivering Sustainability Through the Core Business*, Springer, Heidelberg, 2015.

Dumas, M. *Fundamentals of Business Process Management*, Springer, Heidelberg, 2013.

Figge, F., Hahn, T., Schaltegger, S. and Wagner, M. *The Sustainability Balanced Scorecard – Linking Sustainability Management to Business Strategy*, 30th october 2018, https://doi.org/10.1002/bse.339.

Heragu, S. and Klumpp, M. *Operations, Logistics and Supply Chain Management*, Springer International Publishing, Cham 2018.

Idowu, S. *Sustainable Business Models: Principles, Promise, and Practice*, Springer, Cham, 2018.

Ivanow, D., Schönberger, J. and Alexander, T. *Global Supply Chain and Operations Management: A Decision-Oriented Introduction to the Creation of Value*, 2. Edition, Springer, Heidelberg, 2018.

Kirchmer, M. *Value-Driven Business Process Management: The Value-Switch for Lasting Competitive Advantage*, McGraw-Hill Education, New York, 2013.

Leleux, B. and Van Der Kaaij, J. *Winning Sustainability Strategies: Finding Purpose, Driving Innovation and Executing Change*, Palgrave Macmillan, Springer, Basingstoke, 2018.

Mangan, J. and Lalwani, C. L. *Global Logistics and Supply Chain Management*, 3. Edition, John Wiley & Sons Inc, New York, 2016.

Myerson, P. *Lean Supply Chain and Logistics Management*, Pearson, London, 2016.

Ray, P. *Economics, Management and Sustainability: Essays in Honour of Anup Sinha*, Springer Singapore, Singapore, 2018.

Rushtown, A. *The Handbook of Logistics and Distribution Management: Understanding the Supply Chain*, 6. Edition, Kogan Page, London, 2017.

Slack, N., Brandon-Jones, A. and Johnston, R. *Operations Management*, 7. Edition, Pearson Education Limited, London, 2013.

# HR/Learning/Innovation/Knowledge

Adam S. M. and Jacob, F. A. Balanced Scorecard, Activity-Based Costing And Company Performance: An Empirical Analysis. *Journal of Managerial Issues*, 15(3), 2003, pp. 283–301.

Ahn, H. *Applying the Balanced Scorecard Concept: An Experience Report. Long Range Planning*, Elsevier, 34(4),2001, pp. 441–461.

Ahn, H. *How to Individualise Your Balanced Scorecard. Measuring Business Excellence*, 9(1), 2005, pp. 5–12.

Bohlander, G. W. and Morris, S. *Managing Human Resources*, 17. Edition, Cengage Learning, Boston, 2015.

Bremser, W. G. and Barsky, N. P. *Utilizing the balanced scorecard for R&D performance measurement. R&D Management*, Wiley Online Management, 2004, 34(3).

Brown, A. *Human Resource Management: Innovation and Performance*, Palgrave Macmillan, Basingstoke, 2016.

Craig, J. and Moores, K. Balanced Scorecards to Drive the Strategic Planning of Family Firms. *Family Business Review*, 2005.

Decoene V. Strategic Alignment and Middle-Level Managers' Motivation in a Balanced Scorecard Setting. *International Journal of Operations & Production Management*, 26(4), 2006, pp. 429–448.

Dowling, P. J. and Engle, A. D. *International Human Resource Management*, Cengage Learning, Hampshire, 2013.

Huang, H. C. *Designing a knowledge-based system for strategic planning: A balanced scorecard perspective. Expert Systems with Applications*, Elsevier, January, 2009, pp. 209–218.

Jelenic, D. The Importance of Knowledge Management in Organizations- With Emphasis on the Balanced Scorecard Learning and Growth Perspective.s.l., *Management, Knowledge and Learning*, 2011.

Kaplan, R. S. The Balanced Scorecard: Comments on Balanced Scorecard Commentaries. *Journal of Accounting & Organizational Change*, 8(4), 2012, pp. 539–545.

Kim, J., Suh, E. and Hwang, H. A Model for Evaluating the Effectiveness of CRM Using the Balanced Scorecard. *Journal of Interactive Marketing*, 17(2), 2003.

Kim, J. A. Measuring the Impact of Knowledge Management. Korea, *SAGE Journals*, 2006, pp. 362–367.

Malik, A. *Strategic Human Resource Management and Employment Relations: An International Perspective*, Springer, Singapore, 2018.

Mondy, W. *Human resource management*, Pearson, Munich, 2014.

Sim, K. L. and Koh, H. C. Balanced Scorecard: A Rising Trend in Strategic Performance Measurement Measuring Business Excellence, *Emerald*. 5(2), 2001, pp. 18–27.

Voelpel, S. C., Leibold, M., Eckhoff, R. and Davenport, T. The Tyranny of the Balanced Scorecard in the Innovation Economy. *Journal of Intellectual Capital*, 7(1), 2006, pp. 43–60.

Wu, A. The integration between Balanced Scorecard and intellectual capital. *Journal of Intellectual Capital*, 6(2), 2005, pp. 267–284.

Zeuch, M. *Handbook of Human Resources Management*, Springer Reference, Berlin/Heidelberg, 2016.

# Index

**Note:** The number of the starting page of each KPI profile is emphasized in bold type. KPI groups and categories are also emphasized in bold with ff.
All other references are shown in normal type.

https://doi.org/10.1515/9783110598094-012

www.ingramcontent.com/pod-product-compliance
Lightning Source LLC
Chambersburg PA
CBHW081044220326
41598CB00038B/6972